Carnal Knowledge and Imperial Power

ONE WEEK LOAN

Carnal Knowledge
and Imperial Power

Race and the Intimate in Colonial Rule

ANN LAURA STOLER

'A girl playing with dolls in front of the house. Probably Java,' ca. 1920. KIT album 705/13, neg. 1084/45.

University of California Press

BERKELEY   LOS ANGELES   LONDON

University of California Press
Berkeley and Los Angeles, California

University of California Press, Ltd.
London, England

Library of Congress Cataloging-in-Publication Data

Stoler, Ann, Laura.
   Carnal knowledge and imperial power : race and the intimate in
colonial rule / Laura Ann Stoler.
       p.   cm.
   Includes bibliographical references and index.
   ISBN 0-520-23110-4(alk. paper).—ISBN 0-520-23111-2 (pbk. : alk.
paper)
   1. Race relations.   2. Sex customs.   3. Colonialism.   4. Europe—
Colonies.   I. Title.

JV105.S79   2002

303.48/2171904 21—dc21   200200540

Manufactured in the United States of America

10   09   08   07   06   05   04   03   02   01

10 9 8 7 6 5 4 3 2 1

*In memory of my mother, Sara Stoler; my sister,
Barbara Stoler Miller; and my dearest friend,
Joanne Lukomnik. Their love and wisdom
continue to shape my life and work.*

Contents

Acknowledgments

Each chapter carries its own acknowledgments, reflecting the contributions I have enjoyed from friends and colleagues, foundations and universities that have supported me over the past fifteen years. But preparing and extending earlier essays and writing new ones over the past two years warrants special acknowledgment of its own. Julia Adams, Jay Bernstein, Victoria Ebin, Julie Skurski, Anna Tsing, and Gary Wilder helped me to intellectually and historically situate the introduction and epilogue. Doris Sommer's and Nancy Cott's close readings and insightful comments helped further hone both content and form. Participants in graduate seminars I taught at Stanford University; University of California, Berkeley; University of California, Santa Cruz; and most importantly the University of Michigan—Ann Arbor asked hard questions and taught me how to ask better ones. Thanks go to my editor Stanley Holwitz who, despite waiting far longer than he would have liked, maintained his commitment to the volume. Laura Pasquale and Cindy Fulton, also of the University of California Press, have guided the manuscript through its many stages with patience and expertise. Genese Sodikoff and Andrienne Young did the indispensible work of formatting and standardizing the extensive endnotes and bibliography. Proofreading is rarely a satisfying task, but Monica Patterson, who also helped with final editorial changes, came remarkably close to making this work a pleasure. During 1999–2000 as a fellow of the Center for Advanced Study in the Behavioral Sciences in Stanford, I benefitted from its unique intellectual comradery. I thank Eric Ketelaar for drawing my attention to the photograph that appears on the book's cover, and thank both

Karen Strassler and Sameer Pandya for helping me think about the politics of using colonial photographs in general and in this volume in particular. My family—Larry Hirschfeld, Tessa Hirschfeld-Stoler, Bruno Hirschfeld-Stoler, and Guenn Alison Miller—curtailed by obsessions and celebrated my passion in making this book a political and personal labor of love.

Note on Illustrations

Most of the photographs reproduced here are from family albums. Wherever captions appeared in the albums, I have included them in double quotation marks. I have indicated captions supplied by the library and museum collections of the Koninklijk Instituut voor de Tropen in Amsterdam (KIT) and the Koninklijk Instituut voor Taal-, Land-, en Volkenkunde in Leiden (KITLV) in single quotation marks. Captions without quotation marks are my own. The skewed colonial vision these images display gives some sense of how frequently a similar *tableau vivant,* in which servants figured prominently, appeared in family photographs. As a portrait archive of domestic life, they underscore what some people wanted to remember and how they wanted to remember it.

I use these photos as a visual counterpart to the textual discourses and practices analyzed throughout this book. While portraits in the late nineteenth and early twentieth century were most often taken in studios, these portraits of home life in the Indies were not, in part because so many of the privileges and pleasures of a colonial life (servants, cars, comfortable homes) could not be captured in a studio scene.

I want to thank Leo Haks, who made his collection of family albums available to me and generously provided me with negatives and reproductions.

The photographer is unknown unless specified.

1 Genealogies of the Intimate
Moments in Colonial Studies

L'homme reste homme tant qu'il est sous le regard d'une femme
de sa race.[1]

In 1929, one of the principal architects of French colonial educational policy, Georges Hardy, warned a group of prospective functionaries that "A
man remains a man as long as he stays under the gaze of a woman of his
race." The statement is compelling on several counts. Both declarative and
imperative, it threatens, prescribes, and assures, succinctly capturing a set of
assumptions and anxieties about life in the colonial tropics for European
men and the European women recruited to follow and care for them. Its
conditional clause signals a caution: racial vigilance and virility were domestic and household affairs, and vulnerabilities of body and mind were
tightly bound to the conjugal and sexual arrangements in which Europeans
lived. It reminds the reader that the colonial "gaze" (*le regard*, in French)
was to be at once broad, reflexive, and intimate. It was a regard fixed on the
colonized but just as squarely on Europeans themselves. It was directed not
only at those susceptible, recalcitrant, and marginal Europeans but as much
at the well-heeled entrepreneur and Paris-schooled polytechnician, at the
colony's "old hands" and Leiden-trained greenhorns, at the foot soldiers of
empire—at the high and low among them.

Hardy's homily has the ring of received wisdom, but it was nothing of the
sort. Most strikingly, as I argue throughout this book, it mandated a set of behaviors, a template for living, a care of the self, an ideal of domesticity that few
European men in the colonies were ever able to realize, want, or afford. It
boldly contradicted the unspoken norm that students of colonialism have documented so well: European men should "take on" native women not only to
perform domestic work but to service their sexual needs, psychic well-being,
and physical care. European manhood in the colonies, whether measured by
"character" and civility or by position and class, was largely independent of
the presence of European women. This discrepancy between prescription and

1

practice suggests not only more tangled stories of colonial expansion than imperial historians once allowed (among others, that European women followed men only *after* specific colonial regions were made politically, medically, and physically "safe") but also a radically different set of plots.

Not least, the disjuncture between prescription and practice is a forceful reminder that white endogamy was neither an inevitable development nor even a norm. It was a strategic policy whose timing was planned, a reactive gesture, a contested site—and in many colonial contexts, a relatively late invention. It is also a reminder that the demographics of European expansion tell little in themselves. Ratios of men to women *followed* from how sexuality was managed and how racial categories were produced rather than the other way around. Interpretations of what it took to "remain a [European] man" in colonial Indonesia changed over time and varied widely—as did the photographic poses and placement of persons and objects by which this might be conveyed. Photographs like those in figures 1 through 6, most from family albums, made to be sent or brought back to the Netherlands, suggest comportment, dress, and service relations in those parts of the domestic order that people sought to archive and share.

Hardy's injunction is important for what it says but equally arresting for what it does not. White-on-white domesticity was framed in opposition to more prevalent sorts of unions on which colonialisms thrived. These unions included the forced and financed arrangements of domestic and sexual service by housekeepers kept as live-in lovers and by live-in maids whose children were fathered by their European employers. These arrangements and exchanges of goods and services were made by local women who were labeled "Asian," "African," "colored," or "black." Hardy's solution—"white women looking after white men"—was commonly used to counter what was also increasingly seen as a social problem and political danger in the French and Dutch empires of the early twentieth century: a growing population of mixed-blood children born out of these "mixed" unions, of men who had "gone native" or simply veered off cultural course, of European children too taken with local foods, too versed in local knowledge.

Moreover, heterosexual unions based on concubinage and prostitution across the colonial divide were defended as a "necessary evil" to counter those deemed more dangerous still—carnal relations between men and men. The question is not whether these were real dangers and thus whether their claims were true or false. The task is rather to identify the regimes of truth that underwrote such a political discourse and a politics that made a racially coded notion of who could be intimate with whom—and in what way—a primary concern in colonial policy. The colonial measure of what it took to

Figure 1.   A calling card from Java, ca. 1890s. Leo Haks Collection.

Figure 2.   'The doctor's family J. Kunst in Batavia, Java,' 1899. KIT album 680/7, no. 16.

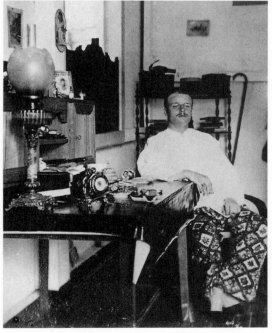

Figure 3. From a family album, ca. 1900. Leo Haks Collection.

Figure 4. 'F. J. G. Janssens, Major in KNIL [Netherlands Indies army] in pajamas, Bandjermasin, 1889.' KITLV no. 10.605.

Figure 5. 'A father and his daughter,' ca. 1935. Photos like this one (and like fig. 6)—of European men in the Indies alone with their children—are rare, and even more so for the nineteeth century. KIT album 583/31.

Figure 6. 'A father and his child,' ca. 1935. KIT album 583/23.

be classified as "European" was based not on skin color alone but on tenuously balanced assessments of who was judged to act with reason, affective appropriateness, and a sense of morality.

Hardy's focus was on a European male identity at risk and in the making, but his warning was not for men alone. Creating and securing the European community's borders took on special significance when cultural, political, and sexual contagions were conjured everywhere—where European and native sensibilities and desires brushed against one another as they were borrowed and blurred. If grown men were at risk, their children were more so. Concubinage could be banned by colonial administrations (and at different times and in different colonial contexts it was), but the quotidian comforts of colonial life created by the constant presence of native nursemaids and housekeepers, washerwomen and watchmen, cooks and gardeners—who serviced and nurtured these European selves—could not. As colonial housekeeping manuals from the 1920s and 1930s show and as Javanese women and men who once worked as domestics in Dutch colonial homes recount today, it was in the disarray of unwanted, sought after, and troubled intimacies of domestic space that colonial relations were refurbished and their distinctions made.

Hardy's warning underscores that the personal was highly political by invoking a set of associations among beliefs about European manliness, racial membership, sexual morality, and the management of empire that this book explores. Tracing the discrepancies between prescription and practice turns attention to the changing criteria by which European colonials defined themselves and to the uncertain racialized regimes of truth that guided their actions. Assessments of civility and the cultural distinctions on which racial membership relied were measured less by what people did in public than by how they conducted their private lives—with whom they cohabited, where they lived, what they ate, how they raised their children, what language they chose to speak to servants and family at home.

When Dutch children in the colonial Indies were forbidden to play with the children of servants because officials thought they might become too comfortable "babbling and thinking in Javanese," when Javanese nursemaids were instructed to hold their charges away from their bodies so that the infants would not "smell of their sweat" (as women who worked as domestics in Dutch households tell it so many decades later), there was more going on than peevish squabbles over cultural style. These were part of a wider set of standards framed to ensure that European children in the colonies learned the right social cues and affiliations—and did not "metamorphize" into Javanese. These were part of the colonial state's investment in knowledge about the carnal, about sense and sensibility, what I have referred to elsewhere as its enduring commitment to "the education of desire."

I pursue these connections between the broad-scale dynamics of colonial rule and the intimate sites of implementation not because the latter are good illustrations of this wider field or because they provide touching examples of, or convenient metaphors for, colonial power writ large. Rather, it is because domains of the intimate figured so prominently in the perceptions and policies of those who ruled. These are the locations that allow us to identify what Foucault might have called the microphysics of colonial rule. In them I locate the affective grid of colonial politics.

These chapters represent a series of studies in a decade-long project on the colonial order of things in the Netherlands Indies of the late nineteenth and early twentieth century. I am concerned with those patterns and rhythms of rule that were at once particular to that time and place but that are also resonant with colonial contexts in a wider comparative and global field. Not surprisingly, these chapters trace both a shared and an idiosyncratic research agenda. Although some dovetail with that wave of interdisciplinary scholarship animating studies of the colonial in the 1990s, they also chart their own peculiar course. My coordinates are located in the Javanese heartland of colonial Indonesia in the mid-nineteenth to early twentieth century and in Deli, its rich North Sumatran plantation belt.[2] The chapters focus on the disjunctures experienced by those who lived in the Indies and those who imagined it only from afar, both the watched and those watching: Dutch schoolteachers, Javanese housemaids, Belgian plantation managers, Dutch journalists in Amsterdam and Surabaya, Semarang housewives, and Leiden lawyers, civil servants, and civilians who advised on policy and those at odds with them. I have asked why they raised the questions they did and what delusions and fears prompted their aversions or actions. Their questions—and refusals to question—have incited my own.

Books based on long-term projects often prompt a search to impose coherence retrospectively. But this one is marked by persistent recuperations: a dogged pursuit of recurrent themes, a sustained focus on the same archival densities and absences, an insistent return to hauntingly similar quotes, and a repeated underscoring of certain tensions and tactics. All of the chapters turn on domestic arrangements, affective ties, and the management of sex. I make no effort to edit out these reiterations. On the contrary, I draw directly on them to trace how frequently the political and the personal were meshed, to identify what was created as private and public, and to ask what affections were perceived as cultural defections on colonial terrain.

Here I try to make sense of why connections between parenting and colonial power, between nursing mothers and cultural boundaries, between servants and sentiments, and between illicit sex, orphans, and race emerge as central concerns of state and at the heart of colonial politics. Each chapter is an effort to discern what made those connections at once so pertinent and consequential and so invisible and effaced in how colonies were ruled and in their historiographies of them. Each in turn grapples with the discrepancies between hard-line prescriptions and messier practices, between the densities of the archives and the emphases of historians. I am interested here in an archival state that recorded and documented the intimacies of empire in ways that historians of the Netherlands Indies—until recently—assiduously have not.[3]

My concern is both with the logics that underwrote the colonial record and with the assumptions that underwrite contemporary analyses of them. In this introduction, I trace some of the concerns that have marked each chapter and draw on each chapter to locate how studies of the intimate and the colonial have shifted over the last twelve years. In the epilogue, I take the opportunity to address what questions these chapters begin to raise and some other directions we might go. Each chapter considers why the micromanagement of sexual arrangements and affective attachments was so critical to the making of colonial categories and deemed so important to the distinctions between ruler and ruled. Thus each turns on the racialized politics of classification.[4] My focus here is on both implicit and explicit colonial categories—on the histories of their making, the exclusions they enabled, and violences they condoned. Each bears historical witness to Ian Hacking's contention that the power of categories rests in their capacity to impose the realities they ostensibly only describe.[5] Classification here is not a benign cultural act but a potent political one. On that argument, I look closely at the paradox and political consequence of racialized categories that were fixed and fluid, precise and protean, received and malleable, all at the same time.[6] This was so, both for ostensibly clear-cut social kinds like "Dutchmen" and "European" and for interstitial kinds like those labeled "poor white" and "mixed-blood" whose members might fall or veer toward either side of the colonial divide or remain awkwardly in between.

All the chapters wrestle with the conceptual fixity of categories and the fluidity of their content. But in working through a disparate corpus of colonial practices, the book seeks to make a broader claim. It insists on the protean character of the categories themselves. Each chapter questions, through different venues, a common assumption: because certain category labels endured, their membership too remained the same. Colonial categories were binding but unbound by those within them, were excessively rigid and exceeded their limits, had nuanced criteria for inclusion that were reworked by people who made them and by those they could not contain.

TRACKING THE INTIMATE

In-ti-mate. adj. 1. Marked by close acquaintance, association or familiarity. 2. Pertaining to or indicative of one's deepest nature. 3. Essential; innermost. 4. Characterized by informality and privacy. 5.a. very personal. b. of or having sexual relations. [Lat. *Intimatus,* p. part. of *intimare,* to intimate]. In-tim-ate. Tr.v. 1. To communicate with a hint or other indirect sign. 2. To announce; proclaim. [Lat. *intimare/* Lat. *intimus,* innermost]

The American Heritage Dictionary

As the citation above indicates, the notion of the "intimate" is a descriptive marker of the familiar and the essential *and* of relations grounded in sex. Its Latin etymology ("innermost"), which it shares with its homograph "to intimate," is more telling still. It is "sexual relations" and "familiarity" taken as an "indirect sign" of what is racially "innermost" that locates intimacy so strategically in imperial politics and why colonial administrations worried over its consequence and course.

As in any intellectual venture, the questions that inform this book are and are not my own. Studies of the colonial over the last decade have been shaped by political economy, feminism, and cultural Marxism. Alternatively, one might locate the range of questions that have animated colonial studies in the convergence of a new cultural history, subaltern studies, and new approaches to historical ethnography. Another possibility would be to trace deeper genealogies of the political and the intimate through Fanon, Freud, and the biopolitics of Foucault.[7] However differently interest in the intimate is mapped, this work reflects a basic commitment to identifying the political stakes lodged in what is defined as public or private, to studying the quotidian shaping of racialized colonial worlds and their disparate sites of production. These approaches take the creation of specific kinds of subjects and bodies to be fundamental to the making of a body politic. Most treat the racial and sexual politics of empire as a history of the present with reverberating postcolonial effects.[8]

But what student of colonialism at the beginning of the twenty-first century would imagine it to be otherwise? If some questions I raise here are yet to be addressed, others are starting points in colonial studies today. No longer fixed on the colonized alone, colonial studies has increasingly been concerned with historical variability in the making of racialized categories. No longer convinced that colonialism was a successful hegemonic project, students of colonial histories now direct their archival energies to the instabilities and vulnerabilities of colonial regimes, to the internal conflicts among those who ruled, and to the divergent and diverse practices among them. As this book suggests, few students of the colonial would claim that colonialism was more an economic venture than a cultural one or that studies of the colonial can be bracketed from the making of the modern, of Europe and its nation-making projects. No one would claim that colonial effects were confined to areas of physical conquest alone.

Critical colonial studies, or the "new imperial history," starts from the premise that colonizing bodies and minds was a sustained, systemic, and incomplete political project in colonial regions *and* in Europe. In a range of colonial contexts, that project has come to be seen as one with unanticipated effects. In the end, there was no panoptic imperial state but only a partially realized range of efforts to specify the use of and access to public space and to dictate which cultural affinities and styles, and what distribution of affections, would prevail in the street and in the home.[9]

A feminist-informed cultural studies places questions of homo- and heterosexual arrangements and identities not as the seedy underside of imperial history—as Britain or France's dirty secret exported to the colonies—but as charged sites of its tensions.[10] Studies of gender, empire, and colonial sexualities are no longer a cottage industry but a major one, evident in the staggering range of subjects and sensibilities they engage and the agencies they recognize and seek to convey.[11] That this research moves so easily between manliness and maternity wards, breast milk and racial contamination, antislavery and feminism, paternity suits and citizenship, signals a broad rethinking of imperial effects and of those practices and persons that confirmed or subverted colonial agendas.[12] Like the broader field of colonial studies, such work bridges metropole and colony, lingering on the ambivalences of those caught on the margins of empire or in middle passage.

What marks this literature is the range of questions, methods, and sources its students have been willing to entertain. In *Social World of Batavia*—a misleadingly modest title for a luminescent book—Jean Taylor sets a standard nearly two decades ago in her portrayal of the political landscape in colonial Indonesia of the seventeenth through nineteenth centuries.[13] Moving deftly between the privatized and the public, between patterns of rule and specificities of context, Taylor combined an ingenious use of source material, eclectic methods, and exquisite craftsmanship to look at the mestizo cultural core of the Indies and the crucial part that alliances through and by women played in it. In her story of mestizo manners and macropolitics, Taylor traced family genealogies five generations deep to detail the web of kith and kin that made up the Indies' changing colonial elite. She located colonial politics in commonplaces, in markers of display and discretion in public and at home: how prominent Indies wives styled their verandas, what language they spoke in private, who slept in their beds, where they were born and buried, and where and by whom their children were raised.

Taylor's questions were Indies-specific, but her story anticipated comparative concerns in colonial studies today: how a relationship between the organization of the domestic and that of the state together shaped colonial cultures that were at once homespun and worldly, reformist and racist, and both self-identified as of a singular nation—the Netherlands—and pan-European. Her work is suggestive on another front, for it points with ethnographic subtlety to the sorts of alliances on which the Dutch colonial state was built—alliances that blurred the very boundaries created by it.[14] Students of colonialism have sought to identify the ways in which the demographic demands of the state for particular kinds of colonizing populations were thwarted or supported by the range of condoned and unsanctioned domestic arrangements that colonialism itself engendered. Taylor's work, like that of Verena Stolcke's for nineteenth-century Cuba, Patricia Seed's for eighteenth-century colonial Mexico, and Raymond Smith's for the colonial West Indies, has underscored how illegitimate unions between native women and European men were woven into the fabric of colonial governance, sometimes circumventing the strictures of governance, elsewhere defining the social distinctions that colonial policy accentuated and brought into play.[15]

Taylor's insights remind us that colonials came in many sizes, that one's tailoring and tastes marked more than style, and that prescribed cultural distinctions were costly and not always easy to learn. Such insights are confirmed in literature, as anyone familiar with colonial belles lettres might attest. Permeable and impervious colonial categories created the pathos of colonial romance, the butt of its derisive humor, and the tragic grist of its stories. Sexual desires transgressed racial boundaries; class boundaries incited prurient desires. Undeclared affections and professed disaffections were distorted by category boundaries as they crossed and redrew those lines.

But the alienations of affection and cultural defections that so animate this literature seem to slip through our scholarly hands. Hungry for "what happened, where, why, and when," we brush by the sentiments that informed the colonial state's policies—and that its form of rule, in turn, helped to produce. Unused to pushing the affective up against the political, we leave sentiments to literature, dismiss references to them as the emotive fluff rather than the real stuff of official archives.

Fiction set in colonial India, Indonesia, Vietnam, and elsewhere is peopled with subjects who made much of their rightful class and national and racial membership while deriding the unrightful inclusion of others—but who were unsure where they themselves were "at home" and most belonged.[16] Madelon Székely-Lulofs's novels of a Sumatran planter's wife in the 1930s, Rudyard Kipling's chameleonic and restless Kim, Marguerite Duras's descriptions of a dysfunctional and impoverished French *colon* family outside Saigon, Louis Couperus's story of the indiscretions and breakdown of a Dutch Indische colonial family and its patriarch's ruin, Pramoedya Ananta Toer's chronicle of being native, educated, and out of place in late colonial Java, and George Orwell's district officer in colonial Burma who fears being mocked in "Shooting an Elephant" (and pointlessly kills an elephant to avoid that fate) all have something powerful in common. All portray sensibilities, sentiments, and states of distress that remain outside our history writing, that haunt and hover on the descriptive fringes of scholarly histories of the colonial, as if evading our hermeneutic finesse.[17] This is not to argue that colonialisms were more complex than we once imagined (true but trivial in itself). Rather, it is to argue that how power shaped the production of sentiments and vice versa is a subject that still begs for more analytic attention. We need to dwell in the disquiets, in the antipathies, estrangements, yearnings, and resentments that constrained colonial policies and people's actions, compelled their fears, and shaped what they imagined they should but could not do.

Colonialism is not *a* story, nor do I tell one. Instead, these chapters explore a set of interconnected and intersecting plots. Like that field of carnality and colonialism itself, they move across disciplines, understanding the colonial through a range of sources, locating colonial effects in microsites and at times unexpected domains. What did it mean to be "European" for colonials who had never set foot in the Netherlands, England, or France? How could children identify with a Dutch homeland when many spoke Dutch less often and with less ease than they did Malay or Javanese? How fixed was the notion of being "European" if a Dutch woman who chose to marry a native man could lose her Dutch citizenry rights because of that desire?

These chapters treat contingent and changing affiliations of colonizer and colonized, European and white, as political subjects—objects of critical history rather than givens of analysis. From this vantage point, they reconsider the spaces of colonial governance: why some intimate sites were more politically charged and relevant to rule than others and thus what we may count as colonialism's archival terrain. Each offers too a reminder that in histories situated on the peripheries of empire where "whiteness" was a palpable obsession, the crafting of chromatic identities has long been a troubled subject. Studies of whiteness have mushroomed in mainstream social science over the past decade, but feminists studying empire have dealt with anxieties concerning the definition of whiteness for a longer time.[18]

SITUATING THE CHAPTERS:
MOVEMENTS IN COLONIAL STUDIES

Chapter 2 begins an argument that informs all the chapters that follow and that has become a departure point of colonial studies today. Looking back over the anthropology of colonialism in the 1970s and 1980s, it argues that students of colonialism, anthropologists in particular, have taken the politically constructed dichotomy colonizer/colonized as a given rather than as a historically shifting pair of social categories that needs to be explained. It treats racism as a central organizing principle of European communities in the colonies, arguing that racial thinking was part of a critical, class-based logic that differentiated between native and European and that was part of the apparatus that kept potentially subversive white colonials in line. The representation of colonialism as white rule rather than class power had framed my earlier work on the tensions between "European underlings" and Sumatra's plantation elite.[19] But this piece differs in making explicit the argument that race was a primary and protean category for colonial capitalism and that managing the domestic was crucial to it.

Researched and written in the mid-1980s, chapter 2 argues for a deeper historical engagement with the range of practices in which racisms were produced and thus with the cultural framing of political categories. It treats colonial discourses as more than a reflection or legitimation of European power but as a site of its production, taking up Edward Said's call to examine the taxonomic conventions of colonial knowledge, how those conventions have shaped contemporary scholarship, and why students of colonialism had not sought to ask about them. It takes Benedict Anderson's notion of "imagined communities," by which he had characterized the social and political networks of anticolonial (and other) nationalisms, to track the movements and imaginings of a different population: the perceptions and practices that policed the membership criteria among European colonials themselves. In focusing on the internal structures of colonial authority and the dissensions that were disallowed, it registers recognition of the sustained political and cultural work that went into crafting the layered distinctions of colonial rule and its moving categories. In thinking through these issues, while often buried under piles of plantation archives, labor histories, Said's *Orientalism*, and Foucault's *History of Sexuality*, George Lakoff's study of categories, *Women, Fire and Other Dangerous Things*, was never far from my desk.

An ethnographic history, this chapter tells a story of the plantation industry in North Sumatra whose contemporary landscape could be traced through its history of contested categories: over what and who were defined as politically dangerous and what and who were not, over company policies on "family formation" that restricted marriage and condoned concubinage for some while encouraging marriage for others. Such policies produced skewed and tense gender dynamics with racialized effects that pitted Chinese workers against Javanese, Javanese against Dutch, and Europeans against Europeans. It subjected women, both Javanese and European, and the ratio of women to men to intense regulation in the industry's strategies of labor control. Finally, in questioning the lack of consensus within the European community, "Rethinking Colonial Categories" invites the reader to look to the vulnerabilities of European hegemony and the cultural ground on which it fashioned its unities.

The title piece, "Carnal Knowledge and Imperial Power," takes up the intimate from yet another perspective: it treats sexual matters not as a metaphor for colonial inequities but as foundational to the material terms in which colonial projects were carried out. I ask explicitly why such projects were riveted on the intimate and so concerned about sex. The piece was written during a year I lived in Paris, in the shadow of the Bibliothèque Nationale and its nearby nineteenth-century arcades, when I first consciously took in the fact that so many of Paris's quintessentially modern and "European" architectural feats were colonial artifacts, principally funded as colonial displays. I read Duras's *The Sea Wall* over and over that year and imagined that if one could so viscerally taste the white underside of colonial Vietnam and the pathos of mildewed and dust-covered lives in a semiautobiographical novel of growing up poor, enraged, and white in 1930s Indochina, the historiography would be rich as well.

But French scholarship on Indochina was then and often remains marked by a stubborn colonial aphasia, with room for little else than the chic, cool white linen nostalgia Catherine Deneuve embodies in the film *Indochine* and the steamier pedophilic pleasures of Duras's more recent book made into the colonial soft porn film *The Lover*. That nostalgia is in striking contrast to the stark and sinister picture Duras paints in *The Sea Wall*, where in 1950 she described whites in the colonies:

> [They] learned to wear the Colonial uniform, suits of spotless white, the color of immunity and innocence[,]...white on white, making distinctions among themselves and between themselves and the others who were not white.... White is, in effect, a color very easily soiled. Thus the whites became ever whiter, taking their baths and their siestas in the cool gloom of their villas, behaving much as do great beasts of prey, beasts with sleek and fragile pelts.[20]

The anthropology of French colonialism has steered clear of the cultural distinctions that made up Duras's racialized landscape and has rarely touched on the social relations that allowed for such sensibilities or their postcolonial effects. Ethnographic history at the time was a study of the colonized. Similarly, historians of French colonialism have looked at colonial policy and its local consequences, not at the kinds of racialized subjects and practices created by that politics. Attention to the "pluriculturelle" (the 1980s version of French "multiculturalism") encouraged studies of immigration as a "modern" problem rather than a (post)colonial phenomenon. The colonial politics of race that produced policies on concubinage and gave rise to orphanages for abandoned mixed-blood children was deemed outside of national history. By bracketing the history of colonial racism, the popularity of the National Front's extreme Right racism in the 1990s could be dismissed as aberrant in France's social history rather than as part and parcel of the extensive and explicit colonial debates over citizenship rights and *métissage*.[21] Frantz Fanon's work on colonial sexualities in the 1950s was taken as a political manifesto for revolution (which it was), not as a lesson in critical methodology. Albert Memmi's insistence (also written during the Algerian war) that colonialism produced both colonizer and colonized in the stylized movements of the everyday had more political impact than historical resonance. As a pointed reflection on the acute psychological and political dilemma of colonial relationships, its currency was among historians of the colonial in Britain and the United States.[22] In France, Memmi's concerns were not those of ethnography. The intimate interface of colonial relations was still the stuff of fiction and not yet on the historian's or ethnographer's agenda.

The aphasia has been deep. At the colonial archives in Aix-en-Provence, which I first visited in 1987, the contents of dossiers cataloged in the colonial registries dealing with "the traffic in women in Saigon," "the regulation of

European prostitution," "clandestine prostitution in Cochin," "the venereal peril" in Tonkin, "the seduction of women," and "[French] functionaries and native women" were no longer there.[23] Whether burned in Hanoi, shredded in Paris, misplaced en route, pilfered by incriminated functionaries, or reclaimed by insurgents (all theories I was offered), they were delivered empty again and again. Why the systematic void if such issues were inconsequential and marginal to politics? Rightly or not, I took that absence as a provocation. If sexuality was not, in Foucault's phrase, a charged "transfer point of power," why were abandoned *métis/se* children such a problem? Why the incessant effort of authorities to count the uncountable number of mixed unions not recorded in the civil registers? And why was *métis* legal status so well documented and so long debated if nothing was at stake?

Chapter 3 thus turns out from Sumatra to the Indies and beyond. It moves from a critique of the anthropology of colonialism to one that insists on seeing gender-specific sexual sanctions and prohibitions squarely at the heart of imperial agendas. Urging better feminist questions about the making of colonial structures of dominance, it holds that the assertion of European supremacy in terms of patriotic manhood and racial virility was not only an expression of imperial domination, but a defining feature of it. It asks what cultural distinctions went into the making of class in the colonies, what class distinctions went into the making of race, and how the management of sex shaped the making of both. It works off the contention that looking at sex—who had it with whom, where and when—takes us closer to the microphysics of rule as it pushes us to rethink what we think we know about the arenas of colonialism's macropolitics.

My tacking among the Dutch archives in the Hague, Amsterdam, and Leiden and those in Paris, Versailles, Marseille, and Aix-en-Provence prompted me to look at an even wider range of colonial contexts in which the making of racial boundaries turned on the management of sex. But it also recentered my focus from one on the "colonial situation" to one that increasingly encompassed a broader imperial terrain. Colonial bureaucrats moved constantly between metropole and colony, and their perceptions and acquired knowledge of difference traveled as well. It was during these years that I began constructing a different sort of colonial archive of my own, in which it seemed increasingly artificial and strained *not* to consider how the eugenics movement in the Netherlands was tied to that in the Indies, or how discourses of degeneracy resonated in Indochina and then reverberated in France. Studying the ways in which eugenics articulated with metropolitan class politics (and with feminism as well), I was struck by how much its vocabulary was deployed to set new standards of colonial morality, to condemn the domestic arrangements and child-rearing practices of poor whites in the colonies, and ultimately to confirm the rights of *certain* Europeans to rule.

If an explicit eugenics discourse was a latecomer to colonial projects, the fear of racial degeneracy and the harnessing of nationalist rhetoric was not. Both had gender-specific effects that dictated why European men were retired young from the colonial civil service, where European children would be schooled, and why European women needed domestic science to counter the immoral states of colonizing men. No government archives could make clearer that the discourses of European nationalism, middle-class sexual morality, and imperial exigencies were inextricably bound than the detailed protocols outlined in colonial housekeeping manuals. Prescriptions for bathing, breastfeeding, cooking, and sleeping arrangements tied anxieties over personhood, race, and what it meant to be Dutch to the choreography of the everyday.

Chapter 4, "Sexual Affronts and Racial Frontiers," continues this attention to national identity and sets debates over citizenship in both metropole and colony into this broader imperial frame. In it, I take the politics of exclusion to be contingent on sorting the cultural criteria that distinguished who could be considered truly "European." E. D. Hirsch's *Cultural Literacy: What Every American Needs to Know* had come out a few years earlier, and its bold conceit that cultural literacy was the accessible "ticket to full citizenship" in the contemporary United States seemed to rehearse exactly what colonial administrators in the Indies a century earlier too had professed.[24] Access to cultural resources was contingent on already having them: Dutch schools in the Indies were not open to children who were not already fluent in Dutch. Legal access to European equivalence demanded a "complete suitability for European society" and a "feeling" of not "belonging" to a milieu that was Javanese. Cultural literacy and cultural competence were the de facto criteria by which racial membership was assigned. It seemed that comportment and affiliation defined racial distinctions more often than somatics and biology. "Cultural racism" was not a recent, postmodern variation on an old theme but itself a colonial phenomenon.

I was not alone in looking to prescribed sentiments in the making of social hierarchies and in the making of race. Reading Uday Mehta's "Liberal Strategies of Exclusion" in manuscript in early 1990 confirmed my sense that the politics of exclusion relied on affective disposition as well as cultural literacy and that sentiment as well as biology was what race was about. If liberalism and colonial racism were both dependent on identifying those with the proper social credentials, they were also joined by the fact that regulating the intimate and "policing the family" were the reformist practices by which those strategies of governance were secured and worked out. Liberal social reform then was not the antidote to imperial expansion but part and parcel of it.

Along with chapter 4, chapters 5 and 6 traverse metropole and colony, plunge further into the intimate, reconsider the domesticating strategies of empire, and consider the affective as a charged political domain. Each touches tentatively on the politics of emotion, the power relations underwriting indiscretions of feeling, sexual liaisons chanced, parent-child bonds painfully severed and not always remade. The earlier chapters focus more on the relationship between power and sexuality, between colonial technologies of rule and the management of sex. These open to a broader etymology of the "carnal" that includes the sensual and affective, passion and compassion, and the unsanctioned and the flesh.

Many of colonialism's exclusivities were public displays of humiliation—like the signs posted on colonial Jakarta's swimming pools that read "No dogs or natives allowed."[25] But many of the most effective and enduring were not. Chapter 4 turns to the lamentation of a French father over the misdeeds of his wayward *métis* son to discuss how cultural competencies defined the exclusions of nation and race. A French father's plea to a Haiphong colonial court that his son was really French—in the face of the court's insistence that he was really not—hinged on affiliations more than skin, on the sense of belonging the boy evinced, and on the cultural knowledge father and son claimed to share.

In moving between the broad and intimate tensions of empire, other bracketed dichotomies slide out of their conventional space. Metropolitan and colonial social policy, liberalism and racism, sexual politics "at home" and "abroad"—domains held distinct both in colonial archives and in historiography—emerged as imbricated and dependent on one another. The cultural criteria for national and racial identities began to look strikingly similar even if the specifics were not the same.

Chapter 5 broaches most directly the colonial state's interest in harnessing sentiment. Looking at the intimate sphere of servants and children, it attends closely to the learning of place and race, to the "sentimental education" in which children destined to be citizens rather than subjects were required to share. And like chapter 4, it asks about the exclusionary practices built into reformist projects. But a focus on state interest in child rearing opens elsewhere: to questions about that early- to mid-nineteenth-century moment in which emergent liberal states as well as colonial ones turned attention and resources to children and to the protected environments in which they were to be raised. Public debates on the early nursery and kindergarten movements in the Indies, the Netherlands, Germany, the United States, and France have distinct chronologies but a common thread. All signal an investment in early childhood attachments, sentiments, and affiliations and a conviction that they were critical to the making of reliable citizens, governable subjects, and modern nation-states. Colonial states, not unlike metropolitan ones, had a strong motivation for their abiding interest in affective politics. In identifying the production and harnessing of sentiment as a technology of the colonial state, this chapter sets a research agenda that drew back to Locke, Hume, and philosophies of affect, to appreciating how much politics of compassion was not an oppositional assault on empire but a fundamental element of it.[26]

Chapter 6 shifts from a "sentimental education" to the broader "education of desire" in the making of colonial governance. In it, I challenge Foucault's history of the carnal while drawing on his genealogy of race. In so doing, I both rehearse and move beyond the argument proposed in *Race and the Education of Desire*, asking not only how the history of empire affects a history of European sexuality but also how its inclusion may alter our understanding of how racism figures in the making of modern states. Most important, this chapter points to the methodological insights that Foucault's histories of racial discourse and biopower afford by underscoring both the "polyvalent mobility" of racial discourse and what might be gained by attending to racial discourses as historical processes of rupture *and* recuperation. It makes theoretically explicit a theme that informs all the chapters: how and why microsites of familial and intimate space figure so prominently in the macropolitics of imperial rule.

The study of colonialism is a history of the present, but chapter 7 puts even that in question. As a response to a political and intellectual impulse in the late 1990s that placed "the politics of memory" at the center of an increasingly broad range of research agendas, it asks whether "the colonial" shapes the memories and recollections of people who live in "postcolonial" Indonesia or India as much as it does those who live in postimperial Holland and Britain today.[27] Unlike the chapters that are archive based—and attend more to how Dutch women and men in colonial Indonesia imagined themselves and the dangers and desires prompted by how they imagined those around them—this one attempts an about-face. It turns away from fears European colonials had about servants to ask how men and women who once worked as domestics remember them, through the recountings of those who in their youth cleaned bathrooms, washed and rewashed floors, and cradled colicky infants in Dutch colonial homes.

Chapter 7, researched and written with Karen Strassler, focuses on how these women and men who worked as nursemaids, cooks, and gofers remembered or retold those relations of proximity and deference on the eve of Suharto's fall in 1996–97—accounts that may be different again if retold in post-Suharto Indonesia today. Their recollections make this chapter a cautionary tale that calls into question both what we think we know about the colonial and what we imagine to be the contemporary relevance and stability of colonial memories. It sits awkwardly between a history of the present and an ethnography of the past, wrestling with the weight of colonial archives and what kind of memories can speak back to them.

Book structures are usually progressive. This one is modular and recursive with key elements that abut and impinge on one another and then pull apart. Each chapter contains incipient, abbreviated discussions of elements of colonial governance that in the latter pieces are more carefully followed. Chapter 2's gesture toward issues of racial boundaries, sex, and the domestic domain opens in chapter 3 to a more explicit engagement with colonialism's sexual politics. The subhead "Children on the Colonial Divide" in chapter 3 reappears as the central concern of chapter 5, devoted to racial boundaries and child care. What surfaces as a series of lengthy footnotes in chapter 4—on the colonial contingencies of national identities in Europe— becomes the center of an analysis of Foucault in chapter 6, on colonial domestic and sexual arrangements in the making of European bourgeois selves. Cultural competencies and fitting sentiments mark definitions of racial membership again and again.

The sequence is logical but not linear. Chapter 2 encourages attention to domestic arrangements as it unravels a set of assumptions about the chronology of colonial settlement, state policy with regard to emigrant white women, and the management of sex. A discussion that highlights the importance of illicit sexual unions in chapter 3 prompts a later consideration in chapter 5 that political authorities were possibly more worried about the racially ambiguous offspring they produced. The latter chapters shift focus from "desire" to the education of it and in so doing move closer to sentiment and farther from sex.

I present the chapters in the order in which they were written. But like other chronologies this one is warped and full of holes, not least because these chapters were interlaced with other related projects. A colonial reading of Foucault that I began in 1993—initially intended as a chapter in this book—became a book and an obsession of its own. A joint project begun in 1987 with Fred Cooper that sought to bring metropole and colony into one analytic domain paralleled and crisscrossed these chapters for nearly a decade. It culminated in the introduction to *Tensions of Empire*, which both drew on some of the chapters here and inspired others. Finally, the opportunity to give the 1996 Lewis Henry Morgan lectures, "Ethnography in the Archives," pushed me to ask more directly, as I do in chapter 7, about archival truths and people's postcolonial memories. This book thus represents a set of sustained strategic efforts to challenge certain givens of colonial history, the historiographies based on them, and the limits of their frames of reference. It develops a set of working concepts that might account for the resilience of colonial categories, their changing criteria, and their moving parts.

2 Rethinking Colonial Categories

European Communities and the Boundaries of Rule

In 1945 Bronislaw Malinowski urged anthropology to abandon what he called its "one-column entries" on African societies and to study instead the "no-man's land of change," to attend to the "aggressive and conquering" European communities as well as native ones, and to be aware that "European interests and intentions" were rarely unified but more often "at war."[1] Four decades later few students of colonialism have yet heeded his prompting or really examined his claim.[2]

The anthropology of colonialism has been a prolific yet selective project, challenging some of the boundaries of the discipline but remaining surprisingly respectful of others. As part of a more politicized scholarship in the early 1970s, it reexamined how colonial politics affected both the theory and method of ethnography and the histories of our subjects.[3] Influenced by the work of Andre Frank and Immanuel Wallerstein, it investigated how the structural constraints of colonial capitalism not only shaped indigenous changes in community and class but also by turns destroyed, preserved, and froze traditional relations of power and production and as frequently reinvented and conjured them up.[4]

Initially this work looked to the impact of colonialism on agrarian structure, household economy, kinship organization, and community life.[5] A second wave, turning away from the determinism that some of those approaches applied, sought to identify the active agency of colonized populations as they engaged and resisted colonial impositions and transformed the terms of that encounter. The contours of these communities and the cultural practices of their inhabitants (exemplified in the preservation of "little traditions," "reconstituted peasantries," and "moral economies") have appeared double-edged—explainable neither solely by their functional utility to colonialism nor by their defiance of it, but as the product of a historically layered set of encounters.[6]

In attending to both global processes and local practices, the units of analysis have also shifted to the extra–village, regional, national, and global ties that bind seemingly discrete peasant populations to the world economy[7] and to a rejection of the notion that categories such as nation, tribe, and culture are, as Eric Wolf put it, "internally homogenous and externally distinctive and bounded objects."[8] Curiously, despite this innovation, the objects of study, if not the units of our analysis, have remained much the same. When students of the colonial have turned their attention to world market forces and examined European images of the Other, it has been to better explain the impact of perceptions and policy on people, on a particular subject community, and on anthropology's ethnographic subject: the colonized.[9] And even when examining the politics of colonial discourse and its local lexicon, the texts are often assumed to express a shared European mentality, the sentiments of a unified, conquering elite.[10]

With few exceptions, even when we have attended to concrete capitalist relations of production and exchange, colonialism and its European agents appear as an abstract force, as a *structure* imposed on local practice. The terms *colonial state, colonial policy, foreign capital,* and *white enclave* are often used interchangeably, as if they captured one and the same thing. While such a treatment encourages certain lines of novel inquiry, it closes off others. The makers of metropole policy become conflated with its local practitioners. Company executives and their clerks appear as a seamless community of class and colonial interests whose internal discrepancies are seen as relatively inconsequential, whose divisions are blurred.[11] In South Africa and in white settler communities more generally, where conflicts between imperial design and local European interests were overt, such glosses are less frequent, but these communities have been less often the subjects of colonial ethnographies.[12]

More sensitized to the class, ethnic, and gender distinctions among the colonized, anthropologists have taken the politically constructed dichotomy of colonizer and colonized as a given rather than as a historically shifting pair of social categories that needs to be explained. Anthropologists have not ignored the ambiguity and manipulation of racial classification.[13] But this interest has rarely been coupled with a focus on European communities or the powerful cultural idioms of domination in which they invest.[14] As a result, colonizers and their communities are frequently treated as diverse but unproblematically viewed as unified in a fashion that would disturb ethnographic sensibilities if applied to ruling elites of the colonized. Finally, the assumption that colonial political agendas are self-evident precludes an examination of the cultural politics of the communities in which colonizers lived.

Colonial cultures were never direct translations of European society planted in the colonies but unique cultural configurations, homespun creations in which European food, dress, housing, and morality were given new political meaning in specific colonial social orders.[15] Formal dress codes, sumptuary laws, and military display did more than reiterate middle-class European visions and values. They were responsive to class tensions in Europe and created what Anderson calls a "tropical gothic," a "middle-class aristocracy" that cultivated the colonials' differences from the colonized while maintaining social distinctions among themselves.[16] The point is that colonial projects and the European populations to which they gave rise were based on new constructions of what it meant to be European. These communities were artificial groupings—demographically, occupationally, and politically distinct. White settlers, but also the more transient European residents, were occupied with social and political concerns that often pitted them against policy makers in the metropole as much as against the colonized.[17] Colonizers themselves, however, were not by nature unified, nor did they inevitably share common interests and fears; their boundaries—always marked by whom those in power considered legitimate progeny and whom they did not—were never clear. On the contrary, colonial Europeans constructed imagined communities as deftly as the nationalist colonized populations to whom they were opposed.[18] These were European communities consciously fashioned to overcome the economic and social disparities that might separate and set their members in conflict.

Racism is an inherent product of the colonial encounter, fundamental to an otherwise illegitimate access to property and power.[19] But studies of the colonial have only begun to recongnize that the *quality* and the *intensity* of racism have varied enormously in different contexts and at different moments in any particular colonial encounter. In situations as diverse as India, New Guinea, the Netherlands Indies, Cuba, Mexico, and South Africa, increasing knowledge, contact, and familiarity lead not to a diminution of racial discrimination but to its intensification and to more rigid boundaries. Understanding those sharpened racial pressures has entailed, among other things, identifying heightened forms of anticolonial resistance and increased demands by those given limited access to certain privileges but categorically denied others.

But colonial racism was more than an aspect of how people classified each other, how they fixed and naturalized the differences between We and They.

It was also how people identified the affinities they shared, how they defined themselves in contexts in which discrepant interests, ethnic and class differences, might otherwise weaken consensus.[20] That sense of community served colonial authority and a particular set of relations of production and power. Racist ideology, fear of the Other, preoccupation with white prestige, and obsession with protecting European women from sexual assault by Asian and black males were not simply justifications for continued European rule and white supremacy. They were part of a critical, class-based logic; not only statements about indigenous subversives, but directives aimed at dissenting European underlings; and part of the apparatus that kept potentially recalcitrant white colonials in line.

This is not to say that without white ruling-class manipulations, subordinate white colonials would necessarily have joined social forces and become politically allied with the colonized. Nor is it to suggest that these subordinates were unwitting practitioners of racist policy.[21] Rather, internal divisions augmented the intensity of racist practice, affected the terrains of contest, and shaped social policies regarding those ruled. Racist rationales permeated the political responses of *both* the corporate elite and their less privileged European class opposition. Here I draw on the case of a European community in North Sumatra in the late nineteenth and early twentieth century to set out some of the issues that the anthropology of colonialism is poised to address—how competing colonial agendas, based on distinct class and gender interests, shaped the politics of race and tensions of rule. Social differences and antagonisms divided East Sumatra's Deli community, but distinct material provisions and cultural conventions were invoked to secure its unity. Sexual and domestic arrangements of European staff were public political and economic issues, not private matters, that sharpened or muted the categories of ruler and ruled. In Deli, the rights to marry and form families were focal points of indigenous and European labor demands and basic to strategies of estate control.

Within the ranks of the European communities, two disparate social groups were closely linked to a European self-image of well-deserved privilege and priority. First was the category of poor or impoverished whites. Efforts to prevent their emergence in the colony, limit their entry, and expedite their repatriation reveal a wider set of colonial concerns and policies. The second category, white women, represented a threat of a different order. The frequency with which white women were barred from early colonial enterprises and the heightened racism that usually accompanied their entry are cited in a range of colonial situations. Attitudes toward poor whites and white women were not unrelated. Both categories marked and threatened the limits of white prestige and colonial control.

THE MAKING OF A COMMUNITY IN DELI

Sumatra's plantation belt—or Deli, as it was known from its "opening" in the late 1860s—was "pioneered" on a scale unparalleled elsewhere in colonial Indonesia. By the early twentieth century it was one of the most lucrative investment sites in Southeast Asia. Covering a fertile lowland plain of some thirty thousand square kilometers, the plantation belt *(cultuurgebeid)* included nearly one million hectares of jungle and swiddens converted within several decades into tobacco, rubber, tea, and oil-palm estates leased to foreign companies. Unlike in Java, where sugar, tobacco, and rice fields were interposed, in North Sumatra, estate holdings were laid out with contiguous borders of complexes ranging from one thousand to several thousand hectares.

Distant and largely autonomous from the Dutch colonial heartland in Java, the foreign community of the plantation belt developed a specific character during its late-nineteenth-century expansion. It had a multinational European membership (rather than a predominantly Dutch one as on Java), an extensive system of concubinage well into the twentieth century, a reputation for labor violence, and what some observers have described as the most marked degree of social discrimination in the Netherlands Indies.[22] Some attributed Deli's heavily racialized characteristics to its proximity to the British Straits colonies; others pointed to the large number of British planters in East Sumatra.[23] In either case, its racialized character was considered to have had little to do with what it meant to be Dutch. Indeed, Deli was frequently contrasted with the more open and hybrid face of Dutch colonial culture on Java, among whom were more creoles—and more mixing—giving European society a stronger inflection of local cast.

But Deli's distinctiveness did not arise from British borrowings alone. Unlike Java, where a Dutch civil service was well established by the mid-nineteenth century, most of Sumatra's plantation belt only came under Dutch political and economic control some fifty years later but with insufficient funds or personnel to carry out the task. Pacification was thus made an international affair, with investors and managers from France, Belgium, Germany, Britain, and the United States at the forefront of the plantation effort. Significantly, these early Deli planters were able to initiate and maintain a level of autonomy from state control over labor conditions and labor relations well into the twentieth century.[24]

With the right to procure land and labor under an open-door policy, the planters were also granted license to protect those assets as they saw fit. Labor recruitment relied on an indentured labor system and a penal code endorsed and enforced by the state. Dependent more on Europe and the Straits settlements than on the administration in Java for personnel and financial support, the early Deli planters were in sustained conflict with Dutch colonial authorities. They both demanded protection and refused, sabotaged, and protested state interference in labor affairs.[25] Claiming prior and privileged knowledge of Deli's conditions, the planters easily circumvented the directives of government agents who were generally young, less experienced, and on short-term assignments in what was then still an outpost.[26]

Memoirs, contemporary press reports, period novels, and government archives display a discursive disjuncture between an emphasis on unity and a subjacent concern with social and political tensions among the Europeans themselves. The proffered image of a rough and rugged cohort of men transforming the primeval forest into a civilized and profitable plantation belt captured the imagination not only of Deli's local Europeans but also of those elsewhere in the Indies and in Southeast Asia. The notion that Deli was an "entirely different idea"[27] and that the Deliaan was a unique type appealed to a pioneering Protestant ethic in which success derived from perseverance and hard work. Descriptions of this planter prototype emphasized a set of common features: perseverance, uncompromising courage, and disregard for class origin.[28]

Celebrations of such heroic personalities were colonial commonplaces. More interesting is how this image played back on the Deliaans themselves, sustaining a sense that their privilege was deserved and their profits well earned and that both were based on hardy, good *character*—not race or class.[29] This notion of "character" did not derive from abstract or universal values. At its heart was a conception of being European that emphasized a bearing, a standard of living, and a set of cultural competencies and practices to which members of the European community were to subscribe and from which the majority of Asians were barred.[30]

Most accounts of Deli describe an early estate administration staffed with an assortment of inexperienced personnel composed of the scions of failed business families, runaways from ill-fated love affairs, defunct aristocrats, and adventurers seeking their fortunes. It was a deeply romanticized portrait, focused more on the few social marginals and fugitives than on the majority of the middling middle class for whom the Indies offered financial hope and social improvement.[31] While the early boom years of tobacco cultivation allowed some to strike it rich, many planters-cum-speculators went bankrupt when the international market failed. Some with good reputations became administrators for the larger companies that bought them out.[32] For the most part, however, the dream of *haute-bourgeois* retirement was something realized by few employed on the estates. In the initial years when staff were trained on the spot, new recruits had some opportunity to work up to higher positions. But this became increasingly rare as multinational companies took over after the turn of the century and as greater technical and administrative skills were needed for higher posts. In short, the Deli planters were rarely gentlemen planters at all but bureaucrats, office workers, industrial specialists, and field foremen in a rapidly expanding, modern corporate hierarchy.

Distinctions among Europeans were commonly couched as *singkeh* (greenhorns) versus old hands and *assistenten* (European field staff) versus senior management, differences that legitimated claims to authority and higher income based on earned seniority.[33] In principle one could move naturally up the corporate ranks. In practice economic mobility was limited and for dissenting personnel, virtually impossible.[34] The social and economic distance that separated directors, administrators, and higher personnel from those Europeans at the bottom was accentuated by the absence of a large "mixed-blood" ("Indo") population who, on Java, constituted much of the low-level office and field staff. Deli's planter elite prided itself on maintaining strict racial distinctions such that many companies refused to employ Indo-Europeans as accountants, scribes, or clerks.[35]

The public facade was white unity, but discontent within the estate hierarchy's lower ranks was evident early on. When the union of European plantation employees (Vakvereeniging voor Assistenten in Deli) was formed in 1909, officials in Batavia, plantation owners in Sumatra, and company directors in Europe viewed it as an outright act of *chantage* (blackmail).[36] With only two hundred members at its start, ten years later, as the union reached outside its Dutch-speaking membership, it had grown to several thousand. Set up in direct opposition to the powerful rubber and tobacco planters' associations and their client press, the union founded an independent and widely read newspaper in which members lodged grievances, criticized government policies, and aired their own interpretations of labor legislation and the causes of violence on Sumatra's East Coast.

Officials and planters attributed increased coolie assaults to the poor quality of European recruits. But the employees' union saw the problem coming from elsewhere, from the strains that an indentured labor system placed on daily encounters and working life. Whereas the planters' press blamed labor violence on "mishandling" of coolies by assistants, the latter pointed to excessive production quotas and the pressure of trying to meet them. Whereas company executives advocated a change in recruitment practices and requirements for selecting low-level staff, subordinate whites demanded improved living conditions, job security, and pensions for those already employed.[37]

The union's publication, ironically titled *De Planter*, did more than contest policies that affected employees' private lives. It also lent support to railway strikes among native linemen and to the demands of the Indies' emergent nationalist organizations.[38] Formed at a time when the nationalist movement had increasing presence locally among Javanese on Deli's estates and throughout the Indies, the Assistants' Union was able to force concessions that would later have been less possible. For example, the 1917 Assistants' Ruling accorded European field supervisors some protection from "coolie assaults" and more job security and directly addressed the complaint that their positions were too dependent on the personal whims of their employers.[39] The ruling was passed despite the opposition of estate executives, who argued that the public airing of such issues gave Deli a bad name and tainted its image as a united European front.

THE MARRIAGE RESTRICTION IN DELI

Some sense of those issues and the sorts of solutions sought is evident in one policy contested for nearly fifteen years—the marriage prohibition on incoming European employees. In the late nineteenth century, the major tobacco companies neither accepted married applicants nor allowed them to marry while in service.[40] Corporate authorities held that new European recruits with families in tow would be unable to support them in a proper manner. What they feared they named outright: the emergence of a "European proletariat in Deli."[41] The antimarriage sanction was relaxed in time to a stipulation that an *assistent* could marry after five years of service and then only if he could demonstrate solvency. Concubinary arrangements with Javanese women were considered preferable because they imposed a less onerous financial burden on low-salaried staff and helped newcomers to learn local language and customs quickly. European marriages, on the other hand, threatened to take up too much time and too much of employees' salaries. By refusing to hire married men, the estate industry at once endorsed a system of concubinage long prevalent on Java and condoned its official sanction on the East Coast.

But concubinage was not without local problems. Given a ratio of one Javanese woman for every ten Javanese and Chinese men, competition for sexual and domestic partners among workers and between them and European supervisors was fierce. Fights in the barracks, disputes over women *(vrouwen perkara)*, and assaults on white staff were common. British Malaya authorities too weighed the advantage of households run by native rather than European women. A proliferation of prostitutes and their mixed-blood progeny was viewed as a social blight, but one preferable to the worse alternative: increased numbers of impoverished white men struggling to maintain a properly appointed lifestyle fit for European wives.[42] In both instances, colonial morality was elastic and relative. Interracial sex was seen as more tolerable than European destitution. As John G. Butcher notes, there was a "particular anathema with which the British [in Malaya] regarded 'poor whites.'"[43]

Others assessed the case differently. Some argued that more white women would exert a restraining check on the rowdy and hard-drinking conduct for which Deli's plantation staff were infamous. Jacob Nienhuis, later hailed as Deli's "pioneer" planter, saw marriages to European women as a source of the sort of cozy conviviality *(gezelligheid)* Deli so lacked. In the end it would provide better returns on labor. Not least, he thought the applicant pool would increase if mothers' hearts *(het moederhart)* were assuaged by knowing their children were headed to a place where "cultivated" society reigned.[44]

Throughout *De Planter's* first ten years, the assistants protested the marriage restriction and its infringement on their civil rights. Most important, they took it as a strategic focus for a wider set of demands. If estate directors feared that such unions would impoverish their assistants, the assistants could then argue that improved wages, bonuses, job security, and pensions would ward off such an eventuality. In a language that played on the fears of the colonial elite, the assistants argued for a better standard of living, security from assault, protection of white prestige, and the right to choose their domestic arrangements.

In 1920, after nearly a decade of steady protest, the marriage restriction was rescinded by the major companies, and more white women arrived. The companies held that the change was now possible because Deli was sufficiently prosperous and the industry sufficiently secure to support European families in a fitting manner. But the concession was tied to other events and came at a crucial moment—when estate labor relations had reached a level of tension that threatened European unity on the estates. *De Planter's* editor in chief, C. E. W. Krediet, who had expressed open sympathy for native labor demands and strike actions, was ousted from his post in

1920 and repatriated to Holland. Krediet was replaced by J. van den Brand who was not much better in the eyes of the planters and the colonial administration. Reaction to his sharp critique of Deli's indentured labor system in 1903 had led to the creation of a labor inspectorate on the Deli estates. But, in less than a year, he too was relieved of his post by the governor-general and died a few months later.[45]

Corporate response to staff dissent, both indigenous and European, was basically the same. The recruitment of single male workers from Java and a bachelor staff from Europe was replaced by a policy that encouraged married couples and promoted conditions that would allow "family formation" for both. These parallel policies accentuated divisions and racial distinctions even more than before. On the premise that clear distinctions of standards and salary were safer for whites, in the 1920s European recruits received higher bonuses, better housing, and more fringe benefits. With an added share and stake in the profits, it was hoped they would become more committed to the companies' cause.[46] For Javanese workers, single-family dwellings replaced barracks, and labor compounds were designed with small subsistence plots that would allow a semblance of village life and the growth of a local labor reserve.[47] In turn, the explanations of violence shifted from the poor quality of low-level staff to the clandestine infiltration of communist and nationalist elements among Javanese and Chinese recruits.

As demonstrations against Dutch impositions became more insistent, the divisions within the European enclave were muted by more reforms. Staff were advised to avoid confrontation by maintaining increased physical and social distance from their workers. The predawn roll calls, notorious sites of assaults on Europeans, had already been abolished.[48] Throughout the 1920s, with increasingly mediated chain of command, supervisors were instructed to relay orders through Javanese and Chinese foremen. Such go-betweens *(tussenpersonen)* were expected to ensure that no European would have to risk the wrath that might follow a worker's reprimand. In an about-face, low-level Europeans increasingly sought security in protection *by* the companies rather than in resistance *to* them.

With these changes on the labor front, the supposed commonalties of the European experience in Deli were reinforced and affirmed. Income, housing, and social differentials still set off the lower rungs of estate personnel from those at the top, but the myth of a Deliaan prototype highlighted their common interests. Remembrance and reenactment of Deli's taming and opening was celebrated by the planters' associations and larger companies in gold-embossed commemorative volumes issued every five, ten, and twenty-five years. These corporate stories welded success, hardship, and intrepid personalities. Such volumes produced more than testimony to economic success and heroic achievement. They also invented Deli's official history. The East Coast of Sumatra Institute annually chronicled the expansion of the cultural infrastructure (tennis courts, theater troupes, social clubs, hill stations, and charities), assuring itself and its overseas investors that the European enclave was stable and strong.

Official discourse was laden with military metaphor, bolstered by brass-buttoned uniforms, roll calls, and forms of deference and address that seemed designed as much to deter any break in the ranks as to impress the local and estate populace. The quintessential monument to this fashioned history was the 1925 plan for "a tomb to the unknown planter," designed to memorialize those whites who had died by coolie assault or otherwise in the service of the industry.[49] The notion that any European murdered (regardless of circumstance) was the equivalent of a war hero left no doubt as to the common enemy. Homogenizing their shared past blurred differences among Europeans as it reiterated those that set them apart. It was, after all, in struggle against the archetypal Asian coolie run amok that some unknown planter-soldier had pitted himself and died.

CUSTODIANS OF MORALITY:
FEMALE HONOR AND WHITE PRESTIGE

From the outset, Deli's colonial community was defined by cultural criteria that set it off from the colonized. Housing, dress codes, transport, food, clubs, conversation, recreation, and leaves marked a distinct social space in which Europeans were internally stratified but from which Asians were barred. When the industry saw its position threatened, new measures were usually sought to identify its members, and their affinities and common interests, along racial lines.

It is frequently argued that social and political differentiation of the colonized and the colonizer intensified after the entry of European women. Some accounts claim that their increasing numbers in colonial settlements resulted in increased racism not only because of the native desire they excited and the chivalrous protection they therefore required but also because they were avid racists in their own right. Thus, Percival Spear, writing on the social life of the English in eighteenth-century India, asserted that women "widened the racial gulf" by holding to "their insular whims and prejudices."[50] Similarly, Ashis Nandy has argued that "white women in India were generally more racist [than their men] because they unconsciously saw themselves as the sexual competitors of Indian men."[51] Thomas Beidelman wrote, for colonial Tanganyika, that "European wives and children created a new and less flexible domestic colonialism exhibiting *overconcern* with the sexual accessibility or vulnerability of wives, and with corresponding notions about the need for spatial and social segregation."[52] L. H. Gann and Peter Duignan baldly stated that "it was the cheap steamship ticket for women that put an end to racial integration" in British Africa.[53] In short, sources in which colonial women received little or no mention accord to these otherwise marginal actors the primary responsibility for racial segregation.[54]

But the arrival of women was tied to other plans. It often coincided with some immediately prior or planned strategies of political stabilization. The term *stabilization* ambiguously expressed either a securing of empire or a response to its vulnerability. In India, after the Great Rebellion of 1857, "stabilization" meant further segregation from contacts with local Indian groups.[55] In New Guinea, large numbers of white women arrived in the 1920s when officials perceived the threat of an increasing number of "acculturated" Papuans visibly and vocally critical of colonial policy.[56] The White Women's Protection Ordinance of 1926 too "stabilized" the racial divide—a culmination of political tensions advocated less by women than by men.[57]

A denser spread of European women did not inadvertently produce stronger racial divisions. Sometimes their presence was encouraged precisely to enforce the separation between Asians and whites. The timing of their entry reflected "the real or imagined threat to superiority and status that miscegenation implied."[58] Worries over their safety were part of a wider response that came before European women themselves had raised objections to mixed unions and mixed marriages. Sexual relations between European men and Asian women per se were not condemned so much as the social tensions to which they gave rise. Live-in arrangements with native women and the presence of their mixed progeny came to be seen as a danger to the European community at large.[59]

White women arrived in large numbers in Deli in the 1920s, during the most profitable years of the plantation economy but also at a time of mounting resistance to estate labor conditions and Dutch rule more generally.[60] Their presence excused sharper racial divisions but also justified policies already in motion to close ranks and sanction those European men who muddied the distinctions between ruler and ruled. As caretakers of male well-being and guardians of morality, European women found their activities and the social space in which they could operate tightly controlled.[61]

Among Deli's colonial novelists, Madelon Székely-Lulofs—the wife of a Hungarian estate manager—stands out. Her books were widely published and both lauded and criticized for her descriptions of bored European women on Deli's estates, obsessed with company status distinctions, lonely and trapped on the estates and in the "coziness" of their suffocating homes.[62] Lulofs's stories mocked the finely graded pecking order of European males—and their siege mentality vis-à-vis native labor. Novels by men place the emphasis elsewhere: on white comradery triumphing over the temporarily difficult adjustment to managerial work and a colonial way of life. Women authors stayed close to the sustained social tensions and distinctions deriving from relations of work, pressures for promotion, conflicts over sexual affairs, and class and racial orderings that prevailed in the home.[63]

Whether white women made racial tensions worse, they did not create them.[64] Still, colonial women were committed to racial separation for their own reasons and in their own right. In towns and on plantations, it was more difficult even than in Europe to live outside marriage and motherhood. These women championed a moral order that restricted their husbands' sexual activities as they cordoned off house and garden as sites demanding their presence and vigilant control.

The increased number of white women in Deli accompanied a more general realignment of labor relations in which cultural politics played a key role. Such methods of stabilization invariably produced new arenas of vulnerability, more points of possible infringement, more places that could not be invaded, and new demands for deference that all gave reason for more control. As custodians of a distinct cultural and moral community, white women had their honor to protect, an issue on which European men could stand united and agree. As in the post-Reconstruction U.S. South, where black men were lynched in the name of chivalry,[65] any attempted or imagined infringement of that honor came to be seen as a challenge to European, white, and colonial rule.[66] In 1929, at a moment when assaults on European staff occurred nearly every month, the killing of an estate *assistent's* wife by a Javanese worker was seen as a subversive act of "communist agitation" and a direct threat to Dutch authority.[67] Officials reacted by sending army reinforcements to Deli and by expanding intelligence operations on the estates. The fascist-linked Fatherland Club, with a strong following in the plantation belt, gained increased support in succeeding years.

THE STRUCTURING OF EUROPEAN COMMUNITIES AND THE PROBLEM OF POOR WHITES

What at first glance seems artificial in European colonial settlements are the burdensome accoutrements that Europeans brought with them: heavy

clothing that mildewed, rich food and liquor that was hard to digest, furniture that retained the heat and sometimes rotted onboard ship before it arrived. These and other markers of European culture have been captured and
caricatured in the novels of Anthony Burgess, Somerset Maugham, and
George Orwell: the jungle planter sweating through a five-course dinner in
formal attire. But cultural artifices were only part of larger projects to construct communities of particular structure and form. Such communities
were demographically and socially skewed by the small numbers of
European women and children in early colonial settlements and the enclosed social space that was delimited for them once they came.

Disease and lethargy were deemed a threat to all Europeans, but children were thought particularly vulnerable.[68] Physical susceptibility had its
social coordinates. European children were subject to cultural contamination when they played with the children of servants and mimicked local
language, gestures, and customs. Native nursemaids cared for the small
children, but older ones were more often sent to boarding schools in
Europe, packed off to schools and vacation colonies in temperate hill stations, or, as in nineteenth-century Hawaii, confined with their mothers to
walled courtyards in the latter's charge.[69] Deli, like other colonial communities, had only a small representation of older children and adolescents.[70]

Adult men were also unevenly represented. When possible, authorities restricted the presence of nonproductive men and those who might sully the
image of a healthy and "vigorous" race.[71] In Deli, the infirm, the aged, and
the insane were quickly sent home. Insurgents were repatriated, while the
impoverished were sheltered and supported until they too could be shipped
out. British authorities in nineteenth-century India also institutionalized "unseemly" whites (in orphanages, workhouses, mental asylums, and old-age
homes) for much of their lives, out of the view of Indians and Europeans
alike.[72] Proposals to establish agricultural settlements for poor Scottish peasants in India and young Dutch farmers in the Indies met with resistance from
those who stressed the "loss of racial prestige and authority which . . . an
'influx' of poor whites would bring."[73] Plans to settle struggling Dutch farmers in Sumatra's Batak highlands during the Great Depression were strongly
opposed by the planter elite as a "chimera" that would lead to "wretched
[European] pauperism."[74]

The potential and actual presence of poor, "unfit" whites was central to
reformist social policies in colonies across the globe. British, Dutch, and
French colonial businessmen and policy makers designed pay scales, housing, medical facilities, marriage restrictions, and labor contracts to ensure
that colonial ventures appeared a middle-class phenomenon. Some sem-

blance of ease was made possible by the low wages paid to domestic workers and to others who provided local services. Still, bourgeois amenities were
not within the reach of many who held the lowest supervisory posts. These
positions, reserved for Indo-Europeans in other colonies and other parts of
the Indies, were occupied in Deli by those of more modest origins but still
considered "European."

The presence of poor whites was more widespread than most colonial
histories lead us to imagine. In nineteenth-century India, "nearly half the
European population could be called poor whites"; nearly six thousand were
placed in workhouses by 1900.[75] In the Indies, European pauperism was a
concern of the Dutch East Indies Company as early as the mid-eighteenth
century. By the early 1900s, government reports were identifying tens of
thousands of Eurasians ("Indos") and "full-blooded" Europeans as dangerously impoverished.[76] In nineteenth-century Barbados, poor whites (called
"redlegs") made up more than three-fourths of the European population.[77]
In French North Africa, a vast population of petits blancs included many of
non-French European origin whose political interests diverged from both
the French colonial elite and the skilled black Africans with whom they
competed for jobs.[78]

South Africa's poor white population, conservatively estimated at three
hundred thousand in the 1920s, was admittedly of a different order but warrants comparison.[79] A comprehensive investigation carried out by the
Carnegie Commission in 1929–30 was prompted by increasing numbers of
European paupers on the internal labor market and concerns about white
prestige. The commission concluded that wider class distinction among
Europeans was giving rise to more mixing between poor whites and "colored" groups. Blacks were no longer calling poor white farmers "boss" but
by their familiar, Christian names. Poor whites and "colored" were eating
and drinking together, reportedly displaying "no consciousness of the need
for a segregation policy."[80] South Africa represented the extreme of enforced
separation, but it was not an exception. Colonial India and Indonesia were
able to maintain less formal racialized regimes because their numbers of
"unfit whites," their settler communities, and, most important, the class composition of their resident white populations were in check and controlled.
Unlike in South Africa, the dangerous, disabled, or destitute could be sent
home. Colonial India and Sumatra experienced a poor white problem of a
magnitude different from South Africa's, but attempts to contain it and the
debates it animated were motivated by similar fears and priorities.

As early as 1891 a relief fund for "needy Europeans" was established in
Deli to support bankrupt planters and their staff, casualties of the economic

crisis triggered by the halving of tobacco prices on the world market.[81] At the end of World War I, concern over white pauperism again loomed large. With the supply of goods from Europe severely diminished and the prices precipitously increased, many companies were forced to grant a temporary cost-of-living allowance to their lower-salaried European personnel. Despite such efforts, the East Coast of Sumatra Institute reported "scores of Europeans without work and without means of support, at large and roaming around the administrative center of Medan."[82] Some lived on credit from Javanese hotels, others on the hospitality of local people on and off the estates. Both options represented a diminished standard of living, an inappropriate circumstance and an affront to the unspoken rules of European comportment on Sumatra's East Coast. Programs devised to provide aid to impoverished Europeans had insufficient funds to support the large numbers who fell below the *acceptable* standard. During the 1921 malaise, relief funds were again collected for the increasing number of European paupers *(armlastingen)* and vagrants *(landloopers)* until they could be sent home.[83] Those who fell through the cracks ended up in native villages when they had exhausted the largesse of their European friends.[84]

In the 1930s, white pauperism, like the depression itself, was of crisis proportions.[85] For the first time, repatriation was not an option as Europe's economies were as faltering as those in the colonies. The projected cost of reengaging personnel from Europe when the crisis passed was considered exorbitant. Moreover, many of these people had nowhere to go. In 1931, of the 240,000 Europeans in the Indies, some ten percent were unemployed.[86] Some reports estimated more than 5,500 unemployed Europeans in 1932, of which 3,238 were listed as "in straitened circumstances."[87] In Deli, the situation was worse. Of nearly 1,700 Europeans working on the estates, half were dismissed within the first few years of the depression; more than 400 were low-level staff.[88]

With the threat of so many Europeans living on the edge, relief agencies arose to feed and board them at some semblance of a European standard. Hotel owners housed them for nominal rent, while hill station resorts were converted into social service centers where courses were given in modern languages and bookkeeping.[89] Their children received free schooling and free lunches. The Salvation Army put scores of families in abandoned hill station villas, and the Support Committee for European "Crisis-Victims" provided funds to more than a thousand European adults and children. Remedies that were used in the United States and Europe to deal with economic crisis—the "make-a-job" and "odd-job" campaigns to keep the working classes occupied at typically menial tasks, scavenging work, and public utilities maintenance—were considered unsuitable for a middle-class colonial elite.[90] Some of those who were out of work tried to help themselves, setting up makeshift colonies on forestry reserves for small-scale agriculture and husbandry, but they were few in number.[91] Impoverished Indo-Europeans fell between the cracks of both the indigenous and the European support systems. Ironically, those who attempted to sustain themselves on subsistence farming were barred from doing so "owing to the traditional policy of excluding from agriculture all who ranked as Europeans."[92]

The handling of the worldwide crisis accentuated certain local social distinctions and political alliances in Deli while downplaying others. First, it wiped out the dissident voice of subordinate whites. In 1931, the Assistants' Union was merged with the Sumatra Cultuur Bond, created by and representing the plantation companies.[93] Two years later, the 1917 Assistants' Ruling was abolished and absorbed into a "planters' ruling" that encompassed lower- and higher-level staff alike. Both moves undermined whatever was left of an independent politics for low-level staff. Affirming the "community of interest" that all Europeans shared, company directors maintained that an "economic class struggle" was not in the interests of unemployed assistants, owners of industry, or the colonial state.[94]

Second, the depression produced a wave of reaction against the increasing number of non-Dutch Europeans employed as estate staff and their recruitment was curtailed. Third, it created a more solid alliance between the plantation elite and the colonial administration. As the economy recovered in the mid-1930s, a more rationalized estate industry, devoid of indigenous "dangerous elements" and with an air of "military discipline," resumed full operation.[95] But unemployment did not disappear with the crisis. In 1935, nearly twenty thousand Europeans who could no longer be classed as crisis victims remained out of work in colonial Indonesia.[96] The astute criticism of government policy regarding white pauperism that appeared in 1931 in *Onze Stem* (one of the early dissident Indo newspapers) was still on the mark: "The important principal fault of the Government is that it only wants to see European employment as a crisis-phenomenon" when in fact it had a much longer history and wider social spread.[97]

EXCLUSION AND ENCLOSURE OF COLONIAL CATEGORIES

The preceding discussion points to a major problem with accounts that speak of "the British" in Malaya or "the Dutch" in the East Indies. It forces our attention to internal differences peculiar to each of these European colonial communities and to their idiosyncratic membership requirements. Something as apparently basic as who could legally be deemed a European differed across colonial contexts, revealing discrepant and *changing* criteria by which racial superiority and attendant European privilege were assigned. For example, in the Netherlands Indies during the early twentieth century, the legal category "European" paralleled only loosely the idea of ethnic European origin. Included within it were Japanese, Jews, Arabs, Armenians, Filipinos, naturalized Javanese, Sudanese wives of Dutch-born bureaucrats, recognized children of mixed marriages, and Christian Africans.[98] To acquire European legal equivalence *(gelijkgestelde)* in 1884, one had to (1) be Christian, (2) speak and write Dutch, (3) have a European upbringing and education, and (4) demonstrate a suitability for European society.[99] Or one could acquire European status by virtue of marriage to or adoption by a European.

The distinctions that set the colonized apart from the colonizer were further complicated by the movement of "Europeans" from one colonial context to another. In British-ruled Malaya in the 1930s, for instance, those designating themselves European outnumbered those who were considered part of the colonizing community proper. The sons and daughters of mixed marriages in Indochina and the Netherlands Indies—persons who were often regarded as part of the native population in their home countries— might list themselves as French, Dutch, or Portuguese when resident outside the colonies from which they came.[100] Such a shifting and arbitrary assignment of social membership makes clear that "European" and "colonizer" were not always synonymous categories.[101]

What is striking when we look to identify the contours and composition of any particular colonial community is the extent to which control over sexuality and reproduction was at the core of defining colonial privilege and its boundaries. Whether incoming European colonials married, lived with, or bedded native women, early colonial communities commonly produced a quotidian world in which the dominant cultural influence in the household was native.[102] That prohibitions against interracial marriage were commonly late rather than early colonial inventions (in such diverse contexts as Mexico, Cuba, India, Indonesia, and the U.S. South) suggests that it was not interracial sexual contact that was seen as dangerous but its public legitimation in marriage. Similarly, it was not the progeny of such unions who were problematic but the possibility that they might be recognized as heirs to a European inheritance. The point should be obvious: colonial control and profits depended on a continual readjustment of the parameters of European membership, limiting who had access to property and privilege and who did not.

Given such disparate origins and circumstances, not all who were classed as European were colonial practitioners or colonialism's local agents.

Thousands were drawn from the middle ranks of the colonized and were neither "cultural brokers" nor natural "intermediaries." The populations that fell within these contradictory colonial locations were subject to a frequently shifting set of criteria that allowed them privilege at certain moments and pointedly excluded them at others. This is not to deny that sharp distinctions divided those who were ruled and those who did the ruling but to highlight the fact that these divisions were not as easily (or permanently) drawn as the official discourse might lead one to imagine.

While Beidelman's contention that "anthropological curiosity [has] stopped at the color bar"[103] may be exaggerated, much evidence supports his claim. For the most part, it has not been progressive social scientists who have sought to describe colonial mentalities but postcolonial intellectuals who have broached the psychology and political economy of rulers and ruled. Frantz Fanon, Albert Memmi, Aimé Césaire, and Ashis Nandy[104] have sought to identify a colonial consciousness that entrapped the defenders of empire as well as its more passive middling participants. The colonial everyman they paint is often a politically conservative composite of middle-class moralism and what V. S. Naipaul once called " B-rate mediocrity."[105] It is also they who have pointed to the intimate injuries of empire for the colonized: hypermasculinity, guilt, alienation, rage at and acceptance of a system that nurtures violence. White women appear as racist accomplices, defined by proxy to their men.

Such caricatures effectively capture certain features of colonials but are limiting. Some colonial administrations selected for mediocrity; others produced it. Middle-class moralism, as we have seen, comprised a wide range of substitutable prohibitions and standards, given new meanings by the changing political agenda to which it was applied. Still, their combined sensibilities suggest that a liberatory political analysis was contingent on locating racism, class tensions, and sexual subordination as key to the everyday cultural idioms of colonial domination. For anthropology, it suggests that we take seriously Memmi's insistence that colonialism creates both the colonizer and the colonized. Attending to the internal structures of colonial authority makes it harder to ignore those features of European class and gender perceptions and practice that were selectively refashioned to create and maintain the social distinctions of empire and the cultural boundaries of rule.

3 Carnal Knowledge and Imperial Power

*Gender and Morality
in the Making of Race*

Over the past fifteen years the anthropology of women has fundamentally altered an understanding of colonial expansion and its consequences for the colonized. In identifying how European conquest affected valuations of women's work and redefined their proper domains, feminist scholars have sought to explain how changes in household organization, the sexual division of labor, and the gender-specific control of resources within it have modified and shaped how colonial appropriations of land, labor, and resources were obtained.[1] Much of this research has focused on indigenous gendered patterns of economic activity, political participation, and social knowledge and on the agency of those confronted with European rule—but less on the distinct agency of those women and men who carried it out.

More recent attention to the structures of colonial authority has placed new emphasis on the quotidian assertion of European dominance in the colonies, on imperial interventions in domestic life, and thus on the cultural prescriptions by which European women and men lived.[2] From an earlier focus on how colonizers have viewed the indigenous Other, more work is beginning to sort out how Europeans in the colonies imagined themselves and constructed communities built on asymmetries of race, class, and gender—entities significantly at odds with the European models on which they were drawn.

Feminist attempts to engage the gender politics of Dutch, French, and British imperial cultures converge on some strikingly similar observations; namely, that European women in these colonies experienced the cleavages of racial dominance and internal social distinctions very differently than men precisely because of their ambiguous positions, as both subordinates in colonial hierarchies and as agents of empire in their own right.[3] Concomitantly, the majority of European women who left for the colonies in the late nineteenth and early twentieth century confronted frequent constraint on their domestic, economic, and political options, more limiting than those in metropolitan Europe at the time and in sharp contrast to the opportunities open to colonial men.[4]

In varied form these studies raise a basic question: in what ways were gender inequalities essential to the structure of colonial racism and imperial authority? Was the strident misogyny of imperial thinkers and colonial agents a by-product of received metropolitan values ("they just brought it with them"), a reaction to contemporary feminist demands in Europe ("women need to be put back in their breeding place"), or a novel and pragmatic response to the conditions of conquest? Was the assertion of European supremacy in terms of patriotic manhood and racial virility an expression of imperial domination or a defining feature of it?

In this chapter I further pursue the premise that imperial authority and racial distinctions were fundamentally structured in gendered terms. I look at the administrative and medical discourse and management of European sexual activity, reproduction, and marriage as part of the apparatus of colonial control. Here I attend more to the dominant male discourse (less to women's perceptions of the constraints placed on them), arguing that it was how women's needs were defined, not by but for them, that most directly shaped specific policies.[5] The very categories "colonizer" and "colonized" were secured through forms of sexual control that defined the domestic arrangements of Europeans and the cultural investments by which they identified themselves. Treating the sexual and conjugal tensions of colonial life as more than a political trope for the tensions of empire writ small but as a part of the latter in socially profound and strategic ways, this chapter examines how gender-specific sexual sanctions and prohibitions not only demarcated positions of power but also prescribed the personal and public boundaries of race.

Colonial authority was constructed on two powerful but false premises. The first was the notion that Europeans in the colonies made up an easily identifiable and discrete biological and social entity—a "natural" community of common class interests, racial attributes, political affinities, and superior culture. The second was the related notion that the boundaries separating colonizer from colonized were thus self-evident and easily drawn. Neither premise reflected colonial realities. Settler colonies such as those in Rhodesia and Algeria excepted—where inter-European conflicts were violent and overt—tensions between bureaucrats and planters, settlers and transients, missionaries and metropolitan policy makers, and petits blancs and monied entrepreneurs have always made European colonial communities more socially fractious and politically fragile than many of their members professed.[6] Internal divisions grew out of competing economic and political agendas—conflicts over access to indigenous resources, frictions over appropriate methods for safeguarding European privilege and power, competing criteria for reproducing a colonial elite and for restricting its membership.

The shift away from viewing colonial elites as homogenous communities of common interest marks an important trajectory in the anthropology of empire, signaling a major rethinking of gender relations within it. The markers of European identity and the criteria for community membership no longer appear as fixed but emerge as a more obviously fluid, permeable, and historically disputed terrain. The colonial politics of exclusion was contingent on constructing categories. Colonial control was predicated on identifying who was "white," who was "native," and which children could become citizens rather than subjects, on which were legitimate progeny and which were not.

What mattered was not only one's physical properties but also who counted as "European" and by what measure.[7] Skin shade was too ambiguous. Bank accounts were mercurial. Religious belief and education were crucial markers but never clear enough. Social and legal standing derived from the cultural prism through which color was viewed, from the silences, acknowledgments, and denials of the social circumstances in which one's parents had sex. Sexual unions based on concubinage, prostitution, or church marriage derived from the hierarchies of rule. But, in turn, they were provisional relations, based on contested classifications, that could alter individual fates and the very structure of colonial society.[8] Ultimately, inclusion or exclusion required regulating the sexual, conjugal, and domestic life of both European colonials and their subjects.

POLITICAL MESSAGES AND SEXUAL METAPHORS

Colonial observers and participants in the imperial enterprise appear to have had unlimited interest in the sexual interface of the colonial encounter. No subject is discussed more than sex in colonial literature and no subject more frequently invoked to foster the racist stereotypes of European society.[9] The tropics provided a site for European pornographic fantasies long before conquest was under way, with lurid descriptions of sexual license, promiscuity, gynecological aberrations, and general perversion marking the Otherness of the colonized for metropolitan consumption.[10] Noting the rigid sexual protocols of nineteenth-century Europe, some colonial historians, such as Ronald Hyam, have suggested that imperial expansion itself was derived from the export of male sexual energy.[11] Grann and Duignan saw colonialism as "a sublimation or alternative to sex [for European men]."[12] Both statements misconstrue the case, but one thing is clear: with the sustained presence of Europeans in the colonies, sexual prescriptions of varied sorts and targeting different actors became increasingly central to social policy and subject to new forms of scrutiny by colonial states.

The salience of sexual symbols as graphic representations of colonial dominance is relatively unambiguous and well established. Edward Said, for example, argued that the sexual submission and possession of Oriental women by European men "fairly *stands for* the pattern of relative strength between East and West, and the discourse about the Orient that it enabled."[13] Orientalism was described as a "male perception of the world[,] . . . a male power fantasy," "an exclusively male province," in which the Orient was penetrated, silenced, and possessed.[14] Sexuality, then, serves as a loaded metaphor for domination, but Said's critique was not (nor did it claim to be) about those relations between women and men. Sexual images illustrate the iconography of rule, not its pragmatics. Sexual asymmetries and visions convey what is "really" going on elsewhere, at another political epicenter. They are tropes to depict other centers of power.

If Asian women are centerfolds for the imperial voyeur, European women often appear in male colonial writings only as a reverse image— fulfilling not sexual but other power fantasies of European men.[15] Whether portrayed as paragons of morality or as parasitic and passive actors on the imperial stage, they are rarely the object of European male desire.[16] To assume that European men and women participated equally in the prejudices and pleasures that colonial privilege bestowed on them eschews the fact that European women took part in colonial relations in ways that imposed fundamentally different restrictions on them.

Sexual domination has been more often considered as a discursive symbol, instrumental in the conveyance of other meanings, but less often as the substance of imperial policy. Was sexual dominance, then, merely a graphic substantiation of who was on the bottom and who was on the top? Was the medium the message, or did sexual relations always "mean" something else, stand in for other relations, evoke the sense of *other* (pecuniary, political, or some possibly more subliminal) desires? This analytic slippage between the sexual symbols of power and the politics of sex runs throughout the colonial record—as well as through contemporary commentaries on it. Some of this may reflect the polyvalent quality of sexuality—symbolically rich and socially salient at the same time. But sexual control was more than a convenient metaphor for colonial domination. It was a fundamental class and racial marker implicated in a wider set of relations of power.

Kenneth Ballhatchet's work on Victorian India has pointed in a similar direction.[17] By showing that regulations on sexual access, prostitution, and venereal disease were central to segregationist policy, he linked issues of sexual management to the internal structure of British rule. He convincingly argued that it was through the policing of sex that subordinate European military and civil servants were kept in line and that racial boundaries were maintained. This was a study, then, about relations of power between men and men. Ballhatchet had little to say about constraints on European colonial women as his emphasis was not on relations of power between women and men.

As a critical interface of sexuality and the wider political order, the relationship between gender prescriptions and racial boundaries is a subject that remains unevenly unexplored. While recent work shows clearly that European women of different classes experienced the colonial venture very differently from one another and from men, we still know relatively little about the distinct investments they had in a racism they shared.[18] Feminist scholars have made efforts to sort out the distinct colonial experience of European women, how they were incorporated into, resisted, and affected the politics of their men.[19] Studies of the intervention of state, business, and religious institutions in the reproductive decisions of colonized populations are now joined by those that examine the work of European women in these programs, the influence of European welfare programs on colonial medicine, and the reproductive constraints on colonial women themselves.[20]

Most of these contributions have attended to the broader issue of gender ideologies and colonial authority, not specifically to how sexual control has figured in the fixing of racial boundaries per se. Although feminist research across disciplines has increasingly explored the "social embeddedness of sexuality" and the contexts that "condition, constrain and socially define [sexual] acts,"[21] this emphasis has not refocused attention on the *racial* "embeddedness of sexuality" in colonial contexts as one might expect. Important exceptions include recent work on southern Africa, where changing restrictions on colonial prostitution and domestic service were explicitly class-specific and directly tied racial policy to sexual control.[22]

The fastening of sexual control to racial tensions is both obvious and elusive. Take, for example, Ronald Takaki's[23] assertion that sexual fear in nineteenth-century America was at base a racial anxiety. Few scholars would disagree, but nothing in the assertion accounts for why it is through sexuality that such anxieties are expressed. Winthrop Jordan sought some sort of answer in proposing that in the nineteenth-century American South, "the sex act itself served as a ritualistic re-enactment of the daily pattern of social dominance."[24] Sander Gilman has argued more generally that sexuality is the most salient marker of Otherness and therefore figures in *any* racist ideology.[25] Like skin color, he contended, "sexual structures, such as the shape of the genitalia, are always the antithesis of the idealized self's."[26] If we accept Gilman's claim there should be no surprise that colonial agents and colonized subjects expressed their contests—and vulnerabilities—in these terms.

This notion of sexuality as a core aspect of social identity has figured importantly in analyses of the psychological motivation of and injuries incurred by colonial rule.[27] Here, sexual submission substantiates colonial racism, imposing fundamental limits on personal liberation. Among colonial and postcolonial male authors, questions of virility and definitions of manliness have been placed at political center stage. The demasculinization of colonized men and the hypermasculinity of European males are understood as key elements in the assertion of white supremacy. But these are studies concerned with the psychological salience of women and sex in the subordination of men by men. They only incidentally deal with sex*ism* and racism as well as racism and sex.[28]

An overlapping set of discourses has provided the psychological and economic underpinnings for colonial distinctions of difference. These discourses tie fears of sexual contamination, physical danger, climatic incompatibility, and moral breakdown to the security of a European national identity with a racist and class-specific core. Colonial scientific reports and the popular press are filled with assertions varying on a common theme: native women bear contagions, white women become sterile in the colonies, colonial men are susceptible to physical, moral, and mental degeneration when they remain in the tropics too long. What work do such statements perform? To what degree are they medically or politically grounded? We need to unpack what is metaphor, what is perceived as dangerous (is it disease, culture, climate, or sex?), and what is not.

SEX AND OTHER CATEGORIES OF COLONIAL CONTROL

Though sex cannot of itself enable men to transcend racial barriers, it generates some admiration and affection across them, which is healthy, and which cannot always be dismissed as merely self-interested and prudential. On the whole, sexual interaction between Europeans and non-Europeans probably did more good than harm to race relations; at any rate, I cannot accept the feminist contention that it was fundamentally undesirable.[29]

The regulation of sexual relations was central to the development of particular kinds of colonial settlements and to the allocation of economic activity within them. Who bedded and wedded whom in the colonies of France, England, Holland, and Iberia was never left to chance. Unions between Annamite women and French men, between Portuguese women and Dutch men, between Inca women and Spanish men produced offspring with claims to privilege, whose rights and status had to be determined and prescribed. From the early 1600s through the twentieth century the sexual sanctions and conjugal prohibitions of colonial agents were rigorously debated and carefully codified. It is in these debates over matrimony and morality that trading and plantation company officials, missionaries, investment bankers, military high commands, and agents of the colonial state confronted one another's visions of empire and the settlement patterns on which it would rest.

In 1622 the Dutch East Indies Company (VOC) arranged for the transport of six poor but marriageable young Dutch women to Java, providing them with clothing, a dowry on marriage, and a contract binding them to five years in the Indies.[30] Aside from this and one other short-lived experiment, immigration of European women was explicitly restricted for the next two hundred years. VOC shareholders argued against female emigration on multiple counts. First, they maintained that the transportation costs for married women and daughters were too high.[31] Second, they argued that Dutch women (with stronger ties than men to the Netherlands?) might hinder initiatives for permanent European settlement. By goading their burgher husbands to quick profits through nefarious trade, they would then press for repatriation to display their newfound wealth.[32] Third, the VOC feared that Dutch women might engage in private trade and encroach on the company's monopoly.[33] Fourth, the objection was raised that European children would become sickly, force families to repatriate, and deplete the font of permanent settlers.[34]

The East Indies Company regulated against female migration by selecting bachelors as their European recruits and by promoting both extramarital relations and legal unions between low-ranking employees and imported slave women.[35] There were some Euro-Asian marriages among the colonial elite, but government regulations made concubinage a more attractive option by prohibiting European men from returning to the Netherlands with native wives and children.[36] For the middling colonial staff, the East Indies Company firmly discouraged Euro-Asian marriages. Households based on Euro-Asian *unions*, by contrast, were seen to bear distinct advantages. Individual employees would bear the costs of dependents, mixed unions would produce healthier children, and Asian women would make fewer financial and affective demands. Finally, men would be more likely to remain if they established families with local roots.

Concubinage served colonial interests in other ways. It permitted permanent settlement and rapid growth by a cheaper means than the importation of European women. Salaries of European recruits to the colonial armies, bureaucracies, plantation companies, and trading enterprises were carefully calibrated and kept artificially low. Eliminating expenses for family support and transportation costs was only part of the story. As important, local women provided domestic services for which new European recruits would otherwise have had to pay. In the mid-nineteenth century such arrangements were de rigueur for young civil servants intent on setting up households on their own.[37] Despite clerical opposition (the church never attained a secure and independent foothold in the Indies), by the nineteenth century concubinage was the most prevalent living arrangement for European men.[38] Nearly half of the Indies' European male population in the 1880s were unmarried and living with Asian women.[39] Government decrees designed to limit barrack concubinage in 1903 were never enforced.[40] It was only in the early twentieth century that concubinage was more actively condemned.[41]

The administrative arguments from the 1600s invoked to curb the immigration of European women, on the one hand, and to condone sexual access to indigenous women, on the other, bear a striking resemblance to the sexual politics of colonial expansion in other times and places. Colonized women living as the concubines of European men—referred to as *nyai* in Java and Sumatra, *congai* in Indochina, and *petite épouse* throughout the French empire—formed the dominant domestic arrangement in colonial cultures through the early twentieth century. Unlike prostitution, which could and often did increase the number of syphilitic and therefore nonproductive European men, concubinage was considered to stabilize political order and colonial health. It kept men in their barracks and bungalows rather than in brothels or hospitals or, worse, in "unnatural" liaisons with one another.[42] Although prostitution served some of the colonies for some of the time, it often proved medically and socially problematic. It had little appeal for those administrations bent on promoting permanent settlement,[43] and venereal disease was difficult to check even with the elaborate system of lock hospitals and contagious-disease acts developed in parts of the British empire.

Across Asia and Africa, colonial decision makers counted on the social services that local women supplied as "useful guides to the language and other mysteries of the local societies."[44] Their medical and cultural know-how was credited with keeping many European men alive in their initial, precarious confrontation with tropical life.[45] Handbooks for incoming plantation staff bound for Tonkin, Sumatra, and Malaya urged men to find a bed-servant as a prerequisite to quick acclimatization.[46] In Malaysia commercial companies encouraged their European staff to procure local "companions" for psychological and physical well-being, as protection against the ill health that sexual abstention, isolation, and boredom were thought to bring.[47] Even in the British empire, where the colonial office officially banned concubinage in 1910, it was tacitly condoned and practiced long after.[48] In the Indies a similar sanction against concubinage among civil servants was only selectively enforced. It had little effect on domestic arrangements outside of Java and no real impact in Sumatra's new plantation belt where Javanese and Japanese *huishoudsters* (as Asian mistresses were sometimes called; lit. "housekeeper") remained the rule rather than the exception.[49]

Concubinage was the prevalent term for cohabitation outside marriage between European men and Asian women. But the term ambiguously covered a wide range of arrangements that included sexual access to a non-European woman as well as demands on her labor and legal rights to the children she bore. If glossed as companionship or cohabitation outside marriage, it suggests more social privileges than most women who were involved in such relations would have enjoyed.[50] They could be dismissed without reason, notice, or severance pay. They might be exchanged among Europeans and "passed on" when men left for leave or retirement in Europe. The Indies Civil Code of 1848 made their position poignantly clear: native women "had no rights over children recognized by a white man."[51] Some women combined sexual and domestic service with the abject status of slave or coolie and lived in separate quarters. On East Sumatra's plantations, where such arrangements were structured into company labor policies, Javanese women picked from the coolie ranks often retained their original labor contracts for the duration of their sexual and domestic service.[52]

Most of these women remained servants, sharing only the beds of European staff. But some combined their service with varied degrees of independence and authority and used their positions to enhance their economic and political standing. In Indochina and the Indies, officials complained that local women provided employment to their own kin, making sure that the

Figure 7. Lithograph, "The Nyai or Native Huishoudster,"
from the portfolio of K. Fuhri, 1853. KITLV no. 35 B 185.

houses in which they served were peopled with gardeners, washerwomen, and night watchmen from their own families. Working for colonial men of higher station, these huishoudsters might run parts of the businesses of the men with whom they had arrangements, hire and fire the servants, and manage shopping budgets and other household affairs.[53] Javanese women (like the European-born in a later period) were called on to keep men physically and psychologically fit for work, to keep them satisfied without distracting them or urging them out of line.[54] Women who worked in such capacities in remote districts and plantation areas provided for the daily needs of the lower-level European staff without imposing the emotional and financial obligations that European family life would demand.[55]

Concubinage reinforced the hierarchies on which colonial societies were based and made those distinctions more problematic at the same time. In North Sumatra, grossly uneven sex ratios often made for intense competition among male workers and their European supervisors for women who would perform these services.[56] Javanese women were not the only ones requisitioned for such jobs. Elsewhere in the Indies, impoverished Indo-European women lived in situations that blurred the boundaries between companionship, concubinage, and paid-for sex. And it was that very blurring that disturbed the racial sensibilities of the Dutch-born elite.[57] Metropolitan critics were openly disdainful of these liaisons on moral grounds—all the more so when these unions became sustained and emotionally significant relationships. Such affective ties defied the racial premise of concubinage as no more than an emotionally unfettered convenience.[58]

The tension between concubinage as a confirmation of racial hierarchy and as a threatening compromise to that order was nowhere more visible than in reactions to the progeny that it produced. Mixed-bloods, poor Indos, and abandoned *métis* children straddled the division of ruler and ruled as they threatened to blur that divide. Referred to by the common Dutch term *voorkinderen* (children from a previous marriage or union), in the colonies the term was racially marked to signal illegitimate children of a mixed union. Economically disadvantaged and socially invisible, they were sent "back" to native *kampongs* or shuttled into the shoddy compounds of impoverished whites.[59]

Concubinage was a domestic arrangement based on sexual service and gender inequalities that "worked" efficiently by some criteria and badly by others. When European identity and supremacy were thought to be vulnerable, in jeopardy, or less than convincing, concubinage came under more direct attack. At the turn of the century and increasingly through the 1920s, colonial elites responded by clarifying the cultural criteria of privilege and the moral premises of their unity. Sex in the politically safe context of prostitution and where possible in the more desirable context of marriage between "full-blooded" Europeans, replaced concubinage.[60] As in other colonial regions, the ban on concubinage was not always expressed in explicit racist language. On the contrary, difference and distance were often coded to mark race in culturally clear but nuanced terms.[61]

Restrictions on European Women in the Colonies

Most accounts of colonial conquest and settlement concur in suggesting that European women chose to avoid early pioneering ventures, but the choice was rarely their own.[62] In the Indies, a government ordinance of 1872 made it impossible for any soldier below the rank of sergeant major to marry. Even above that rank, conditions were very restrictive.[63] In the Indies

Figure 8.   'A picnic at Daoen Lassi,' from photo album titled "Souvenirs of Ternate," 1903. Note the range of women of different dress and different hue, wearing Javanese dress on an "outing." KITLV no. 10.311.

army, marriage was a privilege of the officer corps, with barracks concubinage instituted and regulated for the rank and file. In the twentieth century, formal and informal prohibitions set by banks, estates, and government services operating in Africa, India, and Southeast Asia restricted marriage during the first three to five years of service, while some prohibited it altogether. In Malaya, the major British banks required their employees to sign contracts agreeing to request permission to marry, with the understanding that it would not be granted in less than eight years.[64]

Many historians assume that these bans on employee marriage and on the immigration of European women lifted when specific colonies were politically stable, medically upgraded, and economically secure. But marriage restrictions lasted well into the twentieth century, long after rough living and a scarcity of amenities had become conditions of the past. In India as late as 1929, British employees in the political service were still recruited at the age of twenty-six and then prohibited from marriage during their first three probationary years.[65] In the army, marriage allowances were also denied until the same age, while in the commercial houses, restrictions were frequent but less overt.[66] On the Ivory Coast, employment contracts in the 1920s denied marriage with European women before the third tour, which meant a minimum of five years' service, so that many men remained unmarried past the age of thirty.[67]

European demographics in the colonies were shaped by these economic and political exigencies and thus were enormously skewed by sex. Among the laboring immigrant and native populations as well as among Europeans in the late nineteenth and early twentieth century, the number of men was, at the very least, double that of women and sometimes exceeded it by twenty-five times. Although in the Indies the overall ratio of European women to men rose from 47:100 to 88:100 between 1900 and 1930, representing an absolute increase from 4,000 to 26,000 Dutch women,[68] in outlying islands the ratios were kept far more uneven. On Sumatra's plantation belt in 1920, there were still only 61 European women per 100 men.[69] On Africa's Ivory Coast, European sex ratios through 1921 were still 1:25.[70] In Tonkin, European men sharply outnumbered European women as late as 1931, when there were 14,085 European men (including military) to 3,083 European women.[71] While these imbalances were usually attributed to the physical hazards of life in the tropics, political explanations are more compelling. In controlling the availability of European women and the sorts of sexual access allowed, colonial state and corporate authorities avoided salary increases as well as the proliferation of a lower-class European settler population. Such policies did not mute the internal class distinctions within the European communities. On the contrary, they shaped the social geography of the colonies by fixing the conditions under which European privileges could be attained and reproduced.

As in North Sumatra, the marriage prohibition was both a political and an economic issue, defining the social contours of colonial communities and the standards of living in them.[72] But, as importantly, it revealed how strongly the conduct of private life and the sexual proclivities individuals expressed were tied to corporate profits and the security of the colonial state. Irregular domestic arrangements were thought to encourage subversion as strongly as acceptable unions could avert it. Family stability and sexual "normalcy" were thus concretely linked to political agitation or quiescence.

Domestic arrangements varied as government officials and private businesses weighed the economic versus political costs of one arrangement over another, but such calculations were invariably meshed. Those in high office saw white prestige and profits as inextricably linked, and attitudes toward concubinage reflected that concern.[73] Colonial morality and the place of concubinage in it was relative. Thus in Malaya through the 1920s, concubinage was tolerated precisely because "poor whites" were not. Government and plantation administrators argued that white prestige would be imperiled if European men became impoverished in attempting to maintain middle-class lifestyles and European wives. In late-nineteenth-century Java, in contrast, concubinage itself was considered a major source of white pauperism, condemned at precisely the same time that a new colonial morality passively condoned illegal brothels.[74]

What constituted morality vacillated, as did what defined white prestige—and what its defense should entail. No description of European colonial communities fails to note the obsession with white prestige as a basic feature of colonial thinking. Its protection looms as the primary cause of a long list of otherwise inexplicable postures, prejudices, fears, and violences. But what upheld that prestige was not a constant; concubinage was socially lauded at one time and seen as a political menace at another. White prestige was a gloss for different intensities of racist practice, gender-specific and culturally coded. Although many accounts contend that white women brought an end to concubinage, its decline came with a much wider shift in colonial relations along more racially segregated lines—in which the definitions of prestige shifted and in which Asian, creole, and European-born women were to play new roles.

Colonial communities were not generic; sharp demographic, social, and political differences existed among them. Colonies based on small administrative centers of Europeans (as on Africa's Gold Coast) differed from plantation colonies with sizable enclave European communities (as in Malaya and Sumatra) and still more from settler colonies (as in Algeria) with large, heterogeneous, and permanent European populations. But these "types" were less fixed than some students of colonial history suggest, such as Winthrop Jordan, who argued that the "bedrock demographics" of whites to blacks and the sexual composition of the latter "powerfully influenced, perhaps even determined the kind of society which emerged in each colony."[75] North Sumatra's European-oriented, overwhelmingly male colonial population, for example, contrasted with the more sexually balanced mestizo culture that emerged in the seventeenth and eighteenth centuries in colonial Java.

But these demographics were not the bedrock of social relations from which all else followed. Sex ratios themselves derived from the particular way in which administrative strategies of social engineering collided with and constrained people's personal choices and private lives. These demographic differences, and the social configurations to which they gave rise, still need to be explained, as do some of the common politically charged issues that a range of colonial societies shared. Some of the similar—and counterintuitive—ways in which the construction of racial categories and the management of sexuality were inscribed indicate new efforts to modernize colonial control.[76]

EUROPEAN WOMEN AND RACIAL BOUNDARIES

Little is as striking in the sociological accounts of European colonial communities as the extraordinary changes that are said to accompany the entry of white women. These adjustments are described as shifts in one direction: toward European lifestyles accentuating the refinements of privilege and new etiquettes of racial difference. The presence of European women was said to put new demands on the white communities to tighten their ranks, clarify their boundaries, and mark out their social space. The material culture of European settlements in Saigon, outposts in New Guinea, and estate complexes in Sumatra were retailored to accommodate the physical and moral requirements of a middle-class and respectable feminine contingent.[77] Housing structures in the Indies were partitioned, residential compounds in the Solomon Islands enclosed, servant relations in Hawaii formalized, dress codes in Java altered, food and social taboos in Rhodesia and the Ivory Coast codified. Taken together these changes encouraged new kinds of consumption and new social services that catered to these new demands.[78]

The arrival of large numbers of European women coincided with new bourgeois trappings and notions of privacy in colonial communities. And these, in turn, were accompanied by new distinctions based on race. European women supposedly required more metropolitan amenities than did men and more spacious surroundings for them. Women were claimed to have more delicate sensibilities and therefore needed suitable quarters—discrete and enclosed. Their psychological and physical constitutions were considered more fragile, demanding more servants for the chores they should be spared. In short, white women needed to be maintained at elevated standards of living, in insulated social spaces cushioned with the cultural artifacts of "being European." Whether women or men set these new standards and why they might have both done so (and for different reasons) is left unclear. Who exhibited a "need for" segregation? In Indochina, male doctors advised French women to build their homes with separate domestic and kitchen quarters.[79] Segregationist standards were what women "deserved" and, more important, what white male prestige required that they maintain.

Racist but Moral Women, Innocent but Immoral Men

Recent feminist scholarship has challenged the universally negative stereotype of the colonial wife in one of two ways: either by showing the structural reasons why European women were racially intolerant, socially vicious, abusive to servants, and prone to illness and boredom, or by demonstrating that they really were not.[80] Some scholars have attempted to confront what Margaret Strobel calls the "myth of the destructive female" to show that these women were not detriments to colonial relations but crucial to bolstering a failing empire and to maintaining the daily rituals of racialized rule.[81]

Colonial discourses about white women were full of contradictions. At the same time that new female immigrants were chided for not respecting the racial distance of local convention, an equal number of colonial observers accused them of being more committed racists in their own right.[82] Insecure and jealous of the sexual liaisons of European men with native women, bound to their provincial visions and cultural norms, European women, it was and is argued, constructed the major cleavages on which colonial stratification would rest. Writing about French women in Algeria, the French historian Pierre Nora once claimed that these "parasites of the colonial relationship in which they do not participate directly, are generally more racist than men and contribute strongly to prohibiting contact between the two societies."[83] Similarly, Octavio Mannoni noted "the astonishing fact" that European women in Madagascar were "far more racialist than the men."[84] For the Indies, "it was jealousy of the dusky sirens . . . but more likely some say . . . it was . . . plain feminine scandalization at free and easy sex relations" that caused a decline in miscegenation.[85]

Such bald examples are easy to find in colonial histories of several decades ago. Recent scholarship has been more subtle but not so different. For the French Ivory Coast, the ethnographer Alain Tirefort contended that "the presence of the white woman separated husbands from indigenous life by creating around them a zone of European intimacy."[86] Gann and Duignan attributed the decline of racial integration to, as we saw in the previous chapter, the decline in the price of steamship tickets to British Africa.[87] Such conclusions are not confined to metropolitan men; Ashis Nandy tied the racism of white women to the homosexual cravings of their men.[88]

What is striking here is that women, otherwise supporting players on the colonial stage, are charged with reshaping the face of colonial society, as in the case of Africa, and imposing their racial will on, a colonial world where "relatively unrestrained social intermingling . . . had been prevalent in earlier years."[89] Similarly, in Malaya, the presence of European women put an end to "free and easy social intercourse with [Malayan] men as well," replacing it with "an iron curtain of ignorance . . . between the races."[90] European women were not only the bearers of racist beliefs, but hard-line operatives who put them into practice. It was they who destroyed the blurred divisions between colonizer and colonized, who encouraged class distinctions among whites while fostering new racial antagonisms, formerly muted by sexual access.[91]

What underwrites these assessments? Are we to believe that sexual intimacy with European men yielded social mobility and political rights for colonized women? Or less likely, that because British civil servants bedded Indian women, Indian men had more "in common" with British men and enjoyed more parity? Colonized women could sometimes parlay their positions into personal profit and small rewards, but these were *individual* negotiations with no social, legal, or cumulative claims. Sex was not a leveling mechanism but a site in which social asymmetries were instantiated and expressed.[92]

European women were positioned as the bearers of a redefined colonial morality. But to suggest that they fashioned this racism out of whole cloth is to miss the political chronology in which new intensities of racist practice arose. In the African and Asian contexts already mentioned, the arrival of large numbers of European wives, particularly the need for their protection, followed from new terms and tensions in the colonial contract. Their presence and safety was repeatedly invoked to clarify racial lines. It coincided with perceived threats to European prestige,[93] increased racial conflict,[94] covert challenges to colonial politics, outright expressions of nationalist resistance, and internal dissension among whites themselves.[95]

If white women were the force behind the decline of concubinage, as is often claimed, they did so as participants in a broader racial realignment and political plan.[96] This is not to suggest that they were passive in this process, as the dominant preoccupations in many of their novels attest.[97] Many European women opposed concubinage but not because they were categorically jealous of and threatened by Asian women.[98] More likely, it was because of the double standard concubinage condoned for European men.[99] Some Dutch women championed the cause of the wronged nyai, while others urged improved protection for nonprovisioned native women and children as they did for themselves. Still, few went so far as to advocate the legitimation of these mixed unions in legal marriage.[100] Significantly, what European women had to say had little resonance and little effect until their objections coincided with a realignment in both racial and class politics in which they were strategic.

Race and the Politics of Sexual Peril

If the gender-specific requirements for colonial living imposed specific restrictions on women, they were also racialized assessments of danger that assigned a heightened sexuality to colonized men.[101] Although novels and memoirs position European women as categorically absent from the sexual fantasies of European men, these very men imagined their women to be desired and seductive figures to others. Within this frame, European women needed protection from the "primitive" sexual urges aroused by the sight of them.[102] In some colonies that sexual threat remained an unlabeled potential. In others, it was given a specific name. The "Black Peril" referred throughout Africa and much of the British empire to the professed dangers of sexual assault on white women by black men.

In southern Rhodesia and Kenya in the 1920s and 1930s, preoccupations with the Black Peril prompted the creation of citizens' militias, ladies' riflery clubs, and commissions to investigate whether African female domestic servants would not be safer to employ than men.[103] Some colonial states went further still: in New Guinea the White Women's Protection Ordinance of 1926 provided "the death penalty for any person convicted for the crime of rape or attempted rape upon a European woman or girl;"[104] and in the Solomon Islands authorities introduced public flogging in 1934 as punishment for "criminal assaults on [white] females."[105]

What do these cases have in common? First, the proliferation of discourse about sexual assault and the measures used to prevent it had virtually no correlation with actual incidences of rape of European women by men of color. Just the contrary: there was often no ex post facto evidence, or any at the time, that rapes were committed or attempted.[106] Sexual assaults may have occurred, but their incidence had little to do with the fluctuations in anxiety about them. Moreover, the rape laws were race-specific. Sexual abuse of black women was not classified as rape and therefore was not legally actionable, nor did rapes committed by white men lead to prosecution.[107] If these accusations of sexual threat were not prompted by the fact of rape, what did they signal, and to what were they tied?

Allusions to political and sexual subversion of the colonial system went hand in hand. The term "Black Peril" referred to sexual threats, but it also connoted the fear of insurgence, and of perceived nonacquiescence to colonial control more generally.[108] Concern over protection of white women intensified during real and perceived crises of control—threats to the internal cohesion of the European communities or infringements on its borders. Thus colonial accounts of the rebellion in India in 1857 detailed descriptions of the sexual mutilation of British women by Indian men although no rapes were recorded.[109] In Africa too, although the chronologies of the Black Peril differ—on the Rand in South Africa peaking a full twenty years earlier than elsewhere—we can still identify a patterned *sequence* of events.[110] In New Guinea, the White Women's Protection Ordinance followed a large influx of acculturated Papuans into Port Moresby in the 1920s. Resistant to the constraints imposed on their dress, movement, and education, whites perceived them as arrogant, "cheeky," and without respect.[111] In post–World War I Algeria, the political unease of *pieds noirs* (local French settlers) in the face of "a whole new series of [Muslim] demands" manifested itself in a popular culture newly infused with strong images of sexually aggressive Algerian men.[112]

Second, rape charges against colonized men were often based on perceived transgressions of social space. "Attempted rapes" turned out to be "incidents" of a Papuan man "discovered" in the vicinity of a white residence, a Fijian man who entered a European patient's room, or a male servant poised at the bedroom door of a European woman asleep or in half-dress.[113] With such a broad range of behaviors defined as dangerous, most colonized men were potentially threatening as sexual and political aggressors.

Third, accusations of sexual assault frequently followed on heightened tensions within European communities—and renewed efforts to find consensus within them. Rape accusations in South Africa, for example, coincided with a rash of strikes between 1890 and 1914 by both African and white miners.[114] Similarly, in Rhodesia, after a strike of white railway workers in 1929, otherwise conflicting members of the European community came together in a common cause. The threat of native rebellion produced a "solidarity [that] found sustenance in the threat of racial destruction."[115] When labor actions by Indonesian workers and European staff were most intense, Sumatra's white community did the same. They expanded their vigilante groups, intelligence networks, and demands for police protection to ensure their women were safe and their workers "in hand."[116]

Subsidized sponsorship of married couples was accompanied by new incentives for family formation *(gezinvorming)* in both groups, a policy explicitly designed to weed out "undesirable elements" and the socially malcontent. Higher salaries and bonuses, upgraded housing, and a more mediated chain of command between field-worker and staff differentiated the political interests of European from Asian workers more than ever before.

The remedies sought to alleviate sexual danger embraced new prescriptions for securing white control. These included increased surveillance of native men, new laws stipulating corporal punishment for the transgres-

sion of sexual and social boundaries, and the demarcation of new spaces that
were made racially off-limits. These went with a moral rearmament of the
European community and reassertions of its cultural identity. Charged with
guarding cultural norms, European women were instrumental in promoting white solidarity. But it was partly at their own expense, for on this issue
they were to be almost as closely policed as colonized men.[117]

Policing European Women and Concessions to Chivalry

Native men were the ones legally punished for alleged sexual assaults, but
European women were frequently blamed for provoking their desires. New
arrivals from Europe were accused of being too familiar with their servants, lax
in their commands, and indecorous in their speech and dress.[118] In Papua New
Guinea "everyone" in the Australian community agreed that rape assaults
were caused by a "younger generation of white women" who simply did not
know how to treat servants.[119] In Rhodesia, as in Uganda, sexual anxieties persisted in the absence of any incidents and restricted women to activities within
European enclaves and in their homes.[120] The Immorality Act of 1916 "made
it an offence for a white woman to make an indecent suggestion to a male native."[121] European women in Kenya in the 1920s were dissuaded from staying
alone on their homesteads and discouraged by rumors of rape from taking up
farming on their own.[122] As in the American South, "the etiquette of chivalry
controlled white women's behavior even as [it] guarded caste lines."[123] A defense of community, morality, and white male power was achieved by increasing control over and consensus among Europeans, by reaffirming the vulnerability of white women and the sexual threat posed by native men, and by
creating new sanctions to limit the liberties of both.

European colonial communities in the early twentieth century assiduously
controlled the movements of European women and, where possible, imposed
on them restricted and protected roles. There were, however, European
women who did work. French women in the settler communities of Algeria
ran farms, rooming houses, and shops along with their men.[124] On the Ivory
Coast married European women worked to "supplement" their husbands' in-
comes,[125] while in Senegal the "supplementary" salary of French wives maintained the white standard.[126] Some women missionaries, nurses, and teachers
questioned the sexist policies of their male superiors, but less so the practices
that buttressed the racial order.[127]

In smaller European enclaves, there were often fewer opportunities for
women to be economically independent or to act politically on their own.
The "revolt against chivalry"—the protest of American Southern white

women to lynchings of black men for alleged rape attempts—had no counterpart among European women in Asia and Africa.[128] French feminists urged those women with skills (and a desire for marriage) to settle in Indochina at the turn of the century, but colonial administrators blocked their immigration. Officials not only complained of a surfeit of resourceless widows, they also argued that European seamstresses, florists, and children's outfitters could not possibly compete with the cheap and skilled labor provided by well-established Chinese firms.[129] In Tonkin in the 1930s, "there was little room for single women, be they unmarried, widowed or divorced."[130] Although some colonial widows, such as the editor of a major Saigon daily, succeeded in their own ambitions, most were shipped out of Indochina—regardless of skill—at government expense.[131]

Rejecting expansion based on the "poor white" Algerian model, French officials in Indochina dissuaded colons with insufficient capital from entry and sought to repatriate those who tried to remain.[132] Single women were seen as the quintessential petit blanc. With limited resources and shopkeeper aspirations, they presented the dangerous possibility that straitened circumstances would lead them to prostitution and thus to degrade white prestige at large. In the Solomon Islands lower-class white women were overtly scorned and limited from entry.[133] Similarly, an Indies army high commander complained in 1903 to the governor-general that lower-class European-born women were far less modest than their Indies-born counterparts and posed a greater moral threat to European men.[134] Indies officials themselves identified European widows as among the most economically vulnerable and impoverished segments of the European population.[135]

Professional competence did not protect single European women from marginalization.[136] They were held in contempt along with European prostitutes, on the basis of similar objections.[137] White prostitutes undermined prestige, while professional women needed protection. Both fell outside the colonial space to which European women were assigned: custodians of family welfare and respectability and dedicated and willing subordinates to and supporters of men. These norms were so rigorous precisely because European family life and bourgeois respectability were conceived as the cultural bases for imperial patriotism and racial survival.

WHITE DEGENERACY, MOTHERHOOD, AND THE EUGENICS OF EMPIRE

de·gen·er·ate (adj.) [L. *degeneratus,* pp. of *degenerare,* to become unlike one's race, degenerate < *degener,* not genuine, base < *de-,* from + *genus,* race, kind: see *genus*]. 1. to lose former, normal, or higher qualities. 2. having sunk below a former or normal condition, character, etc.; deteriorated. 3. morally corrupt; depraved– (n.) a degenerate person, esp. one who is morally depraved or sexually perverted– (vi.) -*at'ed, -at'ing.* 1. to decline or become debased morally, culturally, etc. . . . 2. Biol. to undergo degeneration; deteriorate.

Webster's New World Dictionary

European women were vital to the colonial enterprise and the solidification of racial boundaries in ways that repeatedly tied their supportive and subordinate posture to community cohesion and colonial security. That contribution was reinforced at the turn of the century by a metropolitan bourgeois discourse (and an eminently anthropological one) intensely concerned with notions of "degeneracy."[138] Middle-class morality, manliness, and motherhood were seen as endangered by the related fears of "degeneration" and miscegenation in scientifically construed racist beliefs.[139] Degeneration was defined as "departures from the normal human type . . . transmitted through inheritance and lead[ing] progressively to destruction."[140] Degeneracy, brought on by environmental, physical, and moral factors, could be averted by positive eugenic selection or, negatively, by eliminating the "unfit" or the environmental and more specifically cultural contagions that gave rise to them.[141] Eugenic discourse has usually been associated with Social Darwinian notions of "selection," with the strong influence of Lamarckian thinking reserved for its French variant.[142] However, the notion of "cultural contamination" runs throughout the British, U.S., French, and Dutch eugenic traditions.[143] Eugenic arguments used to explain the social malaise of industrialization, immigration, and urbanization derived from notions that acquired characteristics were inheritable and thus that poverty, vagrancy, and promiscuity were class-linked biological traits, tied to genetic material as directly as night blindness and blond hair. This Lamarckian feature of eugenic thinking in its colonial expression linked racial degeneracy to the sexual transmission of cultural contagions and to the political instability of imperial rule.

Appealing to a broad political and scientific constituency, Euro-American eugenic societies included advocates of infant welfare programs, liberal intellectuals, conservative businessmen, Fabians, and physicians with social concerns. By the 1920s, however, it contained an increasingly vocal number of those who called for and put into law if not practice the sterilization of what were considered the mentally, morally, or physically unfit members of the British, German, and North American underclass.[144]

Feminist attempts to appropriate this rhetoric for birth-control programs largely failed. Eugenics was essentially elitist, racist, and misogynist in principle and practice.[145] Its proponents advocated a pronatalist policy for the white middle and upper classes, a rejection of women's work roles that might compete with motherhood, and "an assumption that reproduction was not just a function but the purpose . . . of women's life."[146] In France, England, Germany, and the United States, eugenics placed European women of "good stock" as "the fountainhead of racial strength,"[147] exalting the cult of motherhood while subjecting it to the scrutiny of this new scientific domain.[148]

Eugenics reverberated in the colonies in predictable and unexpected forms. The moral, biological, and sexual referents of "degeneracy" (distinct in the dictionary citation above) were fused in how the concept was actually deployed. The "colonial branch" of eugenics focused on the vulnerabilities of white rule and measures to safeguard European superiority. Eugenics was designed to control the procreation of the "unfit" lower orders and to target "the poor, the colonized, or unpopular strangers."[149] But eugenic thinking reached further. It permeated how metropolitan observers viewed the degenerate lifestyle of colonials and how colonial elites admonished the behavior of degenerates among themselves.[150] Whereas European and U.S. studies focused on the inherent propensity of the impoverished classes to criminality, in the Indies delinquency among "European" children was linked to the proportion of "native blood" that children of mixed unions had inherited from their native mothers.[151] Eugenics provided not so much a new vocabulary as a new biological idiom in which to ground the medical and moral basis for anxieties over European hegemony and white prestige. It reopened debates over segregated residence and education, new standards of morality, sexual vigilance, and the rights of *certain* Europeans to rule.

Eugenic thinking manifested itself, not in the direct importation of metropolitan practices such as sterilization, but in a translation of the political *principles* and the social values that eugenics implied. In defining what was unacceptable, eugenics also identified what constituted a "valuable life" and "a gender-specific work and productivity, described in social, medical and psychiatric terms."[152] Applied to European colonials, eugenic statements pronounced what kind of people should represent Dutch or French rule, how they should bring up their children, and with whom they should socialize. Those concerned with issues of racial survival and racial purity invoked the moral duty of European colonial women to fulfill an alternative set of imperial imperatives. They were to "uplift" colonial subjects through educational and domestic management and attend to the family environment of their men. Sometimes they were simply encouraged to remain in the metropole and to stay at home. The point is that a common gendered discourse was mapped onto different imperial situations that celebrated motherhood and domesticity.

If in Britain racial deterioration was conceived of as a result of the moral turpitude and the ignorance of working-class mothers, in the colonies the dangers were more pervasive, the possibilities of contamination worse. Proposals to secure European rule pushed in two directions. On the one hand, they pushed away from ambiguous racial genres and open domestic arrangements. On the other hand, they pressed for an upgrade and homogenization of European standards as well as a clearer delineation of them. The impulse was clear: away from miscegenation toward white endogamy; away from concubinage toward family formation and legal marriage; away from, as in the case of the Indies, mestizo customs and toward metropolitan norms.[153] As stated in the bulletin of the Netherlands Indies Eugenics Society, "eugenics is nothing other than belief in the possibility of preventing degenerative symptoms in the body of our beloved *moedervolken* [people, populace], or in cases where they may already be present, of counteracting them."[154]

Like the modernization of colonialism itself, with its scientific management and educated technocrats with limited local knowledge, colonial communities of the early twentieth century were rethinking the ways in which their authority should be expressed. This rethinking took the form of asserting a distinct colonial morality, explicit in its reorientation to the racial and class markers of being European. It emphasized transnational racial commonalities despite national differences. Not least it distilled a notion of *Homo europæus* for whom superior health, wealth, and education were tied to racial endowments and a White Man's norm. Thus, Eugene Pujarniscle, a novelist and participant observer in France's colonial venture, wrote: "[O]ne might be surprised that my pen always returns to the words *blanc* [white] or 'European' and never to 'Français'[;] . . . in effect colonial solidarity and the obligations that it entails allies all the peoples of the white races."[155]

Such sensibilities colored imperial policy in nearly all domains. Fears of physical contamination gave new credence to fears of political vulnerability. Whites had to guard their ranks, to increase their numbers, and to ensure that their members respected the biological and political boundaries on which their power was thought to rest.[156] In Europe the socially and physically "unfit," the poor, the indigent, and the insane, were either to be sterilized or prevented from marriage. In the colonies it was these very groups among Europeans who were either excluded from entry or institutionalized while they were there and eventually sent home.[157]

To sustain the notion that good health, virility, and the ability to rule were inherent features of being European, colonial rulers invested in a politics of exclusion that policed their members as well as the colonized. Such strategies and concerns were not new to the 1920s.[158] In the 1750s the East Indies Company had already taken "draconian measures" to control pauperism among "Dutchmen of mixed blood."[159] In the same period, the British East Indies Company enforced policies that discouraged lower-class European migration and settlement and argued that such populations would destroy Indian respect for "the superiority of the European character."[160] Patriotic calls to populate Java with poor Dutch farmers were also blocked for similar reasons in the mid-1800s and then again with new urgency in the following century as successive challenges to European rule were felt more profoundly.

Measures were taken both to avoid poor white migration and to produce a colonial profile that highlighted the manliness, well-being, and productivity of European men. In this equation, evidence of manliness, national identity, and racial superiority were meshed.[161] Thus British colonial administrators were retired by the age of fifty-five, ensuring that "no Oriental was ever allowed to see a Westerner as he ages and degenerated, just as no Westerner needed ever to see himself, mirrored in the eyes of the subject race, as anything but a vigorous, rational, ever-alert young Raj."[162] In the twentieth century, these "men of class" and "men of character" embodied a modernized and renovated image of rule. They were to safeguard the colonies against the physical weakness, moral decay, and inevitable degeneration that long residence in the colonies encouraged and against the temptations that interracial domestic situations had allowed.

Given this ideal, it is not surprising that colonial communities were troubled by men who did not fit the profile. Officials worried over the dangers of unemployed or impoverished Europeans. During the succession of economic crises in the early twentieth century, relief agencies in Sumatra, for example, organized fund-raisers, hill station retreats, and small-scale agricultural schemes to keep "unfit" Europeans "from roaming around."[163] The colonies were neither open for retirement nor tolerant of the public presence of poor whites. During the 1930s depression, when tens of thousands of Europeans in the Indies found themselves without jobs, government and private resources were quickly mobilized to ensure that they were not "reduced" to native living standards.[164] Subsidized health care, housing, and education complemented a rigorous attention to European cultural standards. In affirming those, European women were positioned to play a key role in keeping men *civilisé*.

The Cultural Dynamics of Degeneration

The *colon* is, in a common and etymological sense, a barbarian. He is a non-civilized person, a "new man." . . . [It] is he who appears as a savage.[165]

The shift in imperial thinking evident in the early twentieth century focuses not only on the Otherness of the colonized but also on the Otherness of colonials themselves. In France medical and sociological tracts pinpointed the colonial as a distinct and degenerate social type, psychologically identifiable and with recognizable physical characteristics.[166] Some of that difference was attributed to the debilitating climate and social milieu and from staying in the colonies too long: "The climate affects him, his surroundings affect him, and after a certain time, he has become, both physically and morally, a completely different man."[167] People who stayed "too long" were subject to a sweeping array of maladies. These ranged from overfatigue and physical breakdown to individual and racial degeneration.[168] But cultural contamination had the most serious consequences because it led to neglect of the conventions of supremacy and *disagreement* about what those conventions were.[169] What were identified as the degraded and unique characteristics of colonials by European observers—"ostentation," "speculation," "inaction," and a general "demoralization"—were "faults" contracted from native culture that marked colonials as *décivilisé* as much as the colonized.[170]

Colonial medicine reflected and affirmed this slippage among physical, moral, and cultural degeneracy in concrete ways. The climatic, social, and work conditions of colonial life gave rise to a specific set of psychotic disorders thought to effect *l'equilibre cerebral* and predispose Europeans in the tropics to mental breakdown.[171] Neurasthenia was the most common manifestation, a mental disorder identified as a major problem in French colonies and accounting for more than half the Dutch repatriations from the Indies to Holland.[172] In Europe and America it was "the phantom disease . . . of the late nineteenth century," encompassing virtually all "psychopathological or neuro-pathological conditions, and intimately linked to sexual deviation and to the destruction of social order itself."[173]

In Europe neurasthenia was identified as a consequence of "modern civilization" and its frantic pace.[174] But in the colonies its etiology took the *reverse* form. Colonial neurasthenia was said to be caused by distance from civilization and European community and by proximity to the colonized. Susceptibility was increased by an existence "outside of the social framework to which [a man] was adapted in France, isolation in outposts, physical and moral fatigue, and modified food regimes."[175]

The proliferation of hill stations reflected these political and physical concerns. Developed in the early nineteenth century as sites for military posts and sanatoriums, hill stations provided European-like environments in which colonials could recoup their physical and mental well-being by simulating the conditions "at home."[176] Isolated at cooler altitudes, they took on new importance with the increasing numbers of European women and children, who were seen as vulnerable subjects, susceptible to anemia, depression, and ill health.[177] Vacation bungalows and schools built in these "naturally" segregated surroundings provided cultural refuge and regeneration.[178]

Some doctors considered the only treatment *le retour en Europe*.[179] Others prescribed a local set of remedies, advising adherence to an ethic of morality and work that valorized sexual moderation, abstemious diet, and physical exercise. The "regularity and regimentation" of work was coupled with *European* camaraderie that was to be buttressed by a solid (and stolid) family life with European children and a European wife.[180]

Guides to colonial living in the 1920s and 1930s reveal this marked shift in outlook. Dutch, French, and British doctors now denounced the unhealthy, indolent lifestyles of "old colonials," instead extolling the energetic and engaged activities of the new breed of husband and wife.[181] Prone to neurasthenia, anemia, and depression, women were exhorted to involve themselves in household management and child care and divert themselves with botanical collections and "good works."[182]

Children on the Colonial Divide: Degeneracy and the Dangers of Métissage

[Young colonial men] are often driven to seek a temporary
companion among the women of color; this is the path by which,
as I shall presently show, contagion travels back and forth,
contagion in all senses of the word.[183]

Racial degeneracy was thought to have social causes and political consequences, both tied to the domestic arrangements in which Europeans lived. Métissage generally and concubinage in particular were viewed as dangers to racial purity and cultural securing of racial identity. Through sexual contact with native women, European men "contracted" disease as well as de-

based sentiments, immoral proclivities, and extreme susceptibility to uncivilized states.[184]

By the early twentieth century, concubinage was denounced for undermining precisely what it was charged with fortifying decades earlier. The
weight of competing discourses on local women shifted as well. While in earlier portrayals their negative attributes had been overshadowed by their role
as protectors of the well-being of colonial men, in the new equation they became the primary vectors of sinister influences on physical and mental
health. Adaptation to local food, language, and dress, once prescribed as pos-
tive signs of acclimatization, were now the signs of contagion and loss of
(white) self. The benefits of local knowledge and sexual release gave way to
the more pressing demands of respectability, the community's solidarity, and
its mental health. Increasingly, French men in Indochina who kept native
women were viewed as passing into "the enemy camp."[185] Concubinage became the source of individual breakdown, racial degeneration, and political
unrest. Children born of these unions were "the fruits of a regrettable weakness,"[186] physically marked and morally marred with "the defaults and
mediocre qualities of their mothers."[187]

Concubinage was not as economically tidy or politically neat as policy
makers had hoped. It involved more than sexual exploitation and unpaid
domestic work. It also involved children—many more than official statistics
revealed—and questions of who was to be acknowledged as a European and
who was not. Concubine children posed a classificatory problem, imping-
ing on political security and white prestige. The majority were not recognized by their fathers, nor were they reabsorbed into local communities as
authorities often claimed. Although some men legally acknowledged their
progeny, many repatriated to Holland, Britain, or France and cut off ties and
support to mother and children.[188] Native women had responsibility for but
attenuated rights over their own offspring.[189] The legal system favored a
European upbringing but made no demands on men to provide it. The more
socially asymmetric and perfunctory the relationship between man and
woman, the more likely the children were to end up as wards of the state,
subject to the scrutiny and imposed charity of the European-born community at large.

Concubine children invariably counted among the ranks of the European
poor, but European paupers in the late-nineteenth-century Netherlands
Indies came from wider strata of colonial society than that of concubines
alone.[190] Many Indo-Europeans, as well as creole children born in the Indies
of European parents, had become increasingly marginalized from strategic
political and economic positions in the early twentieth century, despite the

fact that new educational facilities were supposed to have provided new opportunities for them. In Java, volumes of official reports were devoted to documenting and alleviating the proliferation of a "rough" and "dangerous pauper element" among (Indo-)European clerks, low-level officials, dismissed soldiers, and vagrants.[191] In the 1920s and 1930s youths born and educated in the Indies had few economic options. They were uncomfortably squeezed between an influx of new recruits from Holland and the educated *inlander* (native) population with whom they were competing for jobs.[192]

European pauperism in the Indies reflected broad inequalities in colonial society that underscored the social heterogeneity of the category "European" itself. But it was still concubinage that was seen as the principal source of *blanken-haters* (white-haters).[193] Equated with a progeny of "malcontents," of "parasitic" whites, idle and therefore dangerous, concubinage raised the political fear that its progeny would demand economic access, political rights, and seek alliance with (and leadership of) organized opposition to Dutch rule.[194]

The politics of compassion and charity was racially marked as well. Prejudice against métis was often, as in the Belgian Congo, "camouflaged under protestations of 'pity' for their fate, as if they were *'malheureux'* [unhappy] beings by definition."[195] The protection of métis children in Indochina was a cause célèbre of European women at home and abroad. The French assembly on feminism, organized for the colonial exposition of 1931, devoted a major part of its proceedings to the plight of *métis* children and their native mothers, echoing the campaigns for *la recherche de paternité* by French feminists a half century earlier.[196] The assembly called for "the establishment of centers [in the colonies] where abandoned young girls or those in moral danger could be made into worthy women."[197] European women were urged to oversee the "moral protection" of métis youths, to develop their "natural" inclination toward French society, to turn them into "collaborators and partisans of French ideas and influences" instead of revolutionaries.[198] The gender breakdown was clear. Moral instruction would avert sexual promiscuity among métisse girls and political precocity among métis boys, who might otherwise become militant men.

Orphanages for abandoned European and Indo-European children were a prominent feature of Dutch, French, and British colonial cultures. In the Indies by the mid-eighteenth century, state orphanages were established to prevent "neglect and degeneracy of the many free-roaming poor bastards and orphans of Europeans."[199] By the nineteenth century, church, state, and private organizations had become zealous backers of orphanages, providing some vocational education and strong doses of moral instruction. In India, the military orphanages of the late eighteenth century expanded into a nineteenth-century variant in which European and Anglo-Indian children were cared for in civil asylums and charity schools in "almost every town, cantonment and hill-station."[200] In French Indochina in the 1930s, virtually every colonial city had a home and society for the protection of abandoned métis youth.[201]

Whether these children were in fact "abandoned" by their Asian mothers is difficult to establish. That métis children living in native homes were sometimes *sought out* by state and private organizations and placed in these institutions suggests other possibilities.[202] Public assistance in India, Indochina, and the Indies was designed to keep fair-skinned children from running barefoot in native villages but also to ensure that the spread of European pauper settlement was controlled.[203] Emphasis on religious and secular education and socialization was symptomatic of broader fears. Children would grow into *Hollander-haters,* patricides, and anticolonial revolutionaries. As adults, girls would fall into prostitution. And as boys grew into adult men, their affective and lasting ties to native women and indigenous society would turn them into enemies of the state, *verbasterd* (degenerate) and décivilisé.[204]

European Women, Race, and Middle-Class Morality

Rationalizations of imperial rule and safeguards against racial degeneracy in the colonies converged on particular moral themes. Both entailed a reassertion of European conventions and middle-class respectability. Both promoted stronger and more frequent ties with the metropole and a restatement of what was culturally distinct and superior about how colonials ruled and lived. For those women who came to join their spouses or to find husbands, the prescriptions were clear. Just as new plantation staff were taught to manage the natives, women were schooled in colonial propriety and domestic management. French manuals, such as those on hygiene in Indochina, outlined the duties of colonial wives in no uncertain terms. As "auxiliary forces" in the imperial effort, they were to "conserve the fitness and sometimes the life of all around them" by ensuring that "the home be happy and gay and that all take pleasure in clustering there."[205] The Koloniale School voor Meisjes en Vrouwen, established in The Hague in 1920, provided adolescent and adult women with preparatory courses in home management and child care as well as lectures on Javanese custom and culture. Practical guides to life in the Belgian Congo instructed (and warned) *la femme blanche* that she was to keep "order, peace, hygiene and economy"[206] and "perpetuate a vigorous race" while preventing any "laxity in . . . administrative mores."[207]

This "division of labor" contained obvious asymmetries. Men were considered more susceptible to moral turpitude than were women, who were thus held responsible for the immoral states of men. European women were to safeguard prestige and morality and insulate their men from the cultural and sexual contamination of contact with the colonized.[208] Racial degeneracy would be curtailed by European women charged with regenerating the physical health, the metropolitan affinities, and the imperial purpose of their men.[209]

At its heart was a reassertion of racial difference that harnessed nationalist rhetoric and markers of middle-class morality to its cause.[210] George Mosse has characterized European racism as a "scavenger ideology," annexing nationalism and bourgeois respectability to a racist project in which the management of sexuality was central to all three.[211] If the European middle class sought respectability "to maintain their status and self-respect against the lower classes and the aristocracy," in the colonies respectability was a defense against the colonized and a way of more clearly defining themselves.[212] Good colonial living now meant hard work and physical exercise rather than sexual release, which had been one rationale for condoning concubinage and prostitution in an earlier period. The debilitating influences of climate could be surmounted by regular diet and meticulous personal hygiene over which European women were to take full charge. British, French, and Dutch manuals on European household management in the tropics provided detailed instructions in domestic science, moral upbringing, and employer-servant relations. Adherence to strict conventions of cleanliness and cooking occupied an inordinate amount of the time of colonial women and those who served them.[213] Cleanliness itself served as a "prop to a Europeanness that was less than assumed."[214] Both activities entailed a constant surveillance of native nursemaids, laundrymen, and live-in servants while demanding a heightened domesticity for European women themselves.

Leisure, good spirit, and creature comforts became the obligation of women to provide, the racial duty of women to maintain. Seduction of their men by native women would be curtailed by a happy, *gezellig* (cozy) family life much as "extremist agitation" among plantation workers in Sumatra was to be averted by selecting married recruits and providing family housing. There too men would feel "happy and content" *(senang)* and "at home."[215] Moral laxity would be eliminated through the example and vig-

Figure 9.   'Milking the cow in the doctor's family J. Kunst in Batavia, Java,' 1899. This practice would have been neither encouraged nor deemed necessary by the 1930s. KIT album 680, no. 17.

ilance of women whose status was defined by their sexual restraint and dedication to their home environments and to their men.

Imperial Priorities: Motherhood versus Male Morality

The European woman [in Indochina] can only fulfill her duties to bear and breast-feed her children with great hardship and damage to her health.[216]

The perceptions and practice that bound women's domesticity to national welfare and racial purity were not confined to colonial women alone. Child rearing in late-nineteenth-century Britain was hailed as a national, imperial, and racial duty, as it was in France, Holland, the United States, and Germany at the same time.[217] In France, where declining birthrates were of public concern, fecundity itself had become "no longer something resting with couples" but with "the nation, the state, the race."[218] Popular colonial authors such as Pierre Mille hailed the production of children as women's "essential contribution to the imperial mission of France."[219] With motherhood at the center of empire building, pronatalist policies in Europe forced some improvement in colonial medical facilities, new maternity wards, and more attention to the reproductive conditions of both European and colonized women. Maternal and infant health programs instructed European women bound for the tropics in the use of milk substitutes, wet nurses, and breast-feeding practices in an effort to encourage more women to stay in the colonies and to prepare the many more that came.[220] But the belief that the colonies were medically hazardous for white women meant that motherhood in the tropics was not only a precarious but also a conflicted endeavor.

Real and imagined concern over individual reproduction and racial survival contained and compromised white colonial women in concrete ways. Tropical climates were said to cause low fertility, prolonged amenorrhea, and permanent sterility.[221] Belgian doctors held that "the woman who goes to live in a tropical climate is often lost for the reproduction of the race."[222] Colonial conditions were associated with high infant mortality, such that "the life of a European child was nearly condemned in advance."[223] Illnesses ranging from fragile nerves to debilitating fevers were thought to hit women and children hardest.[224]

These perceived medical perils called into question whether European-born women and thus the "white race" could reproduce if they remained in the tropics for an extended time. An international medical community cross-referenced one another's citations of racial sterility by the second or third generation.[225] Such a dark view of climate was less prevalent in the Indies, but psychological and physical adaptation was never a given. Dutch doctors quoted German physicians, not to affirm the inevitable infertility among whites in the tropics, but to support their contention that European-born women and men should limit their colonial status.[226] French observers would flatly state that unions among creole Dutch in the Indies were sterile after two generations.[227] Medical studies in the 1930s, such as that supported by the Netherlands Indies Eugenics Society, were designed to test whether fertility rates differed by "racial type" between Indo-European and European-born women and whether "children of certain Europeans born in the Indies displayed different racial markers than their parents."[228]

Like the discourse on degeneracy, the fear of sterility had less to do with the biological survival of whites than with their political viability and cultural reproduction. Such concerns heightened in the 1930s when white unemployment was high in the colonies and Europe. The depression made repatriation of impoverished Dutch and French unrealistic, prompting speculation as to whether European working classes could be relocated in the tropics without causing further racial degeneration.[229] White migration to the tropics was reconsidered, but poor white settlements were rejected on economic, medical, and psychological grounds. The reproductive potential of European women was the focus of debate again and again, prompting questionnaires concerning their "acclimatization" and detailed descriptions of their conjugal histories and sexual lives.

Imperial perceptions and policies fixed European women in the colonies as "instruments of race-culture" in what proved to be personally difficult and contradictory ways.[230] Child-rearing decisions faithfully followed the sort of racist principles that constrained the activities of women charged with child care.[231] Medical experts and women's organizations recommended strict surveillance of children's activities[232] and careful attention to those with whom they played. Virtually every medical and household handbook in the Dutch, French, and British colonies warned against leaving small children in the unsupervised care of local servants. In the Netherlands Indies, it was the "duty" of the "modern white mother" *(hedendaagsche blanke moeder)* to take the physical and spiritual upbringing of her offspring away from the native nursemaid *(babu)* and into her own hands.[233]

Precautions had to be taken against "sexual danger," against the uncleanly habits of domestics, against a "stupid negress" who might leave a child exposed to the sun.[234] Even in colonies where the climate was not considered unhealthy, European children supposedly thrived well "only up to the age of six,"[235] when native cultural influences came into stronger play. Thus in late-nineteenth-century Hawaii, native nursemaids commonly looked after American children until the age of five. At that point "prattlers" were confined to their mothers' supervision, prevented from learning the local language, and kept in a "walled yard adjacent to the bedrooms [that was] forbidden to Hawaiians."[236]

In the Indies, educational facilities for European children were considered moderately good. Still, it was deemed imperative to send them back to Holland to avoid the "precocity" associated with the tropics and the "danger" of contact with *Indische* youths not from "full-blooded European elements."[237]

> We Dutch in the Indies live in a country which is not our own. . . . We feel instinctively that our blonde, white children belong to the blonde, white dunes, the forests, the moors, the lakes, the snow. . . . A Dutch child should grow up in Holland. There they will acquire the characteristics of their race, not only from mother's milk but also from the

influence of the light, sun and water, of playmates, of life, in a word, in the sphere of the fatherland. This is not racism.[238]

Patriotic images such as those above culturally coded racial distinctions in powerful ways. Dutch identity was represented as a common (if contested) cultural sensibility in which class convention, geography, climate, sexual proclivity, and social contact played central roles.

In many colonial communities, school-age children were packed off to Europe for education and socialization, but this was rarely an unproblematic option. When children could not be left with kin who were still in Holland, it meant leaving them for extended periods in boarding schools or, when they attended day schools, in boardinghouses catering to Indies youths. Married European women were confronted with a difficult set of choices: separation from their children or separation from their husbands.[239] Frequent trips between colony and metropole not only separated families but also broke up marriages and homes.[240]

Not surprisingly, how and where European children should be properly educated was a primary concern of women's organizations and a major theme in magazines right through decolonization. The rise of specific programs in home education (such as the Clerkx-methode voor Huisonderwijs) may have been a response to this new push for women to accommodate their multiple imperial duties—to surveil their husbands and servants while remaining in control of the cultural and moral upbringing of their young. Such conflicting responsibilities profoundly affected the social space European women (not only wives) occupied, the tasks for which they were valorized, and the economic activities in which they could feasibly engage.

The Strategies of Rule and Sexual Morality

The political etymology of colonizer and colonized was gender- and class-specific. The exclusionary politics of colonialism demarcated not just external boundaries but also interior frontiers, specifying internal conformity and order among Europeans themselves. The categories of colonizer and colonized were secured through notions of racial difference constructed in gender terms. Redefinitions of acceptable sexual behavior and morality emerged during crises of colonial control precisely because they called into question the tenuous artifices of rule *within* European communities and what marked their borders.

Even from the limited cases reviewed here, several patterns emerge. First and most obviously, colonial sexual prohibitions were racially asymmetric and gender coded. Sexual relations might be forbidden between white women and men of color but not the other way around. On the contrary, interracial unions (as opposed to marriage) between European men and colonized women aided the long-term settlement of European men in the colonies while ensuring that colonial patrimony stayed in limited and selective hands. Second, interdictions against interracial unions were rarely a primary impulse in the strategies of rule. For India, Indochina, and South Africa, colonial contexts usually associated with sharp social sanctions against interracial unions, "mixing" in the initial period of colonialization was tolerated and even condoned.

The focus here has been on late colonialism in Asia, but colonial elite intervention in the sexual life of their agents and subjects was not confined to this place or period. In sixteenth-century Mexico, mixed marriages between Spanish men and Christianized Indian women were encouraged by the crown until midcentury, when colonists felt that "the rising numbers of their own mestizo progeny threatened the prerogatives of a narrowing elite sector."[241] In eighteenth- and early-nineteenth-century Cuba, mild opposition to interracial marriage gave way to a "virtual prohibition" from 1864 to 1874 when "merchants, slave dealers and the colonial powers opposed [it] in order to preserve slavery."[242]

Changes in sexual access and domestic arrangements have invariably accompanied major efforts to reassert the internal coherence of European communities and to redefine the boundaries of privilege across the colonial divide. But sexual union in itself did not automatically produce a larger population legally classified as "European." On the contrary, even in early-twentieth-century Brazil, where miscegenation had made for a refined system of gradations, "most mixing [took] place outside of marriage."[243] The important point is that miscegenation signaled neither the presence nor the absence of racial discrimination. Hierarchies of privilege and power were written into the *condoning* of interracial unions, as well as into their condemnation.

The chronologies vary from one context to another, but parallel shifts are evident in the strategies of rule and in sexual morality. Concubinage fell into moral disfavor at the same time that new emphasis was placed on the standardization of European administration. This occurred in some colonies by the early twentieth century and in others later on, but the correspondence between rationalized rule, bourgeois respectability, and the custodial power of European women to protect their men seems strongest during the interwar years. The success of Western technological achievements was being questioned.[244] British, French, and Dutch policy makers had moved from an assimilationist to a more segregationist, separatist stance. The re-organization of colonial investments along corporate and multinational lines brought with it a push for a restructured and more highly productive labor force. With it came more vocal nationalist and labor movements resisting those demands.

An increasing rationalization of colonial management produced radical shifts in notions of how empires should be run, how agents of empire should rule, and where, how, and with whom they should live. Thus French debates concerning the need to systematize colonial management and dissolve the provincial and personalized satraps of "the old-time colon" invariably targeted and condemned the unseemly domestic arrangements in which they lived. British high officials in Africa imposed new "character" requirements on their subordinates, designating specific class attributes and conjugal ties that such a selection implied.[245] Critical to this restructuring was a new disdain for colonials too adapted to local custom, too removed from the local European community, and too encumbered with intimate native ties. As in Sumatra, this hands-off policy distanced Europeans in more than one sense. It forbade European staff both from personal confrontations with their Asian field hands and from the limited local knowledge they gained through sexual and domestic arrangements.

Medical expertise increasingly confirmed the salubrious benefits of European camaraderie and frequent home leaves. A *cordon sanitaire* surrounded European enclaves, was wrapped around mind and body, around each European man and his home. White prestige became redefined by the conventions that would safeguard the moral, cultural, and physical well-being of its agents, with which European women were charged. Colonial politics locked European men and women into routinized protection of their physical health and social space in ways that bound gender prescriptions to the racial cleavages between "us" and "them."

It may be, however, that we should not be searching for congruent colonial chronologies attached to specific dates but rather for similar shifts in the rhythms of rule and sexual management, for similar internal patterns within specific colonial histories themselves.[246] For example, following the Great Rebellion in India, political subversion was tied to sexual impropriety in new ways. Colonial politicians and moral reforms stipulated new codes of conduct that emphasized respectability, domesticity, and a more carefully segregated use of space. All of these measures focused on European women. Virtually all resonate with those developed in Africa and Southeast Asia but were instituted a half century earlier than in colonies elsewhere. Looking to a somewhat longer *durée* than the colonial crises of the early twentieth century, we might consider British responses to the 1857 rebellion not as an exception but as a template for colonial responses elsewhere. The modular quality of colonial perceptions and policies was built on new international standards of empire and specific metropolitan priorities. New standards in turn were responsive to local challenges of those who contested life and labor under European rule.

Sexual control figured in the substance, as well as the iconography, of colonialism's racial policies. But colonial politics was not just concerned with sex; nor did sexual relations reduce to colonial politics. Sex in the colonies had to do with sexual access and reproduction, class distinctions and racial demarcations, nationalism and European identity—in different measure and not all at the same time. Major shifts in the positioning of women were not, as we might expect, signaled by the penetration of capitalism per se but by subtler changes in class politics and imperial morality and in response to the failures of specific colonial projects. Ethnographies of empire should attend both to changing sensibilities and to sex, to racialized regimes that were realized on a macro and micro scale. They may begin to capture how European culture and class politics resonated in colonial settings, how class and gender discriminations were transposed into racial distinctions that reverberated in the metropole as they were fortified on colonial ground. Such investigations may show that sexual control was both an instrumental image for the body politic—a salient part standing for the whole—and itself fundamental to how racial policies were secured and how colonial projects were carried out.

4 Sexual Affronts and Racial Frontiers

Cultural Competence and the Dangers of Métissage

This chapter is concerned with the construction of colonial categories and national identities and with those people who ambiguously straddled, crossed, and threatened these imperial divides. It begins with a story about métissage and the métis progeny to which those unions gave rise in French Indochina at the turn of the century. This story has multiple strands—about people whose cultural sensibilities, physical being, and political sentiments called into question the distinctions of difference that maintained the neat boundaries of colonial rule. Its plot and resolution defy the treatment of European nationalist impulses and colonial racist policies as discrete projects, because here it was in the conflation of racial category, sexual morality, cultural competence, and national identity that the case was contested and politically charged. In a broader sense, it addresses a tension of empire that this chapter only begins to sketch: the relationship among the discourses of inclusion, humanitarianism, and equality that informed liberal policy at the turn of the century in colonial Southeast Asia and the exclusionary practices that were reactive to, coexistent with, and perhaps inherent in liberalism itself.[1]

Nowhere is this relationship between inclusionary impulses and exclusionary practices more evident than in how métissage was legally handled, culturally inscribed, and politically treated in the contrasting colonial cultures of French Indochina and the Netherlands Indies. French Indochina was a colony of commerce occupied by the military in the 1860s and settled by colons in the 1870s with a métis population that numbered no more than several hundred by the turn of the century.[2] The Netherlands Indies, by contrast, had been peopled since the early 1600s with those of mixed descent or born in the Indies—numbering in the tens of thousands in 1900. They made up nearly three-fourths of those legally designated as European.

Their Indische mestizo culture shaped the contours of colonial society for its first two hundred years.[3] Conventional historiography defines sharp contrasts between French, British, and Dutch colonial racial policy and the particular national metropolitan agendas from which they derived. But what is more striking is that similar discourses were mapped onto such vastly different social and political landscapes.[4]

In both the Indies and Indochina, with their distinct demographics and internal rhythms, métissage was a focal point of political, legal, and social debate. Conceived as a source of subversion, it was seen as a threat to white prestige, an embodiment of European degeneration and moral decay.[5] The so-called mixed-blood problem was not of the same intensity in both places or resolved in all the same ways, but the issues raised reveal a patterned set of transgressions that have not been sufficiently explored. Both situations were so charged in part because such mixing called into question the criteria by which Europeanness could be identified, citizenship accorded, and nationality assigned. Métissage represented not the dangers of foreign enemies at national borders but the more pressing affront for European nation-states, what the German philosopher Johann Gottlieb Fichte so aptly defined as the essence of the nation, its "interior frontiers."[6]

The concept of an interior frontier is compelling precisely because of its contradictory connotations. As Etienne Balibar has noted, a frontier locates a site of both enclosure and contact, of observed passage and exchange. When coupled with the word *interior,* frontier carries the sense of internal distinctions within a territory (or empire). At the level of the individual, frontier marks the moral predicates by which a subject retains his or her national identity despite location outside the national frontier and despite heterogeneity within the nation-state. As Fichte conceived it, an interior frontier entails two dilemmas: the purity of the community is prone to penetration on its interior and exterior borders, and the essence of the community is an intangible "moral attitude," "a multiplicity of invisible ties."[7]

Viewing late-nineteenth-century representations of a national essence in these terms, we can trace how métissage emerged as a powerful trope for internal contamination and for challenges to rule that were morally, politically, and sexually conceived.[8] The changing density and intensity of métissage's discursive field outlines the fault lines of colonial authority. In linking domestic arrangements to the public order, family to the state, sex to subversion, and psychological essence to racial type, *métissage* might be read as a metonym for the biopolitics of empire at large.

In both Indochina and the Netherlands Indies métis was never a legal category. But that very rejection only intensified how the politics of cultural difference were played out in other domains.[9] In both colonies, the métis-Indo problem produced a discourse that rejected facile theories of racial hierarchy as it confirmed the practical predicates of European superiority. The early Vietnamese and Indonesian nationalist movements created new sources of colonial vulnerability, and some of the debates over the nature and definition of Dutch and French identity must be seen in that light. The resurgence of European nationalist rhetoric was partly a response to displays of anticolonial sentiment. But it cannot be accounted for by that alone,[10] for in French Indochina, discourses about the dangers of métissage were as evident in periods of quiescence. There were connections between native protest and concern over the politics of those of mixed parentage.[11] But challenges to French rule in Indochina, contrary to the discourse that characterized the métis as a subversive vanguard, were never predominantly led or peopled by them. And in the Indies, where persons of mixed descent made up a potentially powerful political constituency, the bids they made for social reform and political representation were more often in contradistinction to the demands of the native population, not in alliance with them.

The content of the métis problem was partially in response to popular threats to colonial rule, but the particular form that the securing of white privilege took was shaped in Europe as well. The focus on moral unity, cultural genealogy, and language joined the imagining of European colonial communities and metropolitan national entities in fundamental ways. Both visions embraced a moral rearmament, centering on the domestic domain and the family as sites in which state authority could be secured or irreparably undermined.[12]

At the turn of the century, in both metropole and colony, the liberal impulse for social welfare, representation, and protective legislation focused expert energy on the preparatory environment for civic responsibility: on domestic arrangements, sexual morality, parenting, and more specifically on the moral milieu of children at school and at home.[13] Both education and upbringing emerged as national projects, but not as we might expect, with a firm sense of national identity imported to the periphery from the metropolitan core. As Eugene Weber has argued for late-nineteenth-century France, "patriotic feelings on the national level, far from instinctive, had to be learned."[14] As late as 1901, six out of every ten French army recruits had not heard of the Franco-Prussian War.[15] Thus the Gallicization of France and its colonies through compulsory education, moral instruction, and language was not a one-way process, with a consensual template for that identity forged in the metropole and later transported by new metropolitan recruits to colonial citizens. Between 1871 and 1914, French authorities were preoccupied with the threat of national diminishment and decline, and the study of national character was a "veritable industry in France."[16]

Historians commonly attribute French anxieties over national identity to the loss of Alsace-Lorraine in 1870, but of perhaps equal import was the collective assimilation of more than 100,000 Algerian Jews under the Crémieux Decree of the same year.[17] Debates over who was really French and who was not intensified over the next twenty years as increasing numbers of working-class Italians, Spanish, and Maltese in Algeria were accorded French citizenship. A declining birthrate (accelerating in the 1880s) placed a premium on expanded membership in the French national community but prompted a fear of internal aliens and pseudocompatriots as well.[18] Out of 200,000 "Française d'Algerie," more than half were of non-French origin. Coupled with the 20,000 Parisian political undesirables deported to Algeria by the Second Republic in 1851 (referred to alternately as "les sans-travail," "les révoltés," "les déracinés"), the equivocal national identity of Algeria's French colonial population was reopened for question. The Dreyfus affair coupled with concerns over the suspect loyalties of these new citizens gave particular urgency to debates about what it meant to be French.[19]

Heightened debates over the mixed-blood question in the Dutch context converged with domestic and colonial social reform that targeted the "dangerous classes" in both locales. In the Netherlands, it was the paupered residuum (distinct from the respectable working class). In the Indies, it was the growing population of impoverished (Indo-)Europeans, the majority of whom were of mixed descent but legally classified as European. The metropolitan project joined liberals and conservatives, Protestants and Catholics, in a shared mission, concentrated on the "uplifting" of the working-class family and its moral reform. This "civilizing offensive" focused in large part on child welfare and particularly on those "neglected" and "delinquent" children whose "upbringing" ill prepared them for "their future place in the social system" and marked them as a danger to the state.[20]

National anxieties were not as pitched as in France, but there is evidence that at the turn of the century Dutch national feeling—what Maarten Kuitenbrouwer has called an "extreme nationalism"—"underwent something of a revival," only to subside again.[21] In tandem with the domestic offensive was an imperial one that spanned concerns about both Dutch paupers in the Indies and "vagabond Hollanders" in South Africa. Efforts to counter "the perils of educational failure" and the increased mixing, marrying, and interaction of poor whites with colonized populations in the two locales prompted increased investments in educating the children of poor whites and in reforming the parenting those children received at home.[22] The securing of Dutch influence in South Africa on the eve of the Boer War centered on strategies to instill a cultural belonging to a "Greater Netherlands" that was to embrace Flanders, South Africa, and the Indies.[23] In both metropolitan and imperial projects, questions of national identity, child rearing, and education were high on the public agenda.

Who might be considered truly French or Dutch resonated from core to colony and from colony to core.[24] In the Indies and Indochina, cultural milieu, represented by both upbringing and education, was seen to demarcate which métis children would turn into revolutionaries, patricides, loyal subjects, or full-fledged citizens of the nation-state. As T. H. Marshall once argued, "when the State guarantees that all children shall be educated, it has the requirements and the nature of citizenship definitely in mind."[25] Métis education was a risky undertaking. At issue were the means by which European civilization *(beschaving)* would be disseminated without undercutting the criteria by which European claims to privilege were made.

Thus the discourses about métissage expressed more pervasive if inchoate dilemmas of colonial rule and a fundamental contradiction of imperial domination: the tension between a form of authority simultaneously predicated on incorporation and distancing.[26] This tension expressed itself in the so-called métis problem in quintessential form. Some métis were candidates for incorporation. Others were categorically denied. In either case, the decision to grant citizenship or subject status could not be made on the basis of race alone as all métis shared some degree of European descent by definition. How then could the state distinguish those candidates to be excluded from the national community while retaining the possibility that others would be granted inclusion because French and Dutch "blood prevailed in their veins"? I explore that question here by working through a seemingly disparate set of texts and contexts: a criminal court proceeding in Haiphong in 1898; the Hanoi campaign against child abandonment in the early 1900s; the protracted debate on mixed marriage legislation in the Indies between 1887 and 1898; and finally, the confused and failed efforts of the Indo-European movement in the Indies to articulate its opposition to "pure-blood" Dutch by calling on race, place, and cultural genealogy to make its demands.

In each of these texts, class, gender, and cultural markers deny and designate exclusionary practices. But which of these is privileged at any given moment cannot be sorted out by fixing the primacy of race over gender or gender over class. On the contrary, these made up an unstable and uneven set of discourses in which certain institutional authorities claimed priority of one over another in accordance with other authorities' attempts to designate how political boundaries were to be protected and assigned. If in mid-Victorian England discourses about gender identity were gradually displaced in the 1850s by those of national identity, imperial contestations over métissage suggest nothing linear about these developments.[27] Rather, class distinctions, gender prescriptions, cultural knowledge, and racial membership were simultaneously invoked and strategically filled with different meanings for varied projects.

Patriarchal principles were not always applied to shore up government priorities. Colonial authorities with competing agendas agreed on two premises: children had to be taught both their place and their race, and the family was the crucial site in which future subjects were to be made and loyal citizenship was to be learned. With this frame, the domestic life of individuals was increasingly subject to public scrutiny by a wide range of private and government organizations. These charged themselves with the task of policing the moral borderlands of the European community and the psychological sensibilities of its marginal as well as its supposedly full-fledged members.

At the heart of this tension between inclusionary rhetorics and exclusionary practices was a search for essences that joined formulations of national and racial identity—what Benedict Anderson has identified as the contrary dreams of "historical destinies" and "eternal contaminations."[28] Racism is commonly understood as a visual ideology in which somatic features are thought to provide the crucial criteria of membership. But racism is not really a visual ideology at all. Physiological attributes only signal the nonvisual and more salient distinctions of exclusion on which racisms rest.[29] Racism is not to biology as nationalism is to culture. Cultural attributions are powerfully invoked for both. Cultural competencies index psychological propensities and moral susceptibilities that are seen to shape which individuals are suitable for inclusion in the national community and whether those of ambiguous racial membership are to be classified as subjects or citizens within it. The epidemiologies of racist and nationalist thinking can both be traced to cultural logics that underwrote the relationship between fixed, visual representations and invisible protean essences. This convergence of national and racial thinking achieves particular clarity in the colonial legal and social debates that linked parenting styles and domestic arrangements to the hidden psychological requirements for access to French and Dutch citizenship in this period.

CULTURAL COMPETENCE, NATIONAL
IDENTITY, AND MÉTISSAGE

In 1898 in the French Indochinese city of Haiphong, the nineteen-year-old
son of a French minor naval employee, Sieur Icard, was charged with as-
saulting without provocation a German naval mechanic, striking his temple with a whip, and attempting to crush his eye. The boy was sentenced by
the tribunal court to six months in prison.[30] Spurred by the father's efforts
to make an appeal for an attenuated prison term, some higher officials subsequently questioned whether the penalty was unduly severe. Clemency
was not accorded by the governor-general, and the boy, referred to by the
court as "Nguyen van Thinh dit Lucien" (Nguyen van Thinh called Lucien),
was sentenced to serve his full term. The case might have been less easily
dismissed if it were not for the fact that the son was métis, the child of a
French citizen and a Vietnamese woman who was a colonial subject and his
concubine.

The granting of a pardon rested on two assessments: whether the boy's
cultural identity and his display of French cultural competence supported
his claim to French citizenship rights. The governor-general's letters listed
the boy as Nguyen van Thinh dit Lucien, thereby invoking the double naming of the son and privileging Nguyen van Thinh over Lucien. This suggested the dubious nature of his cultural affinities, giving the impression
that his real name was Nguyen van Thinh, although he answered to the
name Lucien. The father, Sieur Icard, attempted to affirm the Frenchness of
his son by referring to him as Lucien and eliminating reference to Nguyen.
But the angry president of Haiphong's tribunal court used only the boy's
Vietnamese name. Dropping Lucien altogether, he put the very kinship between father and son in question by naming Icard as the "alleged" father.

Icard's plea for pardon, which invoked his own patriotic sentiments as
well as those of his son, was carefully conceived. Icard protested that the
court had wrongly treated the boy as a *vulgaire annamite* (a common
Annamite) and not as the legally recognized son of a French citizen. Icard
held that his son had been provoked and only then struck the German in re-
taliation. But, more important, Lucien had been raised in a French patriotic
milieu, in a household in which Germans were held in "contempt and disdain." He pointed out that their home was full of drawings of the 1870
(Franco-Prussian) war and that like any impressionable (French) boy of his
age, Lucien's youthful imagination was excited by these images.

The tribunal's refusal to accept the appeal confronted and countered
Icard's claims. At issue was whether Nguyen van Thinh dit Lucien could re-

ally be considered culturally and politically French, inculcated with the patriotic feelings and nationalist sentiments that might have prompted such a loyal response. The tribunal argued that Icard was away sailing too much of the time to impart such a love of *patrie* to his son and that Icard's "hate of Germans must have been of very recent origin since he had spent so much time sailing with foreigners."[31] The boy's non-French inclinations were firmly established with the court's observation that he was illiterate and knew but a few French words. Icard's argument was further undermined, because Icard himself "spoke no Annamite" and therefore shared no common language with his child.

These counterarguments may have been sufficient to convince the governor-general not to grant leniency. But another unclarified and more damning reason was invoked to deny the son's case and the father's appeal: the "immoral relations which could have existed between the detainee and the one who declared himself his father."[32] Or as put by Villeminot, the city attorney in Haiphong investigating Icard's appeal, the boy deserved no leniency because "his morality was always detestable" and the police reports permitted one "to entertain the most serious suspicions concerning the nature of the relations which Nguyen van Thinh maintained with his alleged father."[33]

Whether these were coded allegations of homosexuality or referred to the possibility that Icard only pretended to be the boy's father is unclear. Icard's case came up at a time when acts of "fraudulent recognition" of native children were said to be swelling the French citizenry with a bastard population of native poor.[34] Perversion and patriotism, like immorality and nationalist sentiments, were clearly considered mutually exclusive categories. As in nineteenth-century Germany, adherence to middle-class European sexual morality was one implicit requisite for full-fledged citizenship in the European nation-state.[35]

But with all these allusions to suspect and duplicitous behavior, perhaps what was more unsettling in this case was another unspeakable element—that Icard felt such a powerful sentiment for his son and that he went so far as to plead the case of a boy who had virtually none of the exterior qualities (skin color, language, or cultural literacy) and therefore could have none of the interior attributes of being French at all. What the court condemned was a relationship in which Icard could have shown such dedication and love for a child who was illiterate, ignorant of the French language, and spent most of his time in a cultural milieu that was much less French than Vietnamese. Under such circumstances, Icard's concern for Lucien was inappropriate and improper: his fatherly efforts to excuse his son's misdeeds were lauded neither by the lower courts nor by the governor-general. On the contrary, paternal love and responsibility were not to be disseminated carelessly, as Icard had obviously done by recognizing his progeny but allowing him to grow up Vietnamese. In denying the father's plea, the court passed sentence both on Icard and on his son. Both were guilty of transgressing the boundaries of race, culture, sex, and country. If Icard (whose misspellings and profession belied his lower-class origins) was unable to raise his son in a proper French milieu, then he should have abandoned him altogether.

What was deemed duplicitous in the relationship were matters of misplaced affect and affiliation: (1) the boy could be both Nguyen van Thinh in cultural sensibilities and Lucien to his father; and (2) Lucien's non-French physical and cultural affinities did not stand in the way of the father's love. Like the relationship with the boy's unnamed mother, a liaison easily attributed to its carnal cast, Icard's choice to stand up for his son was reduced to a motive of base desires, sexual or otherwise. Neither father nor son had demonstrated a proper commitment to and identification with those invisible moral bonds by which racist pedigrees were marked and colonial divides were maintained.

CULTURAL NEGLECT AND THE RACIAL POLITICS OF ABANDONMENT

Icard's story invokes the multiple tensions of colonial cultures in Southeast Asia and would be of interest for that alone. But it is all the more startling because it so boldly contradicts the dominant formulation of the "métis question" at the turn of the century. The métis issue was conceived in simple terms—as a problem of "abandonment," of children culturally on the loose, sexually abused, economically impoverished, morally neglected, and politically dangerous. European feminists took up the protection of abandoned mixed-blood children as their cause, condemning the irresponsibility and double standards of European men.[36] But so too did colonial officials, who argued that these concubinary relations were producing a new underclass of European paupers, of rootless children who could not be counted among the proper European citizenry. With sartorial trappings that merely masked their cultural incompetence, they did not know what it meant to be Dutch or French. The consequences of mixed unions were collapsed into a singular moral trajectory. Without state intervention, it would lead to a future generation of Eurasian paupers and prostitutes, affront European prestige, and contribute to national decay.

But what was identified as "abandonment" had cultural and historical peculiarities that prompted the specific response to Icard's case. In a comprehensive history of child abandonment in western Europe, John Boswell wrote that "abandonment" commonly referred to "the voluntary relinquishing of control over children by their natal parents or guardians" and to children who were left at the doors of churches or in other public spaces and less frequently to those intentionally exposed to death.[37] Boswell may have been right that abandonment was conflated with infanticide more than the evidence warrants, but perceptions and policies on abandonment often were tied to issues of child mortality. According to Jacques Donzelot, in nineteenth-century France abandonment often led to high rates of child mortality that morally justified intensified policing of families.[38] Neither of these formulations suggests that abandonment always led to death or that this was its sole intent. Still, the contrast with its colonial usage is striking, for discussions of abandonment in the colonies rarely raise a similar concern for infanticide or even obliquely address this eventuality.

In the colonial context, the abandonment of métis children invoked, not a biological, but a social death. It conjured a severing from European society, a banishment of "innocents" from the European cultural milieu in which they could potentially thrive and in which some reformers contended they rightfully belonged.[39] Those officials who wrote about métis children understood "exposure" in a different sense. It was not "exposure" to the natural elements but to the native milieu and to the immoral influence of native women whose debased characters inclined them to succumb to such illicit unions in the first place. Moreover, abandonment was not necessarily voluntary, nor did both parents, despite the implication in Boswell's definition, participate in it. The statutes of the Society for the Protection and Education of Young French Métis of Cochinchine and Cambodia defined the issue of abandonment in the following way:

> Left to themselves, having no other guide than their instincts and their passions, these unfortunates will always give free rein to their bad inclinations, the boys will increase the ranks of vagabonds, the girls those of prostitution. Left to their mothers and lost in the milieu of Annamites, they will not become less depraved. It must not be forgotten that in most cases, the indigenous woman who consents to live with a European is a veritable prostitute and that she will never reform. When, after several years of free union with Frenchmen, the latter disappear or abandon her, she fatally returns to the vice from which she came and she nearly always sets an example of debauchery, sloth, and

immorality for her children. She takes care of them with the sole purpose of later profiting from their labor and especially from their vices.

For her métis son, she seeks out a scholarship in a school with the
certainty that when her child obtains a minor administrative post, she
will profit from it. But, in many cases, the child, ill-advised and ill-
directed, does not work and when he leaves school, abandons himself to
idleness and then to vagabondage; he procures his means of existence
by extortion and theft.

Abandoned métisse girls are no better off; from the cradle, their
mothers adorn them with bracelets and necklaces and maintain in them
a love of luxury innate in the Annamites. Arriving at the age of
puberty, deprived of any skills which would help them survive, and
pushed into a life by their mothers that they have a natural tendency to
imitate, they will take to prostitution in its diverse forms to procure the
means necessary to keep themselves in luxury.[40]

Here, abandonment has specific racial, cultural, and gender coordinates.
Most frequently, it referred to the abandonment of métis children by
European fathers and their abandonment of the children's native mothers
with whom the men lived. The gaze of the colonial state was not directed at
children abandoned by native men but only at the progeny of mixed unions.
Most significantly, the child, considered abandoned whether he or she remained in the care of the mother, was so frequently classified precisely because the child was left to a native mother and to the cultural surroundings
in which she lived.

But the term *abandonment* was also used to condemn those déclassé
European men who chose to reside with their mixed-blood children in a native milieu. In designating cultural rather than physical neglect, abandonment carried at least two judgments: a proper French father would never
allow his offspring prolonged contact or identification with such a milieu,
and the native mother of lower-class origins would only choose to keep her
own children for mercenary purposes.

If abandonment by European men of their métis offspring was considered morally reprehensible, the depraved motives of colonized women who
refused to relinquish their children to beneficent state institutions were considered worse. Thus, in 1904 the president of the Hanoi Society for the
Protection of Métis Youths noted that "numerous mothers refuse to confer
their children to us . . . under the pretext of not wanting to be apart from
them, despite the fact that they may periodically visit them at school."[41]
But if maternal love hid mercenary quests to exploit their young for profits

and pleasure, as was often claimed, why did so many women not only refuse to hand over their children but also reject any form of financial assistance for them? Cases of such refusal were not uncommon. In 1903 the
Haiphong court admonished a métisse mother who was herself "raised with
all the exterior signs of a European education" for withdrawing her daughter from a government school "for motives which could not be but base
given the mother's character."[42]

Resistance also came from youths themselves. In 1904 the seventeen-
year-old métisse daughter of an Annamite woman who was cohabiting with
the French employer of her mother's Annamite lover, declared that she will-
ingly accepted and preferred her own situation over what the Society for
the Protection of Métis Youths could offer.[43] Numerous reports are cited of
métisse girls forced into prostitution by *concubin,* that is, by native men
who were the lovers of the girls' native mothers. These cases expressed another sexual and cultural transgression that social reformers in France and
colonial authorities both feared: "traffic in *filles françaises*" for the Chinese
and Annamite market, not for Europeans.[44]

The portrait of abandonment and charitable rescue was seriously flawed.
It missed the fact that the channeling of abandoned métis children into special state institutions was part of a larger (if failed) imperial vision. These
children were to be molded into colonial citizens of a particular kind. In one
scenario, they were to be the bulwark of a future white settler population,
acclimatized to the tropics but loyal to the state.[45] As proposed by the French
feminist caucus at the National Colonial Exposition of 1931, métisse young
women could

> marry with Frenchmen, would accept living in the bush where young
> women from the metropole would be hesitant to follow their
> husbands, . . . [and would form] the foundation of a bourgeoisie,
> attached at one and the same time to their native land and to the France
> of Europe.[46]

This perspective on mixed marriages was more optimistic than some. But it
echoes the commonly held view that if métisse girls were rescued in time,
they could be effectively educated to become *bonnes ménagères* (good
housekeepers) of a settled Indochina, wives or domestics in the service of
France. In the Indies too similar proposals met with little success. In both
contexts, the vision of fortifying the colonial project with a mixed-blood
yeomanry was informed by the same concern. Would this mixed population
of ambiguous positioning and torn affiliations become adversaries or partisans of the colonial state?

FRAUDULENT RECOGNITIONS AND
OTHER DANGERS OF MÉTISSAGE

The question of what to do with the métis population prompted a number of different responses that all hinged on the same issue: whether métis should be classified as a distinct legal category subject to special education or so thoroughly assimilated into French culture that they would pose no threat. Administrators sought answers within empires but also across imperial borders. In French Indochina, the Indies model had appeal and currency. In 1901, when Joseph Chailley-Bert, director of the Union Colonial Française, went to Java to report on the status of métis in the Indies and on the efficacy of Dutch policy toward them, he left Batavia immensely impressed and convinced that segregation was not the answer. Overwhelmed by the numbers of persons of mixed descent who enjoyed some degree of high station, wealth, and cultivation that he thought rivaled those of many "full-blooded" Europeans, he argued that the Dutch decision not to segregate those of mixed descent or distinguish between illegitimate and legitimate children was the only humane and politically safe course to pursue. On returning to Indochina, he recommended that abandoned métis youth should be assigned European status until proof of filiation was made, that private organizations in each legal grouping (i.e., European and native) should be charged with poor relief rather than the government, and that European standing should not be confined to those with the right "dosage of blood." He noted that such a ruling would be impossible in the Indies where so much of colonial society was métis. Such a distinction "would allow a distance between the Aryan without mix and the Asiatic hybrids."[47]

One Monsieur A. July, writing from Hanoi in 1905, similarly applauded "the remarkably successful results" of the Indies policy that rejected the legal designation "métis" as a caste apart. While he argued that France's abolition of slavery and call for universal suffrage had wiped out racial prejudice, he was less sanguine that France's political system could permit a similar scale of naturalization as that practiced by the Dutch. Not all young métis could be recognized as *citoyens françaises* for reasons he thought better not to discuss. Firmin Jacques Montagne, a senior conductor in the Department of Roads and Bridges, also urged that French policy makers follow the Indies path. The Dutch, as he saw it, had not only "safeguarded their prestige but also profited from a force that if badly directed, could turn against Dutch domination."[48] Based on the account of a friend who administered a plantation on Java, he recommended that métis boys, as in the

Indies, be schooled in special institutions for soldiering and later for modest jobs in commerce or on the estates.

These appeals to Dutch wisdom are curious, not least because they reflected neither the treatment of the mixed population in the Indies nor what administrative quandaries were then facing Dutch authorities. In the very year of Chailley-Bert's visit to Batavia, the Indies government was to initiate a large-scale investigation of European pauperism and its origins. Between 1901 and 1903 several thousands of pages of government reports outlined the precarious economic conditions and political dangers of a population legally classified as European but composed of impoverished widows, beggars, vagrants, and abandoned children who were mostly Indo-Europeans.[49] The commission identified an "alarming increase" of Europeans born in the Indies or of mixed parentage, who could not compete for civil service positions with the influx of "full-blooded" Dutch educated in Europe or with the growing number of better-educated Indonesians now qualified for the same jobs.[50]

The commission's focus was partly on Indo-European adult life and labor but as much on children and their upbringing in the parental home *(opvoeding in de ouderlijkewoning)*.[51] Among the more than seventy thousand legally classified Europeans in the Indies in 1900, nearly 70 percent knew little Dutch or none at all. But there was a more disturbing finding: many of them were living on the borderlands of respectable bourgeois European society in styles that indicated not a *failed* version of European culture but an outright rejection of it.[52] The cause was found in concubinage among subaltern European military barred from legal marriage and among civil servants and estate staff for whom marriage to European women was either forbidden or made economically untenable.

Both the Indies administration and private companies relaxed the restrictions on female immigration from Europe after the turn of the century, but mixed unions did not disappear. The pauperism commission targeted concubinage as the primary source of a transient "rough and dangerous pauper element," with danger defined by three conditions: (1) they lived off the native population when they could, (2) they were a disgrace to European prestige, and (3) they created a financial burden to the state.[53] In Indochina too, that French officials had to issue repeated warnings against concubinage from 1893 to 1911 (just when the societies for protection of métis youth were most active) suggests that another generation was in the making who did not know where they properly belonged.[54]

But concubinage was only part of the story. The pauperism inquiry revealed an educational system that was racialized and exclusionary. European youths educated in the Indies were categorically barred from high-level administrative posts, while Indo-Europeans of modest means were offered only a rudimentary training in Dutch, a basic requisite for any white-collar job.[55] European public (free) schools in the Indies, like those in Indochina, were largely schools for the poor *(armenscholen)*, attended by and really only designed for a lower class of indigent and mixed-blood Europeans.[56]

The problems of concubinage and educational inequities were met with some minor measures for reform. But European pauperism was seen to be linked to a more unsettling problem with deeper roots. This was the growing fear of a surreptitious penetration of inlanders into the legal category "European."[57] French and Dutch officials offered a long list of reasons for why there was such a "rush" to the civil registries and what one French official called a "spontaneous generation" of those claiming European membership.[58]

In the Indies European legal standing provided access to education, jobs, privileges, and social services. It exempted men from labor service and from the harsher penal code applied to those of native status. In the colonial army it meant a higher pay scale and better housing. It opened access to European schools, to jobs, and to travel without the written permission of local authorities. On the father's death, a mixed child recognized by a European father would be placed in a European rather than a native orphanage and educated by the state. But the increase of youths claiming European parentage was not coming only from the native population as one might expect.

According to government officials, "false recognitions" were being instigated by certain Europeans. Officials described a white underclass of soldiers and civilians engaged in a profitable racket of recognizing native children who were not their own for an attractive fee. Reports on the issue provided pointed examples such as one that described "a certain Heer van der Hijde" who had acknowledged seven children born between September 28, 1880, and June 4, 1896, and another "certain Heer Jansen" who "in just one day acknowledged seven children born between September 27, 1872, and October 23, 1896!"[59] Both French and Dutch authorities blamed reprehensible Europeans for fostering the practice, and ambitious native mothers as well. The Indies Pauperism Commission concurred and drew another conclusion: European impoverishment was more limited than the statistics indicated. By its account, the European civil registers were grossly inflated by lowlife mercenaries and, as in Indochina, by "des sans-travail" (the unemployed) who might register as many as thirty to forty children who were not their own.[60]

The issue of fraudulent recognition spoke to other colonial anxieties. Like concubinage, it pointed to the fear that children were being raised in cultural fashions that blurred the distinctions between ruler and ruled. It also suggested the possibility that young, uneducated native men were acquiring access to Dutch and French nationality by channels that circumvented state control. Such practices were seen to be contingent on a class of European men willing to facilitate the efforts of native mothers who sought such arrangements.

It is impossible to know whether there were as many fraudulent recognitions of métis children in Indochina or "artificially fabricated Europeans" *(kunstmatig gefabriceerde Europeanen)* in the Indies as authorities claimed. The repeated reference to fictitious, fraudulent, and fabricated Europeans expressed an underlying preoccupation of colonial authorities, shared by many others in the European community, that illicit incursions into the Dutch and French citizenry extended beyond those cases explicitly referred to by those terms. We should remember that Nguyen van Thinh dit Lucien's condemnation was never explicitly argued on the basis of his suspect parentage but on the more general contention that his behavior was that of an *indigene* in disguise, not a citizen of France. Similarly, Annamite women who had lived in concubinage were accused of clothing their métisse daughters in European attire while ensuring that their souls and sentiments remained deeply native.[61]

Colonial officials wrestled with the belief that the Europeanness of métis children could never be assured, despite a rhetoric affirming that education and upbringing were transformative processes. Authorities spoke of abandoned métisse daughters as "les filles françaises" when arguing for their redemption. But when making a case for segregated education, the same authorities recast these youths as the "fruits of a regrettable weakness," as physically marked and morally marred with "the faults and mediocre qualities of their [native] mothers."[62] Such children represented both the supplement to empire and its excess. They were evidence of the sexual transgressions and indiscretions of European men and reminders of the dangers of a degenerate *(verwilderen)* subaltern class. They were also seen as a threat to male authority. Here was a population that officials saw as "lacking paternal discipline" *(gemis aanvaderlijke tucht)*, inhabiting a contrary colonial world in which mothers took charge.[63] To what extent the concern over these children was about both the negative influence of the native milieu and the threat of single-mother families (as in Europe and America in the same period) is difficult to tell.[64] The absence of male authority in households of widows and native women who had exited from concubinary domestic arrangements was clearly seen as a threat to moral upbringing, sanctioning intervention of the state. Métis children undermined the principles on which national identity thrived—those *liens invisibles* (invisible bonds) that all men shared and that so clearly and comfortably marked off *pursang* (pure-blood) French and Dutch from those of the generic colonized.

The option of making métis a legal category was debated in international colonial forums through the 1930s but was rejected ultimately on political grounds. French jurists argued that legal segregation would infect the colonies with a "class of déraciné, déclassé," with "our most dangerous enemies," with "insurgents, irreconcilable enemies of our domination."[65] Rejection of the legal designation hardly diminished the concern about them. On the contrary, it fueled an intensified racial discourse in which cultural markers of difference were honed and more carefully defined.

This was particularly clear in legal debates about what criteria should be used to assign French or native nationality to children of unknown parentage.[66] Under a 1928 *décret*, all persons born in Indochina (i.e., on French soil) of unknown parents, of which one was presumed to be French, could obtain recognition of "la qualité de français."[67] Presumed Frenchness rested on two sorts of certainty: evaluation of the child's "physical features or race" by a "medico-legal expert" and a "moral certainty" derived from the fact that the child "has a French name, lived in a European milieu and was considered by all as being of French descent."[68] Thus French citizenship was not open to all métis but restricted by a "scientific" and moral judgment that the child was decidedly not indigene.[69] As noted in the case of Nguyen van Thinh dit Lucien, even this was not enough. His French name, Lucien, the acknowledged paternity by Icard, and the patriotic ambience of the household were only sufficient for the child to be legally classified as French, not for him to be treated as French by a court of law. Inclusionary laws left ample room for implementation based on exclusionary principles and practices.

The outrage against abandonment introduced new problems for those who ruled: métis youth had to be morally upraised but educated in ways that would not produce unreasonable expectations. Education was to modulate their desires for privilege, temper aspirations deemed above their station, and remind them that colonial privileges did not follow because European "blood flowed in their veins." The aim of the Hanoi Society for the Protection of Métis Youth was "to inculcate them with our sense of honor and integrity, while only suggesting to them modest tastes and humble aspirations."[70] In the Indies, there was a similar assessment and fear of sentiments and desires out of range and out of place. Pauperism was often attributed to the "false sense of pride" of Indos who refused to do manual labor or take on menial jobs, who did not know that "real Dutchmen" in the Netherlands worked with their hands. The assault was double-edged. It blamed those impoverished for their condition but also more subtly suggested that if they were really Dutch in spirit and drive, such problems of pauperism would not have arisen.

THE CULTURAL FRONTIERS OF THE NATIONAL COMMUNITY

Fears of white impoverishment in the colonies were expressed by many different constituencies—by social reformers concerned with child welfare and by European feminists opposed to the double standard of European men. Colonial officials too worried over whether increased education would diffuse the discontents of the European poor or, as with the French peasantry, turn them against the state.[71] Such concerns were grounded in the belief that those Europeans who did not subscribe to Dutch middle-class conventions of respectability would waver in their allegiance to the cultural distinctions of European rule.

Mixed-bloods were not the only target. At the height of the Ethical Policy, a prominent doctor warned that those Europeans born and bred in the Indies, the *blijvers* (those who remained), lived in surroundings that stripped them of their *zuivere* (pure) European sensibilities, which "could easily lead them to metamorphize into Javanese."[72] Worry over degeneracy among the creole Dutch was not new, but in this moment of liberal reform it took on more force with specific moral coordinates. It was an unease about poor whites living on the cultural borderlands of the *echte* (true) European community, about some European men who married native women, about all European women who chose to marry native men, and about both European and Indo-European women who cohabited with but chose not to marry men of other nationalities.

That unease may have been intensified by the surge of political activity at the turn of the century, coalescing around an Indische population of "mixed-blood" and "pure-blood" Dutch of Indies origin. Their distinct economic interests, cultural style, and legal positioning produced equivocal loyalties to Dutch rule. The Indische voice, evident in a range of new publications and associations, identified itself in two ways: by its cultural rooting in the Indies rather than the Netherlands and by an ambiguous appeal to the notion of race. At a moment when the native nationalist project was barely emergent, this Indische press articulated a new notion of a fatherland loyal to but distinct from the Dutch fatherland and firmly opposed to the Dutch-born elite who managed the state. Between 1898 and 1903 various Indische groups rose, fell, and reassembled as they each sought viable programs to promote the "uplifting" of the Indo-European poor without linking their own fate to them. To do so, they resorted to principles of racial hierarchy that accorded those of a certain upbringing, sexual morality, and cultural sensibility a right to privilege and to rule.[73]

What underwrites this common discourse is a new collusion between race and culture. As race dropped out of certain legal discriminations, it reemerged, marked by specific cultural criteria, in other domains. The contemporary discourse on Europe's new racism situates "cultural racism" as a relatively recent and nuanced phenomenon, replacing the physiological distinctions on which earlier racisms had so strongly relied.[74] The "novelty" of the new racism is often located in its strong cultural inflection, embedded in wider structures of domination, based in the family, and tied to nationalist sentiments in ways that make it more relevant to a wider constituency and therefore more pervasive, insidious, and difficult to weed out.[75] But these features of the "new" racism are familiar colonial conventions firmly rooted in earlier discourses that linked race, culture, and national identity, discourses elaborated in Europe's "laboratories of modernity"—the colonies—not at home.[76]

The concept of cultural surroundings (*milieu* in French, *omgeving* in Dutch) was critical to the new legal stipulations on which racial distinctions and national identity were derived. Paul Rabinow makes the case that the concern about "milieu" in French colonial thinking on education, health, labor, and sex in the late nineteenth century must be understood in terms of the scientific episteme on which it relied.[77] Medical guides to acclimatization in tropical regions warned that Europeans would lose their physical health and cultural bearings if they stayed in the tropics too long. Debates over whether European children should be schooled in France or the Netherlands were prompted by efforts to create the social habitus in which sentiments and sensibilities would be shaped.[78]

These debates drew not so much on Darwin as on a popular neo-Lamarckian understanding of environment in which racial and national essences could be secured or altered by the physical, psychological, climatic, and moral surroundings in which one lived. This understanding underwrote colonial legal discourse on the criteria for European status. The importance of omgeving was not inscribed in the laws themselves, which self-consciously disclaimed racial difference, but in the cultural and racial logic of the legal arguments.

What is apparent in these legal documents is a tension between a belief in the immutability and fixity of racial essence and a discomforting awareness that racial categories were porous and protean at the same time. Moreover, the essences that defined colonized and colonizer were asymmetric. Thus Javanese or Vietnamese might at any moment revert to their natural indigenous affiliations, while a Dutch essence was so fragile that it could unwittingly transform into something Javanese.

JUS SOL, JUS SANGUINIS, AND NATIONALITY

In the civilized world, no one may be without a relationship to the state.[79]

J. A. Nederburgh, one of the principal architects of Indies colonial law, engaged the question of national identity and membership more directly than many of his contemporaries. He argued that in destroying racial purity, colonialism had made the criteria of *jus soli* (place of birth) and *jus sanguinis* (blood descent) obsolete for determining nationality. Colonial *vermenging* (mixing or blending) had produced a new category of "wavering classes," large groups of people whose place of birth and mixed genealogies called into the question the earlier criteria by which rights to metropolitan citizenship and designations of colonial subject had once been assigned. Taking the nation to be those who shared "morals, culture, and perceptions, feelings that unite us without one being able to say what they are," Nederburgh concluded that one could not determine who had these sensibilities by knowing birthplace and kinship alone. He pointed to those of "pure European blood" who "for years remained almost entirely in native surroundings [*omgeving*] and became so entirely nativized [*verinlandschen*] that they no longer felt at ease among their own kind [*rasgenooten*] and found it difficult to defend themselves against Indische morals and points of view."[80] He concluded that surroundings had an "overwhelming influence," with "the power to almost entirely neutralise the effects of descent and blood."[81]

Nederburgh's claim may seem to suggest a firm dismissal of racial supremacy, but this was not the case. He was among the more staunchly conservative legalists of his time, a firm defender of the superiority of Western logic and law.[82] By his account, Europeans who remained too long in the Indies, especially children, "who because of their age are most susceptible and often the most exposed" to native influence in school and native servants at home, "could only remain *echte-Europeesch* [truly European] in thought and deed with much exertion."[83] While insisting that he was not "against Indische influence per se," he recommended that the state allocate funds to bring up European children in Holland.[84] Some eight years later, at the height of the Ethical Policy, another prominent member of the colonial elite made a similar but more radical recommendation to close all schools of higher education in Batavia and replace them with state-subsidized education in Holland to improve the quality of the colored *(kleuringen)* in the civil servant ranks.[85] Both proposals derived from the same assumption: it was "impossible for persons raised and educated in the Indies to be bearers [*dragers*] of Western culture and civilization."[86]

Attention to upbringing, surroundings, and milieu did not disengage personal potential from the physiological fixities of race. Distinctions made on the basis of *opvoeding* (upbringing) merely recoded race in the quotidian circumstances that enabled acquisition of certain cultural competencies and not others. The focus on milieu naturalized cultural difference, sexual essence, and moral fiber of Europeanness in new ways. In chapter 3 we saw how the shift in the colonies away from concubinage to white endogamy coupled with an intensified surveillance of native servants and European children marked out the cultural borders of the European community. It also indicated how much political security was seen to reside in the choices of residence, speech, and cultural style that individuals made. Personal cirteria for inclusion as citizens of the Dutch state were as stringent and intimate as those that defined the exclusion of subjects. The wide gap between prescription and practice suggests why the former were so insistently reiterated, updated, and reapplied. Among those classified as European, there was little agreement on these prescriptions, which were contested if not openly defied.

In 1884 legal access to European equivalent status in the Indies required a "complete suitability *[geschiktheid]* for European society," defined as a belief in Christianity, fluency in spoken and written Dutch, and training in European morals and ideas.[87] In the absence of an upbringing in Europe, district authorities were charged with evaluating whether the concerned party was "brought up in European surroundings as a European."[88] But European equivalence was not granted simply on the display of competence and comfort in European norms. It required that the candidate "no longer feel at home" *(niet meer thuis voelt)* in native society and have already "distanced" himself from his native being *(Inlander-zijn)*. In short, the candidate could neither identify nor retain inappropriate senses of belonging or longings for the milieu from which she or he came.[89] The mental states of potential citizens were at issue, not just their material assets. But who were to be the arbitrators? Suitability to which European society and to which Europeans? The questions are disingenuous because the coding is clear: cultural competence, family form, and middle-class morality became the salient new criteria for marking subjects, nationals, citizens, and different kinds of citizens in the nation-state. As European legal status and its equivalent became accessible to an ever broader population, the cultural criteria of privilege were more carefully defined. European women who subscribed to white endogamy were made the custodians of a new morality, but this was not the case for those "fictive" European women who rejected these norms.

Colonial practices contradicted and complicated the moral designations for European national and racial identity in blatant ways. Those practices prompted an uncomfortable question: which European morality was to be celebrated? Was it that embraced by European men who cohabited with native women, adopted native speech and dress, and supported their offspring? Or was it to be the morality of European men who retained their Dutch manners and cuts of cloth, lived with native women who were the mothers of their children, and then departed for Europe unencumbered when their contracts were done? Was the moral high ground occupied by colonial officials who barred the filing of paternity suits against European men by native women? Or more rightly so by those who argued for it on the grounds that it would hinder legal recognitions of "natives in disguise" by lower-class European men? What can we make of the ruling on European equivalence for non-native residents that stipulated candidates must be from regions or states that subscribed to a monogamous family law?[90] How did this speak to the thousands of Indische Dutch men for whom concubinage was the most frequently chosen option?

If national identity was, as often stated, "an indescribable set of invisible bonds," the fact that a European woman on marriage to a native man was legally reclassified to follow his nationality could make a mockery of that pretension. As we shall see, these invisible bonds, in which women only had a conjugal share by proxy to their husbands, were those enjoyed by some but not all men. The paradox is that native women married to European men were charged with the raising of children, with the formative making of Dutch citizens, and with culturally encoding the markers of race. Colonial cultures created problematic contexts in which patriarchal principles and citizenship criteria seemed to be at fundamental odds. At a time when European feminists were turning to motherhood as a claim to citizenship, this notion of "mothers of citizens" meant something different in the colonies. There definitions of proper motherhood served to clarify the blurred boundaries of nation and race.[91]

THE MIXED-MARRIAGE LAW OF 1898

The mixed-marriage law of 1898 and the legal arguments that surrounded it are of special interest on several counts. Nowhere in the Dutch colonial record was the relationship among gender prescription, class membership, and racial category so contentiously debated and so clearly defined. Nowhere was the danger of certain kinds of mixing so directly linked to national image while references to race were repeatedly denied.[92] The mixed-marriage debates were framed as part of a liberal discourse ostensibly about the protection of native (men's) rights. In later years these debates were taken as paradigmatic examples of progressive colonial ethics on the argument that they were motivated by an effort to equalize and synchronize colonial and metropolitan law. But, as Willem Wertheim noted forty years ago, they did far more to buttress racial distinctions than to break them down.[93]

Legal attention to mixed marriages was not new in the Indies but had never been formalized as it was to be now.[94] Mixed marriages had been regulated by government decree and church decretals soon after the East Indies Company established its first Batavia settlement. The decree of 1617 that forbade marriage between Christian and non-Christian remained intact for more than two hundred years. With the Civil Code of 1848, religious criteria were replaced with the ruling that marriage partners of European and native standing would both be subject to European law.

The legislation on mixed marriages before 1898 was designed to address one kind of union but not others. The 1848 ruling allowed European men already living in concubinage with non-Christian native women to legalize their unions and the children born from them. The civil law of 1848 was derived from the Napoleonic civil code, but the defining principle of the civil code had been curiously ignored. This was the stipulation that on marriage, a woman's legal status was made that of her husband. Dutch jurists were to argue a half century later that because mixed marriages had then been overwhelmingly between European men and native women, the latter's legal incorporation could be easily assumed.

But this was no longer the case in the 1880s when Indies colonial officials noted two troubling trends. First, more women classified as European were choosing to marry non-European men. Second, concubinage continued to remain the domestic arrangement of choice over legal marriage.[95] While legal specialists argued that concubinage was a primary cause of Indo-European impoverishment, the mixed-marriage rulings, as they stood, were so complicated and costly that people continued to choose cohabitation over conjugality. But there was a more disturbing outcome still. Some European, Indo-European, and native women were opting to retain their own legal standing, thereby protecting their material assets and those they could bestow on their children. These women were rejecting marital arrangements altogether.[96]

Colonial lawyers were thus faced with a conundrum. How could they implement a ruling that would facilitate certain kinds of mixed marriages (over concubinage) and condemn others? Two basic premises were accepted on all sides: the family was the bulwark of state authority, and the unity of the family could only be assured by its unity in law.[97] Thus legitimate children could not be subject to one law and their father to another, nor could women hold native status while their husbands retained that of a European.[98] Given this agreement there were two possible solutions. Either the "superior European standing" of a spouse would determine the legal status (and nationality) of the other, or the patriarchal principle that a woman follow her husband's legal status—regardless of *his* origin—would be applied. Principles of cultural and male supremacy seem opposed. Let us look at why they were not.

Those who argued that a European woman should retain her European standing in a mixed marriage did so on the grounds that without such a stipulation European prestige would be compromised. The liberal lawyer, J. H. Abendanon, held that a European woman would be placed in a "highly unfavorable and insecure position." Being thereby subject to native *adat* law, she risked becoming no more than a concubine if her native husband took a second wife as polygamy under Islamic law was not justification for divorce. Others pointed out that she would be subject to the penal code applied to those of native status. Should she commit a crime, she would be treated to "humiliating physical and psychological punishment," for which her "physical constitution" was unsuited. Relegation of European women to native status would thus cause an "outrageous scandal" for all Europeans.[99]

That argument rested on one central but contested assumption: all women classified as European deserved the protection and privilege of European law. But those who made the countercase—that the patriarchal principle be applied regardless of origin—argued that the "quality of women" with European standing was not the same. The state commission noted that mixed marriages between European women and native men were relatively few but also noted their "steady increase among certain classes of the inhabitants,"[100] unions that were all but unthinkable in midcentury. Why Indo-European and even full-blooded European women now were choosing them reflected a broader trend of increasing impoverishment and declining welfare of these women themselves. Some authorities opined that their choices might also have been motivated by the improved "intellectual and social development" among certain classes of native men. But this possibility was overshadowed by the more dominant contention that women who made such choices were neither well bred nor deserving of European standing.[101]

Some legalists made the case more forcefully than others. The lawyer Taco Henny argued that the category "European" was a legal fiction that neither applied to many women who enjoyed the cultural and moral life of the European community nor described the majority who were "outwardly and inwardly indistinguishable from natives." Fundamental to the debate was the question of class. Henny contended that because these women tended to be of lower-class origin or mixed racial descent and were already native in culture and inclination, they needed no protection from a milieu in which they rightly belonged. Nor was their possible subjection to the native penal code reason for scandal since it was appropriate to their actual station, one that was so far removed from Dutch society proper that it would cause no alarm.

Pastor van Santen made the case in even bolder terms: "The European woman who wants to enter into such a marriage has already sunk so deep socially and morally that it does not result in ruin, either in her own eyes or those of society. It merely serves to clarify her situation."[102] The argument rested on an interior distinction between "real" Dutch women and those only classified as such, in whose veins "very little European blood actually flowed." His claim that this latter group had *already* fallen from cultural and racial grace had its "proof" in yet another observation: "[I]f she was still European in thought and feeling, she would never take a step that was so clearly humiliating and debasing in the eyes of actual [*werkelijk*] European women."[103] This reasoning (which won in the end) marshaled the patriarchal tenets of the civil code to exclude women of a certain class and cultural milieu from Dutch citizenship rights without directly invoking race in the legal argument.

But this gendered principle did more work still and could be justified on wider grounds. It defined a "true" European woman in specific cultural terms—by her spousal choice and then by her maternal sentiments. She was to demonstrate that she put her children's interests first by guarding their European standing, which would be lost to her future progeny if she married a non-European under the new law. In this way the law strongly dissuaded "true" European women from choosing to marry native men. This was its implicit and, according to some advocates, its explicit intent.

The proposed legislation also was said to speak to the interests of well-to-do native men by protecting their access to agricultural land and other privileges passed from fathers to sons under adat law.[104] It also was claimed to discourage concubinage by guarding the customary rights of native men who would not be tempted to live with Indo-European and "full-blooded" European women outside of marriage. In short, the proposed law prevented the infiltration of increasing numbers of native men into the Dutch citizenry and may have been directed precisely at men of the middling classes considered to have little to lose and much to gain by acquiring a Dutch nationality. Others who supported "uplifting" native men to European status through marriage would in effect encourage marriages of convenience at the expense of European women drawn to such unions and those who prided themselves on the cultural distinctions that defined them as European.[105] Here again, as in the fraudulent recognitions of métis children, at stake was the undesirability of increased numbers "of persons who would only be European in name."[106]

In the end, the mixed-marriage ruling and the debates surrounding it were more an index than a cause of profound changes in thinking about sexual practice, national identity, and colonial morality. Mixed marriages increased between 1900 and 1920. This was evident in fewer acknowledgments of children born out of wedlock and in increased numbers of single European men who now sought to marry the native women in their domestic service.[107]

Condemnation of concubinage came simultaneously from several sources. The Pauperism Commission had provided new evidence that concubinage was producing an underclass of Indos that had to be curbed. By treating prostitution and the huishoudster system as similar phenomena, the Nederlandschen Vrouwenbond (Dutch Women's Association) conflated the distinct options such arrangements afforded women and rallied against both.[108] The Sarekat Islam, Indonesia's earliest nationalist organization, also campaigned against concubinage on religious grounds that probably discouraged some native women from such unions.[109] Still, in 1920 half the métis children of a European father and native mother had been born outside of marriage. After 1925 the number of mixed marriages fell off again as the number of Dutch-born women coming to the Indies increased fourfold.

Hailed as exemplary liberal legislation, the mixed-marriage ruling was applied selectively in ways that attended carefully to class, gender, and racial distinctions. By reinvoking the Napoleonic civil code, European men were assured that their "invisible bonds" of nationality remained intact regardless of their legal partner. European women, on the other hand, were summarily (but temporarily) disenfranchised from their national community on the basis of conjugal choice alone.[110] Those mixed marriages that derived from earlier cohabitations between European men and native women were not the unions most in question, and jurists of different persuasions stated as much throughout the debate. These marriages were considered unproblematic on the assumption that a native woman would be grateful for and proud of her elevated European status and content with legal dependence on a European man. Whether native women were so easily granted European legal status and Dutch citizenship because there was no danger that they could or would fully exercise their rights was never discussed because racial and gender privileges were aligned.

But what about the next generation of métis? Although the new ruling effectively blocked the naturalization of native adult men through marriage, it granted métis children European standing by affixing their nationality to their father's. Would this generation be so assuredly cut from their mother's roots? The persistence in the 1920s and 1930s of discussions of social environment, upbringing, class, and education suggests resounding doubts. As noted in the preceding chapter, the Eugenics Society designed studies to test whether children of Indies-born Europeans might display different "racial markers" than their parents.[111] Eugenicist logic consolidated discussions about national identity and cultural difference in a discourse of "fitness" that located the interior frontiers of the nation. It reaffirmed yet again that upbringing and parenting were critical in deciding who would be marked as a fictive compatriot or a true citizen.

The race criterion was finally removed from the Indies constitution in 1918 under native nationalist pressure. But debates over the psychological, physical, and moral makeup of Indo-Europeans became even more intense in the 1920s and 1930s. A 1936 doctoral dissertation at the University of Amsterdam could still "explain the lack of energy" of Indo-Europeans by the influence of a sapping and warm, dank climate, by the bad influence of the "devitalized Javanese race" on Indo-Europeans, and by the fact that "half-bloods" were not descended from the "average European" and the "average Javanese."[112] In the 1920s the European-born Dutch population was visibly closing its ranks, creating new cultural boundaries while shoring up its old ones.

Racial hatred *(rassenhaat)* and representation were watchwords of the times but hardly new to the vocabulary of the Indies-born Europeans.[113] As early as 1908 contributors to the Indische press accused the European-born

Dutch both of doubting Indo identification as "Hollanders" and of outright racial discrimination.[114] But now there was evidence of a renewed disdain for Indos that heightened in the depression as the nationalist movement grew stronger and as unemployed "full-blooded" Europeans found "roaming around" in native villages blurred with the ranks of the Indo poor. How the colonial state distinguished these two groups from one another and from "natives" on issues of unemployment insurance and poor relief underscored how crucial these interior frontiers were to official thinking about welfare policy and to the emergent ideas about a welfare state.[115]

INDO-EUROPEANS AND THE QUEST FOR A FATHERLAND

The slippage between race and culture, as well as the intensified discussions of racial membership and national identity, were not invoked by the "real" Europeesche population alone. Despite the huge numbers of Europeans of mixed parentage and substantial economic means, the term *Indo* was usually reserved for that segment who were *verindische* (indianized) and poor. Less clear are the cultural, political, and racial criteria by which those of mixed descent identified themselves. The contradictory and changing criteria used by the various segments of the Indo-European movement at the turn of the century highlight how contentious and politically charged these deliberations were.

There was a lot in a name, and the use of different designations changed as quickly as did racial politics. It is no accident that *Indo-European* is difficult to define. In the Indies it applied to those of *mengbloeden* (mixed blood) of European and native origin, to Europeans born in the Indies of Dutch nationality and not of native origin, and to those "pure blood" Europeans born elsewhere who referred to the Indies as a "second fatherland."[116] The semantics of mixing thus related to blood, place, and belonging to different degrees and at different times. *Soeria Soemirat*, one of the earliest publications of the educated Indo-Europeans in the late 1890s, included among its members all Indies-born Europeans and took as its central goal the uplifting of the (Indo-) European poor. The Indischen Bond, formed in 1898, was led by Indies-born Europeans who spoke for the Indo poor but whose numbers were rarely represented in their ranks. At the heart of both organizations was the push for an *Indisch vaderland*, contesting both the popular terms of Indonesian nationalism and the exclusionary practices of the Dutch-born *(totok)* society.[117] Some used the term *Indiers* or *Indische Nederlanders* to underscore their Dutch affiliations.

The Indo-European movement never developed as a nationalist one. It was as "socially thin" as Anderson suggests its creole counterpart was in the Americas. It could neither enlist a popular constituency nor dissociate from its strong identification with the European-born Dutch elite. The Indisch movement often made its bids for political and economic power by invoking Eurasian racial superiority to inlanders while concurrently denying a racial criterion for judging their status vis-à-vis European-born Dutch. The subsequent effort in 1912 to form the Indische Partij (with the motto "Indies for the Indiers") was stridently antigovernment, with a platform that addressed native as well as poor Indo welfare. Despite inclusionary rhetoric, its native and poor Indo constituency were categorically marginalized and could find no common political ground.[118]

By 1919, when native nationalist mobilization was gaining strength, the need for a specifically Indo organization took on new urgency and meaning. As its founder argued, it would be a *class-verbond* (class-based association) to support the interests of the larger Indo group.[119] This organization, eventually called the Indo-Europeesch Verbond (IEV), with more than ten thousand members in 1924, continued to plead the cause of the Indo poor while remaining unequivocally loyal to the Dutch colonial state. This truncated version of a much more complicated story should illustrate at least one unsettling point. Poor Indos never gained a political voice, however large their numbers. They were eventually rejected from the Indonesian nationalist movement, in part because their demands were based largely on claims to a cultural and racial alliance with those Dutch who ruled.[120]

Cultural, racial, and national affiliations were particularly charged around proposals for Indo-European agricultural settlements. This utopian project for white settler communities that would be colonized with those of mixed descent joined persons of widely disparate political persuasions in curious ways. In 1874 and 1902 state commissions on European pauperism had begun to explore the agricultural possibilities for the Indo poor. Their proposals focused on beggar colonies, self-sufficient rural confinements in which (Indo-)European paupers would be housed, fed, and kept out of sight. Other, more ambitious schemes advocated intensive horticultural and small-scale estates that would not compete with either native peasant production or the agribusiness industry.

These rural solutions, entertained in both the Indies and Indochina, were based on a common set of assumptions about who mixed-bloods were: native blood ties would make them more easily acclimatized to tropical agriculture, while their European heritage would provide them with the reasoning capacity and drive for success. Thus brawn combined with brains, tropical know-how joined to European science, would make for a hybrid and dynamic innovation. Government assistance and private initiative were to come together to produce an economically self-sustaining, morally principled, and loyal *volk*. The Indische Bond first and the IEV later made land rights and agricultural settlements for needy Indos principal features of their platforms. Conservative and fascist-linked organizations concerned with European unemployment in Holland and European prestige in the colonies also proposed a New Guinea settled by whites that would serve their imperial plan. As a province of a "Greater Netherlands" (Groot Nederland), New Guinea might absorb an economically weak underclass in the metropole, alleviate Dutch unemployment, and foster a settler colonialism in the Indies for a more stabilized form of rule.[121]

The vision of turning potential patricides into pastoral patriots never worked. But its discussion raised critical issues for different interest groups. The state viewed the poor Indo population as out of place, rootless, and dangerous. The Indisch movement clearly could not claim a fatherland without territorial rights and roots within it (since many Indo-Europeans had European standing, they could not own land). The movement's appeal to an Indisch nationalism faltered in the absence of mass-based support or a homeland on which to rest its claims. For the conservative Fatherland Club, rural settler colonies in the 1930s were envisaged as a defense against a Japanese invasion and as a means to reduce overpopulation in the Netherlands. The Fatherlands' Club and the IEV made a short-lived alliance to support the settler schemes, to oppose the *ontblanking* (unwhitening) of the Indies, and to attack the Ethical Policy, which had placed more educated Javanese into subaltern civil service jobs. But their joint venture collapsed as the IEV became increasingly vocal in their criticisms of the European-born elite and their conflicting images of the future fatherland became difficult to deny.[122]

For the Indo-European movement, their *vaderland* was an Indisch one independent of Holland. For the Indies fascists, who defined their task as the self-purification of the nation *(zelfzuivering der natie)*, their notion of the fatherland conjured "a tropical Netherlands" that would unite the Netherlands and Indies into a single state.[123] Neither of these visions concurred with that of the native nationalists who were to oppose them both.

ROOTLESSNESS AND CULTURAL RACISM

With rootedness at the center stage of nationalist discourse, the notion of rootlessness captured a range of dangers about métissage.[124] Abandoned métis youths were generically viewed as vagrants in Indochina, as child delinquents in the Indies, as de facto stateless subversives without a country.[125] In times of economic crisis "free-roaming European bastards" were rounded up for charity and goodwill in efforts to avert a racial disgrace. Liberal colonial projects spent decades creating a barrage of institutions to incorporate, inculcate, and insulate abandoned métis youths. But the image of rootlessness was not only applied to those who were abandoned.

In 1938 government officials in Hanoi conducted a colony-wide inquiry to monitor the physical and political movements of métis. The Resident of Tonkin recommended a comprehensive state-sponsored social rehabilitation program to give them the means to function as real citoyens on the argument that with "French blood prevailing in their veins," they already "manifested an instinctive attachment to France."[126] But many French in Indochina must have been more equivocal about their instinctive patriotic attachments. The fear that métis might revert to their natural inclinations persisted. So did a continuing discourse on their susceptibility to the native milieu, where they might relapse to the immoral and subversive states of their mothers.

Fears of métissage were not confined to colonial locales. We need only read the 1942 treatise, *Les métis,* of René Martial who combined his appointment on the faculty of medicine in Paris with eugenic research on the *anthro-biologie des races.* For him, métis were categorically persons of physical and mental deformity. He saw métis descent as a frequent cause both of birth defects in individuals and of the contaminated body politic of France. As he put it,

> Instability, the dominant characteristic of métis, is contagious, it stands in opposition to the spirit of order and method, it generates indeterminable and futile discussion and paralyzes action. It is this state of mind that makes democracies fail that live with this chimera of racial equality, one of the most dangerous errors of our times, defended with piety by pseudo-French who have found in it a convenient means to insinuate themselves everywhere.[127]

That Martial's spirit continues to thrive in contemporary France in the rhetoric of the radical Right is not coincidental. The discourses on *métissage* in the early twentieth century and on immigrant foreigners today are both about external boundaries and interior frontiers. Both discourses are permeated with images of purity, contamination, infiltration, and national decay. For both Martial and the French National Front's former leaders, cultural identities refer to human natures and psychological propensities inimical to the identity of the French nation and a drain on the welfare state.[128]

CULTURAL HYBRIDITY AND THE POLITICS OF REFUSAL

The historically disparate discourses on métissage are striking in how similarly they encode it as a political danger predicated on the psychological liminality, mental instability, and economic vulnerability of culturally hybrid minorities.[129] But would these discourses look different from another perspective, by asking whether it was weakness that métissage entailed? Recast, these anxious documents may have been more about the fear of empowerment, not about marginality at all. These were debates about groups that straddled and disrupted cleanly marked social divides and whose diverse membership exposed the arbitrary logic by which the categories of control were made.[130]

Nor were they unlike those about Indische women themselves. In disparaging their impoverished and hybrid Dutch and non-European tastes, authorities eclipsed the more compelling reality that they could, as Jean Taylor has put it, "sometimes pass between ethnic communities, cross lines drawn by color and caste and enter slots for which they had no birthright, depending on their alliance with men."[131] Taylor's final clause is critical. It was through these varied sexual contracts that citizenship rights were accorded and métis identities were contested and remade.[132] The management of sexuality, parenting, and morality was at the heart of the late imperial project. Cohabitation, prostitution, and legally recognized mixed marriages slotted women, men, and their progeny differently on the social and moral landscape of colonial society. These sexual contracts were buttressed by pedagogic, medical, and legal evaluations that shaped the boundaries of European membership and the interior frontiers of the colonial state.

Métissage was first a name and then made a thing. It was so heavily politicized because it was understood to destabilize both national identity and the Manichaean categories of ruler and ruled.[133] The cultural density of class, gender, and national issues that it invoked converged in a grid of transgressions that touched the nerves of both metropolitan and colonial politics. The sexual affront that it represented challenged middle-class family order, racial frontiers, norms of child rearing, and conjugal patriarchy. As a sexual affront, it became increasingly difficult to distinguish between true nationals and their sullied, pseudocompatriots. The issue of fraudulent recognition could be viewed in a similar light. Poor white men and native women who arranged legal recognition of their own children or those of others, defied the authority of the state by using the legal system to grant Dutch and French citizenship to a younger generation.[134]

The turn of the century represents one major breaking point in the nature of colonial morality and in national projects. In both the Indies and Indochina, a new humanitarian liberal concern for mass education and representation was coupled with newly recast social prescriptions for maintaining separatist and exclusionary cultural conventions regarding how, where, and with whom European colonials should live. Virtually all of these differentiating practices were worked through a psychologizing and naturalizing impulse that embedded gender inequalities, sexual privilege, class priorities, and racial superiority in a tangled political field. Colonial liberalism in its nationalist cast opened the possibilities of representation for some while for others it set out moral prescriptions and affixed psychological attributes that partially closed those possibilities down.

5 A Sentimental Education
Children on the Imperial Divide

What goes for our cigars and furniture, holds for our children.
They can remain in good condition here, but it is more difficult to
do so.[1]

In tracking the ambiguous allegiances, affiliations, and cultural competencies of the Indies European population, Dutch authorities, as we have seen, did not cast their disquieted eyes on adults alone. Children were the focal point of their concerns about white poverty and politics, about sex and subversion, about the preferability of white endogamy over mixed marriages. For officials and civilians of diverse political persuasion, the moral and physical contaminations to which European children were subject in the Indies served to measure how effectively domestic arrangements might confirm or undermine the moral tenets of European privilege and the security of rule. Contamination was conceived as physical and sexual but affective as well. While evidence of rationality, reason, and progress was certainly a measure invoked to define privilege and distinction, European colonial communities policed their borders by other criteria, attended to with equal care. Here I look more closely at the moral landscape of a racializing and reformist colonial regime for whom child rearing and affective attachments were defining features and affairs of state. At issue was the *learning* of place and race. A focus on children underscores which elements of difference were considered necessary to teach—and why agents of empire seemed so convinced that the lessons were hard to learn.

If Foucault was correct that the supervisory state proclaimed visual surveillance as its triumphant mode in the late nineteenth century, it is striking that colonial state authorities became increasingly invested in controlling the nonvisual domain. Their political energies were directed at more than the "empire of the night," the secreted sexual liaisons between native women and European men. As in the last chapter, pervasive concern for what defined European membership rested on the identification of invisible bonds, those attachments "that unite us without one being able to say what

Figure 10. 'Brother and sister playing with a doll in front of the house,' Java, ca. 1925. KIT album 582/27c.

Figure 11. 'Son of the family Kunst, 4 years of age,' 1902. The practice of decorating a chair with paper flowers to celebrate a birthday was and remains a common Dutch practice. In this photo from the Indies, the child is enshrined with live foliage rather than paper flowers. KIT album 680/12, no. 25.

they are" that might distinguish "real Frenchmen" and the "truly Dutch" from their suspect false compatriots.[2]

But access to European equivalent status in the Indies, as we also saw, was not granted simply on the display of competence and familiarity with European norms. It required evidence of estrangement of another kind— that the candidate "no longer felt at home" in native society, that she or he showed evidence of feeling "distanced" from that native part of his or her being and its cultural sensibilities.[3] It was the internal states of those on the colonial divide that were at issue, not material or cultural accoutrements alone. As in the case of Nguyen van Thinh dit Lucien, sentiment and sensibility granted some candidates the right to be treated as European that it did not grant others. Underwriting colonial anxieties was the sustained fear that children of mixed parentage would always remain natives in disguise, fictive Europeans, fabricated Dutchmen, affectively bound to the sentiments and cultural affiliations of their native mothers.

EUROPEAN CHILDREN AND CULTURAL
CONTAGIONS: A RECURRENT FRAME

The everyday jeopardy that children of mixed parentage were thought to face in the Indies provided enduring and powerful images in the repertoire of stories that concerned Dutch reformers exchanged among themselves. Over the span of more than a century, between the 1830s and 1940s, thousands of pamphlets, scientific articles, popular books, and newspaper editorials described the dangers to which European children were subject in schoolyards, in the streets, and in their homes.

This archive on children is dense with refrains, recurrent themes, and cross-references. The same charged vocabulary of distress, neglect, dismay, and disorder appears again and again. As ethnographic description, its redundancy might suggest that nothing changed. Jean Taylor, for example, has noted an "unbroken tradition" in the colonial history of the Dutch in Indonesia that attributed "defects of character to the habit of leaving child-rearing to Asian subordinates."[4] At one level Taylor's observation is not incorrect. The tradition was "unbroken," but shared images did not signal unchanging fears. How do we treat invariant incantations that are mobilized to different ends? As Carolyn Steedman reminds us, "a perception of childhood experience" may provide "the lineaments of adult political analysis."[5] Discourses on child rearing in the Indies shared themes across generations, but the political uses to which they were put were not the same.

By way of example, let us look at two seemingly identical descriptions of child rearing in the Indies separated by nearly seventy years. The first, a pamphlet published in 1849, was part of a broader critique of European schools in the Indies and of an inadequate educational system. Its author, Albertus Wilkens, was a schoolteacher and a Javanologist and was credited as joint author of the first comprehensive Javanese-Dutch dictionary. Born in Gresik, educated in Weltevreden, and buried in Soerabaya, his Indies career spanned some forty years.[6] Wilkens's account is not only the earliest description of its sort—of a day in the life of a European child raised in Java. It is also characteristic of that emergent genre in reformist literature that drew on the pathos of ethnographic anecdote to make its evidentiary claims. Wilkens wrote:

> It is not possible for us to sketch all the nuances of the ways in which children in the Indies are raised. We will limit ourselves to the darkly (not the darkest) colored, and take those households as a general standard where the parents and the children speak Malay.
>
> At six or six-thirty in the morning the children usually get up, neither say good morning to the father nor mother, and meander in the garden in *sarong* and *kebaya* until their grumbling nursemaid, threatening, pushing and pinching them takes them to the well, washes them, brings them to their rooms and puts them each into their clothes. Next, they receive some money from the mother for breakfast, consisting of rice with condiments. A native rice seller comes to the backdoor of the garden and serves the children with her rice, or the nursemaid goes to the corner of the street and buys it in a foodstall. Before the clock strikes 8, the nursemaid brings the children to school with slates and books under her arm and picks them up again when school is out. Once at home, they eat, sometimes with the parents, sometimes separately, before or after them. Prayer and thanks are sometimes said, if the children eat with the parents, otherwise it depends on the desire of the children themselves, and some do not know what it [prayer] is. After they eat they undress themselves under the direction of the nursemaid.
>
> Some parents like to have their children take a nap as they do themselves, so as to avoid them playing in the streets, or conversing with the servants which would happen most of the time if the children stayed up. Others give the child money to buy snacks, more out of custom than from fear that they, who have eaten an hour before, would starve of hunger. In the evening, when it is time to be dressed it is the nursemaid who, as in the morning, does it again.
>
> As soon as they are dressed, they sit in front of the door, rather than inside, play on the street or in the garden or go wandering about as they please and sometimes receive money again. In houses where there is a fixed hour for the children to eat, they sit at the table together; oth-

erwise they do it irregularly, one after the other, and go to the kitchen to ask for food. After the evening meal, they undress. Then they play a little again in their *sarong* and *kebaya* until they get sleepy and finally, wishing neither mother nor father goodnight, go to bed. Neither evening nor morning prayers accompany going to bed or getting up.[7]

The passage is compelling on several counts. The children are getting something wrong, and it is assumed that the reader knows what it is. Wilkens confirms the credibility of his "day in the life" narrative with a footnote telling the reader that his account is based on "his own life as a youth and that of his children." There are no boldface signposts as to how the passage should be read. For Wilkens and his Dutch readership, the message was clear. Parental negligence is evident at every turn. Indies parents relinquish too much of the material care of their children to native domestics and pay insufficient heed to their children's moral upbringing. The children are not taught parental respect. The lack of religious training is evident in the sporadic observance of morning and bedtime prayers. They are left to their own whims and worse, to those of a servant.

Neglect comes in oblique forms. The dispensing of money punctuates the child's days, replacing parental care. The children are bought off with small change to forage for their breakfasts, to distract them during the parents' midday nap, and again in the evening when they are left to "wander" the streets. Children do not learn self-reliance or respect, and thus they cannot learn to whom respect should be given. They are bereft of the tenderness in which they should share. Instead, the "grumbling" native nursemaid ministers to their needs. She dresses and grooms them, cajoles them from sarong to Dutch attire and back to native dress again. It is her hands who tend to their physical needs and to her quarters that they retreat in quiet hours. Wilkens's indictment was framed as a broader assault on the Indies educational system, but the dangers identified are those found in the home.

Commentaries of this sort on the domestic milieu were not uncommon in the decades that followed. But this one is ambiguous about whose behavior it condemns. The pamphlet's title, *Het Inlandsche Kind in Oost-Indie en Iets over den Javaan*, does not refer to natives or to children as we might expect. Nor is its target those Europeans born and bred in the Indies who lived in a Dutch-speaking milieu. Rather it refers to those families partially descended from Europeans, those "darkly (but not darkest) colored children" born out of mixed unions—Malay-speaking Dutchmen cohabiting with native women whose "attachments" *(gehechtheid)* to the fatherland Wilkens questioned, defended, and questioned again. Its target is those who never set eyes on the "motherland" and lacked the knowledge to respect its civilities. In earlier years that Indo-European population was referred to disparagingly by the Dutch born as "liplaps," in later years by "Indo" and other pejorative names.

Wilkens's compassionate interest in the lives of these borderline Europeans was widely shared. In the same year he wrote, the Indies commissioner of education dispatched a circular to his regional offices with an urgent appeal for the creation of European nurseries to protect those "young children dangerously at risk of entirely degenerating and later being unfit for learning and civilization because of how they are reared."[8] And just a few years later, speaking before members of the Netherlands' foremost philanthropic association, the Society for Public Welfare (Maatschappij tot Nut van 't Algemeen), its prominent board member, P. J. Veth, emphatically urged the opening of European nurseries in the Indies as a political priority to counter the "direly neglected upbringing" of its European youth.[9] In colony and metropole, parenting practices and education were key political issues on the reformist agenda.[10]

But consider another version of this scenario that appeared in 1917 in a pamphlet by A. de Braconier accounting for the rise of juvenile criminality among Europeans.

> In the morning, the European *kampung* [village] child was given a few cents to buy breakfast in a local village food stall that he or she ate along the side of the road. After getting dressed, the mother sent the child to school. However the little *"njo"* [Indo boy] or *"nonnie"* [Indo girl] did not carry the school bag, but was followed by a *babu* [native nursemaid] or young native girl who carried the things for them. . . . As school is out at one in the afternoon and the child is at home, the most dangerous time begins. There [the child] plays with his friends in the village or in the gardens. There we see both native and European boys playing brotherlike [*broederlijke*] together and so begins hooliganism and small thefts.[11]

The scene captures a site of Dutch anxieties about life in the Indies that survives the social transformations of those seventy years. The two accounts are similar, but Braconier's is framed by a different set of associations. It is less Christian piety that is at issue than the spread of pauperism. Child neglect by poor, "degenerated Indos" is what "incites" children to crime.[12] In Wilkens's account, "neglect" is evinced in money that passes between mother and child. In Braconier's version, it is "weak, immoral [*zwakke, moreel-willooze*] European paupers without occupation" that feed the environments in which delinquents thrive. For Wilkens, "rearing" is the problem, not the legality of sexual union. For Braconier, the sexual depravity of barrack concubinage thwarts any semblance of "family life." Parental attention is elsewhere; children wallow in a destitute street life of immorality and petty crime. Where Wilkens blamed both parents, Braconier attributed the causes of European poverty to those debased "native mothers" who sapped the energy of boys and men by procuring native lovers for their sons at a tender age. "Both [Indo-]European and native mothers" were guilty of leaving their children to their own devices and "on their own."[13]

For Braconier, sex was a source of dangerous political inclinations, and sexual depravities show up again and again. Indische girls are no longer "safe" in their parental homes. Barrack life exposes children to a precocious knowledge of sex, to things they should not "see and hear."[14] Children of deceased European fathers are forced to live in native villages "where they are exploited for unfit practices" by their mothers and native or Indo stepfathers at an early age. Wilkens's narrative addressed a social world that condoned concubinage and mixed unions. Braconier's addressed one that increasingly condemned racial proximity and concubinage as a source of crime.

What distinguishes these two descriptions, then, is not their content; in fact, the second almost seems a paraphrase of the first. Both target what Wilkens refers to as the pitiful upbringing of Indies Europeans. Both fear the "hostile inclinations" of mixed-blood youths.[15] But the causal arguments and political contexts are not the same. Wilkens's account was mobilized to promote Indies-based education, from nurseries to high schools, in which Europeans *and* "inlandsche kinderen" would be joined. Braconier's was testimony to the need for strictly segregated reformatories that would separate "pure" Europeans from the Indo poor. Wilkens encouraged a moderately inclusionary policy. Braconier took exclusion as a given of his argument.

But both share a similar idiom in another sense. Both worry over children, sentiments, and politics. Colonial civil servants, lawyers, doctors, and other professional elites were psychologically attuned observers who imagined domestic sensibilities as the breeding ground of political ones. Cultural competence was the observable criterion for access to the European community but only because it measured what was far more difficult to gauge: the affective dispositions and political attachments of middling, poor, and borderline Europeans. Appropriate sentiments figured prominently in their recommendations, while misdirected sentiments provided the rationale for excluding even those with legal right to membership.

Their concern for the harnessing of sentiment should not be surprising. Nationalism speaks in a language of love, pride, affront, and enduring affection.[16] By Benedict Anderson's account, the common experience of educational pilgrimage, in which Indonesia youths traveled, met, and created *fraternal* bonds, was to animate the nationalist movement.[17] But hostile anti-Dutch communities of political sentiment developed in other less public sites, as colonial authorities knew only too well. Schooling may have produced a shared affect among Western-educated, peripatetic Indonesian youths in the 1920s and 1930s, but it was in poor and middling Indo households at an earlier period where authorities feared that mixed-blood boys would grow into confused, resentful, and subversive men.

Officials' assessments of sentiment showed up in predictable places: in legal debates over paternity, child neglect, and custody rights. But a discourse of sentiment appeared in less obvious places as well: in debates over mixed-marriage laws and nationality and in discussions of criminality and educational reform. Officials assessed the maternal sentiments of native women who refused to give *up* their children to European institutions and on that basis refused them state aid. This practice can be seen in Icard's case: his affections for his son were the very grounds on which Haiphong's court denied their bid for clemency.

Dutch colonial authorities were undecided and wavering partisans in the nurture/nature debate. They understood the realm of sensibilities and sentiment, not unlike race, in two very different ways. On the one hand, certain sentiments were understood almost as inherent endowments, elements of one's given psychological inclinations and mental state. On the other hand, sentiments were sometimes construed as a set of acquired sensibilities that had to be cultivated and that were not ready-made. These two paradigms informed competing views of race, reform, and what could be changed in mixed-blood children.

LEARNING ONE'S PLACE, LEARNING ONE'S RACE

The fears which grown-ups consciously or unconsciously induce in the child are precipitated in him and henceforth reproduce themselves more or less automatically. The malleable personality of the child is so fashioned by fears that it learns to act in accord with the prevailing standard of behavior, whether these fears are produced by direct physical force or by deprivation, by the restriction of food or pleasure. And men-made fears and anxieties from within or without finally hold even the adult in their power.[18]

Children are of course bearers of adult culture but, contra Norbert Elias's statement above, only in partial and imperfect ways. They learn certain normative conventions and not others and frequently defy the divisions that adults are wont to draw. In contrast to Elias's notion of an "automatically" channeled production of fear, European children in diverse colonial contexts seemed often to have gotten their categories "wrong." They chose Malay over Dutch, chose to sit on their haunches and not on chairs, and chose Indo and Javanese playmates. Socialization in colonial norms was not as straight-forward a transmission process as Elias would have it. Colonial officials in-tuitively knew what cognitive psychology is convinced of today: children's cognitions undergo complex reorganization as they acquire the social rep-resentations in which adults share.[19]

Children were seen to be particularly susceptible to degraded environ-ments, and it is no accident that colonial policy makers looked to upbring-ing and education, to schools and homes, to the placement of servant quar-ters, and thus to the quotidian social ecology of children's lives. Medical guides, housekeeping manuals, educational periodicals, and women's mag-azines addressed a readership devoted to thinking about how, where, and by whom European children should be schooled and raised. As prescriptive texts, they outlined formulas for the psychological, physical, and moral well-being of adults as well as of the children whose European identities they were intent on protecting.

Such concerns were not Indies-specific. On both sides of the North Atlantic, childhood and children in the mid- and late nineteenth century became the subjects of legislative attention and were at the center of social policy as they had never been before.[20] In Europe and the colonies, the lib-eral impulse for social welfare and political representation focused atten-tion on the preparatory environment for civil responsibility, on domestic arrangements, sexual morality, parenting, and more specifically on the moral milieu in which children lived. Debates about child welfare were transnational, long-standing, and bound to modernizing political rational-ities.[21] As students of European state formation have noted, by the eigh-teenth century socialization was already seen as a key to adult character. But attention to child welfare increased exponentially when it became linked to national interest in the period that followed.[22]

Child welfare discussions in the colonies shared their concerns but in a different frame. Colonial officials expressed the profound fear that the "Europeanness" of children of mixed parentage could never be assured, de-spite their rhetoric affirming that education was transformative and that upbringing was a socially acquired process. The concern over child neglect alternately emphasized the "negative influence" of the native milieu and the specific hazards of mixed children raised by their native mothers. But even in households with fathers, similar concerns were raised. Subaltern white men—soldiers and middling civil servants—were seen to exert less cultural and moral influence over their children's dispositions than did the native women with whom they lived.

"Indo uplift" (*verheffing van de Indo*) was a principal focus of Dutch philanthropic organizations but in very selective ways. Child protection agencies in the colonies were *not* directed at "uplifting" native mothers, considered beyond redemption, but with removing métis children from their care.[23] In Europe and the United States, corresponding agencies placed children in institutions for limited periods and then usually returned them to the natal homes and to their mothers.[24] But Indies authorities could not decide whether such families were worthy of state aid because they could not decide whether the children were better classified as European or Javanese. Regardless of whether funding would eventually come from private charities or the state, the education offered in private and public institutions for such children had a shared aim: as stated in 1900, "to remove the child as early as possible from the influence of native and Malay speaking mothers"; and as restated in 1941, "[to] withdraw the child from the milieu in which it was raised."[25]

COLONIAL NURSERIES, LANGUAGE, AND THE POLITICS OF RACE

Would not such a nursery school be a blessing for children of the Indische popular class that frequently vegetate in a village house in the midst of chickens and dogs, tended—not raised—by a mother who does not know what rearing is?[26]

A defining feature of the Indies discourse on European children was the direct line drawn from language acquisition to motherhood to morality. This concern placed political attention on household environments, on servants, on the language in which parents communicated, and on whether children took their cultural and linguistic cues while playing in the streets, from what they saw and heard in the servants quarters, or from more acceptable role models in their homes. Authorities were disquieted by the fact that European children were more comfortable speaking Malay than Dutch and naturally "chose" the former over the latter. Some accounted for the preference on the argument that Malay was a "simple, childlike language," easier to master than the more difficult pronunciation and more highly developed lexicon of Dutch. Language was seen to provide proper content and form: the structure, idioms, ways of thinking, and cultural referents in which children's "character formation" would take shape.

The conflict between home environment and school milieu informed much of the discussion of child welfare in the Indies in the second half of

Figure 12.   'The nursery class of Mrs. Proper in Bandung, Java,' 1927. KIT album 500/57F, neg. 740/15.

the nineteenth century. The social anxieties that tied child rearing to European identity were nowhere more clearly expressed than in the nursery school debates. In the Indies these politically charged debates were discussed in classified state documents, public addresses, and scientific proceedings and were dominated not by women but by men. In 1900 a prominent Indies physician addressed the opening of Batavia's first European high school not with a speech about career prospects and job placement but with one devoted to nurseries and early childhood development. The Pauperism Commission too gave over large sections of its reports to preschool learning and nursery education. In some ways these nursery initiatives were not unlike those in the United States designed to eradicate prostitution and crime.[27] Both were about cognitive development. Both were about how to make subjects of a particular kind. What was different was their specific inflections on race.[28]

Nursery schools in England, Belgium, Germany, Holland, and France first spread on a large scale in the 1830s and again after 1848.[29] Supported by political liberalism, they were envisioned as a "training ground" where children of the working-class residuum could be rescued from an adult life

Figure 13. 'A class from the 'Koningin Emma School, a Christian European School,' ca. 1935. Most of the students in this "European" Froebel school seem to have been of mixed parentage. KIT album 583/45.

of immorality.[30] From their inception, nurseries reflected the class and gender politics of the time. In Holland as in Germany they took on two distinct forms. While the early day care centers–nurseries (*bewaarscholen*) in the 1840s were confined to children whose mothers could show proof of a need to work, the later middle-class kindergarten crusade explicitly turned away from the custodial (*bewaar*) model toward one designed to create a morally and intellectually nurturing environment. Inspired by the German educator Friedrich Froebel, preschool education would no longer instill rigid discipline but rather foster creativity through perceptual stimulation and play.[31] Just as in the antebellum United States, the shift was from "overt physical coercion to psychological maneuvering."[32]

The *froebelscholen* had a wider class appeal than the earlier bewaarscholen, but both shared a basic assumption—the conviction that women from the popular classes, either as mothers or as nursemaids, could offer neither the intellectual nor the moral requisites for child development and proper care.[33] Froebel's conclusions were also widely shared; that is, that infants and toddlers were better off in kindergartens than under the negligent supervision of servants and unschooled nursemaids.

But middle-class women were also seen as neglecting their maternal duties. Conservative politicians attacked the kindergartens as subversive institutions, aimed at replacing rather than supplementing familial authority.[34] Spurred by the admonishments of educators that uneducated nursemaids were unsuited to raise future burghers, middle-class women responded by seeking out young women from their own class (*kinderjuffrouw*) and by promoting a trained cohort "better equipped" to care for their young. In the Indies fears of racial degeneration redirected the crusade and shifted its pool of advocates.

The dating of nurseries in the Indies was similar to that in Europe, but nursery initiatives in the colonies were reformist projects that were racially defined. Not intended for the native population, their primary concern was European and Indo households and those "habits of the heart" taught in the home. Several private nurseries for indigent European children were set up in Java's European-populated centers (notably Batavia and Semarang) in the 1830s, but it was only in the 1850s that anxieties about the home milieu prompted a nursery campaign on a broader scale. Commissions on educational reform argued that a proper upbringing and knowledge of Dutch were both lacking in the European Indische homes. Infants were being left to the care and training of "uncultured and untrained" native servants, unsuitable replacements for proper mothers who, by "nature," provided their children with "food for the body and food for the soul."[35]

Parental negligence showed up in the fact that many children could speak no Dutch or only one "mixed with the bastardized Malay" that they heard at home.[36] Worse still was the spurious Dutch of children whose parents worked in distant government posts and isolated estates where they learned it from the children of "Indo clerks" who themselves had no idea of the sound of "pure" Dutch. "Negligence" (*veronachtzaming*), then, was culturally coded: it referenced the absence of a Dutch-speaking environment and exposure to and engagement with one that was tinged with Malay words and tarnished by the cadences of Javanese.

Preschool children were a principal concern for an important reason: the majority of the three thousand "European" children in attendance at the public elementary schools in the 1850s had such rudimentary skills that their Dutch-speaking teachers claimed they could neither communicate with nor discipline and educate their charges. Teachers and inspectors complained that

Figure 14. A "European" school in Ternate, the majority of whose students were probably children of mixed marriages or Christian *inlander* with European equivalent legal status, ca. 1903. KITLV, no. 10.309.

school attendance was absurdly low. Private nurseries were set up, but with meager subsidies they quickly closed down. The *bewaarschool* in Batavia that opened in 1850 and lasted for five years admitted thirty children between the ages of two and six with two aims: to make them fluent in Dutch (which was not successful) and to remove them from the "damaging influence of native servants."[37] Despite a Dutch-born director and rave reviews in the initial year, few parents sent their toddlers to the school, and enrollment declined. Some attributed the decline to the indifference of parents, others to overly protective ones who were uncomfortable leaving their little ones in "strangers' hands." Some parents seemed to have been discouraged by how the school was run, but the real problem was attributed to native mothers who remained unconvinced of the use for a day care center. Was it that they saw no reason to have their children schooled in Dutch? Or was it that the very "native servants" from whom authorities sought to protect the children were, in fact, the children's mothers?

Figure 15.   Another "European" school (the "Ligthartschool," a Carpentier-Alting Institute) with a very different racial composition, ca. 1935. KIT album 583/38A.

Over the next thirty years there were efforts to establish preschool centers in at least seven other Indies cities, but absenteeism was high and the number of students enrolled always remained low. Another commission on education in 1874 concluded that Indische children were lacking a Christian upbringing and any basic knowledge of Dutch. Children, it held, were only being fed *(gevoed)* by their mothers, not nurtured or reared *(opgevoed)*.[38] Schools that had once graduated students at least suitable for rote clerical work were now producing a discontented class, "grumbling over their rights."[39] The age of seven was now considered too late to begin cultivating European sensibilities and European knowledge. But again these accounts were not concerned with formal education. New recommendations to open bewaarscholen reaffirmed the purpose of removing children from the "damaging influence of native servants or of undeveloped mothers" *(schadelijken invloed van Inlandsche bedienden of van te weinig ontwikkelde moeders)*. The mandate of these schools, alternately referred to as *pratenscholen* (lit., "talk schools"), was to make sure the children spoke Dutch while promoting "truthfulness, love for order, and a moral sensibility"—the markers of Dutch character.[40]

Figure 16.   'A school class with mostly native and a few European children, Semarang, Central Java,' ca. 1925. KITLV, no. 16.766.

Figure 17.   'A classroom with European children,' 1945. Note the military uniform of the teacher and the poem on the board about an "organ grinder," a figure not familiar on the Indies landscape. KITLV, no. 6762.

Again in 1902, the Indies Pauperism Commission recommended the establishment of nurseries as a weapon in the war against European impoverishment. In reviewing the failure of past efforts, it singled out the state's repeated refusal to provide anything more than moral support for preparatory education. State funds were withheld throughout most of the nineteenth century on the argument that similar institutions were under private auspices in the Netherlands and could remain so in the colonies as well. Criticizing the state's narrow focus on formal education in the fight against pauperism, the commission opined that it "neglect[ed] to begin at the beginning" with the "intimate cause of the situation," with the fact that children needed to be removed "as early as possible from the parental home."[41] Over and again commission members warned authorities that "preparatory education had a far greater influence than people thought."[42] If state funds were in such short supply, the commission recommended that resources for "intellectual development" be reallocated to programs for "moral training" in which nurseries would play a key role.

The social impetus for the day care centers was clear. It derived from a racial logic that attributed the intellectual inferiority of Indo-European children to what they had inherited from their maternal side. But sometimes the nursery campaigners had other targets. As in Dr. D. W. Horst's account above, nurseries also could be a conservative weapon against social policy that was seen as excessively liberal. Do-good reformers, he argued, were undermining the Dutch "spirit" (geest) and what it meant to be Dutch.[43] Indos were being granted Dutch legal equivalence with too much ease. His recommendation was to police the racial borders more sharply than before to guard against a future population of degenerate Europeans. Some went further, such as "Pa" van der Steur who urged the government to curtail its "hospitality" toward needy Europeans and stop non-Dutch immigration to the Indies altogether.[44]

Horst's speech was full of anxious premonition and racial doom in a way that Wilkens's of fifty years earlier was not. For Horst, the "Asiatic tint" of Indo-Europeans was not limited to their complexions. It was their views and ideas that were tinged as well. The real danger was that "they feel themselves more world citizens [wereldburger] than citizens of the Netherlands." Their loyalties were feared not to be to a Dutch fatherland but to notions of liberty and representation. Colonial authorities had worried over such tendencies fifty years earlier in the wake of the 1848 revolutions in Germany and France.[45] Once again the specter of "world citizens" was informing their assessments of child care and racialized social policy.

The fear of misguided sentiments focused primarily on the indigent European population but on the middle class as well. Among them too children were not only speaking Malay first but learning "to think and express themselves" in this "little developed" language. Authorities were convinced that if a child had to choose between the language spoken by his mother or his nursemaid, the child would "always choose [the nursemaids'] Malay."[46] Horst proposed that the choice itself be retracted and that the child, from its first stammering, be forced to speak Dutch, thereby "driving out the little devil of Malay."

The goal of the nurseries was thus twofold: to provide an environment in which children would be strongly encouraged, if not compelled, to speak Dutch and to provide them with the moral environment that their parental homes neither fostered nor allowed. But language training entailed more than written and verbal fluency. Language was seen to fix the parameters of children's perceptions, enabling them to think certain sentiments and not others. Linguistic fluency was a necessary, not sufficient, condition for citizenship rights and without the appropriate moral referents, of little use at all. As one French colonial official put it, French literacy was a subversive weapon if not accompanied and tempered by a French *éducation du coeur*.[47]

The Pauperism Commission had some public support but hardly enough to initiate the kind of kindergarten crusade that spread in Europe and the United States. Absent was the support of either comfortably situated Indische women or that of the thousands more Dutch-born women now entering the Indies. They may have looked on the bewaarscholen, as did women in the Netherlands, as lower-class institutions, designed for the residuum and not themselves.[48] But perhaps more important was the shift in colonial policy that now brought more Dutch women to the Indies and made the nursery issue less politically pressing than it had been before. The concerted "Dutchification" of colonial society, the encouragement of white endogamy, and the increased density of Dutch in urban centers and on inland estates meant that more Dutch children were growing up in the "cozy" and segregated environments that would foster a "pure Dutch" competence and healthy distance from things Javanese.

Alternatives to the nurseries were appearing as well. The Clerkx-Methode for home education of European children was being used by 1909 throughout the Indies. Its organization provided a guide in home schooling for European mothers. Letters of thanks from "Clerkx-mothers" describe the method as a blessing to those women who saw themselves stranded on distant plantations and outposts far from the European urban centers.

Moreover, the reassuring lessons of the guide brought their children—and them—a little closer to "home." [49]

Rather than take up the Pauperism Commission's recommendations, educational policy shifted in another direction. The concern for early childhood development was redirected to the scientific management of the home. Stricter guidelines for servant-child contact accompanied the professionalization of child care. Prospective brides and wives of men whose careers took them to the Indies came bearing new prescriptions for household management and modern motherhood. The proliferation of housekeeping guides was both a manifestation of this trend in the Indies and a response to the many more European women there. Women's pages of the major Indies dailies did their part as well in counseling and guiding European mothers on what to feed their infants, what to teach them, and what they both should wear. By the 1930s the Indies association of housewives had branches throughout the colonial heartland, from North Sumatra to East Java.

The idea of preparatory institutions for European toddlers of Indische and native mothers was replaced by a preparatory structure for Dutch-born mothers themselves. The Colonial School for Women, which opened in the Hague in 1921, provided "knowledge of domestic and social issues of use to women in the colonies." Working with the support of Holland-based feminist and housewives' associations, the school offered three-month courses that included infant care, sewing and cooking, advice on home nursing, and instruction in Malay. Government officials came to speak on select subjects ("prostitution" and "colonial education"), and retired colonial hands and their wives were invited to lecture on cultural themes of their choice ("the Javanese women" and "Balinese dance"). Advertisements for the courses emphasized the school's "national interest." While the courses were designed to ease the cultural shock of life in the Indies for new wives and young mothers, women with experience living in the Indies saw it as a way to save marriages. Letters of appreciation from some of the seven hundred women who passed through the school between 1921 and 1932 suggest that it met with success. While the school was open to "independent unmarried women," its archives give no sign that professions were on its agenda. It was domestic management, servant relations, and child care that were principally addressed.

ON PARENTING AND SCHOOLS FOR THE EUROPEAN POOR

The conflict between home environment and school milieu continued to preoccupy the Indies educational commissions at the turn of the century.

Commissioners expressed exasperation with European parents of the poor and middling classes who could provide neither the material circumstances (proper clothing, shoes, and food) nor the moral atmosphere and Dutch-speaking environment that would keep their children in school. Educators again blamed the laxity with which parents allowed their children to mix with native servants.[50] But the main issue that brought "European" school and "Indo" home into open conflict was a racialized quandary. If poor whites were living side by side with members of the native population in urban settlements, then could they also sit side by side with "pure-blood" European children in European schools? Many authorities and parents thought not.

Conflicts over educational policy for mixed-blood youths captured a basic colonial dilemma—a fundamental ambivalence about the advantages and disadvantages of pursuing policies of incorporation or exclusion and whether both could be pursued at the same time. As discussed in chapter 3, efforts to nurture patriotic affinity to European culture were coupled with limited access to it. While some efforts were made to integrate mixed-blood children into European schools, this was often in the face of strong resistance from those parents who refused to have their children in close proximity to lower-class and "mixed-blood elements." When the first European schools were established in the Indies more than half of their students had nonpaying "gratis" status.[51] By the 1860s a two-tiered educational system had developed: "first-rank" European public schools designed for those who could pay and a "second-rank" set of *armenscholen* (schools for the poor) for those impoverished Europeans and their mixed-blood descendants who could not. Educational policy was not explicitly discussed in racial or class terms because the *cultural criteria* for admission made it unnecessary. Because only children with a good knowledge of Dutch *by the age of seven* could be admitted to the "first-rank" school, all Indo children who did not speak Dutch as a first language at home were excluded de facto.[52]

If nurseries were envisioned as early sites of social engineering, it was because parenting among different segments of the European population was under scrutiny in different ways. The brunt of the accusations of parental immorality fell on Asian mothers of two sorts: those who cohabited outside of marriage in native kampongs with poorer European men and those who assumed full custody of their mixed-blood children by choice or force. But the Indo-European woman living in legal marriage with a European man was not exempt from accusations of child neglect.

Educational reform was designed to structure children's days and to keep them out of native kampongs, off the streets, and in the home. To this end, recommendations were made for two hours of mandatory religious instruction daily and for the creation of afternoon schools to keep Indo boys from "loitering" and Indo girls out of the villages and *away* from their homes. Mrs. L. J. Hissink-Snellebrand, addressing the Indische Genootschap in 1910, argued that young Indo women of fourteen and fifteen were "unsafe" in their parental homes because "seduction, concubinage and prostitution" confronted them at every turn.[53] References to a "white slave trade" were supported with stories of girls sold to wealthy Chinese and Arab traders. Hissink-Snellebrand's call for the protection of Indische girls recommended the establishment of special institutions to teach them how to be "good, upstanding mothers." More pragmatic voices rejected her plan as unrealistic and naive, as such palliatives would have little effect on the girls once they ventured home. Proposals for foster care programs also met with little favor on the curious argument that the Indies did not have enough respectable European families to go around.[54]

Moral critiques were directed at Asian mothers, but European fathers of certain classes were also targeted. Some authorities argued that child neglect and European pauperism would be alleviated if concubinage was eradicated. But both conservative and more progressive critics rejected the claim of liberal reformers that marriage was a cure-all. Conservatives urged a ban on miscegenation, but socialists like H. H. van Kol held that marriage would do little good to a European soldier with four to six children to support on a daily wage of thirty-three cents.[55] Others proposed that marriage requests be made contingent on auditing of the prospective groom's financial ability to maintain a wife and children on his own.

Moral recriminations against European fathers of Indo children were indictments of values—a lack of patriarchal sentiment and little sense of responsibility—not found among more respectable European men. Advocates who argued for abolition of the ban on paternity suits did so in the belief that runaway fathers should be forced to pay for their indiscretions and support the children they fathered.

But the moral assault on lower-class European men was as frequently vented toward those who did *not* abandon their children as those who did. Hissink-Snellebrand characterized the "Netherlands Indies father as a moral weakling" who probably had no mother himself and thus never learned to value women in his youth.[56] Such men were admonished for their desires and *chosen* lifestyles as much as for their poverty, condemned as much for their contentment in native villages, as were those men who expressed discontent with their lot. Both represented affronts to the categories in which

European men belonged. Braconier's recommendation that the government take sharp measures against "the thousands of European paupers without occupation" who lived as parasites in native villages expressed another recrimination: European men who "lived off" native women could not be counted as "family heads" and thus not as proper men.[57]

The moral attack on European mothers who left their children with native servants was particularly strong at the turn of the century, marking a shift in how European children in the colonies were to be raised. Mothering was now a full-time occupation, entailing vigilant supervision of a moral environment in which European women were to take full charge. The prescriptions for proper parenting detailed the domestic protocols for infant and child care with regard to food, dress, sleep, and play. Condemnation of concubinage and the view of Dutch-born women as the custodians of morality understandably eclipsed the bewaarscholen debate, but it perhaps even escalated the related fear of contamination, transgression, and dependence that servants inspired.

SERVANTS AND CHILDREN IN THE EUROPEAN COMMUNITY

If we take care that our children hear a cultured, pure speech there
is no reason to despair of forming good Dutch-speaking people;
teach them that their place is in the family circle, and not in or
near the servants' quarters; teach them that our natives have
moral beliefs that are vastly different from ours, but teach them to
treat your servants as people[;] . . . teach our children as quickly as
possible to care for themselves, . . . to go to school on their own
and never to let a servant carry their books and slates for them.[58]

To understand why servants were such a charged site of European anxieties in the Indies is to understand how they both shaped and made up the habitus in which European colonials and their children lived. Servants policed the borders of the private, mediated between the "street" and the home, and occupied the inner recesses of bourgeois life; they were, in short, the subaltern gatekeepers of gender, class, and racial distinctions that by their very presence they transgressed. There is nothing novel about these observations, nor were all these trangressions particular to the colonies.[59]

What marks the Indies context as unique is the central fact that native women who served as domestic servants, mistresses, and living partners of European men often bore the children of those men and continued to live with them. Thus domestic servants as huishoudsters represented more than the

Figure 18.   From a family album with the caption "Child-Joy! 1914 Polonia" (an estate in North Sumatra). Leo Haks Collection.

Figure 19.   From a family album. Leo Haks Collection.

Figure 20. "Baboe, Batavia," West Java, 1904. This unusual
studio portrait of a servant seems to draw on two photographic
genres: Javanese "types" that showed typical occupations and
were mass produced as postcards and the bourgeois studio portrait reserved for Europeans, wealthy Chinese, and aristocratic
Javanese.

"domesticated outsiders of the bourgeois imagination."[60] The servant issue in the Indies contained a social critique of mixed unions, anxiety about the security of European norms, and a direct assault on native mothers. Up through the turn of the twentieth century, more than half of the European men in the Indies lived in domestic arrangements with women who were their servants, sexual partners, concubines, household managers, and sometimes wives and sometimes lovers. In conflating servitude and sexual service, cohabitation and conjugality, domestic service and motherhood, these colonial domestic arrangements continually raised the possibility that some European men were indifferent to bourgeois civility and not even aspiring to it.

That servants were identified in both metropole and colony as the "uncivilized" and "immoral" source of child corruption suggests that the nursery campaign spoke to a common concern—control over the social environments in which children could be fashioned into citizens and in which national identities were to be made. But here again, the distinct politics of the "servant problem" warrants closer examination. While nursemaids in Holland were considered a damaging influence on children of the comfortable and well-to-do, in the Indies Javanese nursemaids could effect the very formation of racial character. Idioms of contamination and contagion were common to both contexts, but the susceptibility of European colonial children was of a different kind. They too, as in Holland, might not become "stolid burghers," but in the Indies they risked lacking those cultural sensibilities that would allow them to manage in a European milieu. The notion of being "spoiled" in the colonies referred to more than sexual depravity. Children could be "spoiled" by servants who taught the children dependence rather than self-reliance and who allowed children to order them about and did not instill self-discipline. For both Wilkens in 1849 and Braconier in 1917, a signature moment of such "spoilation" was captured in the fact that children did not even carry their own books to school.

Colonial authorities admonished native fathers for taking advantage of their Indo girls and former huishoudsters, who turned to prostitution when their white patrons left. But the attack was on "mixing" itself as a threat to the making of abstinent and morally tempered women and men. Among poor whites, it was the "Indischized" domestic milieu with which schools had to contend. Among Europeans of "good standing," colonial anxieties fixed the native nursemaid with a central role. Critical of the negligence of an early generation of European mothers in the Indies, child care manuals of the turn of the century warned of the babu's "pernicious" influence. Nor were the sexual accusations oblique. As one doctor put it, babus lulled their charges to sleep "by all sorts of unnatural means [and] unbelievable practices that alas occur all too often, damaging these children for their entire adult lives, and that cannot be written here."[61] As I have argued elsewhere, such imagined moments of sexual intimacy probably belied another story of personal touch, alienation of affection, and cultural familiarity that parents feared more.[62] In the 1930s, when many more European schools were open to native students, one of the hallmarks of a top-grade institution was that students "never come in contact with native personnel."[63] The Brestagi school in Sumatra prided itself on rigorous rules that forbade children from entering their own sleeping quarters if native servants were present. In 1941 contact with native servants still was seen to pose a "great danger for the physical and moral well-being of . . . children."[64]

MAKING RACE AND THE ACQUISITION OF CIVILITY

Adult perceptions about children capture the visionary quality of social engineering, where the conflict between prescription and practice was often played out. These debates about nursemaids and nurseries suggest what was seen as subversive about the domestic domain and why the production of sentiment was so relevant to state control.

Cognitive psychologists increasingly concur that categorization is a mental process that proceeds not by identifying a set of specific attributes (e.g., that all Europeans in the colonies speak Dutch, eat voluminous amounts of meat, and do no manual labor) or by recognition of similarities alone ("they're all white"). Rather these attributes and similarities are "driven" by a "knowledge-based theory" about the world that prescribes which attributes will be singled out and to *which* similarities people will attend.[65] While such a line of inquiry focuses on *mental* representations, we might also think about such processes in political terms. How do children learn which social categories are salient? How do they learn to attend to the politically relevant inclusions and exclusions that shape the imagined communities in which adults live? Colonial authorites were obsessed with just such concerns, and few took socialization to be unproblematic. This is more than evident in their sustained efforts to identify those features of cultural life (language, dress, schooling, and upbringing) that would guarantee children's easy access to and acquisition of what it took to remain or become "truly " European. How children acquire social categories, what social environmental conditions shape their choices, and how they distinguish "we" from "they" were questions posed by colonial policy makers in varied forms again and again.[66]

In the Indies, the ability to define which essences made up collective affiliations informed complex assessments of child development that had high political stakes. But the notion of essence was not based on a blanket belief in an immutabile personhood and racial fixity that could not be transformed. Native and mixed-blood "character" was viewed as fixed in a way that European "character" was not. Officials worried openly that "mixed-blood" children of European fathers and native mothers, schooled and raised in a European cultural milieu, would turn their backs on those cultural acquisitions and "revert" to their native allegiances, becoming patricides, revolutionaries, and enemies of the state. The warning of A. de Braconier, an outspoken commentator on the political dangers of increasing prostitution and concubinage and the relationship of both to a new generation of Indo paupers bent on subversion and crime, was widely shared:

> This category of children, left behind by their European fathers, whether or not [legally] recognized [by them], are *par droit de naissance* [birthright] European-haters and the "Urhebers" [authors] of Indische crime. In the future, they will be the anarchists and extremists of Indische society if Dutch lawmakers do not intervene in a timely manner to extend their protective hand to these "outcasts."[67]

Anxieties about the children of "full-blooded" European parents were not the same. They suggest that the "moral essence" of Europeans was more fragile and less secure. As Dr. J. J. Nieuwenhuis reminded his readers, education in the Indies had to address more than linguistic fluency. It had to cultivate (*aankweekt*) "colonial qualities": a stronger body, greater mental endurance, and stronger nerves. It had to foster a "strong sense of solidarity" and "an inner and outer refinement." [68] Did people such as the prominent lawyer, Nederburgh, or the physician, J. H. F. Kohlbrugge, really believe that in the absence of a properly controlled environment a European child could actually "metamorphose" into a Javanese?[69] Did they truly imagine that the child of a Javanese mother and a European father would remain Javanese, while the child born of European parents in the colonies might not? School authorities questioned whether European children could ever attain that Dutch "spirit" if their first thoughts and babblings were not in Dutch.[70] Right up to World War II, guides to the Indies still debated whether children raised in good colonial homes would not be contaminated in school by sexually precocious Indische youths not of "full-blooded European" origin.[71]

The social geography of empire underwent profound restructuring in the early twentieth century as the lines between colonizer and colonized and between subject and citizen were redrawn. Cultural literacy and distributions of sentiment defined the exclusionary politics of European colonial communities and metropolitan nation-states. European households in the colonies confronted threats to those distinctions at every turn. Language was considered a crucial source of national belonging, but "European" children in the Indies were repeatedly missing their linguistic cues or getting them wrong. A full staff of servants was a marker of privilege and class, but the very presence and proximity of so many servants compromised what white children needed to ingest: what it meant to be Dutch and to know they belonged. Mothers were the makers of moral citizens, but here too Indies homes were tainted at their heart. Did authorities really think that children risked losing their national identity if cradled in native hands or lulled to sleep in a language that was not their mother's? If they did, it is because they knew then what postcolonial theorists have just begun to grasp: power was constituted in the forming of subjects; the harnessing of sentiment was a crucial site of political contest; and how children acquired thoughts and feelings was a key to colonial strategies that looked more to consent than coercive control. If we take their cue, we might think to look further at children in the making of "communities of sentiment" and at the reasoned strategies of affective recruitment to them.[72]

6   A Colonial Reading of Foucault

Bourgeois Bodies and Racial Selves

In each of the preceding chapters, Foucault has figured as a shadow presence, first as a source of inspiration, then as a source of reflection and critique. My initial thinking about knowledge and power, like so many others in colonial studies, was transformed by him. For two decades and through different venues, I have worked off and reworked his insistence on sexuality as "an especially dense transfer point for relations of power."[1] All of the earlier chapters here turned on thinking with Foucault and feminism about colonial power and the management of sex. How colonial authorities chose to speak about the carnal and iterate its dangers did more than substantiate his general claim. In later work more directly on colonial discourses that positioned sex as "the truth" of the racialized self, it was to Foucault that I turned again.

But as a blueprint for understanding what joined carnality to power in the nineteenth-century Netherlands Indies, Foucault's contentions made only partial sense. His assertion that sexuality was "originally, historically bourgeois" seemed at once more reasonable and more questionable the more time I spent in the colonial archives. What was absent, obviously so in retrospect, was the issue of race. My work on colonial regimes played off his arguments but drew more on his conceptual frame as I skirted his historical claims.

For a student of the colonial, reading Foucault incites and constrains. Volume 1 of the *History of Sexuality* is an uncomfortable reminder of how much empire and its colonial landscapes have remained in the peripheral vision of even critical European history—much less more conventional historiographies of race. It is this reflection that frames the challenge of this chapter. In it I revisit a question that informed *Race and the Education of Desire* to ask how the making of a European bourgeois self might look different when that history is rendered less self-referential, when imperial politics is placed center stage.

My colonial reading of Foucault draws on cumulative contributions to colonial studies to ask what implications such a rereading might have for how we think about the intimacies of empire, European history, and the colonial etymologies of race. I return to some arguments of my book, but that return is selective. Here I am interested in why Foucault's elusive and suggestive treatment of race still remains so marginal to what colonial historians take from him today.

Writing *Race and the Education of Desire* led me to pursue some issues that were more predictable than others. Engaging the interface of Foucault's work on the nature of racial discourse and on the history of sexuality prompted rethinking the technologies of colonial rule and their sites of production. Questions about the "education of desire" turned me less to sexual desires per se than to the wider array of sentiments that carnal knowledge may express.[2] Working back through Foucault's Nietzschean bent in a colonial context not least raised some hard questions and left them unanswered: How does one guard against history writing in "the comfort zone"?[3] What would make up a discomforting colonial history of the present?[4]

Foucault's constant return to the political entailments of knowledge production has been disruptive and useful at a number of registers. Take, for example, the critique it might offer of "comparative colonialisms." What could be more reassuring than the argument on which comparative studies of colonialism has thrived; namely, that differences in colonial policies derive from European distinctions of national character. In such a model, some country's legacy was always more benevolent, another's violences were truly atrocious, and yet another's integrative efforts were more effective or more benign. The positioning may shift with perspective, but the structure of the narrative stays the same. Such comparisons signal more about the national underpinnings of comparison than they do about significant differences in strategies of rule. These are not "wrong" answers so much as unproductive questions.

Attention to the perceptions and practices of colonial regimes in different times and places could start with other kinds of questions. What are the premises and "ready-made syntheses" that have made comparative studies of colonialism possible? Can one compare colonialisms without defining the protean criteria for assessing race? What sorts of comparisons are invidious, and which are not? What assumptions allow a comparison between "mixed-bloods" in the Indies and "coloreds" in South Africa and métis in Indochina? What sorts of colonial racial grammars made architects of imperial policy think they could—and us today think we should with a different political agenda—do so? At the heart of such questions is an inquiry into the politics of knowledge that makes comparisons possible. This inquiry questions those units of analysis that—often inadvertently—have reflected the sharply bracketed frames of nineteenth-century national historiographies.

The task of writing new genealogies of the colonial, then, is an opportunity of many sorts. It presses us to learn from Foucault as we push past his insights and push our own further. Some have argued that his influence has been pernicious—apolitical, anti-Marxist, and fundamentally contrary to a feminist agenda. I have no interest in refuting those claims. I am interested in drawing on his insights to think harder about how the making of race has figured in placing sexuality at the center of imperial politics.

I ask about the colonial state's investments in managing the assessment of what was normal and what was not; how the management of sexuality in part framed what sentiments could be expressed and to whom they could be directed. Colonial states had a strong interest in affective knowledge and a sophisticated understanding of affective politics. While concern with the politics of sentiment is more mine than Foucault's, I ask what we might glean from his insights and where we have not yet taken them.

WHERE IS RACE IN FOUCAULT?

Race and the Education of Desire was based on some simple questions. At a time when Foucault's work has had an enormous impact on a range of disciplines and on the discursive and historic turn within them, why have contemporary scholars dealt in such an oblique way with the slimmest—some might argue the most accessible—of his major works, *The History of Sexuality*? More precisely, why has colonial studies, where issues of sexuality and power are now so high on the intellectual and political agenda, had so little to say about it? In a field in which reading that volume has been de rigueur and reference to it conferred intellectual authority, what accounts for this striking absence of an engagement that is simultaneously analytically critical and historically grounded?

Race and the Education of Desire was meant initially to be a colonial reading of *The History of Sexuality*, one that questioned both Foucault's account of the making of European bourgeois subjects and the centrality of empire and race to that process. But what seemed an exciting but straightforward task got abruptly halted in midprocess. This was when I first heard about and then sat riveted in Paris at the Saulchoir library listening to the scratched tapes of his then unpublished lectures from 1976 given at the Collège de France. These were eleven full lectures devoted to theorizing the history of racisms, of racial discourses and racisms of the modern state. More startling still was the fact that they were delivered the very winter that the first volume of *The History of Sexuality* was in press. Here was Foucault, in just two years, engaged in two parallel histories and sequential pursuits: a history of sexuality and a treatise on power through a genealogy of race.

The lectures at once confirmed Foucault's Europe-bound vision but as quickly unsettled a quick dismissal of him for sidestepping issues of race. They placed racism more centrally in his thinking than any of his then published work would suggest. But they also prompted a rush of questions. Did this work on race really represent a "turning point" in Foucault's intellectual itinerary?[5] What should we do with his often-repeated statement that all his writings were autobiographical? Was it significant that he had spent 1966 through spring 1968 in Tunisia—a former French colony—where he wrote *The Archaeology of Knowledge,* wrote friends about anti-Semitism, and had his work repeatedly interrupted by student strikes against the governing policies of a newly empowered state?[6] In writing *Race and the Education of Desire,* I intentionally avoided discussing the stark discrepancy between his knowledge of the postcolonial in Tunis and the absence of the colonial in his work. With a sense that it was too easy to point out, I did attempt to answer the question. I have begun to rethink that position today.[7]

Indeed, what was his relationship to the colonial, and what has colonial studies at any particular moment imagined is a "usable" Foucault? Why does *Discipline and Punish* more often provide a model than the nuanced methodological insights of *The Archaeology of Knowledge*? Why is there so much recent work on colonial "governmentality" but so little on the complex ways in which he understood the movements of subjugated knowledges and their "resurrections"? And why, until very recently, is there even less on race?[8]

This is *not* a prelude to the argument that we have all missed the "real" Foucault. Identifying the tensions between the lectures and his written work is only part of a more general effort—to ask what Foucault offers for our understanding of the bourgeois underpinnings of colonial regimes and in turn how attention to colonial sites refigures his parameters and challenges what gets counted as part of European historiography.

There are two basic arguments of *Race and the Education of Desire* that are relevant here. First, the proliferating discourses of sexuality that Foucault registers in Europe in the eighteenth and nineteenth centuries simply cannot be chartered in Europe alone but through a more *circuitous* imperial route than he suggests. These were refracted by men and women whose affirmation of a bourgeois self was contingent on imperial products, perceptions, and racialized Others that they produced. I argued that you could not get from eighteenth- to nineteenth-century technologies of sex in Europe without tracking them across colonial ground. I thus approached *The History of Sexuality* through several avenues by comparing its chronologies and strategic ruptures to those in the colonies. But, as important, I argued that a "comparison" of these two seemingly dispersed technologies of sex in colony and in metropole might miss the extent to which they made up parts of one another and were tightly bound.

Second, following this line of reasoning, I argued that racial entailments were not relevant in the colonies alone. By bringing anxieties and struggles over citizenship and nation back within our frame (as Foucault did not), bourgeois identities in metropole and colony emerge as tacitly and emphatically coded by race. In rerouting the history of sexuality through the history of empire, modern racism appears less "anchored" in European technologies of sex than Foucault claimed. Both racial and sexual classifications appear as ordering mechanisms that *shared* their emergence with the bourgeois order of the early nineteenth century. Racial thinking was not subsequent to the bourgeois order but constitutive of it.

The implications are several. First, racism was not a colonial reflex, fashioned to deal with the distant Other, but part of the very making of Europeans themselves. "Internal colonialism," in this perspective, was not a peculiar form of empire building (a variant frequently used to describe the expansion of the American West) but, according to Foucault, its earliest and enduring incarnation. Second, racisms have rarely adhered to the visual and social clarity of difference among widely disparate groups. They have flourished in similar, contiguous populations. Racisms have riveted on ambiguous identities—racial, sexual, and otherwise—on anxieties produced precisely because such crafted differences were not clear at all. Such a formulation adds weight to the claim I have made elsewhere: racisms gain their strategic force, not from the fixity of their essentialisms, but from the internal malleability assigned to the changing features of racial essence.[9] In the nineteenth-century Indies cultivation of a European self was affirmed in proliferating discourses on pedagogy, parenting, and servants—microsites in which bourgeois identity was rooted in notions of European civility, in which designations of racial membership were subject to gendered appraisals, and in which "character," "good breeding," dispassionate reason, and proper rearing were part of the changing cultural and epistemic indexing of race.

HISTORIES OF SEXUALITY/HISTORIES OF RACE

For a long time, the story goes, we supported a Victorian regime,
and we continue to be dominated by it even today. Thus the image
of the imperial prude is emblazoned on our sexuality, restrained,
mute and hypocritical.[10]

While there have been several colonial readings of Foucault, for the most
part they have applied the *general principles* of a Foucauldian frame to a
specific ethnographic time and place, engaging the outlines of his analytic
apparatus more than the historical content of his analysis. This sort of passion for Foucault's general strategies is apparent in readings of each of his
texts—nowhere more than in treatments of *La volonté du savoir*, or *The
Will to Power*, which has been rendered in English as volume 1 of *The
History of Sexuality*.

That book engages a disarmingly simple thesis: why, if in nineteenth-
century Europe sexuality was indeed something to be silenced, hidden, and
repressed, was there such a proliferating discourse about it? Foucault tells
us in the first line of the first chapter that we have gotten the story wrong:
the "image of the imperial prude . . . emblazoned on our restrained, mute
and hypocritical sexuality" misses what that regime of sexuality was all
about. It did not seek to restrict a biological instinct, to overcome a "stubborn drive," nor was it an "exterior domain to which power is applied."[11] For
Foucault, sexual discourse is not opposed to and subversive of power but a
"dense transfer point" of it, charged with "instrumentality."

Although we have caught the gist of the message well, much recent
work, including my own, has turned with varied inflection on a similar
premise—that the management of the sexual practices of colonizer and
colonized was fundamental to the colonial order of things and that discourses on sexuality at once classified colonial subjects into distinct human
kinds while policing the domestic recesses of imperial rule.[12] Such readings take seriously the fact of a relationship between colonial power and
the discourses of sexuality but neither confirm nor confront the specific
chronologies Foucault offers or the selective genealogical maps his works
suggest.

Students of empire have shown little interest in Foucault's most basic
rejection of Freud's repressive hypothesis. On the contrary, we have exhibited strong allegiance both to a Foucauldian perspective on power and to
implicit Freudian assumptions about the psychodynamics of empire and the
sexual energies "released." We have applied an ejaculation theory of history to how such regimes extend and work.

Some of the problems are Foucault's, some our own. *The History of Sexuality* seems to impede an alternate venture. Tracing the deployment of sexuality within an analytic field confined to Europe—to "modern Western sexuality"—Foucault presents a familiarly pat binary world of *ars erotica* (the Orient) and *scientia sexualis* (the West).[13] The opening image of the "imperial prude" is the first and only reference to empire. For Foucault, that image of the prude is a mainstay of our misguided reading of nineteenth-century sexuality that is dismissed, replaced, and not discussed further. Overseas empire disappears along with its caricature. For him, the discursive energy surrounding sexuality remains an internal European matter.

Such origin myths of the making of European cultural practices are less credible today as the bracketed domain of European history has been unsettled, its sources reassessed, its boundaries blurred. More than two decades after *The History of Sexuality* first appeared, as colonial studies has turned to tensions that cut across metropolitan and colonial sites of imperial rule, we are prompted to ask whether the shaping of bourgeois subjects can be located outside those force fields in which imperial knowledge was promoted and desiring subjects were made. Foucault's impulse to write a history of Western desire that rejects desire as a biological instinct or as a response to repressive prohibitions pushes colonial studies in a direction feminism has long urged, to question how shifts in the imperial *distributions* of desiring male subjects and desired female objects might shape that story as well.

Moreover, in re-viewing the colonies as more than sites of exploitation but as "laboratories of modernity," what constitutes metropolitan versus colonial inventions and importations has precipitously shifted course. Timothy Mitchell, in a study of colonial Egypt, places the Panopticon, that supreme model institution of disciplinary power, as a colonial invention that appeared first in the Ottoman Empire, not northern Europe.[14] Gwendolyn Wright and Paul Rabinow have argued that the modern was played out in colonial settings, that French policies on urban planning were experimented with in Paris and Toulouse but probably in Rabat and Haiphong first.[15]

Mary Louise Pratt stretched back farther to argue that those modes of social discipline taken to be quintessentially European may have been inspired by seventeenth-century imperial ventures and only then refashioned for a later bourgeois order.[16] Such reconfigured histories have pushed a rethinking of European cultural genealogies across the board. They prompt us to ask whether those most treasured icons of modern Western culture—liberalism, nationalism, state welfare, citizenship, culture, and "Europeanness" itself—were not clarified among Europe's colonial exiles in Asia, Africa, and Latin America and only then brought "home."

But the point here is not simply to turn the tables and thus argue that "modernity" or "capitalism"—fill in the blank as you will—was invented in the colonies rather than in Europe, as some studies of the colonial now so eagerly contend. It is rather to imagine new ways of subverting deeply statist historiographies by tracing people's transnational itineraries and circuits of knowledge production through movements of global breadth.

Students of colonialism should be spurred to work out Foucault's genealogies on a broader imperial map because of this glaring absence alone. But that crucial element of *The History of Sexuality* that does speak to the imperial world of the nineteenth century has been largely ignored. This is his strategic linking of the history of sexuality to the construction of race. Contrary to the received account—that the book is about sexuality and biopower—references to racism appear in virtually every chapter. It is surprising that few of Foucault's interlocutors have noticed or noted them given that the final two sections of the book deal directly with the "instrumentality" of sexuality in the rise of racisms and the convergence of both with the biopolitical state. One could argue, as Etienne Balibar does, that racism is what the concept of biopower sets out to explain.[17] The 1976 lectures, and the one published in *Temps modernes* in 1991 with the subtitle "La naissance du racisme" (The Birth of Racism), give weight to Balibar's argument while rendering the silence more profound.

This silence may reflect the constraints of a political and intellectual field in which Foucault was situated at the time, a field in which the concept of class and the sort of social transformations to which capitalism gave rise remained foundational in critical social and political theory. Race and racial theory were not. Histories of racism occupied a different space, bracketed off in U.S. scholarship as a subtheme in the history of slavery, in Britain as a politically anesthetized, ahistorical field of "race relations," in France as a history of Jewish genocide, and in Germany as a history of Teutonic particularism that produced a history of horrors to dispose of that were over and past.

What is more, after this short-lived turn to the history of racisms, Foucault precipitously abandoned the project. The "war of races," the explicit discussion of "state racism," disappears from his subsequent lectures and his written work. Whether he was "deadlocked" on theorizing racism, as one of his close colleagues suggests, is hard to know. Whatever the case, in his lectures racism is situated squarely at the core of state and societal processes of normalization and regularization, processes that were to occupy him for many years before and after. In the lectures racism was a normalizing feature of a range of state formations, not an aberrant feature of them.

But the refusal in France to engage him on racism may have little to do with Foucault. It may reflect a long-standing and more widespread refusal to consider racism as fundamental to France's contemporary history. The surge in the 1990s in publications and public discourse on the force of the far Right contrasted sharply with its confined and limited treatment earlier.[18] It was really only in that period—following the National Front's regional electoral victories—that a wider intellectual constituency has sought to account for the Front's diverse appeal and acknowledge French racism as more than an uncharacteristic blip on its political horizon.[19] While many commentators have sought to emphasize the foreign and singularly marginal status of the National Front's adherents, more convincing analyses have described it as a movement spawned on French soil with a deep history and solidly "made in France."[20] Even among the latter, none explore or entertain a relationship between French racism and the making of a French modern state.

Whether coincidental or not, it is also only recently that the lectures have been published by France's two major publishing houses, Seuil and Gallimard, in a series intended to include Foucault's seminars between 1970 and 1982. Although the inaugural volume starts not with his first lectures but with his 1976 seminar on race,[21] its introduction makes no reference to the seminar's principal subject: genealogies of race and racisms of the state.[22] Foucault remains decidedly off the radar of those in France writing on race, despite the fact that the discourses he describes—those of a "war of the races" and of a "defense of society" against itself—are familiar refrains in the National Front's claims to defend the nation and to protect a French society at "civil war."

But Foucault's contention in the 1976 lectures that racisms are basic to the way biopower develops in all modern states was not well received, nor was it twenty years later when they were published. A review in *Le Monde des Livres* in 1997 refers to this aspect of Foucault's argument as a surprising and disturbing "sursaut" (a leap with the sense of an abrupt, almost involuntary start), making the point that Foucault had gone too fast ("Il va soudain trop vite"), and too far. Philosophers too apparently have placed the lectures aside. The first journal articles devoted to them (and featured as a special section, "Michel Foucault: The War of the Races to Biopower") appeared in 2000.[23]

If some surprises in the lectures were ill received, as an exemplar of Foucault's thinking, other surprises are in store that concern his methodology. First, for those who understand his notion of power as always capillary and micro rather than concerned with the state's macro-monopolies, the lectures should give pause. Here his focus is on modern biopolitical states and the conditions of possibility that produce and condone state-sanctioned disenfranchisement and murder within them.

Second, rather than a focus on the discontinuous epistemic rupturing in history—for which he has been so well known—here Foucault alerts us to a more complex process. This is one that includes the simultaneous "reinscription," "encasement," and "recovery"—terms he uses repeatedly in the lectures—of older racial discourses as they are reshaped into new ones, understood as a layering of sedimented hierarchical forms. It is through this tension between recuperation and rupture that Foucault explores racisms' tactile and "polyvalent mobility." Attention to Foucault's thinking on racism, then, is not a presentist reading of his work. Racism is a complex subtext of how he understood biopower and thought about states. The lectures show his strained efforts to grapple with racism and elide it in a historical frame so locked in Europe that "colonial genocide" (a term he uses only once) could by his account derive from Europe's internal politics, subsumed and unexplained.

References to racism in *The History* are neither incidental nor perfunctory but carefully signposted in each part of the book—which makes sense since that volume was the blueprint for what was never realized, the six volumes he had set out to write, with volume 6 to be titled *Population and the Races.* Although references to racism are sparing in *The History,* the fact of modern racism is fundamental to it. In Foucault's genealogy, racial discourse was a part of the technologies of sex that arose in the eighteenth century to regulate sexual conduct and by which populations could be expanded and controlled. These would become "the anchorage points for the different varieties of racism of the nineteenth and twentieth centuries." It was the scientific arbitrators of sex who authorized the "hygienic necessity" of cleansing and invigorating the social body in forms, he writes, that "justified the racisms of the state, which at the time were on the horizon." Note here that racism is a potential waiting to be born, not yet on the terra firma that produced the rigid racial taxonomies of the late nineteenth century.[24]

A colonial perspective could offer a different chronology with other prefigurings—of which Foucault was clearly aware. Colonial technologies of rule bear witness to explicit racially based policies of earlier date and widespread use. Why then did he categorically reject the standard story of nineteenth-century sexuality but embrace this version of the history of race? *The History* hints at some reasons, but the lectures provide more. Colonialisms were outside his purview, as were their racialized systems of social classification. But, as importantly, as the lectures make clear, Foucault was concerned with "state racism," and it was to this form alone that he thought the term "racial discourse" should be applied.

Not least, Foucault set out to explain the Nazi state and the final solution it embraced. (In the lectures it is Stalin's Soviet state as well.) Neither apartheid Africa nor the segregationist United States is mentioned. The teleology of his argument is to account for a state's right and obligation to kill not only its external enemies but its internal enemies as well. His concern was with those discursive forms and those categories that made common sense of purgings within, how a state establishes that right and then turns it into a moral obligation. It is a discourse, he argues, that confers on a citizenry the right to kill its own designated members as an act of beneficent purification. The 1976 lectures, titled "To Defend Society," take this discourse of defense as a mobilizing point for society at large.

These issues are not spelled out in The History, but in the 1976 lectures they frame his project. There he traces the transformation and reversal of a discourse on the unjust state that will reappear in the nineteenth century. "The state" he argues in his fourth lecture in January 1976, "is and must be the protector of the integrity, the superiority, the purity of the race."[25] Modern racism is born out of this conversion from a discourse on races to a discourse on race, from a discourse directed against the state to one organized by it. In The History racism is embedded in early discourses on sexuality but not yet in explicit form. It is only in the late nineteenth century that the "series composed of perversion-heredity-degeneracy" comes to make up the "solid nucleus" of a new technology of sex that "took the exasperated but coherent form of state-directed racism."[26]

Such references may seem to suggest a progressive story of racism emerging out of earlier technologies of sex, but Foucault's story is more complicated. In the final chapter of The History the concept of biopolitics and its ties to racism are the focus of his argument. "Biopower" is identified as having two distinct forms: one concerned with the life of the individual, the other with that of species. It is the micromanagement of the individual body and the macrosurveillance of the body politic—and the circuits of control between them—that linked the fate of the two. Note here the crucial link: the "encasement" of a disciplinary power targeting the individual within a state power targeting the social body. It is this that allows for racism in its contemporary form.

If we turn to colonial terrain these formulations are compelling but in ways that make what Foucault does not say about gendered coordinates of colonialism more pronounced. In the Indies, in South Asia, and in the North and South American colonies, the sexual arrangements of company officials, subaltern military, and settlers were monitored if not successfully regulated early on in ways that repeatedly positioned women of different hue as desired objects and more obliquely as unruly desiring subjects as well. Connections among the making of racial categories, the prescribing of women's reproductive functions, and the managing of sexuality are hard to miss.

By the mid-nineteenth century, as we have seen, Dutch children in the Indies—abandoned, illegitimate, and of mixed blood—had become the sign and embodiment of what needed fixing in colonial society. More clearly defined bourgeois prescriptions that encouraged white endogamy, attentive parenting, Dutch-language training, and surveillance of servants made up the web of directives designed to shore up the state's priorities. Together these discourses of sexual and racial transgression provided social reformers with ready evidence that colonial policies had to distinguish between the "real" Dutch and those assimilated natives, Indos, and poor whites considered of "fabricated" European status, between citizens and subjects, and between colonizer and colonized.

FROM A SYMBOLICS OF BLOOD
TO AN ANALYTICS OF SEXUALITY

In *The History* Foucault writes:

> Beginning in the second half of the nineteenth century, the thematics of blood was sometimes called on to lend its entire historical weight toward revitalizing the type of political power that was exercised through the devices of sexuality. Racism took shape at this point (racism in its modern, "biologizing" statist form).[27]

A description of the reappearance of a "symbolics of blood" in nineteenth-century science as a technology that worked to consolidate racism is not an unfamiliar story. What is dissonant is the selective Europe-bound genealogy Foucault derives for it. He traces it solely through an aristocratic symbolics of legitimacy and descent, with no sign of an imperial politics of exclusion worked out earlier and reworked later on colonial ground. Science and medicine may have fueled the reemergence of the beliefs in blood, but so did a folk theory of cultural contagions, as threatening as those of bodily ones.

The revival of a symbolics of blood derived from the imperial logic that cultural hybridities were subversive, that subversion was contagious, and that native sensibilities and affiliations were the invisible bonds that could position those of "mixed blood" against "full-blooded" Europeans who claimed the right to rule. For Foucault, modern racism appears as a consequence of that class body in the making. In my perspective race was constitutive of it. We may have so few colonial readings of *The History* because questions of what constituted European identities in the colonies, who counted as European and could claim to be white, are only now foregrounded in critical cultural theory and analysis.

COLONIAL CULTIVATIONS OF THE BOURGEOIS SELF

Colonialism was not a secure hegemonic bourgeois project.[28] It was only partly an effort to import cultured sensibilities to the colonies but as much about the *making* of them. Indeed, most of the European population in the Indies never enjoyed the privileges of what Benedict Anderson has labeled a "bourgeois aristocracy" at all. That ill-defined population included poor whites, subaltern soldiers, minor clerks, mixed-blood children, and creole Europeans whose economic and social circumstances made their ties to metropolitan bourgeois civilities often tenuous at best.

These were neither players absent from the colonial stage (as some official histories would have it) nor the rebel vanguard against European rule (as some authorities claimed). Rather they were people precariously poised, economically vulnerable, and socially askew. Effaced from view and then pushed to center stage at strategic moments, these were people about whom colonial officials virulently disagreed. Where they were placed in the state's racial taxonomy affected the extent of the state's financial responsibility for the impoverished and the reach of its moral authority. Note here that colonial comparative statistics on indigent Europeans in South Africa, Australia, India, and the Indies were never simply intended to count which Europeans were poor but which of the poor were really European and should be included as such. Statistics was a moral science, and these were fundamentally moral judgments about the deserving and undeserving poor. They were also assessments that depended on a definition of race. Only then could officials construct social policy for European welfare and a definition of poverty.

Our blind spots are one issue, Foucault's another. His account of what sexuality meant to the eighteenth-century bourgeoisie refused what he saw as a facile economic reductionism—emphasis on the exploitation of the Other. Thus he wrote:

The deployment of sexuality *must be seen as the self-affirmation of one class rather than the enslavement of another;* a political ordering of life[,] . . . it provided itself with a body to be cared for, protected, cultivated, and preserved from the many dangers and contacts, to be isolated from others so that it would retain its differential value.[29]

Note how even the syntax absents key actors. Foucault makes no room for the fact that these bourgeois bodies were produced in practices never contingent on the will to self-affirmation alone. This "body to be cared for, protected, cultivated, and preserved from the many dangers and contacts" required other bodies that would perform those nurturing services and provide the leisure for such self-absorbed administerings and self-bolstering acts. It was a gendered body and a *dependent* one, on that intimate set of sexual and service relations between French men and Vietnamese women, Dutch women and Indo men and shaped by the politics of race. Native women who served as concubines, servants, nursemaids, and wives in European households at once threatened the "differential value" of adults' and children's bodies that they were there to protect and affirm.

There was a set of fundamental tensions: between a culture of whiteness that cordoned itself off from the native world and a set of domestic arrangements and class distinctions among Europeans that produced cultural proximities, intimacies, and sympathies that transgressed them. The family, as Foucault warned, was not a haven from the sexualities of a dangerous outside world but the site of its production. Colonial authorities knew it only too well. They were obsessed with moral, sexual, and racial affronts to European identity in prisons, in schools, and in hospitals but most definitively where they had equivocal control—in the home.

As evinced in earlier chapters, medical manuals and pedagogic journals insisted that mixed-blood children in poor white households needed to be salvaged from their domestic surroundings and severed from their native mothers. European children of the well-to-do too were at risk if the proper habitus was not assured, if socializing with poorer children of mixed parentage was not monitored and certain social protocols were not met. The risk for both was that their sense of "belonging" and their longings allowed in too much that was locally acquired and Javanese.

Foucault wrote as if one could easily assume that the middle class was sure of what it was affirming. But I think it was not. These strategies of identity making and self-affirmation were labile, affirmed by a cultural repertoire of competencies and sexual prescriptions that altered as states weighed profit-making strategies against the stability of rule. Self-discipline, sexual morality, and self-control were visual signs of middle-class rearing, indexing what was invisible and harder to test—namely, what defined the essence of being European and whether creole and "Indo" affinities for things Javanese were a threat to it.

One might argue that such racialized notions of the bourgeois self were colonial idiosyncrasies and applicable there alone. But racial and imperial metaphors were applied to class distinctions in Europe at a very early date. While social historians generally have assumed that racial logics drew on the ready-made cultural disparagements honed to distinguish between middle-class virtues and the immorality of the poor and between the "undeserving" and the "respectable" poor, it may very well be that such social etymologies were sometimes reversed.

The lexicon of empire and the sexualized images of it may have provided for a European language of class as often as the other way around. From Montaigne to Mayhew, in Britain, the Netherlands, and France, imperial images of the heightened erotics of the colonized saturated the discourses of class. Nor is it first in the mid-nineteenth century that those parallels were made between the immoral lives of the British underclass, Dutch dirt farmers, Irish factory workers, and primitive Africa or Southeast Asia. To argue this case is not to embrace unwittingly the comparative categories used by colonial states. It should rather encourage a tracking of the histories of these comparisons themselves. It should prompt us to ask what kinds of equivalencies would have to be made and what truth-claims would allow or disallow such comparisons to be drawn.

Empire figured too in the bourgeois politics of liberalism and nationalism in ways we have only begun to explore. As Uday Mehta has argued, eighteenth-century bourgeois liberalism had written into it a politics of exclusion based on race.[30] The most basic universalistic notions of "human nature" and "individual liberty," so dear to Locke and Mills, rested on breeding and the learning of "naturalized" habits that set off those who exhibited such a "nature" and were endowed with the sensibilities that would allow them to exercise such liberty from the racially inferior—and in their cases, the South Asian colonized world. Discourses of sexuality, racial thinking, and rhetorics of nationalism used visual markers to (poorly) index the cultural and affective attributes on which these folk theories of difference were based.

The quest to define moral predicates and invisible essences tied the bourgeois discourses of sexuality, racism, and nationalism in fundamental ways. Nationalist discourse staked out those sexual practices that were nation building and race affirming, marking, as Doris Sommer notes, "unproductive eroticism[,] . . . not only [as] immoral, [but also as] unpatriotic."[31] In such a frame, European women were cast as the custodians of their morally vulnerable men and of national character. By not engaging the nineteenth-century discourses of nation and empire, cultivation of the bourgeois self and its gendered assignments appear routed in Europe and *inside* the nation rather than as part of the making of them.

CHILDREN'S SEXUALITY AND
THE ALIENATION OF AFFECTIONS

It was not the child of the people, the future worker who had to
be taught the disciplines of the body, but rather the schoolboy, the
child surrounded by domestic servants, tutors and governesses,
who was in danger of compromising not much his physical
strength as his intellectual capacity, his moral fiber, and the obligation to preserve a healthy line of descent for his family and his
social class.[32]

Foucault's attention in *The History* to what he calls the "pedagogization of children's sexuality" is schematic, uneven, and only broadly framed. But the subject was central to his conception of a biopolitical state. In fact, his planned volume 3 of the projected six-volume *History* was to be titled *The Crusade for Children* (Croisade des enfants). He never finished that project, but what he did have to say about the discourse on children and masturbation makes sense of its colonial variants in interesting ways. If this was one of the principal discursive sites where bourgeois culture defined and defended its interest, in colonial perspective it was also one of the key sites where racial lines were transgressed and national identities were formed. It was a discourse in which the distribution and education of desire was lodged in the home, as Foucault put it, in that "tiny, sexually saturated, familial space."[33]

In the Indies these discourses were animated not by fears of children touching their own bodies but by fears of their affections for those bodies that should not touch them. Foucault rightly observed that the profusion of child-centered prescriptions and protocols affirmed a bourgeois self in the making. But it was that "cast" of stereotypical Others shadowed in these narratives against which the quotidian boundaries of the cultivated self were drawn. As he was to explain in his *Resumé des cours* for his 1974–75 lectures on "Les anormaux" (The Abnormals), authorities saw children's transgressions as the fault of parents who entrusted them to "wet nurses, domestics, tutors, all these intermediaries regularly denounced as the initiators of debauchery."[34]

Liberal philosophers, colonial policy makers, and nationalist thinkers could not agree more. They shared a political preoccupation with the dispositions of very small children, the malleabilities of their minds, and the training of habituated practices that would "appear natural" to them as adults later on. Strict surveillance of domestic servants was one way to protect children. Removal of children from the home was another, as the proliferation and state endorsement of kindergartens and nurseries in the nineteenth century attest. Both moral philosophers and policy makers were spurred by the conviction that bourgeois households were providing poor child management and that toddlers and even infants were better off in nurseries than in a servant's care.

In the Indies virtually all of the debates about masturbating and sexually precocious European children were about whether these children would be able to acquire the sensibilities that would allow them to grow up European. Schooling was proffered as a protection against the risks to which girls were exposed outside the family but more dangerously within it.

These discourses did not target the sexuality of children so much as the dangers posed by alien cultural longings and affective estrangements, disrupting the culturally contained milieus in which European children rightfully belonged. Children required an environment cordoned off from those conduits of sentiment that would disincline them to "feel at home" in a European setting and, as one colonial official put it, "to think and feel" not in Dutch but in Malay or Javanese. Servants could steal more than the sexual innocence of European children. They could redirect their cultural longings, the smells they preferred, the tastes they craved, and their sexual desires.

Judith Butler has called *The History of Sexuality* a history of Western desire, but I am still not convinced this is the case. From volume 1 we learn little about what sorts of passions are produced and what people actually did with them. We learn even less about how pleasure was distributed, how desire was motivated and power displayed. But those of us who study sexuality and empire do not do much better. All might agree that carnality has underwritten European folk theories of race for more than two centuries. But in colonial studies the carnal often is suspended as a precultural instinct, given and unexplained. Such analyses often proceed, *not* from a Foucauldian premise that sexual cravings are a social construct and sex a nineteenth-century invention, but from an implicitly Freudian (and imperial) one. In this narrative, colonialism expressed the sublimated sexual outlet of virile and homoerotic men. White women, by and large, display affective pains and pleasures but no sexuality at all.

The sexual stories that European colonials and their metropolitan observers told about their own desires and what distinguished themselves turned on instantiating class-specific sensibilities. Thus the sexual susceptibility of European children in the tropics demanded vigilant education of their desires and care that native contacts were controlled. European colonial women whose conjugal choices were deemed unfit, as we have seen in chapter 4, could be stripped of the European community's protection of their womanhood and disavowed as true Europeans.

Similarly, colonial discourses of desire contrasted lower-class men of passion and bourgeois men of character. They did not silence talk of sex but knowingly detailed its social etymologies. These discourses attributed sexual excesses to those of creole, lower-class, and mixed-blood background—"fictive" and not properly embourgeoised Europeans. Such representations hinged on the presence of other actors, on a marking of their sexuality as the truth of the self, as an index of the social category to which they truly belonged. British, French, and Dutch moralizing missions produced discourses contrasting desire and reason, native instinct and white self-discipline, subversive unproductive sexuality and productive patriotic sex, but these lines could never be drawn—nor were they meant to be drawn—with racial clarity.

These assessments of the sexuality of masturbating children, of promiscuous servants, and of degenerate white men and intruders in the bourgeois home congeal around what constituted the threat in these transgressive moments. Sexual intimacy and precocity were at issue, but not them alone. Evidence of emotional ties, confusions of blood and milk, impudence, disrespect or indifference were as dangerous as carnal knowledge and tainted blood. Nor was reference to particular sentiments just another way of talking about what "really mattered"—sex. Subversions of the bourgeois order were those that threatened that repertoire of sensibilities glossed as "personal character" and that marked who was eligible to be classed as white. These contexts of "cultural contagion" might disrupt dichotomies of ruler and ruled as they clarified and confused what being respectable and properly colonial was supposed to be about. Desire may have been reduced to the sexual, but the desires at issue embodied other powerful sensibilities. Cultivation of a self that was self-reliant, without pretensions, and morally pure was thought to define the interior landscapes of "true" Europeans and the interior frontiers of the superior polities to which they were constantly reminded they rightfully belonged. Thinking about "the education of desire" more broadly may help to avoid a quandary, that is, reproducing the very terms of high imperial discourse that reduced and read all desires as sexual ones. It offers another option—looking to a wider range of affective dispositions and cultural trangressions that informed what was unspeakable and what had to be said.

FURTHER REFLECTIONS

Race and the Education of Desire turned out to be more useful than I hoped for some, less accommodating to others. Scholars in a range of fields also have been smitten with Foucault and troubled by him. Some have shared my concern with how few people have pushed his chronologies up against those in the colonies and enthusiastically joined me in asking why he did not. Some students of the colonial have joined to query the articulation between European biopower and colonial racisms in both contiguous empires and those "overseas." Fewer have sought to ask whether a language of race developed out of the language of class (as nineteenth-century racial discourse suggests) rather than the other way around.

But curiously the focus on Foucault has caused more trouble than I could have imagined. However much colonial studies in Britain and the United States has drawn on Foucault, Dutch historians of the colonial by and large have not. For them, the book is not about Dutch empire but about Foucault. For Foucauldians of a philosophical bent, the book is about colonialism and race. It has been reviewed by neither. One critic noted my "overconfidence in empirical forms of analysis"; another suggested that the book was insufficiently mired in the native and empirical world. It has been referred to as eminently readable and overcongested. Some have embraced my rereading of European sexuality through empire; others have criticized it for being a "racially deterministic" one.

Many people curiously have suggested that I was too generous to Foucault. Reading the book as colonial ethnography, some have gently queried whether Foucault could have been omitted altogether. Most recently, a well-disposed male colleague questioned why yet another "theoretically inclined woman" sought to frame her contribution "through a male actor." Disenchantment with Foucault is neither new nor my concern. But clearly something was missed. I am interested in why, despite a wide readership, what I still see as some of the book's more critical concerns—and those of Foucault's—seem muted if not ignored.

Not least among these concerns is the one I have already mentioned: Foucault's efforts to think through a specific genealogy of discourses on race. As important is the emphasis he placed in the 1976 lectures on modern racism as an inherent feature of contemporary states. Foucault's focus was decidedly not on some generic notion of racism but on what he alternately referred to as "state racism" or "racism in its statist form," racism as part of the normalizing apparatus of capitalist, fascist, and socialist states. Such a shift in analytic emphasis does two things: it reconceives racism not as an aberrant, pathological development of state authority in crisis but as a fundamental "indispensable" technology of rule—as biopower's operating mechanism. This demands a further question: How could this be so? How could racism serve such a wide spectrum of political agendas at the same time?

That question is in many ways basic to the progression of the 1976 lectures. For where Foucault began his exegesis was not with a discussion of racism, as one might expect, but with a more general set of observations about the nature of power, erudite knowledge, and discursive formations. As he did in the methodological project of *The Archaeology of Knowledge,* he once again refutes—and refuses—the notion that a discursive formation can be identified by its unity and coherence; rather it can be identified by "the different possibilities that it opens of reanimating already existing themes, of arousing opposed strategies, of giving way to irreconcilable interest, of making it possible with a particular set of concepts, to play different games."[35]

It is different manifestations of this "polyvalent mobility" that Foucault tracks in the race seminar. Beginning in the first two lectures with the assertion that discourses are composed of both erudite and subjugated knowledge, he makes a striking point: seemingly unified discourses are historically layered with oppositional discourses, permeated with resurrected subjugated knowledges that may resurface with them. In short, racial discourse is neither always a tool of the state nor always mobilized against it. Racial discourses diffuse over a broad field. Their geneaological histories should track their "spaces of dissension" and unique sites of dispersion.[36]

The first two lectures have been canonized (indeed fetishized) as Foucault's work that speaks most directly to the study of subaltern history. But they do so in a very specific way—by setting out a counterintuitive proposition. Disqualified knowledge can be of different sorts. Like the field of phrenology, it can be valorized at one historical moment and dismissed at another, without undermining its basic principle; namely, an alignment between the physiology and the inner states that determine race. But disqualified knowledge can work against itself and serve erudite knowledge instead. Racial discourse, for example, accrues its force not because it is a scientifically validated discourse but just the opposite. It is saturated with sentimentalisms that increase its appeal. Disqualified knowledge can do something else. It can usurp the place of erudite knowledge and in its "resurrection" turn the world upside down. Thus the first two lectures that address this resurrection introduce a specific kind of history, a genealogy of race.

A second important point worth more attention: Foucault draws on the notion of polyvalent mobility to account for why racial discourse is rarely consistent in its political affiliation or strategic claims. It may serve a reactionary political agenda or a reformist one. It may be mobilized against the state at one historical moment and usurped by the state at another. Recognition of this quality may help to account for its resilience and enduring relevance over time. I have tried to argue elsewhere that this very fact—that racial discourses contain, comply with, and coexist with a range of political agendas—is not a contradiction but a fundamental historical feature of their *nonlinear* political genealogies.[37]

This analytic focus on how counternarratives and disqualified knowledges may resurface within official discourses links to a third theme, one critical to Foucault's understanding of the resilence of racial discourses and the force of discursive formations. This is the tension he posits between processes of rupture *and* recuperation. It remains striking how much Foucault's philosophical and historical project continues to be characterized as one concerned with historical discontinuity, abrupt fissures, and dispersions in unexpected time and place. Many scholars take this as his defining contribution and the hallmark of his work.

But from the lectures it is clear that discursive formations are never built on epistemic rupture alone. Discourses about race and how race is known— that is, the popular and erudite theories that inform knowledge of it—are plural not singular, are sedimentary not linear. It is within these sedimented folds that new planes and surfaces reemerge. These preserved possibilities account for why racial discourses so often appear as new and renewed at the same time. But what accounts for those specific features that are available for recuperation? What qualifies some for recodification and not others? What makes the contemporary discourse of the European extreme Right on citizenship, foreigners, or national education look so similar to the wider consensual discourse on these issues *and* not dissimilar to that of racist demagogues a hundred years earlier?

No one would argue that the 1976 lectures offer a comprehensive analysis either of racial discourses or of racisms of the state. On the other hand, few others have asked such discomforting questions about modern state formations or explored the reversibilities of racial discourses and the process of reversal. If Foucault pressed on some questions more than others, it is for us twenty years later to take on the ones he could and did not.

It is for us to understand the conditions of possibility that give racial thinking its continuing and refurbished currency, to dissect the forms in which racist visions pronounce themselves as relevant to the twenty-first century, to understand what charges them with populist and oppositional appeal. Foucault's notion that state policies are directed at "the defense of society" against itself has chilling resonance in extreme Right discourse in Europe today. Understanding more fully what joins racisms, biopolitics, and modern states may be one way of participating in doing what Foucault encouraged—the writing of histories that nourish reversals, recuperations, and insurrections within them. The chapter that follows is an effort in that direction.

7 Memory-Work in Java

A Cautionary Tale

With Karen Strassler

Throughout these essays, I have worked off and with a specific set of colonial perceptions and practices: how concubinage was seen by Dutch authorities, how servants were viewed by their employers, how Dutch women were made ready for their tasks as good modern housewives—and why all of these mattered so much to colonial authorities. But this chapter does something different. It attempts an about-face. It turns to the ways in which Javanese women and men who worked as servants in late colonial Indonesia saw their Dutch employers. The about-face then is directed at colonial inscriptions of the quality of those domestic relations.

But this chapter is also an about-face of another kind, for it situates memories of domestic service by those who served against the density of the archives about them. Its tenor and tentativeness responds to Doris Sommer's injunction that scholars should "proceed with caution" in their treatment of colonial narratives, temper their interpretive license, and not imagine that all encounters can be unpacked with hermeneutic finesse. As Michel-Rolph Trouillot put it in his book cover comments, Sommer upsets the "false intimacy of the liberal embrace." This chapter speaks to these issues and asks what such a cautionary reflection may say about what we think we know about colonial memories.

At no time has there been more fascination with the contrast that memories of colonialism afford between the "elegance" of domination and the brutality of its effects.[1] While images of empire surface and resurface in the public domain, colonial studies has materialized over the last decade as a force of cultural critique and political commentary and, not least, as a domain of new expert knowledge. One could argue that the entire field has positioned itself as a counterweight to the waves of colonial nostalgia that have emerged in the post–World War II period in personal memoirs, coffee table picture books, tropical chic couture, and a film industry that encourages "even politically progressive [North American] audiences" to enjoy "the elegance of manners governing relations of dominance and subordination between the races."[2] Still, Nietzsche's warning against "idle cultivation of the garden of history" resonates today when it is not always clear whether some engagements with the colonial are raking up colonial ground or vicariously luxuriating in it.[3]

From the vantage point of the postcolonial, the notion of a history of the present has strong resonance and appeal. Colonial architecture, memorials, and archives and the scientific disciplines that flourished under the guidance of colonial institutions are dissected as technologies of rule whose "legacies" and "influences" are embodied in our comportments and leisures, lodged in our everyday accoutrements, and embedded in the habitus of the present. Remembering—and reminders of—past colonial relations of power has emerged as fundamental to a range of postcolonial intellectual and political agendas that make the recording, rewriting, and eliciting of colonial memories so pertinent and charged.

Yet what remains surprisingly muted in ethnographic histories written "from the bottom up" and elite histories viewed upside down is an explicit engagement with the nature of colonial memories—not only with what is remembered and why but also with how the specifically "colonial" is situated in popular memory at all. This chapter rests on a relatively simple but disconcerting observation: "the colonial" is invoked with such certitude of its effects by those studying it and "colonial memory" with such assuredness of its ever presence that both are treated as known and knowable quantities rather than as problematic sites of inquiry in themselves.

But this was not where this project began. It was initiated as a response to that specific archive on the colonial domestic order, documented and celebrated in personal memoirs and public records of Europeans, particularly the Dutch, who lived and worked in late colonial Indonesia. We have seen how enduring these images of family life were and how centrally servants figured in them. Thus this memory project addressed the two most tenacious forms in which servants were cast in Dutch renderings: the threatening image offered in housekeeping guides, child-rearing manuals, and medical handbooks warning against the contaminating influence of servants on European children; and, in stark contrast, the favored image (recurrent in colonial memoirs devoted to fond reminiscences of affections shared) of the servants in whose company childhoods were spent.[4] Our questions worked around these images: What resonances did these castings have in people's lives? What was remembered by those whose touch, smell, and gestures were the very objects of such aroused recollections?[5] Over a period of nearly two years, we talked with Indonesian women and men who had worked between the 1920s and 1950s as gardeners, gofers, kitchen helpers, nursemaids, cooks, housekeepers, and watchmen in Dutch colonial homes.

The memories they chose to recall present a challenge to two prevailing postcolonial stories. One is the popular romance of the beloved and nurturing servant that dominates Dutch memoirs. The other is the story of subaltern memory as the truth of the colonial past. This project adheres to neither. Instead it pushes the accounts of former servants against these Dutch renderings to explore how the dissonance in their perceptions of intimacy and affect may unsettle our certainties about what constituted the colonial and how it figures in people's memories today.

As an opening question, we ask why colonial studies, despite its obvious commitment to questions of memory, has dealt in such circumscribed ways with the nature of remembering and the particular forms that memories of the colonial take. We then turn to the specific recollections of former servants to question how their colonial memories were framed, how concrete and sensory memories of cooking, cleaning, and child care evoke sensibilities that other ways of telling do not. Two concerns grew out of this project: a longer reflection on the politics of interpretive license and what might be gained by making memory-work the subject rather than a given of colonial analysis.

COLONIAL SENTIMENTS AND TACTILE MEMORIES

My recollections of events of this time escape me but there is one thing that will always stick in my mind: how [she] would carry me in a *slendang*[6] at dusk and would rock me to sleep by humming the "Nina Bobo" lullaby. I still remember how heavenly I found that; so entirely "imprisoned" in her *slendang,* in the curve of her arm, flat against her body, rolling with her slow rocking gait, with the veil-like material of her *kebaja* [blouse] gently grazing my cheek and her humming resonating in her breast so that I could feel it with the rise and fall of her voice. It was as if she flowed through me.[7]

She would . . . take me in her lap. The fragrance of her body and her clothes, of her *sarung* especially, I must have intensively inhaled, a sort of preerotic! She caressed me by nestling me against her. . . . Now still I recollect this fragrance, because smells can remind me of it! . . . [S]uch was my relationship to her.[8]

It was like this with the Dutch. . . . I was told to take care of the child. At ten at night I'd go back in and give it something to drink, some milk, then a change of clothes, whatever clothes were wet, you know, . . . then I'd return to the back [servants' quarters] again, like that.[9]

The quotations above, two from Dutch memoirs and one from a Javanese woman who worked as a nursemaid (babu), recall colonial intimacies in distinctive ways. Both Dutch accounts are marked by lush sentimentality, by sensuous evocations of bodily intimacy. The nursemaid's comment also gestures to everyday rhythms, to bodies and substances, smells and spaces. Hers too is strikingly tactile. But it is spare. Emphasizing routines, tasks, and commands, she evokes a place of work, not the coziness of home. If for the remembered Dutch child "home" is the body of the servant, for the nursemaid the place of belonging is out "back."

Our interest was to explore the "structure of feeling" of these "intimate" relations so differently remembered, the emotional economy and the sensory regimes in which those relations were rendered possible, then retold and remade.[10] Students of the colonial know so much more about how European colonials saw their servants than how their servants saw them. On this premise we questioned how Indonesian women and men today remembered "the Dutch" they knew at once up close and only from afar, what language they used to describe those daily exchanges, and how they remembered what struck them at the time as distinctly European. We sought out neither the richest storytellers nor those locally celebrated for their vivid recollections. We were as interested in those who were reluctant to speak as in those who eagerly proffered their stories; as drawn to those who could muster no easy frame, whose recollections would not distill into a storied and ready counternarrative. In most cases, we were struck by an unease in recounting "the colonial," by the singularly uncozy and "charmless" accounts people offered about their jobs and the sensibilities that pervaded Dutch colonial homes. The play of repetitions that seemed so innocuous— that the Dutch were all "so good," that Dutch employers were "so very clean"—drew us to plumb less for the deep grit of their accounts than to follow their surface grain.

It would have been a straightforward task to take "speaking back to the archives" to mean contrasting the sentimentalism of Dutch nostalgia with the distinctly unsentimental remembrances of those who served them. Sentimentalism so underwrites colonial nostalgia that scholars' attempts to

Figure 21.   'Babu with the children of A. F. Fokersma,
Soerabaja, East Java, 1911.' KITLV, no. 15.285.

Figure 22.   'A European child with the babu and house
boy,' ca. 1900–10. KIT album 704/41b, neg. 1084/9.

write against it have tended either to avoid the subject of sentiment or to limit their focus to affective extremes, that is, to conditions of palpable duress, dislocation, and diaspora.[11] In doing so, they have called attention to a variety of technologies of memory: place-names, ritual enactments of subjugation, commemorative events, and the violence of conflicts indelibly inscribed in bodies and minds.

Here instead we address the emotional economy of the everyday: when, where, and with whom sentiments were withheld, demanded, and "freely" displayed. We attend to a more prosaic genre of *aides de memoire*, tied to the non-eventful and the senses.[12] Colonial domestic relations were invoked through recollections of the color and texture of clothes, the taste and smell of unfamiliar foods, the sound of partially understood conversations and commands, and reference to sweat, soaps, chamber pots, and fragrance.[13] Sentiments lay not outside of—or behind—tactile memories but embedded in them.

We asked what these acts of remembering and retelling might signal about the duties and dispositions that went with domestic work and what it meant to be in the service of those who were often inept at "being colonials": provincial brides on their first trip to the Indies, recently transferred government bureaucrats, plantation supervisors climbing the corporate ladder, young doctors on philanthropic missions, and crusty old colonial hands who might just be learning what it meant to be self-consciously European.

MEMORY IN COLONIAL STUDIES:
STORAGE AND THE HYDRAULIC MODEL

Concern with the politics and techomnemonic strategies of remembering permeates a range of disciplines, public debates, and epistemic fields. It might be claimed that only in an extremely narrow, even parochial definition of what constitutes memory could one argue that memory-work is not on the colonial studies agenda. Surely the scholarly study of colonialisms is itself a memory project, as has been that of postcolonial subjectivity.[14] Issues of "memory" have played an increasingly prominent role in how students of colonialism understand the relationship between the facts of the colonial archive and ethnographically elicited historical knowledge, between archival production and the politics of its consumption,[15] between a particular set of memory aids—manuscripts, metaphors, bodies, and objects—and how this stored knowledge may be refashioned by postcolonial populations for their needs today.[16]

Still, the treatment of memory in colonial studies has developed in relation to specific political concerns and thus in particular ways. Some of these bypass important insights about the "fragile power" of memory noted by those who study it more specifically.[17] The storage model, captured in Locke's metaphor of memory as a "storehouse of ideas," has long been discredited.[18] Yet students of the colonial often unwittingly hold to a variant of it: memory as a repository of alternative histories and subaltern truths. This "hydraulic model" rests on the premise that memories are housed as discrete stories awaiting an audience, as repressed or unrecognized sources poised to be tapped.[19]

In colonial studies, memory has been the medium, not the message, the access point to untold stories of the colonized. In efforts to restore a more complete memory of the colonial and struggles against it, oral histories are often invoked to counter official versions and the sovereign status they implicitly give to European epistemologies.[20] Subaltern acts of remembering have not been in question because it is official memory that is on the line; the process of remembering and the fashioning of personal memories are often beside the political points being made—and may in fact be seen to work against them.[21] Oral histories, designed to extract counternarratives of important anticolonial events, document unheralded and heroic popular participation in them. By Ranajit Guha's account, these "small voices" may counter the weight of official discourse because they remain undomesticated and unsullied by "state-managed historiography" and "the monopolizing force of official knowledge."[22] Students of colonial history seem to want to have it both ways: a story of a hegemonic colonial state, saturating both the cultural frame and the cracks in which the colonized live, *and* a story in which deft evasion leaves the memories of these same actors unscathed by state intrusions.[23]

A crucial premise underwrites this hydraulic model: subaltern accounts already possess hidden circuits of movement. Silenced or unsanctioned by the state, these camouflaged "hidden scripts" await decoding. The job of ethnography is then to identify them in their secreted form, whether it be folktale, shaman ritual, scatological humor, midnight gossip, or charivari song.[24] But the very search for those concealed inscriptions of colonial violence and resistance often assumes the production of narrative and the prevalence of telling. Those with whom we talked in Java put that notion of "subaltern circuits" in question again and again.[25] For it was not clear that these circuits were devoted to the historical or specifically clogged with the colonial. Nor was it clear when, where, and whether colonial memories circulated at all.

A commitment to writing counterhistories of the nation has privileged some memories over others. Because it is often restoration of the collective and archived memory of the making of the *post*colonial nation that has been at stake, the critical historian's task has been to help remember what the colonial state—and often the nationalist bourgeoisie—once chose to forget.[26] The assumption is that subaltern narratives contain trenchant political critiques of the colonial order and its postcolonial effects. But this commitment may generate analytic frames less useful for understanding memories that are unadorned with adversaries and heroes, that are not about nationally salient events with compelling plots or violent struggles. This focus on event-centered history may in fact block precisely those enduring sentiments and sensibilities that cast a much longer shadow over people's lives and what they choose to remember and tell about them.

It might be argued that this is all beside the point. Everyone knows that memories are not stored truths but constructions of and for the present. Whether applied to the personal or the social, in this "identity" model memory is that through which people interpret their lives and redesign the conditions of possibility that account for what they once were, what they have since become, and what they still hope to be.[27] Treating memory as a self-fashioning act of the person or the nation places more emphasis on what remembering does for the present than on what can be known about the past.

Yet we are wary of starting from the premise that acts of remembering can and should be reduced to transparencies about the making of the self. Both the identity and the hydraulic models limit what can be learned about how the colonial is remembered. They either reduce acts of memory to constructions of the present or uphold memory as privileged access to a real past. We chose rather to highlight some of the interpretive problems that these models often elide. By treating memory as interpretive labor, the focus is on not only *what* is remembered but *how*. Marking off a colonial, then, from a postcolonial now flattens out a set of intervening and crosscutting points of reference. Instead we emphasize an ongoing and uneven production process. While recoding is obviously a repeated act, it is less obvious how idioms of the past are reworked with a differently inflected but equally active voice in the present. Recursive play occurs in the very terms in which memories are stated, in the possibilities of using a single phrase to "play different games."[28]

DOMESTIC SUB/VERSIONS

Manang, our gardener, smelled of different kinds of smoke. He never hurried and I liked being near him: it was restful. My father and the other men used to return from the tea gardens in shirts dark with sweat, their faces wet. Not Manang. He never

Figure 23. Servant with Dutch children, Java, ca. 1920s(?). Men who worked as gardeners and "houseboys" often appear in Dutch family albums with the children they helped care for and entertain. Leo Haks Collection.

Figure 24. From a family album. Leo Haks Collection.

Figure 25. 'Adrian Wilhelm Weber with the *babu* at Pangkadjene, South Celebes, 28 October 1908.' Photograph by Wah Seng. KITLV, no. 18.090.

Figure 26. From a family album. Infants in a pram with their nursemaid, ca. 1900. Leo Haks Collection.

looked hot. Manang wore faded khaki shorts that used to be my father's, no shirt, and a straw hat that hid his eyes. His large flat feet had spaces between the toes because he didn't have to wear shoes. . . . I wanted feet like that, and his shiny brown skin, and I tried to walk bow-legged like him.[29]

R: Dutch children weren't allowed to be held, [because] later they'd smell of [our] sweat. Holding them wasn't allowed. . . . [T]hey [the Dutch] were afraid [of their children] being soaked in sweat, the sweat of Javanese. . . . [T]he sweat of Javanese is different you know.

D: Why?

R: Javanese people's sweat smells, right.

D: What about Dutch people's sweat?

R: Yeah, Dutch sweat smells worse, 'cause they eat butter, milk, cheese.[30]

These recollections—from a Dutch man's memoir of his Indies boyhood and from Ibu Rubi, a former house servant—allude to the banal intimacies of everyday life, where "sweat" and scent could mark the lines of difference between kinds of people. They could also distill the dangers and pleasures of contact across those lines. In contrast to nation-centered narratives, the domestic occupies a space that is neither heroic nor particularly eventful nor marked by the brash violences in which colonial relationships are more often thought to be located.[31] As significantly, there is no site where Dutch colonial memoirs linger more knowingly, where more nostalgic energy has been placed.[32] It is a familiar story: the feminized, depoliticized home as the locus for a kinder, gentler colonialism.

Dutch stories of former servants are filled with tender anecdotes and demonstrations of affection, loyalty, and mutual recognition. Thus Annie Salomons could write in 1932, with only a touch of irony, "[T]hat washer boy, despite the fact that I could not yet distinguish him from his fellow men, was my dearest friend."[33] Childhood memories of Indies servants are central even when the nostalgia is critical, as in Rudy Kousbroek's sober recollections serialized in the Dutch press and recently made into a much praised film, where he refers to the "entire repertoire [of stories] of [his] loving *babu*" that remained so vividly in his mind.[34] In colonial fiction, memoirs, and children's literature, servants serve as the supporting cast and scenic backdrop and often as the main (and only) source of local knowledge.[35] Sometimes they mark the real and experienced; elsewhere, the imagined and the feared.[36] Dutch accounts of former servants who smuggled food to their imprisoned employers inside Japanese internment camps provide testimony to good treatment repaid and loyal service given long after employers could no longer afford their salaries.[37]

If those who write memoirs and belles lettres subscribe to this imagined vision of domestic bonds, scholars have been taken with another. For the latter, domestic service typifies the Hegelian dilemma and the subaltern condition.[38] In this site of intimate humiliation, contempt, and disdain, subaltern power accrues from the knowledge that those they served were deeply dependent on them.[39]

But both representations are in sharp contrast to the picture of Dutch colonial households conjured by Indonesian women and men who worked as servants. They avoided such expressions of affect, both in how those relations are remembered and in what sorts of emotions are made visible in the telling. Our attempts to elicit "feelings" often fell flat. In response to "How did you feel about working for the Dutch?" Ibu Kilah, a former cook, answered with a blunt, mocking response that emphasized the material rather than the emotional economy of those relations: "My feeling? I was happy because I was paid five and a half silver coins." Later, when asked about her relationship with her employer, she responded: "My relationship? Well, she was my employer, my boss, so I had to do whatever, you know. I had to be obedient, for example, if I was asked to help with this, help with that. . . . [S]o I was cared for, so my relationship was good with my boss."[40]

Ibu Kilah's unsentimental recollections suggest no easy interpretation. Were relations between servants and those they served utterly bereft of tenderness, or were care and nurturing factored into the sale of emotional labor, cherished and valued only by those Dutch who were recipients of it? Students of Javanese culture might argue that this apparent lack of sentiment reflected a more general cultural aversion to emotional display.[41] Or were we deaf to sentiments expressed in unfamiliar ways? We imagine that if this were a more sustained ethnographic project, our elicitations would have been muted and the answers very different.[42] Nevertheless, a focus on memory-work itself opened avenues we had not imagined. As the rest of this chapter suggests, it pointed us repeatedly to "the content of the form":[43] to how and why former servants talk without sentimentality about sentiment and recollect the colonial past without telling scripted, storied narratives.[44]

MEMORIES OUTSIDE THE COMFORT ZONE

That the accounts of former house servants often speak past rather than back to the colonial archive and the nostalgic memoirs of their Dutch employers should not be surprising. People's memories were clearly shaped by dominant historical narratives, by popular literary representations of domestic service, and by contemporary concerns. But if the different orientations of these accounts are predictable, their uneven densities were not. Rather than tap into well-honed, circulating stories, most people seemed unaccustomed to and uneasy relating their colonial experiences. Certainly what people chose to say to *us* was textured by what we inadvertently solicited and by what they thought we wanted to hear. Still, reticence about the colonial seemed to signal a discomfort that extended beyond the interview dynamics. Subtle shifts, evasions, and formulaic responses located the fault lines of memory, the places of discomfort and disinterest as well as those of safety and concern.

Inevitably this reticence was in part the product of a political climate of fear and repression. The research was conducted in the final years of the New Order regime, before the onset of the devastating economic crisis that would bring an end to Suharto's rule in May 1998. Despite growing concern about succession and the 1996 riots over his maneuvers to neutralize an opposition leader, there was little doubt at the time of these interviews that Suharto and his regime were firmly entrenched. So too were certain authorized versions of Indonesian history, within which daily life under the Dutch was marginally placed. When we explained to one former servant's adult granddaughter that we were interviewing people about the Dutch period, she immediately took it to mean that we were looking for revolutionary fighters *(pejuang)*.[45]

Questions about servant life in the 1930s and early 1940s more often provoked a swift change of subject than an unleashing of hoarded narratives. People frequently redirected the interviews to other periods, especially the Japanese occupation.[46] In fact, "the colonial" was rarely a discrete domain of retelling. Again and again we heard that the Dutch were "good" and the Japanese were the ones who were truly "bad." In popular memory and official history, the Dutch and Japanese periods are discursively paired, mnemonically fused, almost inaccessible independently. It is a fusing that upsets one tacit assumption of those who study the colonial—that the key opposition organizing contemporary memories is that between a colonial past and a postcolonial present, as if there was a direct line binding them and little of significance in between.

This fixation on the Japanese occupation was not particular to our interviews. In a country that has celebrated its independence from "three hundred fifty years of Dutch rule" with annual flourish, life under the Dutch regime has been consistently marginal to New Order stories about national beginnings.[47] Instead the brief Japanese occupation stands as the dark period before liberation, with Dutch colonialism typically invoked as a *zaman normal* (a time of normalcy, a term frequently used for the prewar years) and as a benign contrast.

The Japanese occupation was a safe topic of public discourse—as long as it remained circumscribed by a script of sacrificial suffering that was widely known.[48] People vividly recalled eating corn and other foods considered fit for animals and wrapping themselves in palm fibers and banana leaves when cloth was scarce. Detailed descriptions of Japanese soldiers who forced people to bow before them, of arbitrary beatings, abuse, and brutal deaths, were readily offered. Such stories attest to the extremity of those times but also to the sanctioning of certain kinds of memories of violence. Accounts of having gone hungry during the Japanese period were enough to mark one's heroic participation in the nationalist experience. These highly personalized accounts are almost dissonant in Indonesian, a language in which self-reference is avoided. By contrast, in hushed accounts of the 1965 coup and its bloody aftermath—a decidedly dangerous topic—that "I" quickly disappeared, replaced by a discourse of silences and vague allusion.[49]

People seemed less sure what to do with the "I" when it came to memories of the more ambiguous and normalized violences of the Dutch. Narrations of the nation emphasizing exemplary sacrifice and (male) heroism may have made memories of domestic service seem inappropriate to tell. But the hesitancy, thinness, and discomfort when it came to remembering Dutch colonialism was all the more striking because it has not always been so in Indonesia and certainly is not the case elsewhere. The recollection of colonial injustices may express shared nationalist sentiments in other postcolonial contexts, but to Indonesia's New Order government, anti-imperialist sentiments smacked of the "extreme" and demonized leftism of the Sukarno era. Such sentiments were deemed bad for the burgeoning tourist industry and for foreign investments. Capitalizing on the pleasures and pathos of a lost colonial era *(tempo doeloe)* had become a lucrative national industry in the Netherlands and Indonesia, with international appeal. More important in shaping reticence about the Dutch colonial regime, however, may have been the New Order state's own eerie resemblance to it.[50]

If the reasons that popular representations of the nation's history did not dwell on the colonial are complex, the effects are clear. To tell of one's experiences during the Dutch period conferred neither glory nor legitimacy nor "recognition."[51] Those with whom we spoke often assumed our interest in the heroic and actively worked to pull discussion in that direction.

The frequent return to the Japanese occupation as a comparative referent was only partly an effect of official nationalist narratives. As important, the occupation cast a different light on both the quotidian and the extraordinary violences of Dutch rule. For many former servants, the ravages of World War II and the volatility of the revolution years (and subsequent periods) prompted reworked recollections of the *zaman Belanda* (the Dutch period) as one of relative *personal* security.

Witnessing Dutch internment did not erase memories of Dutch control, but it was often a pivotal moment. The experience of having watched their employers taken away and never heard from again, having seen their well-furnished homes emptied of belongings, having watched fathers separated from wives and children, and having seen life behind barbwired internment camps recast many former servants' recollections of their employers.[52] Ibu Kilah, for example, who recalled bringing food in to the camp for her "Nyonya," remembered feeling "pity" that she was living in crowded conditions and growing thinner by the day. Yet in contrast to nostalgic Dutch recollections that dwell more on the loyalty and generosity of Javanese servants during these hard times, she said flatly that she stopped working when her Nyonya's money began to run out and the demands of other Dutch women in the camp became too onerous.[53]

Others called on their experiences during the occupation and the revolution to frame their accounts of working in Dutch homes, thereby both steering the interview to a "safer" moment and emphasizing how radically colonial relations had altered. Before the occupation, Pak Mulyo had worked for seven years as a gardener for the top administrator of a sugar factory outside Yogyakarta. He responded to our opening question about his job by recounting instead his experience on the cusp of independence. First describing how Sukarno provided for the starving and destitute Dutch released from camps after the Japanese surrendered, he linked himself to the nationalist leader by recounting his parallel generosity toward a desperately hungry Dutch man in a refugee camp to whom he brought an egg because he "felt sorry for him." Pak Mulyo remembered refusing the Dutch man's offer to give him something in return and concluded the anecdote, "Yeah, so that was it, working with a Dutch man."[54]

Pak Mulyo took an opening question about working *for* the Dutch as an invitation to tell how he worked *with* one. The context became one in which he could turn the tables and feel the pleasure of pity if not power per se. Noting that "this Dutch man was a good one," he stressed his exercise of choice while justifying his sympathy for a former colonizer. Beginning with this anecdote, his retelling of domestic service moved outside our frame. Instead his story was one of reversed fates and nationalist liberation. Only then did he talk about tending a Dutch man's garden.

There seemed to be no comfortably correct stance to take in relation to the colonial past. But what was unsafe? Recounting work for a Dutch person because one's previous service rendered one's patriotism suspect? Disparaging a colonial European (often, though not always) to a white interviewer? Or merely having an opinion at all?[55] The submerged anxiety that ran through some interviews at times surfaced with clarity, as with Pak Purwo, a man in his eighties from a village outside Yogyakarta. He had worked only briefly and part time as a gardener for a Dutch administrator in a sugar factory, in addition to working on the plantation and in the factory itself. The interview took place in the yard of his home, just several hundred yards from the former site of the factory, which had been burned down during the revolution.

> P: Am I going to be tried, Mas?[56]
>
> D: Oh no, we want to gather stories, Mbah. About the past. For history, not for being tried.
>
> P: Oh, if that's the case, I'll tell a long story.
>
> D: Yeah, Mbah, for history, in the old days how Javanese people worked in the homes of Dutch people. Because there hasn't been a book about it yet.
>
> P: Later I'll tell, OK. Up to the era of Independence, Mas?
>
> D: Oh, just the Dutch period, Mbah.
>
> P: Up to the Japanese period?
>
> D: Yes, the Japanese period.
>
> P: Later I can.
>
> D: You're not going to be tried, Mbah. I'm from UGM [the University of Gadjah Mada, in Yogyakarta], Mbah.
>
> P: Oh, Gadjah Mada.
>
> D: Gathering stories of when Javanese people worked as gardeners.
>
> P: So, nothing's going to happen to me, right?
>
> D: Oh nothing, Mbah. It's for school.
>
> P: Later will I be brought to court?
>
> D: No, Mbah. Only for history, for a book.
>
> P: Don't later say, "That man used to work for the Dutch [*ikut Belanda*]."[57]

D: Oh no, no, it's just for history.

P: Oh, yeah, yeah.

D: So we're just asking for stories.[58]

Uneasy focusing on the Dutch period, Pak Purwo preferred to talk about the Japanese occupation and the Independence period. He was keenly aware that telling the past has political stakes. In New Order Indonesia's "elaborately tended heritage" of fear, one could not be sure what actions and motivations might be attributed to one fifty (or thirty) years later.[59] But his fear may also reference a silenced memory of nationalist violence in which former male servants of the Dutch were often suspected of—and sometimes murdered for—treason against the Republic.[60] Clearly, "history" and "stories" provided neither reassuring nor safe frames for colonial memories.

UNSCRIPTED MEMORIES AND REFUSED SCRIPTS

A common assumption about collecting oral histories is that despite their variations, a good listener can discern a shared (if contested) narrative frame, a cultural schema that underlies how people make sense of their unique histories. But what emerged here was an unhomogenized body of accounts built around the minimal scaffolding of sanctioned formulas. People's recollections moved between concrete detail and pat statement, between rich commentary and terse responses and awkward silences. Their memories could neither call on familiar plots nor be contained in packaged narratives. Many people undermined their own neat encapsulations as soon as they were offered. Ibu Kilah made the sweeping statement that under the Dutch "all Javanese were servants," only to describe in the next breath a highly stratified Javanese society in which elite Javanese could exploit their servants more than did Dutch employers. People seemed unused to talking about and perhaps even recollecting these experiences. In contrast to the elaborated, often-repeated stories of the Japanese occupation that rolled off the tongue, these accounts seemed uncrafted, rough hewn, and apparently unrehearsed.

If this was subjugated knowledge circulating in subaltern spheres, their children and grandchildren seemed to care and know little about it. One woman, who had worked as a housemaid, said that her children were uninterested in her memories and considered her opinions old-fashioned.[61] Here it was both she and the history she had lived that were irrelevant. Another who had worked as a *genduk* (a young girl who cared for and played with Dutch children) said her children never asked about working for the Dutch.

Youthful impatience with stories of the old days is no surprise, but this insistent disregard raised a familiar question: What happens to marginalized memories, excluded from the valued, "usable past"?[62] Was there no common script in part because there was no audience and no forum for their telling? Tapping into subaltern narratives was not the direction to go. Instead that very absence led us to explore the availability and amenability of narrative forms to encompass these recollections.

But the unscripted nature of people's accounts could only partly be attributed to the lack of an appreciative audience. The accounts also took shape in a negative space around the one widely circulated and gendered local script for colonial service: the tale of the sexually exploited and morally debased female domestic. Through evasions and silences people worked to keep their accounts from fitting into this ready mold, even as they alluded to it in whispers. If in Dutch literature colonial servants are either nurturing or threatening, in Indonesian literature they appear as figures of calculating opportunism or pathetic victims of power. It is not the caregiving babu but the seductive nyai, the housemaid-concubine, who dominates portrayals of colonial domestic roles.[63] Merely to state that one had worked in a Dutch home was to invoke such plots, to stir suspicion, to suggest a hidden story. Even to acknowledge having known women who were "kept" or sexually assaulted was to risk being tainted oneself.[64]

Stories of women forced to sexually service Dutch men and their sons emerged only rarely. Most women were reluctant to speak of this subject, and most denied that their employers had ever made sexual advances. Ibu Soekati had been nearly raped by her employer when she was still a teen. In our first interview, she merely mentioned with a chuckle that he had been *nakal,* a word that can suggest inappropriate sexual behavior but is also often used to describe the innocuous antics of a mischievous child. It was only at a later meeting that she recounted how he had chased her around the house when no one else was there. Yet she cast his assaults as the acts of a crazy man, muting both the seriousness of his abuse and the severity of her condemnation.[65] Many others who similarly acknowledged their employers' improprieties emphasized how exceptional their experiences were. These stories were not part of family lore, nor were they topics for humor or moral instruction. Few of the children or grandchildren appeared to know anything of them.

Most people couched the subject of sexual relationships and illegitimate pregnancies in the removed language of rumor. Nearly everyone knew of someone "distant" or had heard "stories" of such things happening in "other places." In the first interview, Ibu Kilah only whispered that "Dutch men liked Javanese women" but in later meetings told of Javanese servants made pregnant by their employers, vague rumors she claimed to have heard from a neighbor rather than from her mother (who had worked as a babu) or from her own experience (although she had worked as a servant all her adult life). She suggested that women who had sex with their employers were just after money, echoing the disdain for concubines so prevalent in Indonesian popular representations. Overly eager to elicit more, we later pushed her to remember again. She acknowledged that Javanese servants might be "forced" to have sex with their employers while insisting on her own immunity to such advances. When we asked if her employer had ever propositioned her, she responded curtly that she was already married (and thus protected) and that before her marriage she had been far too young to have been an object of such desires.[66]

Others, rather than resist the available script, drew on it in ways that reinforced their distance from it. Pak Hardjo, for example, denied knowing anyone sexually involved with a Dutch employer but demonstrated his knowledge of such scenarios by staging an impromptu skit, in which he placed us (the three interviewers) in the roles of "Babu," "Tuan," and "Nyonya."

> H: I don't really know, but I sort of know. For example there is a servant, . . . for example, Karen is the servant of Ann and Ann is the wife of Dias. Then by chance Ann's husband likes Karen.
>
> A: Yes, but I don't like that.
>
> H: You don't know about it.
>
> A: Oh, OK, I don't know.
>
> H: Ann doesn't know, but Karen, well eventually she has relations with Ann's husband. And the Nyonya [Ann] instead of just . . .
>
> A: Later we divorce? Or not?
>
> H: No, she [he points to Karen] is asked to leave. Sent away.
>
> K: And what happens to my child? . . . I take the child with me, or I leave it?
>
> H: It stays with you. The child stays with you.
>
> A: So where are all of those children now? Where are those children now?
>
> H: I don't know.[67]

As frequently happened, Pak Hardjo stopped the conversation short with his disavowal. He said that he heard of this scenario from the babu of the household where he worked, who in turn had heard it from a friend. Did his "drama" reflect a personal memory rather than the wide currency of the script and its familiar cast? Or was the point rather his delight in placing us in these fitting colonial roles?

There are obviously many ways to read the silences, evasions, and careful crafting of recollections of sexual encounters. How far should we take our interpretive license? The accounts could be interpreted as people's refusals to place themselves in plots that readily cast them as pawn or victim. They could also be read more simply as a "strategic refusal" (as Doris Sommer calls it) to entertain our questions.[68] Why share these disturbing memories and why tell a *londo* (a white or Dutch person) about a londo at all? Are such silences, as David Cohen warns, "not a consequence of a forgetting, a loss of knowledge, but rather of powerful and continuous acts of control in both public and private places"?[69]

There were exceptions. Some accounts sliced through the roles accorded servants in local narratives. Ibu Sastro spoke bluntly about being propositioned by an elderly employer as her daughter-in-law and adult granddaughter nodded with recognition, having obviously heard these stories before.[70] She recounted her Tuan's crude manner and rude questions ("Are you married? Marry me, okay?")[71] and laughed to remember that such an old Dutch man could have imagined she would comply. With humor undercutting the pathos of a recollection searing enough to be recalled in minute detail, she evoked acute feelings of both vulnerability and self-possession:

> So he wanted that, but I didn't want it. "I'll give you money later, if you want" [he said]. I didn't say anything. I didn't say I didn't want it, I didn't say anything, I just took my clothes and went home. I didn't say anything, I was afraid. . . . I didn't say anything to anyone, not to the Nyonya, not the cook, not the gardener, I said nothing to anyone. I took my slendang and I went home, afraid.

Her fluid telling now contrasting with her younger self's terrorized silence, she assigns the trauma of the encounter to the past and positions herself as one for whom the event now makes a good story.

> [He said,] "What do you want coming here, asking for money?" . . . He called me a bitch [*bajingan*]. "If you don't want me to have you then you're just a bitch." "Just pay me now!" [I said]. He gave me four

rupiah, four and a half rupiah. "Here's your money, now get out of here! I don't want to see you!" So if he didn't want to see me, fine. . . . He threw that money at me [laughs], I wasn't even allowed to enter the house.[72]

FAMILY FRAMES

It was a cozy house with furniture . . . to our taste and with many books. We felt safe. We had good servants who were with us for years . . . who felt attached to us as we to them. Servants of the good old days, trustworthy and trusted. . . . We ask ourselves often whether [our former housemaid] is still alive or not.[73]

Former servants did not always reject outright the roles cast for them in colonialist narratives. The Dutch refrain that they treated their beloved servants "like family" was (to our discomfort) at times shared by those with whom we spoke. But their recollections of domestic work in the language of family ties were hardly a mirror image of the Dutch accounts. Instead they frequently gestured outside that domestic space to other relations and contexts. The terms might converge, but the distributions of affect did not. Whereas the Dutch invocation of family ties conjured an enclosed realm of cozy intimacy, former servants who spoke of being treated like family evoked their stance of respectful fear and deference. The relationship was more often figured in terms of a common Javanese form of patronage wherein poor relatives serve as quasi-servants in the homes of wealthy kin.

Ibu Tinem recalled that her employers had treated her "like one of their own children," as she in turn treated them "like [her] own parents." She said she "liked" working for her Dutch employers because they were "kind" and "everything was provided." She felt protected when her Tuan insisted that an older male servant accompany her when she wanted to go out. She felt cared for when her Tuan read the letters she received to make sure she was not being seduced at a tender age. She felt privileged to be given clothes and to be taught, unlike people from her village, to be "neat" and "clean"— even as she recalled trembling in fear when her Tuan caught her unawares with her hair not pulled back into the requisite bun.[74]

Ibu Tinem's memories of Dutch domesticity do not gloss over the strictures imposed by a paternalistic employer. Rather they provide a context for her willing submission to them. For her account ultimately was less about her familial ties in this Dutch home than her lack of strong family bonds outside it. She chose to tell us of a difficult childhood in a desperately poor village, of her mother's death and her father's remarriage to a woman who was cruel. She told of a strained relationship with her only sister and of losing her husband in the Japanese occupation. She bitterly recounted how her eldest son, who she feels should be caring for her in her old age, lives far away. To make matters worse he converted to Islam. Her daughter, present at one interview, described her as someone "floating," abandoned, with a life amounting to nothing.

Ibu Tinem recalled a brief interlude of familial care in a lifetime of emotional deprivation and vulnerability. Others spoke of the Dutch household as a place of shelter and economic security. References to Dutch care could tacitly—and sometimes overtly—provide commentary on the unfulfilled promises of the paternalistic New Order regime. Many compared the relative security of the Dutch era to uncertain economic prospects in Indonesia today. Although paid little under the Dutch, they could be sure of a secure income and food to eat. Yet unease with even veiled criticism of the state was such that one woman, after comparing Dutch money to what she called "worthless" money now, expressed anxiety that the Indonesian member of our team would report her to the police.[75]

Stories of the cared-for, loyal servant may have appeared in some former servants' accounts, but another Dutch myth of family ties did not—that of the babu with gentle touch and lilting voice who loved her charges as her own. Some spoke of having been nurtured themselves, but few celebrated their assigned nurturing roles. Ibu Kasan, for example, remembered her employer's car pulling away on the eve of the occupation. She recalled the child's outstretched arms and hysterical shrieks of " 'Genduuuk, Genduuuk," his mother's cold and hurried "good-bye," and her own indifference, in sharp contrast to the cared-for Ibu Patmi, who cried telling of her confusion and desolation when her employers, who had treated her "like their own child," were taken by the Japanese.)[76] Some recalled the children's names but not those of their parents. Others had forgotten both. Ibu Soekati equated caring for Dutch children with caring for their pet dogs: both were fed milk, taken for walks, and given baths. Few of these women and men had maintained any connection with those for whom they had worked.

Nowhere is the clash of memories more striking than in the contrast between the cozy images found in Dutch family albums and former servants' remembrances of performing child care tasks. In Holland today, both nostalgia for and critiques of the colonial feed on a vast archive of images from photo albums, calling cards, and postcards sent home as "proof" of the good life overseas (see figs. 3, 27, and 28).[77] The volume of these images—their material presence and "evidentiary force"—gives powerful credence to Dutch imagin-

Figure 27. 'H. Ch. Douwes Dekker and Mevrouw Douwes Dekker-Jolles at Koetei,' 1901. KITLV, no. 2723.

Figure 28.
Family portrait
with two servants
in (or as)
background, ca.
1915. KITLV, no.
13.289 A 247.

Figure 29.   From a family album: "Lien, [P] and baboe on the veranda, Bioscoop Way 11," December 12, 1920. Leo Haks Collection.

Figure 30.   Standing "houseboy" and empty chairs, from a family album, ca. 1890s. Leo Haks Collection.

Figure 31. Standing servant, empty chair, and two schoolteachers in Pekalongan, Central Java, 1898. KITLV, no. 15.305.

Figure 32. Servants, ca. 1910. Photos of servants on their own (not posed next to their employers) were often taken as here (and as in fig. 33) next to sites and objects (kitchen, laundry, backyard) that marked their work and "place." KITLV, no. 17.847.

Figure 33.   Servants posed with workday objects. Batavia, ca. 1915. KITLV, no. 13.306.

ings of themselves in a beneficent colonial regime. In these private and public mementos of the (good) old days, household servants play a key role.[78]

Familiar colonial stories about racial hierarchy, prescribed comportments, and control were captured and preserved in these photographic *tableaux vivants*. Scores of photos archived in family albums offer testimony to the ease of a colonial life made possible by servants who labor offstage (see figs. 29–33). Some show servants blurred in the background watching a scene of domesticity unfold—as in Dutch literature, crucial to the colonial "backdrop."[79] In some family albums, servants figure at the center of the images, but in the captions they remain unremarked or unnamed (see figs. 36, 37). Many images place servants firmly within the intimacy of family bonds, displaying a domestic order that was comforting and shared (see figs. 34, 36, 38). Most striking is how frequently those whose jobs were not defined as child care are posed with Dutch children (see figs. 22, 23, 24).

But these are images cherished by Dutch colonials from the Netherlands. Family albums of Indo-Europeans are not strewn with servants.[80] Nor are these images cherished by the colonized. Such snapshots are literally and figuratively absent from the memories that servants have of domestic labor and child care and from the stories they choose to tell about it. Colonial iconography is full of images of servants holding Dutch babies in the

Figure 34.   From a family album, ca 1890(?). Infant and nursemaid
flanked by the child's parents. Leo Haks Collection.

Figure 35.   In some family albums, nursemaids figure at the center of
photos but in captions remain unnoted or unnamed. The caption in this
family album reads "Aunt Let with little Arend." Leo Haks Collection.

Figure 36.   The caption in this family album
reads "Ida (4 yrs) and little Paul (3 months)."
Leo Haks Collection.

Javanese manner, wrapped about the woman's body and held there snugly
with a long cloth, known in Indonesian as "to *gendong*" (see figs. 21, 34,
38). Yet the majority of the women with whom we spoke said they had not
been allowed to carry the babies in their care in this way. Being forbidden
to gendong figured centrally in several accounts, epitomizing the contrast
of Javanese and Dutch child-rearing practices. Some invoked it to illustrate
the contexts in which they were criticized and their own disapproval of their
employers. Sometimes, not being allowed to gendong underscored their dis-
inclination to alien habits and practices. Ibu Kamsih recalled that the stric-
ture against carrying her charge was so absurdly rigid that he had to be
placed in a pram to be transported even within the house grounds.[81]

Ibu Rubi too spoke not of cozy intimacy but of how contact between children and servants was carefully controlled. She recalled wet nurses being required to change into clean, crisp white clothes before breast-feeding Dutch
babies so that the infants would be protected from the seep of their sweat.[82] She
remembered being told, "If the little boy cries, just let him be, you must not

Figure 37.

Figure 37–38.   Children, taken on as house servants in training, were called *genduk*. In these photos from a family album, the infant is held in a slendang and the young girl (genduk) is similarly holding a white doll. Leo Haks Collection.

Figure 39.   From family album. "Vic and Sarip,"
date unknown. Leo Haks Collection.

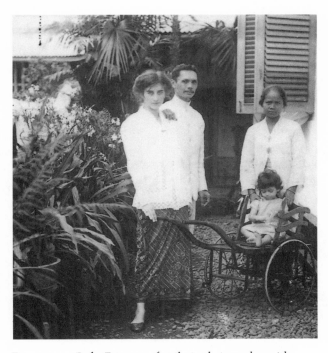

Figure 40.   'Indo-European family in their garden with servant, Batavia, West Java,' ca. 1915. KITLV, no. 13.342. Photographer probably Max Foltynski, Jr.

pick him up, you may not gendong him." When we asked why, she explained as if it were self-evident: "Later, he'd smell of my sweat."[83] Genduk Ginem (who asked us to call her by the name used by her Dutch employers), on the other hand, had been allowed to gendong but did not remember this contact nostalgically. She recalled having to carry children who were too old and heavy to be cradled in a slendang, whose bodies weighed heavily on hers.[84]

When we would mention the numerous photos of servants we had seen in family albums, most women expressed surprise and skepticism because they themselves had never held the children in that way, nor had they been asked to pose for such pictures. Only a few recalled snapshots being taken; no one had a picture of herself with the family for whom she worked. When we asked Bu Darmo if she had been photographed with her employers, she scoffed, "Dutch people would never have wanted a picture with Javanese," because they were simply not allowed to "mix." [85]

Figure 41.   Ibu Sastro with her diploma from
1940, April 1997. Privately owned.

Ibu Sastro remembered that her picture was once taken by an employer,
recalling with evident pleasure that her image had been "brought to
Holland."[86] Yet this photo was for her employer. She was not given a copy.
And when we asked if she had any from her many years of service, she
pulled out the one memento she had preserved: a worn and creased certificate
signed by a colonial officer and dated November 28, 1940. It announced that
she had passed a course in "electric stove cooking." This certificate bears a
small black-and-white photograph showing a young woman of serious expression and smoothly coiffed hair, testimony not to intimate ties but to professional status (fig. 41).

REVERBERATING REFRAINS: ON THE JUDGMENTS OF EXCESS

The difficulty lies in learning to conceive of history in such a way
that the concept no longer excludes repetition but registers its
vitality.[87]

Not surprisingly, Javanese servants' accounts were littered with bits of stories that Dutch colonials liked to tell about their charity and civilities. More interesting was how and when these were invoked, the different work they could do, and where they seemed to fall short. What at first appeared to be easy formulas designed to deflect unwelcome questions arrested us, over time, by the range of critique and comment they conveyed.

The label "good," so flat and empty that we first took it as an obstruction, became an unexpected point of entry. The power of "good" rested in the space left open by its descriptive thinness and blandly approving sense.[88] Calling a Dutch employer "good" clearly could place a dangerous story within a safe frame, as when Ibu Soekati recalled, "In my experience, I mean, all [of the Dutch I worked for] were good," and then immediately described how she had been practically raped by her employer while his wife and children were on vacation.[89]

Calling the Dutch "good" could serve to set them off from the "cruel" Japanese but might also register the finely shaded social (and racial) distinctions among Europeans. The "good" Dutch often meant the totok, or full-blooded Dutch, as opposed to mixed-bloods.[90] Operating as a class term, it could distinguish doctors, teachers, clergymen, and high-ranking government officials from "factory Dutch" ("Belanda fabrik"), "poor Dutch" ("Belanda miskin"), and "retired Dutch" ("Belanda pensionan") who were perceived as stingy and crude. One woman recalled that it was only the "factory Dutch" who had sex with Javanese women servants, never doctors and teachers. Another suggested that only "black Dutch" (Ambonese in the Dutch military) kept Javanese concubines. Those former servants who were Christian might use "good" to distinguish "Christian Dutch" from their less respectable compatriots. Some categories (such as "factory Dutch" and "red Dutch") differed from those found in Dutch colonial writings. But others seemed to reinscribe colonial distinctions, placing "full-blooded" bourgeois Dutch at the top of the colonial social scale.

Besides referencing stratifications in Dutch society, "the good Dutch" also suggested the tenor of specific relations within domestic space. "Good" was more often an assessment of how well an employer adhered to the tacit rules that both obeyed than an endorsement of Dutch character, more often an appraisal of specific comportments than a moral judgment. It could signal that an employer provided one with sufficient money to live and food to eat. For some, it marked those who said "please" before a command, or who called a person by name and not by the job he or she performed. For others, it distinguished those who trusted their servants enough not to bolt their cupboards and closets or inspect for hoarded change when a servant returned from the market. Some people used it to describe those who spoke in Javanese instead of barking commands in Dutch, while others reserved it as a stamp of approval on those Dutch who learned to maneuver the intricacies of high and low Javanese.

Used most often in the sense of "proper," "good" in no way muted the gestures of subordination built into colonial relations. Ibu Sastro, for example, described her colonial employers as "good" and then contrasted them with "today's Dutch," who are more respectful because they recognize that "Java belongs to the Javanese."[91] Even when the rules of "proper" domestic relations were followed, they were hardly fair. A "good" Dutch might get angry only if you had done something wrong. But Ibu Kilah recalled that even if she repeatedly scrubbed a dirty garment, if the stain remained she was "wrong."[92] People expressed anger most directly when speaking of employers who transgressed these tacit rules. Ibu Darmo recalled crying in rage when she was wrongly accused of stealing soap.[93] Ibu Kasan said she quit one evening because after being told no guests were coming for dinner, they did come, and she was berated by the adult daughter for not preparing enough food and accused of "having no brain." The young woman later came to her home and begged her to return, but she refused, saying, "I guess I can't work if I don't have a brain."[94]

Other attributes of the Dutch, their "cleanliness" and their "discipline," were called on in ways that could similarly convey multiple meanings. People's memories often seemed to gel around these catchwords. Ibu Rubi, for example, made Dutch "cleanliness" the leitmotiv of her account. She had worked in the 1930s and early 1940s for both Dutch and Indo employers, for Ambonese soldiers in the Dutch army, and, both before and after Independence, for Chinese-Indonesians.[95] She said of working in a Dutch home, "Everything was clean and healthy, [one had] a strong body. I lucked out."[96] But this apparent endorsement became less self-evident as her repeated statement that the Dutch were "clean" accumulated weight through her interviews. Repetition transformed a seemingly straightforward assessment into something else.

> R: I liked working for the Dutch, it was so perfectly clean. . . . The Dutch were, well, clean, healthy, the food was healthy. If you ate fish, what is it, you know, leftover fish that had been sitting around, they didn't like it. When you cooked, all kinds of things still had to be bloody when you cut into them. I didn't like it, but I was forced, made to eat it, to be healthy.

D: Eventually did you like it?

R: Yeah, I put it in my mouth, later I spit it out.

Ibu Rubi seems to approve concern for her health even as she rejects the attempt to impose that concern on her body.[97] She goes on to talk of clothes that had to be washed three times before they were acceptable to her employers, floors that had to be mopped several times a day, and kitchen utensils subject to daily spot checks. Repetition turns her words from the virtue of cleanliness to the effects of its excess. The more she underlines Dutch cleanliness, the more she seems to mock it. With her words of praise punctuated with anecdotes about servants forced to eat things against their will, the ground shifts to a Dutch obsession borne by those who worked for them. The fastidious concern shown by one of her employers for the cleanliness and health of a wet nurse, she emphasized, was not for the benefit of the servant but for the health of the Dutch infant she nursed. She was given "clean food" and medicine, "told to sleep there, forbidden to go home, because if she went home she'd be dirty. Her breast milk would be dirty."[98]

Yet if praise turned to critique in Ibu Rubi's account, it folded in on itself again when she recalled so absorbing these Dutch notions of cleanliness that she became estranged from her own "dirty" neighborhood (an experience also recounted by others). She told of returning to the village and furiously attempting to clean everything, even trying to mop dirt floors, to the surprise of her neighbors. When asked if they minded she says: "No, it was OK, it was for cleanliness, good health." Ibu Rubi condensed judgments in familiar tropes that could be turned to different ends. Her constant shuttling between praise and criticism unsettles any comfortable interpretation of "cleanliness" in her account.

"Cleanliness" was also ambiguous in Ibu Rubi's account, because the term is as charged in the present as it was in the past. Like "discipline," which also frequently punctuated people's accounts, "cleanliness" was both part of the repertoire of concepts that Dutch household manuals used to prescribe domestic relations and a catchword of the New Order. Government-sponsored billboards urged discipline and "a culture of cleanliness" as requisite virtues for a "developed" Indonesia.[99] Such historically dense vocabularies raise basic problems of interpretive license. To what degree were people's descriptions of the colonial past to be read as commentaries on the postcolonial present? And given that they must be to some extent "about" both, how to calibrate the relative weighting of the two? Ibu

Rubi's account evokes a relation to Dutch sensibilities that shifts over time, that swings between rejection and attraction—both in the colonial past and looking back from her vantage point of the present.

ON SENSE AND SENSIBILITY: MEMORIES OF THE CONCRETE

Our interviews tended to stay close to the mundane rhythms and concrete physicality of everyday life—not only because our questions were directed precisely to the intimacies of domestic work but also because people so resolutely held us there. Those memories recounted with the most energy and engagement were rooted firmly in the senses—in Dutch disciplines imposed on their bodies, in the repugnant or delicious tastes of Dutch foods, or in the clashes over child-rearing styles that so often produced friction between Dutch employers and the women they hired for child care. If telling eventful stories is one way of relating experience, telling the routine and the habitual is another.

That Javanese servants remembered tastes, smells, textures, and sounds so differently from their Dutch employers is unsurprising. This domestic space was, after all, "home" to the Dutch and "workplace" to their servants. Nor is it surprising that recollections of these clashes of sensibility were affectively charged. But the fact that affective memories are called up through the senses is perhaps more widely accepted than the fact that moral and political judgments are as well.[100] Feelings of being imposed on, of being bored, and of being judged and chided were not framed as personal testimonials of political injustice but were embedded in the sensory recall of the unremarkable, in the often minute emotional accommodations of the everyday.

People remembered detailed menus of meals eaten more than fifty years ago and would recite with energy and care each ingredient and each stage of preparation. This clustering of memories around practices of cooking and eating was obviously linked to food's symbolic power and daily importance. At times lists of foods cooked and prepared seemed assertions of specialized knowledge, displays of privileged familiarity, or recitals of sheer tedium, as when Ibu Kilah recalled, "Then, the only food [the Dutch] ate was potatoes, potatoes, always potatoes, potatoes with this, potatoes with that. . . . [P]otatoes, potatoes, potatoes nonstop, . . . with steak."[101] Food talk was a shared idiom, a shorthand to conjure up adaptations and differences muted and sharpened by what one swallowed. To say that a Dutch family "ate rice" was to identify them approvingly as acclimatized to the Indies (or as having some Javanese blood). Genduk Ginem recalled that one of her totok Nyonyas had "become Javanese," as evinced by the fact that she "rarely ate potatoes."[102] For Ibu Rubi to recount that the Ambonese soldiers ("black Dutch") for whom she had once worked slaughtered chickens by crushing their necks under their feet was to offer proof of their uncultured ways.[103]

Our questions about what the Dutch were like were frequently answered with discussions of the foods Dutch people ate. Initially, we took this turn to the concrete as a retreat from judgment, as a way of moving carefully onto neutral ground. What could be less risky than to respond that the Dutch were people who lived on potatoes? But when Ibu Adi said, "Everywhere the white Dutch are all the same. The food is the same,"[104] was she deflecting the question or commenting on the standardized "European" milieu that many totok Dutch so carefully tended and that she—through a different lens—observed?

Memories of eating Javanese food in the back quarters while employers ate Dutch food in the dining room were, for many, signature scenes of a cultural divide in the home. The sharing of food, by contrast, could be invoked to signal that those very differences were overcome or transgressed. Ibu Patmi had worked in her early teens for a Dutch widow and her adult daughter whom she remembered with great affection. She offered a recollection of eating with them at their dining room table as evidence of not being treated like a servant: "I was treated the same." This memory seemed to carry more weight than that of sleeping every night on the floor beside her Nyonya's bed.[105]

Food was remembered as a principal arena in which Dutch fears about contact and contamination were played out but also as a site where the seductive pull of Javanese ways often proved too powerful to resist. Several people recalled that Dutch children were not allowed to eat Javanese food sold on the street or slipped to them by servants in the back of the house. Ibu Sastro imitated her Tuan's warning not to buy his child *gudeg* (a sweet, spicy central Javanese stew) from streetside stands: "Don't give him rice and gudeg, later he'll know how good it is and won't want to eat potatoes."[106] But the child continued secretly to buy it and, she told us with delight, no longer wanted potatoes. Ibu Adi, with similar pleasure, recalled her employers' children sneaking into the kitchen to steal the *tempe* she was preparing for the servants' meal.[107]

Several men drew a comparison between the food they ate and that given to the beloved family dog. A mini-parable of colonial relations, this was one of the rare times that people called on a rehearsed and available narrative. Told almost identically by three of the six men, it detailed daily subordinations with humor and poignancy.[108] Pak Mulyo recalled that the pet dog had its own babu who prepared its special meals:

Even its plate gleamed. Its food, waah, when I saw it, . . . the food, it was just like the boss's. There was meat, there was egg. Stew. Wow, that's what I thought. . . . [S]ometimes I even said to the dog's babu, "Wah, just give it to me, Bu." "Yeah," she replied, "go ahead and help yourself. Later the boss will yank your ear."[109]

But if the subject of food often elicited vivid anecdotes, other questions evoked memories tied to the senses that emerged in less storied forms. Chronological ordering and narrated sequences of events did not dominate these recollections.[110] Storied segments were often overwhelmed by a jumble of lists, names, fragments of dialogue, foreign words, and gestures seemingly unmoored from narrative threads.[111] Litanies of seemingly obscure details contained muted affective strains. Long lists of tasks performed, foods cooked, and schedules imposed were not indifferent recollections. They registered, in ways no story could, the repetitive and often deadening regularity of domestic work.[112] When Genduk Ginem recited her daily routine of sixty years ago by the precise hour, she evoked the rigid and imposed rhythms of Dutch households and habits.[113]

If memories are forged into stories in uneven and incomplete ways, what is missed by focusing so resolutely on their narrative structure? As those who call attention to the sensory nature of memory remind us, oral historians too often focus on the disembodied "voice," a move that edits out inarticulate forms of remembering. In our interviews, gestures often evoked what language could not, as when Ibu Kilah suddenly cringed, her body unmistakably adopting the curled posture of a scared child, as she described witnessing her mother yelled at by an abusive employer. Pak Hardjo demonstrated how, as a young errand boy, he rocked the children in his arms and carried them on his back. When we asked how he felt when his employers left Indonesia, he was silent but used his hands to show how the tears ran down his face. Ibu Patmi frequently patted herself firmly on her head to show how her Nyonya showed approval and affection, saying "goed, goed" as she performed the gesture.

Interrupted with Dutch sounds and physical gestures, people's accounts blurred incomplete and intimate knowledge, invoking both the understood and the foreign. Recitations of remembered Dutch words—"eten, slepen, koken, wassen"—punctuated their accounts as if these words were emblems of the foreign codes they had to learn to work in Dutch homes. Their always partial mastery was expressed in the common assertion that one could understand Dutch but not speak it: the words "wouldn't come out." Ibu Sastro noted that one had to be "gutsy" *(berani)* to work in a Dutch home precisely because one had to confront a language only partially understood.[114] Ibu

Darmo too remembered overhearing her employers talking about which servants were trustworthy but understanding only the gist of their words.[115]

The partial nature of translation was evident in how Dutch curses were transformed into Javanese verbs: for doing something wrong one could be *di-godverdom* or *di-kerdom* or *di-verdoma* (with the Dutch curse "God damn you" here given a Javanese-Indonesian prefix indicating the passive voice). When asked to translate "Godverdom, zeg!" Ibu Rubi glossed it as "Ah, not like this!"[116] More often, people offered no translations when they imitated Dutch commands like "kom hier," conveying meaning instead through harsh tone and imperious gesture.

These concrete and sensory recollections of the everyday called up an intimate landscape of affective ties and asymmetric relations. Neither dramatic tales with sweeping moral judgments nor wrenching testimonials, they registered an uncomfortable space where servants' sensibilities jostled uneasily against those of their employers.

BEYOND THE STORIES WE WANT TO TELL

Ibu Darmo tells us she's eighty-one. With delight I say that my mother is too. She looks at me straight for the first time since we sat down and simply says: "I thought whites [*londo*] were all dead by that age. I didn't know they could live that long."

Ann's fieldnotes, July 12, 1997

Ibu Darmo receives us in a small sitting room behind her grocery store that opens onto the road. We are uncomfortable that there are five of us, and Dias waits outside. Nita and Didi have met with her before and are not as ill at ease as we are. Ibu Darmo is not ill at ease at all. She sits back with her legs crossed, looking us over. She neither satisfies us with redemptive rage and juicy tales nor offers a study of resigned accommodation. She merely tolerates our presence. She is as the French say *correct,* that is, minimally polite. No one makes us feel quite so stopped short. Reading through the transcripts of a previous interview, all five of us are struck by this elderly woman with her blunt phrases and keen memory for details and dialogued scenes. This is someone, we imagine, who might speak back to the archive in interesting ways that we could still hear.

But we imagined Ibu Darmo could speak back to the archives, perversely perhaps, because she more than anyone else with whom we spoke would not speak directly to us.[117] She addressed herself solely to Nita and Didi, as if we were not there. While others politely attended to our questions, she did

not bother to listen or appeared to find them incomprehensible. She had little interest in our venture. She offered no refreshment, by Javanese etiquette an obligatory part of this encounter. We were made to know not only
that we were an intrusion, but that there was little point in apologizing for
our presence or effusing our appreciation here. In response to Ann's misplaced effort to find some common ground in noting that her mother and
Ibu Darmo are the same age, Ibu Darmo halts us with her blunt response:
"I didn't know *londos* lived so long." Beginning and end of discussion.
Recalling for us that both Dutch adults and children called her "Babu" and
not by her own name, she has little interest in making connections with our
kin. Ann's mother was an aged white, an unusual category of persons in
colonial Java, as she noted, but a "londo" nonetheless.

Unlike others whose recollections were more haltingly told, Ibu Darmo
could fluently recount how she first began working for her Tuan, the names
of his children, and her many time-consuming tasks. But the spareness of her
account stood out more than the acuity of her recall. These were not warm
recollections. When we asked if she had since heard from one of the daughters
who had left Java at nineteen, she said indifferently, "I have no idea about her
now, I don't know if she's alive or not, I don't know." She imitated acrimonious
dialogues between the two grown daughters but offered no anecdotes of affection, no grumbling endearments, no kind words. Instead she conveyed how
tedious and burdensome the work had been. She was supposed to be a wash-
erwoman but was called on to sweep, dust paintings, and do ironing that had
to be finished long after she was supposed to go home for the day. She described conflicts between the servants, like the time she advised the cook and
the houseboy not to steal and they gave her the silent treatment for weeks.[118]

Her recollections were neither scripted nor soothing. She was dismissive
rather than degraded, disdainful rather than defiant. We left after a short
visit, disquieted by her willingness to share her memories even as she rejected our eagerness to commiserate and share in them. But to celebrate Ibu
Darmo's refusal to engage us may be to be charmed all over again.

In the past decade, students of colonial studies have turned their attention to representations of colonial pasts and the subaltern voices submerged
within them. That work has sought to resituate popular experience and subjugated knowledge at the center of nationalist histories rather than as marginalized addenda to them. Whether colonial history is conceived as a
"scarce resource" or a marker of the modern, the work of remembering
other colonial pasts in the form of counterhistories carries a sense of urgency as contemporary political demands are fueled by indictments of colonial categories and claims.[119]

We had intended to speak back to the colonial archive and to Dutch nostalgia, to pierce the dense weave of public documents and family archives in which those memories were secured, to counter the literary and archival caricatures that swung between servant as icon of danger and as metonym of the loyal colonized. Yet in talking with people who had worked sporadically as youths, at intervals as married couples, and even as longtime retainers in Dutch colonial homes, it was not "colonial memories" per se that were poised for extracting a different historical rendering. Our attention was instead arrested by the ways in which people moved between formulaic refrains and concrete detail, between Javanese politesse and blunt Dutch curse, from recipe ingredients and dry shopping lists to dramatic reenactments of pointed dialogues. Their recollections of touch, taste, and smell were not shaped into tidy plots, much less congealed as anti-Dutch resistance narratives. Moving fluidly between the 1930s and the Japanese occupation, between the present and the 1950s—between dense layerings of other aspects of people's lives—these accounts refused the colonial as a discrete domain of social relations and politics, of experience and memory.

Attending to memory-work does not mean abandoning entirely the project of speaking back to colonialist histories and nostalgia. It does mean letting go of some received wisdoms and cherished assumptions—that the colonial is ever present in postcolonial lives; that postcolonial subjectivity by definition pivots on the transition from the colonial to the postcolonial; that there are subaltern circuits in which colonial critiques are lodged; that there is resistance in the smallest of gestures and the very lack of gesture at all; and that telling of the colonial past is a therapeutic act. Opening these up as questions to be asked, instead of treating them as foregone conclusions, makes it less easy to take interpretive license, less easy to be sure of what we know about the colonial, and less comfortable with some postcolonial claims. It invites more work on colonial memory itself while making "the colonial" a subject rather than an assumed category of analysis.

Epilogue
Caveats on Comfort Zones
and Comparative Frames

Inspired in part by the feminist insistence that the personal is political, these essays have taken up different tensions produced or played out in sites of the intimate to understand what made the "private" such a charged "public"colonial domain. At one level, the concerns addressed here are now familiar: the making and unmaking of categories; the cultural competencies that went into designations of race. I have tried to steer between an approach that neither dwells on the fixity and immobility of colonial categories nor treats them as radically contingent and wholly up for grabs. My impulse instead has been to focus on the processes in between, on scrutiny of convention as well as moments of crisis that made anxieties and fears into political forces and social things, that escalated concerns about "white prestige" and tied affirmations of "moral respectability" to sexual prescription and the making of race.

I have suggested that dissension within the lower European ranks could unsettle what it meant to be European as did the surreptitious entry of "fabricated Europeans" whose membership was elusive and whose numbers could not be counted or kept in check. I have argued that a sense of longing and belonging rather than skin color alone marked mixed-bloods and impoverished whites as potential subversives, as racialized renegades, and as the "enemy within" whose hearts and minds were on the line. But such uncertainties were not only prompted by those on the racial margins as students of contact zones have learned to expect. Dutch residents in the Indies worried over the interior frontiers of their communities in their ostensibly most cloistered and securest sites, within their families and within their homes.

Like the field of colonial studies itself, this book reflects a rejection of the facile fixity of racial categories, but it has sometimes embraced fixities of other sorts.[1] For even with a recognition of the porousness of social labels, the specific histories of racialized designations and their strategic and sometimes short-lived political uses can get lost nonetheless. At least part of the problem might be sought in how we fashion analytic frames in ways that freeze postcolonial concepts and colonial categories as shortcuts, what Bernard Cohn once referred to as "summary statements," that preclude rather than promote further historical analysis.[2] The challenge is still to account for the *temporary* fixity of terms such as "white prestige," "poor whites," "métissage," and "bourgeois respectability," how they congealed and then were refigured in any given colonial context.

One antidote is to maintain a stronger commitment to a notion of *working* concepts. I mean "working" in several senses of the term: concepts that we *work with* to track variation in their use and usefulness; concepts that *do work* to destabilize received historical narratives; concepts that are "working" in the sense that they are *provisional* rather than placeholders, subject to review and revision rather than fully formed; concepts that invite scrutiny rather than block it. The most important notion of working concepts for colonial studies, then, are ones that are "working" in the sense that they promote analytic openings and are subject to change. Ian Hacking argues that social constructionism has become stale, but I disagree.[3] Indeed, I think we need to take it more seriously, to treat what Foucault called those "ready-made syntheses" that make up the dimensions of interpretation as new objects of analysis.

ON COMPARATIVE FRAMES

My starting point in this book may have seemed curious to students who have been schooled in the Foucauldian credo that knowledge is power and that colonial regimes were masterful at acquiring both. These chapters started from another premise: colonial regimes were uneven, imperfect, and even indifferent knowledge-acquiring machines.[4] Omniscience and omnipotence were not, as we so readily assume, their defining goals. More important, they were part of what I have called "taxonomic states," whose administrations were charged with defining and interpreting what constituted racial membership, citizenship, political subversion, and the scope of the state's jurisdiction over morality.[5]

Preoccupations with taxonomies conjure up censuses and cartographies commissioned by colonial administrations, detailed studies of ethnographic, legal, and botanical minutiae that were the stuff of imperial expertise and social control. But taxonomies demand more than specification and detail.

As Jim Scott too notes, "seeing like a state" may encourage just the oppo-site—that its agents master not sociological fine print but broad simplified sociological generalizations.[6] Taxonomic states may encourage state agents to pay less attention to detail than to sorting codes. Psychologists convinc-ingly argue that taxonomies reduce cognitive expense. Colonial adminis-trators seemed to treat them as technologies that reduced political expense as well. In the Indies, social categories that were "easy to think" pared down what colonial recruits and residents thought they needed to master. Sociological shorthands lessened how much of certain kinds of information one needed to operate and how much one needed to know.

Category-making projects of this sort, by definition, produce commen-surabilities. They facilitate comparisons, but they also flatten out variations across time and space. What they say about colonial states may be different from what we imagine. Colonial bureaucracies invested in selective and strategic comparison, highlighting similarities to some polities and differ-ences from others. Colonial taxonomies produced equivalences based on a mix of prescribed similitudes and cued distinctions—and the implicit man-date that others be ignored. They registered two political fictions—that tax-onomies catalog differences rather than produce them and that taxonomies document social membership rather than create the subject positions and affiliations that made up colonial worlds.[7]

Take such a common element of colonial lexicons as "white prestige." Sometimes it appears in histories of the colonial as a folk category of colo-nial elites, as an internal, culturally located representation of inequities. At other times it appears as an analytic tool, something beyond the use of its colonial practitioners, that can be used by historians to explain colonial proj-ects designed to maintain inequalities. But "white prestige" in itself accounts for too little and too much. How can it provide the raison d'être for main-taining concubinage and the raison d'être for its abolition? How can it ac-count for both the recruitment of European women and their forbidden entry into specific colonies? What does it mean when "the protection of white prestige" is called on to explain why workers were killed in one colo-nial context and why servants are housed in the back courtyard in another? "White prestige" looks less like an explanation than part of a "just so" story—less an analytic tool than a narrative feature in a colonial box.

Still, as a folk category it is invoked in a range of colonial contexts. The question is not how something like "white prestige" *functioned* to main-tain rule and how domestic arrangements functioned for both—an issue on which students of colonialism have dwelled too long. Instead we might ask why the category was so resonant and relevant, what sentiments it mobilized, and what conditions and circumstances were thought to put this *thing* called "white prestige" in jeopardy? What were its attributes? How was it measured? What kinds of subjects did it produce? What was on the line? What did French colons or Dutch civil servants have to believe about what they were doing to imagine that it mattered? Did they use "white prestige" because they believed in it, or did they believe it because they used it? Or was it merely a plausible rationale in the colonial habitus in which they operated for something they did not believe at all? "White prestige" was not a stable signifier that worked this way or that. We need to ask how it circulated, what work it did, and what other social relations it indexed, enabled, and prohibited, and with what specific racial effects.[8]

The category "mixed-bloods" raises a similar problem, as does the notion of métissage. In chapters 3 and 4 I underscore the subversive quality of métissage, arguing that mixed unions were perceived as a political danger because they complicated the criteria by which Europeanness could be identified and nationality assigned. Such unions threatened both to destabilize national identity and the Manichaean categories of ruler and ruled. But this was not always the case. "Mixed-bloods" and the category "mixing" were *not* subversive in themselves.[9] To say that "mixed-bloods" were a threat to the colonial state is to miss the ways in which mixing could provide access to some privileges while it sharply blocked access to others. Flexibility and ambiguity in racial identifications could contribute to racialized distinctions as well. Recurrent debates over who was "mixed" could as easily confirm as contest truth-claims about other bold-faced social categories.[10] These discourses work better as diagnostics of stress points than as metonyms for empire writ large. Whether such discourses are viewed as subversive or as something easily contained—and how fast that could change— are historical questions. Métissage operated on the frayed edges of taxonomies that were at the core of colonialisms' inconsistent racial politics.

This is not to make the obvious point that mixedness meant different things in different places at different times. Rather it is to argue that shifts in the density, frequency, and sequence of attention to mixed unions by those who ruled should turn us in another direction: to the historical specificities of its occurrence, to the rules that governed its appearance, to the ways in which a particular set of relations and discourses about those relations could, as Foucault put it so well, "arouse opposing strategies" and make it possible, "with a particular set of concepts, to play different games."[11]

The problem is not unique to colonial studies, nor are its effects. How do we steer between an adherence to colonialism's folk categories and a misguided sense of commonality based on our own? Are comparative colonial analyses so few because we are unsure what units of analysis are productive to compare? Students of colonialisms engage less in comparison than in parallel play.[12] We juxtapose context, borrow and trade on one another's analytic distinctions, and then claim common patterns and convergent governing strategies.

"Folk" categories such as "mixed-bloods" and "poor whites" beg for wider comparisons because they appear in such a wide range of colonial contexts. But as categories of administrative and scientific expertise they are not unproblematic. As part of the moral science of statecraft in metropolitan and colonial states, these designations derived from the same technology that consolidated statistics, censuses, and their commensurabilities in the nineteenth century. With transnational currency, they produced cross-colonial equivalences that allowed for international conferences and convinced their participants—anthropologists, geographers, doctors, lawyers, policy makers, and reformers—that they were participating in the same conversation if not always talking about the same thing.

If the above is granted, then as historians of the colonial we might think not to ask whether métissage in the Indies and India was really the same or how it differed but to move in another direction—in a more self-consciously critical comparative frame. One task would entail treating these comparative categories more as ethnographic evidence of historically shifting strategies of rule, as part of the cultural expertise that allowed colonialisms to work as both reformist and racist projects.[13] In such a view, we would not compare colonies so much as seek to identify the "grids of intelligibility" that were operating and that allowed specific comparisons to be made when they were.

This in its turn would yield yet another focus—one on the history and politics of comparison, on the political task of comparing and on what features of colonial governance it served. We might ask what the political stakes were in celebrating some similarities and disavowing others. We might ask not about the similarities of particular (racialized) entities but about the common set of *relationships* (to the wider colonial polity and to other racial categories) they shared and that made such comparisons pertinent and possible.[14]

Colonial studies scholarship identifies striking similarities in policy and practice: patterns of panic, discourses reiterated, outrages rehearsed, and fantasies shared. But no one would argue that the former Dutch East Indies, British India, French Indochina, and the Belgian Congo looked everywhere and from anywhere the same. Nor were the strategies of rule forged into or the effects of cohered, transnational plans. The point is rather to pursue the overlapping and crosscutting circuits of persons and policies that made their way from metropole to colony and the other way around (and are readily documented in well-worn archival tracks), as well as those that connected metropolitan centers, cut along horizontal axes within colonized regions, and produced circuits of knowledge production that traversed imperial borders and were not confined by them.[15]

THINKING THROUGH GENDER IN COLONIAL STUDIES

Studies of gender and empire have shown persuasively that key symbols of the colonial state were secured by the ways in which gender was regulated, sexuality was patrolled, and race was policed. Recent studies have given new weight to earlier claims that "domesticity," the "civilizing mission," and the paternalism of liberalism were all endowed with gendered predicates.[16] The analytic vocabulary of empire no longer looks like a lexicon of virile, masculine practices but like a gendered grid of contained and contested tasks that produced a politics of compassion, compliance, and coercion that differently positioned women and men.

Nor have we merely treated the familial domain as a powerful metaphor for the political or as a source of its fantasies. Private sentiments and public policy come together in the colonial not only because family relations provided the vocabulary for political narratives, as Lynn Hunt argues for revolutionary France, not only because the family was a "kind of prepolitical category for organizing political experience," but because domestic and familial intimacies were critical political sites in themselves where racial affiliations were worked out.[17]

But questions remain. If the impetus and energy from work on the intimacies of empire have come from unsettling assumptions about the nature of colonial rule and from refusing to bracket the colonial, what is it that studies of the carnal, the intimate, and the colonial are unsettling today? How does that work stay uncomfortable, as effective history and as a politically accountable act? David Scott asks a similar question of postcolonial criticism: "whether or not [the] questions continue, in the conjuncture at hand, to constitute questions *worth having answers to.*"[18] The issue is important because while the last decade of studies on gender and empire has placed its concerns squarely at the center of broader research agendas, that affirmation has sometimes had a paradoxical effect. Instead of destabilizing and revising colonial histories, its cumulative weight risks conferring a predictability on postcolonial analyses that presupposes the neat fit between gender inequities and colonial rule—that confirms rather than questions, that substantiates rather than subverts. Conceptual frames should not be inert structures that allow historical particulars to be filled in for given contexts but frames of possibility that prompt a reworking of their constituent concepts.

Similarly, studying how colonialisms' gendered metaphors were racially coded takes us only so far. It may point compellingly to how discursive practices shape behavior. But when the language of rule stays constant and policies subtly or violently change, we need to attend closer to the relationship between prevailing metaphors and particular practices. In chapters 2 and 3, I refer to how gendered prescriptions were mobilized to uphold white prestige. But who cared about that prestige, and who talked about it? Those who had it, those on the verge of losing it, those who wanted it, or those who did not? Similarly, European women were positioned as the guardians of morality in a range of imperial contexts. These were gendered assignments that scripted what women were compelled to do as mothers, daughters, sisters, and wives, what marriage choices they made, how they arranged their homes and schooled their young. But the notion of the European woman as moral guardian cannot be called on to make sense of some constraints and be put aside when it does not make sense of others. We should be able to account for when the model was suspended and rendered less relevant, when this gendered language of rule converged or diverged from how living and labor arrangements changed.

All of which raises a troubling question: have the analytic notions of "domestication," "sexual management," and "bourgeois morality" become dead metaphors rather than working concepts that both do work and are subject to change? Rehearsing the instrumentality of gendered divisions to rule or the functional compatibility of domestic arrangements for colonial politics may have disrupted the ready-made syntheses of colonial history a decade ago but may no longer work that way today. If analyses of colonial domesticity produce pat and stable narratives, here again it may be because the vocabulary of domesticity has been assigned too much explanatory weight and remains only loosely tied back to colonialisms' macropolitics. As an analytic convention, it may hollow out the politics of a critique that drew mainstream political history back inside the nursery, bedroom, kitchen, and home. The task is to work harder with the concepts rather than throw them out.

Thus in chapter 3 I point to the range of sexual and social relations that "concubinage" could entail and the different political purposes to which discourses about it were put. But we still know little about the varied relations of intimacy and service that "concubinage" glossed: when it was a viable option for women but disappeared from administrative view; how women manipulated its terms, reinvented its meanings, and constrained how it changed. Similarly, my discussion of "morality" underscored its frequent appearance as a motivation for policy, as a criterion for who might be considered European and who might not. But morality was invoked to discount reasoned judgments in some contexts and appropriate sentiments in others. Like "bourgeois respectability," it explains what motivated colonial policy only if we take the terms of a colonial lexicon to explain itself. It is not a history of terms we need so much as new histories of the changing force fields in which such terms operated.

Much of this literature on gender and empire has tacked tentatively between a feminist concern that focuses on women, their daring or despair, and one that focuses on the ways in which a wider domain was shaped by gendered sensibilities and sexual politics. The first tends to stop at the threshold of women's direct agency and direct presence; the latter does not. The first tends to show how the subordination of women in some fashion functioned for imperial enterprises; the second takes insights about gendered relations to make sense of geopolitics.

Tacking back and forth is not a problem in itself. But as many feminist historians long have argued, a broader gendered history may offer more than women's history tout court. The ways in which colonial intimacies were managed did more than illustrate larger dilemmas. They were, as colonial officials and early welfare state planners clearly placed them, at the heart of racial reasoning and repeatedly invoked in colonial politics.[19] Nor were these discourses the concerns only of those who ruled. As Foucault insisted, official and valorized discourses contain disqualified knowledge. Dominant discourses (like those on racial purity and white women, like Georges Hardy's on white women looking after white men, like that on concubinage as a "necessary evil" to deter men from desiring other men) were constructed out of sanctioned social formulas but also shaped by rejected ones.[20]

Subjugated knowledge, unsanctioned idioms, and disqualified practices were not outside official knowledges but folded as preserved possibilities within them. Such a line of inquiry opens to readings against the grain of colonial archives in ways that lead to alternative perspectives if not subaltern accounts. But it also leads elsewhere—to rejected proposals, to incoherencies of official discourse, to potential disruptions of what counted as knowledge and who qualified as its arbiters. Such a reading along the archival grain turns attention to unexpected perturbations over racial membership, such as those by Javanese and Dutch women who rejected certain measures of civility and status. It turns attention to dislocated persons, to cultural renegades unwilling to be counted among their "kind." It is this range of unruly practices more than the unsullied "small voices" of history that we should expect to find.

Racial taxonomies thus were not the unilateral inventions of colonial and metropolitan states. Their points of contention and densities of debate signaled points of stress and conflict among colonial groups and across their divides. The politics of intimacy showed itself in how people crafted and disregarded convention, affirmed distinctions, adhered to them in public, violated them "in private," and refused the state's bid for public affirmation of private relations again and again. Colonial ethnographies of the affective and intimate press on these disparities. They disallow neat stories; they muddy the waters, confuse the claims; they cloud vision with visceral responses of those—colonial subjects and agents, women and men—who encroached on the boundaries in which they themselves were invested and for which they sometimes had drawn the sharpest lines.

Focusing on carnal knowledge and imperial power does more than bring issues of gender and sexuality from the margins to center stage. Luise White's account in *The Comforts of Home* of how prostitutes in colonial Nairobi organized their work in a restricted urban space invited us to question the extent of colonial interventions in private lives and the state's limits of rule.[21] More recent work on the state regulation of prostitution enjoins us to consider the international traffic in women and children as part of a biopolitics that was both transnational and requisitioned to serve specific colonial social policies.[22] But it was in the informal traffic in sexual and domestic services making up the commonplace habitus of colonial relations between women and men that the contingencies of citizenship, the power of race to determine child custody, and the intimate injuries of empire were played out.

ON THE CARNAL AND COLONIAL SCRIPTS

The Pro Juventute society was one of many social reform groups active in the Indies in the early twentieth century. With branches in the major urban centers of European residence across Java (Bandung, Batavia, Yogyakarta, Malang, Semarang, and Surabaja) and in Padang in Sumatra, it was an organization devoted to children at risk, partly state-subsidized but mostly dependent on private contributions and charitable aid.[23] Pro Juventute was a child relief agency, a clearinghouse that served as a temporary home for juvenile delinquents and abandoned, neglected, homeless, orphaned, abused, and apparently "slow" children who were to be farmed out to mental institutions, boarding schools, reformatories, foster families, and, in some cases, eventually back to their mothers or fathers.

Each annual report included a long list of case reports of no more than a paragraph each. Most were sketchy and unadorned. As a charity-based organization, its reports were solicitations for compassion and financial support. But they may also be read as intimate, if spare, ethnographies of empire that document living arrangements, social acts, and cultural practices that rarely appear in histories of the colonial. They register unexpected sentiments in discrepant details that were the product of colonial categories but defied colonial prescriptions, of attachments that got in the way of benevolent intervention and rescue operations. Here are four case reports, striking because they are so matter-of-fact about illegitimacy and child neglect, because they convey unusual dependencies and arrangements to deal with indigence as if they were ordinary if not banal.

> Case 42 (from 1934): On a visit to the native quarters in Jogjakarta our Officer noticed a very blond girl, apparently a European child, who was living with an old Javanese. The man, an ex-soldier, said that after having been pensioned, he had taken up residence in Singapore. There he had a friend (a Javan) who lived with a poor English woman—of which the girl N . . . must be the child. When both parents died, he took the girl N . . . with him and later returned to Java. The child is very slow and because the man is old and fears that after his death, the girl might fall into bad hands, in accord with the advice of a psychiatrist he has approved that the Pro Juventute will entrust the further care of the little one to the Directress of the Mental Institute in Temanggoeng.[24]

> Case 13 (from 1937): Mother L . . . , a European woman, supported by Poor Relief, died in very poor circumstances with two uncared for little boys left behind. The woman, years ago, had had a relationship with a Javanese, out of which both boys issued. On the demand of the Poor Relief, supported by the police, Pro Juventute intervened in the case and admitted the boys in Our Group House. The oldest, however, was soon taken away by his father, although he had not concerned himself with the children for many years. The youngest boy, badly underfed and sickly, remained in our Settlement house but after some time ran away. In tracking him down, he turned out to be with his father.

> Case 44 (from 1940): L . . . , a European[,] has lived for 21 years with an Indonesian woman. He had legally recognized his child, Erna, who is 9 years old. Recently there have been scenes between the man and woman and he found fault with her in everything she did. It appeared that the man had fallen in love with another woman. The Indonesian woman wanted to leave and returned to her birthplace and because she

was very attached to the child and the child to the mother, Erna was put in the St. Vicentius settlement house in Batavia.

Case 45 (from 1940): At P . . . , deep in the native quarter, lived an old Indonesian women with a small pension from her dead [European] husband. She has in her care two children who have been given European equivalent status. She did not get much pleasure from these children. The oldest, a boy, was lazy; the youngest, a girl of 15, for whom our help was requested, was not too diligent and also impudent. To protect the girl against moral ruin . . . it was urgent that this child have a disciplined environment and more supervision. She was placed in the St. Vicentius settlement house in Batavia.

Few colonial records convey so starkly this range of lifestyles, mixtures of family settings, and movements of people living on the colonial edge. Such stories are the stuff of popular fiction. Few colonial histories linger in these tense and tender sites or dwell on why an Indonesian mother of a mixed-blood child for whom she cared would have to give her up to a settlement house. Few could fill in the story of that estranged Javanese father whose children (considered European) chose to run away from an orphanage for Europeans to live in the native quarter with him. How would one make sense of the boys' choice if the father was cut off and without ties to them as the case report suggests? One could account easily for the currency of a representation that placed a fifteen-year-old European girl "deep in the native quarter" but not the trajectory of such a life. Contemporary histories of the colonial allow for ambiguous categories but not the severed lives that colonialisms' racial policies produced. No histories of colonial Indonesia describe the house visits of child savers who, with reformist zeal, passed judgment on moral environments and then decided when and where to remove light-skinned children from their native mothers. Few could find occasion to draw on the hundreds of cases of "unmanageable children" left by their European fathers with their native mothers who could not acclimatize them to native village life—or why some were allowed to return to their native fathers.

More striking still is the fact that these are not case histories from an old Indische Indies of a discarded, disparaged, and retrograde kind: on the contrary, the Pro Juventute was the product of modern Dutch colonialism, a humanist and philanthropic one on the eve of World War II. Its annual case reports were funded by and consumed along with advertisements contributed by Plymouth car dealers, upscale French toiletry suppliers, electrical home appliance stores, Jewish optometrists, and Chinese law offices on the same pages. The argument that colonialism does not precede modernism but is the underside of it is vividly illustrated here.[25] Students of colonialism have shown that liberalism and colonialism, social reform and colonial racism, were not contradictory political impulses but were woven out of the same imperial cloth. But a social world that so easily juxtaposed "old-time" colonial domestic relations (between native concubine and European colonial) to the fetishes of modernity is something that we have just begun to mark.[26]

What is surprising in these case reports is not only the unfamiliar social landscape but also the breadth of movement in it: the mobility of a Javanese former soldier who decided to live in Singapore and then returned to Java; a "Javan" friend living with but not married to a poor English girl with whom he had a child; a blond-haired, "apparently European," "backward girl" living in a Javanese village until she was "discovered" by a social worker and returned to her "kind"; a psychiatrist (employed by whom?) on call to evaluate the girl's mental and moral condition, with the solution being her permanent residence in a hill station mental institute in central Java. Most of the actors are familiar, but their movements, locations, and scrambled relations are not.

Students of colonialism have concentrated on certain stories of the colonial because we have bought in to colonial scripts themselves. Although we are now better prepared to argue that the categories of colonized and colonizer were never given, we have done less to identify the complicated affective landscape that these protean categories produced. When Foucault wrote that "all sentiments have a history," he offered an invitation without providing a blueprint for the task. Identifying the "structures of feeling" in which race and colonial power were forged is a challenging project that is still being mapped. The sentiments of "false pride" (attributed to poor whites), of the "impudence" of mixed-blood children, or the compassion and display of sympathies so crucial to being white and middle-class were judgments of class status and racial expectation. They were ascriptions of casts of mind and racially loaded affective markers.

Discovering why colonial archives were written can only partially shape how they are later read. Our readings of colonial archives can recoup those sites in which common sense was crafted to understand the vulnerabilities of these imperial projects and the fears they engendered. In such a frame, nursemaids, children, kindergartens, and orphanages no longer seem out of place when they appear as the subjects of state commissions on race, when they are hushed up as state secrets that were both inside and outside colonial control.

We need to appreciate how colonial authority was fashioned, how cultural resources were allocated, and how the production of sentiments worked with and against the production of privilege, allocations of labor, and distributions of wealth. Refocusing on the cultural work that colonial states imagined they could do allows a richer sense of what shaped the colonial landscape and what was decidedly beyond its micromanagement. But people such as those above whose lives cut unfamiliar paths across the distinctions of rule suggest still other structures of feeling in formation, other sites of power to identify, a wider range of sources to consider, and, not least, other kinds of memories to call on and stories to tell.

Notes

CHAPTER 1. GENEALOGIES OF THE INTIMATE

1. Georges Hardy, quoted in C. Chivas-Baron, *La femme française aux colonies* (Paris: Larose, 1929).

2. The Netherlands Indies is by some accounts a unique empire, by others quintessential in just about every way. Similarly, some consider it an "old" colony, others do not. Although Dutch presence in the Indies dates from as early as the late sixteenth century (thus the common statement, "three hundred fifty years of Dutch rule"), the Dutch colonial state did not. It took form only after the collapse of the Dutch East Indies Company (VOC) and at the end of the British interregnum. Building on the administrative work of the VOC, it emerged in the 1820s, coming rapidly into its own in midcentury. See Cees Fasseur, *De Indologen: Ambtenaren voor de Oost, 1825–1950* (Amsterdam: Bert Bakker, 1993). By 1930 there were 50 million people classified as European and 60 million classified as "native" *(inlander)*. On Java alone there were 193,000 "Europeans" in 1930 and 40 million "natives." See Jacobus van Doorn, *De Laatste Eeuw van Indie: Ontwikkeling en Ondergang van een Koloniaal Project* (Amsterdam: Bert Bakker, 1994). On the racial landscape of the Indies, see W. Prins,"De Bevolkingsgroepen in het Nederlandsche-Indische Recht," *Koloniale Studien* 17 (1933): 652–88; A.van Marle, "De Groep der Europeanen in Nederlands-Indie, iets over Ontstaan en Groei," *Indonesie* 5, no. 2 (1952):

77–121; 5, no. 3 (1952): 314–41; 5, no. 5 (1952): 481–507; Cees Fasseur, "Cornerstone and Stumbling Block: Racial Classification and the Late Colonial State in Indonesia," in *The Late Colonial State in Indonesia: Political and Economic Foundations of the Netherlands Indies, 1880–1942*, ed. Robert Cribb (Leiden: KITLV Press, 1994), 31–56.

3. For a recent effort in that direction, see Elsbeth Locher-Scholten, *Women and the Colonial State: Essays on Gender and Modernity in the Netherland Indies, 1900–1942* (Amsterdam: Amsterdam University Press, 2000).

4. Close attention to the categories of colonial rule has had a range of inspirations. One runs from Marx through British labor history (E. P. Thompson and Douglas Hays) to subaltern studies. Another can be traced through Gramsci and Foucault to Said. Yet another was animated by Bernard Cohn's work at the nexus of anthropology and history on censuses and representations of colonial authority ("The Census, Social Structure and Objectification in South Asia," in *An Anthropologist among the Historians and Other Essays* [Delhi: Oxford University Press, 1987], 224–53). Among those who pick up on these latter threads, see Arjun Appadurai's "Numbers in the Colonial Imagination," in *Modernity at Large* (Minneapolis: University of Minnesota Press, 1996), 114–35; Nicholas B. Dirks's work on caste, *The Hollow Crown: Ethnohistory of an Indian Kingdom* (Cambridge: Cambridge University Press, 1987); and Gyan Prakash, "Science 'Gone Native' in Colonial India," *Representations* 40 (1992): 153–78. My own trajectory shifted from a focus on political economy, on the categories that facilitated strategies of labor control in colonial Indonesia, to a broader set of categories of rule and their racial epistemologies. These shifts are evident in Ann Laura Stoler, "Perceptions of Protest: Defining the Dangerous in Colonial Sumatra," *American Ethnologist* 16, no. 4 (1985): 642–58; and "Racial Histories and Their Regimes of Truth," *Political Power and Social Theory* 11 (1997): 183–255. They are discussed further in the 1995 preface to *Capitalism and Confrontation in Sumatra's Plantation Belt, 1870–1979* (New Haven: Yale University Press, 1985).

5. See Ian Hacking's "The Looping Effect of Human Kinds," in *Causal Cognition: A Multidisciplinary Debate*, ed. Dan Sperber, David Premack, and Ann Premack (Oxford: Oxford University Press, 1995), 351–83.

6. For discussion of the "latent" and "patent" in racial epistemologies, see my "Racial Histories," 183–255.

7. These genealogies have been traced elsewhere. See, for example, my 1995 preface to *Capitalism and Confrontation in Sumatra's Plantation Belt, 1870–1979;* Nancy Rose Hunt's introduction to the special issue "Gendered Colonialism in African History," *Gender and History* 8, no. 3 (1996): 323–37; Gyan Prakash's introduction to *After Colonialism: Imperial Histories and Postcolonial Displacements*, ed. Gyan Prakash (Princeton: Princeton University Press, 1995), 3–20. Also see Frederick Cooper's and my introduction to *Tensions of Empire: Colonial Cultures in a Bourgeois World* ("Between Metropole and Colony: Toward a New Research Agenda") (Berkeley: University of California Press, 1997), 1–58; Peter Pels's "The Anthropology of Colonialism: Culture,

History, and the Emergence of Western Governmentality," *Annual Review of Anthropology* 26 (1997): 163–83; and Catherine Hall's introduction to *Cultures of Empire: A Reader*, ed. Catherine Hall (Manchester: Manchester University Press, 2000), 1–33.

8. Some do so more directly than others. See, for example, Vron Ware, *Beyond the Pale: White Women, Racism and History* (New York: Verso, 1992); Robert Young, *Colonial Desire: Hybridity in Theory, Culture and Race* (London: Routledge, 1995); Anne McClintock, *Imperial Leather: Race, Gender, and Sexuality in the Colonial Contest* (New York: Routledge, 1995); Françoise Vergès, *Monsters and Revolutionaries: Colonial Family Romance and Métissage* (Durham, N.C.: Duke University Press, 1999).

9. See Nancy Rose Hunt, " 'Le bébé en brousse': European Women, African Birth Spacing, and Colonial Intervention in Breast Feeding in the Belgian Congo," in Cooper and Stoler, *Tensions of Empire*, 287–321; Jean Comaroff and John Comaroff, "Home-made Hegemony: Modernity, Domesticity, and Colonial Domination in South Africa," in *African Encounters with Domesticity*, ed. Karen Tranberg Hansen (New Brunswick, N.J.: Rutgers University Press, 1992), 37–74; Rosemary M. George, "Homes in the Empire, Empires in the Home," *Cultural Critique* (Winter 1994): 95–127; Vicente L. Rafael, "Colonial Domesticity: White Women and United States Rule in the Philippines," *American Literature* 67 (December 1995): 639–66; McClintock, *Imperial Leather*, esp. chaps. 2, 3; and Julia Clancy-Smith and Frances Gouda, eds., *Domesticating the Empire: Race, Gender, and Family Life in French and Dutch Colonialism* (Charlottesville: University Press of Virginia, 1998).

10. Studies of empire and manliness have multiple genealogies. Some of that work traces through Frantz Fanon's *Black Skin, White Masks*, trans. Charles Lam Markmann (New York: Grove Press, [1952] 1967). Other inspirations come from work on fascism, nazism, and sexuality, most notably George H. Mosse's *Nationalism and Sexuality: Respectability and Abnormal Sexuality in Modern Europe* (New York: H. Fertig, 1985); and Klaus Theweleit's *Male Fantasies*, trans. Stephen Conway with Erica Carter and Chris Turner (Minneapolis: University of Minnesota Press, 1989). On the history of empire building, schooling, and preparations for manhood and examples of the diverse approaches to it, see Graham Dawson, *Soldier Heroes: British Adventure, Empire, and the Imagining of Masculinities* (New York: Routledge, 1994); Mrinalini Sinha, *Colonial Masculinity: The "Manly Englishman" and the "Effeminate Bengali" in the Late Nineteenth Century* (Manchester: Manchester University Press, 1995); Warwick Anderson, "The Trespass Speaks: White Masculinity and Colonial Breakdown," *American Historical Review* 102, no. 5 (1997): 1343–70; Frances Gouda, "Gender and 'Hyper-masculinity' as Post-Colonial Modernity during Indonesia's Struggle for Independence, 1945–49," in *Gender, Sexuality and Colonial Modernities*, ed. Antoinette Burton (New York: Routledge, 1999), 161–74.

11. Besides those already cited above, see, for example, Vicente L. Rafael, *Contracting Colonialism: Translation and Christian Conversion in Tagalog*

Society under Early Spanish Rule (Ithaca: Cornell University Press, 1988); Patricia Seed, *To Love, Honor, and Obey in Colonial Mexico: Conflicts over Marriage Choice, 1574–1821* (Stanford, Calif.: Stanford University Press, 1988); John Dunham Kelly, *A Politics of Virtue: Hinduism, Sexuality and Countercolonial Discourse in Fiji* (Chicago: University of Chicago Press, 1991); Frances Gouda, *Dutch Culture Overseas: Colonial Practice in the Netherlands Indies, 1900–1942* (Amsterdam: Amsterdam University Press, 1995); Antoinette M. Burton, *At the Heart of the Empire: Indians and the Colonial Encounter in Late-Victorian Britain* (Berkeley: University of California Press, 1998); Indira Chowdhury, *The Frail Hero and Virile History: Gender and the Politics of Culture in Colonial Bengal* (New York: Oxford University Press, 1998); Nancy Rose Hunt, *A Colonial Lexicon of Birth , Medicalization, and Mobility in the Congo* (Durham, N.C.: Duke University Press, 1999); Lata Mani, *Contentious Traditions: The Debate on Sati in Colonial India, 1780–1833* (Berkeley: University of California Press, 1999); Eileen J. Suarez Findlay, *Imposing Decency: The Politics of Sexuality and Race in Puerto Rico, 1870–1920* (Durham, N.C.: Duke University Press, 1999); Vicente L. Rafael, *White Love and Other Events in Filipino History* (Durham, N.C.: Duke University Press, 2000); Luise White, *Speaking with Vampires: Rumor and History in Colonial Africa* (Berkeley: University of California Press, 2000).

12. Jean E. Pedersen, " 'Special Customs': Paternity Suits and Citizenship in France and the Colonies, 1870–1912," in Clancy-Smith and Gouda, *Domesticating the Empire*, 43–64.

13. Jean Taylor, *The Social World of Batavia: European and Eurasian in Dutch Asia* (Madison: University of Wisconsin Press, 1983). Although it has had limited readership in the United States, a strong reception in the Netherlands eventually prompted its translation into Dutch.

14. On these issues, see Timothy Mitchell, "The Limits of the State: Beyond Statist Approaches and Their Critics," *American Political Science Review* 85, no. 1 (1991): 77–96; and Akhil Gupta, "Blurred Boundaries: The Discourse of Corruption, the Culture of Politics, and the Imagined State," *American Ethnologist* 22, no. 2 (1995): 375–402. Taylor traces alliances that cut back and forth across the boundaries that divided civilians from civil servants. Most strikingly these blurrings were within families themselves. This attention to family relations in the making of Dutch colonial rule is vindicated by Julia Adams's compelling case that family alliances formed the basis of modern nation-states in "The Familial State: Family Practices and State-making in the Early Modern Netherlands," *Theory and Society* 23, no. 4 (1994): 505–39. Also see Linzi Manicom, "Ruling Relations: Rethinking State and Gender in South African History," *Journal of African History* 33 (1992): 441–65.

15. See Verena Martinez-Alier [Stolcke], *Marriage, Class and Colour in Nineteenth-Century Cuba: A Study of Racial Attitudes and Sexual Values in a Slave Society* (Cambridge: Cambridge University Press, 1974); Seed, *To Love, Honor, and Obey*; and Raymond T. Smith, "Hierarchy and the Dual Marriage System in West Indian Society," in *Gender and Kinship*, ed. Jane Collier and

Sylvia Yanagisako (Stanford, Calif.: Stanford University Press, 1987), 163–96. Also see Ramón A. Gutiérrez, *When Jesus Came, the Corn Mothers Went Away: Marriage, Sexuality, and Power in New Mexico, 1500–1846* (Stanford, Calif.: Stanford University Press, 1991); Muriel Nazzari, "Concubinage in Colonial Brazil: The Inequalities of Race, Class and Gender," *Journal of Family History* 21, no. 2 (1996): 107–24; and for a subtle analysis of how the labeling of mixed children as "orphans" dispossessed birth mothers of their own children, see Indrani Chatterjee, "Colouring Subalternity: Slaves, Concubines, and Social Orphans in Early Colonial India," in *Subaltern Studies X: Writings on South Asian History and Society,* ed. Gautam Bhadra, Gyan Prakash, and Susie Tharu (New Delhi: Oxford University Press, 1996), 49–97.

16. Historical accounts that have treated this angst over "belonging" and the colonial consequences of it include John Comaroff's "Images of Empire, Contests of Conscience: Models of Colonial Domination in South Africa," in Cooper and Stoler, *Tensions of Empire,* 163–97; and Catherine Hall's "Missionary Stories: Gender and Ethnicity in the 1830s and 1840s," in *White, Male and Middle Class: Explorations in Feminism and History* (Cambridge: Polity Press, 1992), 205–54. Such confused sentiments are at the heart of Homi Bhabha's "Of Mimicry and Man: The Ambivalence of Colonial Discourse," in Cooper and Stoler, *Tensions of Empire,* 152–60. His focus is on a generic and widespread phenomenon, not its historical specificities.

17. See Madelon Székely-Lulofs, *Rubber* (Amsterdam: Elsevier, 1931); *De Andere Wereld* (Amsterdam: Elsevier, 1931); Marguerite Duras, *The Sea Wall,* trans. Herma Briffault (New York: Harper and Row, [1952] 1986); Louis Couperus, *The Hidden Force,* trans. Alexander Teixeira de Mattos (Amherst: University of Massachusetts Press, [1900] 1985); George Orwell, "Shooting an Elephant," in *Collected Essays* (London: Secker & Warburg, 1961); and the four novels in Pramoedya Ananta Toer's Buru Quartet: *This Earth of Mankind: A Novel* [Bumi Manusia], trans. Max Lane (New York: Penguin Books, [1975] 1990); *Child of All Nations: A Novel,* trans. Max Lane (Melbourne: Penguin Books Australia, 1984); *Footsteps,* trans. Max Lane (New York: W. Morrow, 1994); and *House of Glass: A Novel,* trans. Max Lane (New York: Penguin Books, 1992). Also see E. M. Beekman's exquisite set of translations of (and his excellent introductions to) E. Breton de Nijs, *Faded Portraits* (Amherst: University of Massachusetts Press, [1954] 1982); Edgar du Perron, *Country of Origin,* trans. Francis Bulho and Elizabeth Daverman (Amherst: University of Massachusetts Press, [1935] 1984); and E. M. Beekman, ed., *Fugitive Dreams: An Anthology of Dutch Colonial Literature* (Amherst: University of Massachusetts Press, 1988).

18. Among those who have looked at (some more directly than others) the sexual and gendered coordinates of white European identity *avant la lettre* of studies of "whiteness" are Amirah Inglis, *The White Woman's Protection Ordinance: Sexual Anxiety and Politics in Papua* (London: Sussex University Press, 1975); Claudia Knapman, *White Women in Fiji, 1835–1930: The Ruin of Empire?* (Boston: Allen and Unwin, 1986); Helen Callaway, *Gender, Culture and*

Empire: European Women in Colonial Nigeria (Oxford: Macmillan, 1987); and Patricia Grimshaw, *Paths of Duty: American Missionary Wives in Nineteenth-Century Hawaii* (Honolulu: University of Hawaii Press, 1989). But for a critique of Knapman and Callaway, see Margaret Jolly, "Colonizing Women: The Maternal Body and Empire," in *Feminism and the Politics of Difference,* ed. Sneja Gunew and Anna Yeatman (Sydney: Allen and Unwin, 1993), 103–27.

19. See my "Perceptions of Protest," 642–58.

20. Duras, *Sea Wall,* 135–36.

21. Pierre-André Taguieff's *La force du préjugé: Essai sur le racisme et ses doubles* (Paris: Découverte, 1988) was a notable exception. For a recent analysis that makes this connection, see Emmanuelle Saada, "Enfants de la colonie: Batards raciaux, batards sociaux," in *Enquête d'Ariel: Discours sur le métissage, identités métisse,* ed. Sylvie Kandé (Paris: L'Harmattan, 1999), 75–96. And on the relationship between "French Algeria" and anti-Arab racism in France today, see Benjamin Stora, *Le transfert d'une memoire: De 'l'Algerie française" au racisme anti-arabe* (Paris: Découverte, 1999).

22. Albert Memmi, *The Colonizer and the Colonized* (Boston: Beacon Press, [1957] 1967).

23. All district and regional reports on "the conditions of women and children" between 1906 and 1925 (for Cochin, Tonkin, and Indochina as a whole) were "unavailable," as were dossiers pertaining to specific accusations against French officers and their sexual liaisons with "native women." However, documents that did not name names (circulars and regulations from 1901 and 1908 on the "cohabitation of functionaries and native women") were there.

24. E. D. Hirsch, *Cultural Literacy: What Every American Needs to Know* (Boston: Houghton Mifflin, 1987).

25. A translation of the title of H. C. Beynon's edited volume, *Verboden voor Honden en Inlanders: Indonesiers vertellen over hun leven in de koloniale tijd* (Amsterdam: Jan Mets, 1995).

26. See Amat Rai's *The Rule of Sympathy* (2002) for a fine analysis of the imperial genealogy of sympathy that ties it to the sustained construction of difference and social inequalities. As I argue here and elsewhere, sympathy is one of a set of sentiments at the core of imperial logic and its governing projects. See my *Along the Archival Grain: Colonial Cultures and Their Affective States* (Princeton, N.J.: Princeton University Press, forthcoming).

27. On the continuing salience of imperial loss for white Britons, see Bill Schwarz's "Decolonizing England," in *Memories of Empire in Twentieth-Century England* (London: Verso, forthcoming).

CHAPTER 2. RETHINKING COLONIAL CATEGORIES

This essay was originally printed in *Comparative Studies in Society and History* 31 (1989): 134–16 and reprinted with permission of Cambridge University Press. It was first written for the symposium, The Categories of Colonialism, at the 1987 American Ethnological Society Meetings, with research funds from the

University of Wisconsin. I thank Talal Asad, Frederick Cooper, Murray Edelman, Linda Gordon, Lawrence Hirschfeld, Gerda Lerner, Nancy Lutkehaus, Aram Yengoyan, Steve Stern, and Steve Feierman for their thoughtful readings of an earlier text. Members of my graduate seminar at the University of Wisconsin–Madison on colonial cultures helped me to clarify many of the issues presented here.

1. Bronislaw Malinowski, "Dynamics of Culture Change," in *Social Change: The Colonial Situation*, ed. Immanuel Wallerstein (New York: Wiley, 1966), 14–15.

2. Malinowski was not alone in noting the conflicts of interest and distinctions among Europeans. Margaret Mead too commented on the social tensions among officials, missionaries, and planters and was acutely sensitive to appropriate dress codes when encountering different sorts of whites in the colonies (*Letters from the Field, 1925–1975* [New York: Harper and Row, 1977], 62–63); also see Hortense Powdermaker, *Stranger and Friend: The Way of an Anthropologist* (New York: Norton, 1966), 102–7. But such observations most often were anecdotal or personal asides and considered irrelevant to the subject of ethnography. Powdermaker, Malinowski's student, is one of the few U.S. anthropologists who, in her work in both northern Rhodesia and Mississippi, attended specifically (if somewhat briefly, as she notes) to Europeans and white society, respectively (*Stranger and Friend*, 183–98, 272–79).

3. See, for example, Kathleen Gough, "Anthropology and Imperialism," *Current Anthropology* 9, no. 5 (1968): 403–7; and the important contributions in Dell Hymes, ed., *Reinventing Anthropology* (New York: Vintage, 1969); Talal Asad, ed., *Anthropology and the Colonial Encounter* (London: Ithaca Press, 1973); Anthropological Research, "Anthropological Research in British Colonies," *Anthropological Forum* 4, no. 2 (1977): 1–112; and Gerald Berreman, *The Politics of Truth: Essays in Critical Anthropology* (New Delhi: South Asian Publishers, 1981).

4. Asad, *Anthropology*; James C. Scott, *The Moral Economy of the Peasant: Rebellion and Subsistence in Southeast Asia* (New Haven: Yale University Press, 1976); Aidan Foster-Carter, "The Modes of Production Controversy," *New Left Review* 107 (January–February 1978): 47–78; Eric Hobsbawn and Terence Ranger, eds., *The Invention of Tradition* (Cambridge: Cambridge University Press, 1983).

5. Julian H. Steward, *The People of Puerto Rico: A Study in Social Anthropology* (Urbana: University of Illinois Press, 1956); Eric R. Wolf, *Sons of the Shaking Earth* (Chicago: University of Chicago Press, 1959); Clifford Geertz, *Agricultural Involution: The Process of Ecological Change in Indonesia* (Berkeley: University of California Press, 1963); Sidney W. Mintz, *Caribbean Transformations* (Chicago: Aldine, 1974); Mona Etienne and Eleanor Leacock, eds., *Women and Colonization: Anthropological Perspectives* (New York: Praeger, 1980).

6. Renato Rosaldo, *Ilongot Headhunting, 1883–1974: A Study in Society and History* (Stanford, Calif.: Stanford University Press,1980); Michael T. Taussig,

The Devil and Commodity Fetishism in South America (Chapel Hill: University of North Carolina Press, 1980); Robert Wasserstrom, "Ethnic Violence and Indigenous Protest: The Tzeltal (Maya) Rebellion of 1712," *Journal of Latin American Studies* 12, no. 1 (1980): 1–19; Jean Comaroff, *Body of Power, Spirit of Resistance: The Culture and History of a South African People* (Chicago: University of Chicago Press, 1985); Ann Laura Stoler, *Capitalism and Confrontation in Sumatra's Plantation Belt, 1870–1979* (New Haven: Yale University Press, 1985); William Roseberry, "Images of the Peasant in the Consciousness of the Venezuelan Proletariat," in *Proletarians and Protest: The Roots of Class Formation in an Industrializing World*, ed. Michael Hanagan and Charles Stephenson (Wesport, Conn.: Greenwood Press, 1986).

7. June Nash, "Ethnographic Aspects of the World Capitalist System," *Annual Review of Anthropology* 10 (1981): 393–423; Joan Vincent, *Teso in Transformation: The Political Economy of Peasant and Class in Eastern Africa* (Berkeley: University of California Press, 1982); William Roseberry, *Coffee and Capitalism in the Venezuelan Andes* (Austin: University of Texas Press, 1983).

8. Eric R. Wolf, *Europe and the People without History* (Berkeley: University of California Press, 1982), 6.

9. Asad, *Anthropology;* John Clammer, "Colonialism and the Perception of Tradition," in *Anthropology and the Colonial Encounter*, ed. Talal Asad (London: Ithaca Press, 1975); Syed Hussein Alatas, *The Myth of the Lazy Native: A Study of the Image of the Malays, Filipinos and Javanese from the 16th to the 20th Century and Its Function in the Ideology of Colonial Capitalism* (London: Cass, 1977); Marshall Sahlins, *Historical Metaphors and Mythical Realities: Structure in the Early History of the Sandwich Islands Kingdom* (Ann Arbor: University of Michigan Press, 1981); Gerald Sider, "When Parrots Learn to Talk, and Why They Can't: Domination, Deception, and Self-Deception in Indian-White Relations," *Comparative Studies in Society and History* 29, no. 1 (1987): 3–23.

10. Alatas, *Myth of the Lazy Native*, 1977; Tzvetan Todorov, *The Conquest of America: The Question of the Other*, trans. Richard Howard (New York: Harper and Row, 1985).

11. French students of colonial history writing about territories in which *pieds noirs* (French born in the colonies) and *petits blancs* (lower-class whites) were a sizable political force have looked at these divisions more carefully. See Robert Louis Delavignette, *Service africain* (Paris: Gallimard, 1946); Pierre Nora, *Les français d'Algérie* (Paris: R. Julliard, 1961); Paul Mercier, "The European Community of Dakar," in *Africa: Social Problems of Change and Conflict: Readings*, ed. Pierre L. Van den Berghe (San Francisco: Chandler, 1965), 283–304. Still, few French anthropologists have taken the lead suggested by Georges Balandier in 1951, to explore the internal structure of European communities and their construction of racial categories ("The Colonial Situation: A Theoretical Approach," in Van den Berghe, *Africa*, 47–49, 53). Other anthropological efforts to examine specific agents of colonialism (and sometimes the tensions among them) are found in T. O. Beidelman, *Colonial Evangelism: A*

Socio-Historical Study of an East African Mission at the Grassroots, (Bloomington: Indiana University Press, 1982); Bernard Cohn, "Representing Authority in Victorian India," in *The Invention of Tradition,* ed. Eric Hobsbawm and Terence Ranger (Cambridge: Cambridge University Press, 1983), 165–210; Comaroff, *Body of Power;* Jean Comaroff and John Comaroff, "Christianity and Colonialism in South Africa," *American Ethnologist* 13, no. 1 (1986): 1–22; Robert J. Gordon and Mervyn J. Meggitt, "The Decline of the Kipas," in *Law and Order in the New Guinea Highlands: Encounter with Enga,* ed. Robert J. Gordon and Mervyn J. Meggitt (Hanover, N.H.: University Press of New England, 1985), 39–70; Sidney W. Mintz, *Sweetness and Power: The Place of Sugar in Modern History* (New York: Penguin, 1985); Jan Breman, *Koelies, Planters en Koloniale Politiek* (Dordrecht: Foris Publications, 1987).

12. Vincent Crapanzano's study of South Africa whites is exception: *Waiting: The Whites of South Africa* (New York: Vintage, 1985).

13. Marvin Harris and Conrad Kottak, "The Structural Significance of Brazilian Radical Categories," *Sociologia* 25 (1963): 203–9; Marvin Harris, *Patterns of Race in the Americas* (New York: Norton, 1964); and "Referential Ambiguity in the Calculus of Brazilian Racial Identity," *Southwestern Journal of Anthropology* 26, no. 1 (1970): 1–14; Sidney W. Mintz, "Groups, Group Boundaries, and the Perception of 'Race,' " *Comparative Studies in Society and History* 13 (Fall 1971): 437–50; Virginia Dominguez, *White by Definition: Social Classification in Creole Louisiana* (New Brunswick, N.J.: Rutgers University Press, 1986).

14. See, for example, R. E. S. Tanner, "Conflict within Small European Communities in Tanganyika," *Human Organization* 23, no. 4 (1964): 319–27. Historians have been more attentive to these issues, although nuanced studies of colonial Europeans are generally distinct from those that deal with the social classifications of race and class. Thus the profusion of "community studies" of the British in India attend to the social rankings of colonial life but not to the internal political tensions among the British themselves. See, e.g., Henry Dodwell, *The Nabobs of Madras* (London: Williams and Norgate, 1926); Thomas George Percival Spear, *The Nabobs: A Study of the Social Life of the English in Eighteenth-Century India* (London: Oxford University Press, 1963); Michael Edwardes, *Bound to Exile: The Victorians in India* (London: Sidgwick and Jackson, 1969); Dennis Kincaid, *British Social Life in India, 1608–1937* (New York: Kennikat Press, 1971). Studies of British and French interaction with the colonized and their philosophies of rule analyze the political priorities informing colonial policy but rarely treat the everyday practice of colonial domination. For French imperialism, see Agnes Murphy, *The Ideology of French Imperialism, 1871–1881* (New York: H. Fertig, 1968); William B. Cohen, *The French Encounter with Africans: White Response to Blacks, 1530–1880* (Bloomington: Indiana University Press, 1980); on the British in Africa, see Lewis H. Gann and Peter Duignan, *The Rulers of British Africa, 1870–1914* (London: Croom Helm, 1978). Efforts to go beyond official debates and examine distinct class interests within the colonial state are few: Frederick Cooper,

From Slaves to Squatters: Plantation Labor and Agriculture in Zanzibar and Coastal Kenya, 1890–1925 (New Haven: Yale University Press, 1980); John Lonsdale and Bruce Berman, "Coping with the the Contradictions: The Development of the Colonial State in Kenya, 1895–1914," *Journal of African History* 20 (1979): 487–505. Studies of European communities in colonial Africa reflect many of the themes addressed here: Helen Callaway, *Gender, Culture, and Empire: European Women in Colonial Nigeria* (Oxford: Macmillan, 1987); Dane Kennedy, *Islands of White: Settler Society and Culture in Kenya and Southern Rhodesia, 1890–1939* (Durham, N.C.: Duke University Press, 1987); David Prochaska, *Making Algeria French: Colonialism in Bône, 1870–1920* (Cambridge: Cambridge University Press, 1990).

Literature on the social construction of race in Latin America provides some insights into differentiation among European colonials (Carl N. Degler, *Neither Black nor White: Slavery and Race Relations in Brazil and the United State* [New York: Macmillan (1971) 1986]; Verena Martinez-Alier, *Marriage, Class, and Colour in Nineteenth-Century Cuba: A Study of Racial Attitudes and Sexual Values in a Slave Society* [Cambridge: Cambridge University Press, 1974]; John Chance and William Taylor, "Estate and Class in a Colonial City: Oaxaca in 1792," *Comparative Studies in Society and History* 19, no. 4 [1977]: 454–87; Patricia Seed, "Social Dimensions of Race: Mexico City, 1753," *Hispanic American Historical Review* 52, no. 4 [1982]: 590–606) but focuses primarily on intermediary racial categories while that on South African apartheid distinctly has not.

15. I owe the term "homespun" to Scott Christensen, a participant in my colonial cultures seminar. See also Malinowski's observation that the white settler "community is by no means a direct replica of its mother community at home" ("Dynamics," 14).

16. Benedict Anderson, *Imagined Communities: Reflections on the Origin and Spread of Nationalism* (London: Verso, 1983), 137.

17. Arghiri Emmanuel, "White-Settler Colonialism and the Myth of Investment Imperialism," *New Left Review* 73 (May–June 1972): 89; Robert Hughes, *The Fatal Shore: A History of the Transportation of Convicts to Australia, 1787–1868* (New York: Knopf, 1987). See, for example, B. J. Moore-Gilbert's thoughtful analysis of colonial fiction that addresses the conflicts and distinct social visions that divided British residents in India from those in Britain: *Kipling and "Orientalism"* (New York: St. Martin's Press, 1986).

18. Anderson, *Imagined Communities*.

19. Albert Memmi, *Portrait du colonisé, precédé du portrait du colonisateur* (Paris: Payot, [1957] 1973); Jean-Paul Sartre, *Critique of Dialectical Reason: Theory of Practical Ensembles*, trans. Alan Sheridan Smith (London: New Left Books, 1976); Ronald T. Takaki, *Pau Hana: Plantation Life and Labor in Hawaii, 1835–1920* (Honolulu: University of Hawaii Press, 1983).

20. Claude Lévi-Strauss, *Le regard éloigné* (Paris: Plon, 1983).

21. But such forms of cooperation between European employees and indigenous workers did exist and were actively opposed by some colonial states

and foreign companies. During the rise of the Javanese labor movement in the 1920s, multiracial trade unions were promoted that, in the case of railway workers, included lower-level Europeans and Indonesian workers. See John Ingelson, " 'Bound Hand and Foot': Railway Workers and the 1923 Strike in Java," *Indonesia* 31 (April 1981): 55. In South Africa, where working-class whites and blacks socialized at home and at work, urban planning in Johannesburg was designed precisely to eradicate "interracial 'slum-yards' " and "increase the growing social distance between white and black miners" (Charles van Onselen, *Studies in the Social and Economic History of the Witwatersrand, 1886–1914* [New York: Longman, 1982], 1:39).

22. Christopher Bagley, *The Dutch Plural Society: A Comparative Study in Race Relations* (London: Oxford University Press, 1973), 44.

23. J. H. Marinus and J. J. van der Laan, *Veertig Jaren Ervaring in de Delicultures* (Amsterdam: J. H. de Bussy, 1929); Bagley, *Dutch Plural Society*.

24. Stoler, *Capitalism and Confrontation*.

25. Marinus and van der Laan, *Veertig Jaren Ervaring*.

26. See my "Perceptions of Protest: Defining the Dangerous in Colonial Sumatra," *American Ethnologist* 12, no. 4 (1985): 642–58, for a discussion of how conflicts between local planters and Dutch government officials affected labor policy. On the inconsistent and incoherent interpretations of Sumatra's plantation violence by officials, estate personnel, and the military in the late nineteenth century, see Ann Laura Stoler, " 'In Cold Blood': Hierarchies of Credibility and the Politics of Colonial Narratives," *Representations* 37 (Winter 1992): 151–89.

27. Roger Nieuwenhuys, *Oost-Indische Spiegel: Wat Nederlandse Schrijvers en Dichters over Indonesie Hebben Geschreven, vanaf de Eerste Jaren der Compagnie tot op Heden* (Amsterdam: E. Querido, 1978), 346–47.

28. Willem Brandt, *De Aarde van Deli* (The Hague: W. van Hoeve, 1948), 186; Ladislao Székely, *Tropic Fever: The Adventures of a Planter in Sumatra* (Kuala Lumpur: Oxford in Asia [1937] 1979), 37. Witness the number of novels, sketches, and memoirs describing the attributes of the "Deli planter"; e.g., Jo Manders, *De Boedjang-Club: Delische Roman* (Gravenhage: H. P. Leopold, 1933); J. Kleian, *Deli-Planter* (The Hague: W. van Hoeve, 1936); H. Gorter, *Delianen: Schetsen uit het Plantersleven op Sumatra's Oostkust* (Amsterdam: L. J. Veen, 1941); Brandt, *De Aarde*; H. Tscherning Petersen, *Tropical Adventure: Sumatra, Land of Loveliness and Stern Destiny*, trans. Eugene Gay-Tifft (London: J. Rolls, 1948); Székely, *Tropic Fever*.

29. The relative importance of character over class in determining colonial status varied widely. References to character pervade the colonial literature with often contradictory formulations. In New Guinea, "class distinctions disappeared and recognition of character took over" (James Boutilier, "European Women in the Solomon Islands, 1900–1942: Accommodation and Change on the Pacific Frontier," in *Rethinking Women's Roles: Perspectives from the Pacific*, ed. Denise O'Brien and Sharon W. Tiffany [Berkeley: University of California Press, 1984], 179), whereas in the administrative service of the Ivory

Coast in the 1920s, character was a class privilege defined by an Oxbridge arrogance if not education (Henrika Kuklick, *The Imperial Bureaucrat: The Colonial Administrative Service in the Gold Coast, 1920–1939* [Stanford, Calif.: Hoover Institution Press, 1979], 26). Whereas character, not class origin, allegedly marked the making of a Deli planter in the early twentieth century, in India at the same time "class distinctions within the British community became more sharply defined" (George Woodcock, *The British in the Far East* [New York: Atheneum, 1969], 163). These differences may reflect historical variation or distinct rhetorical uses of the notion of "character." In any case, character clearly stood in for class as a social marker and was defined by privileges that were largely race- and class-specific. Cf. Robert Hughes (*Fatal Shore*, 323), who states that in the colonization of Australia, "the question of class was all pervasive and pathological." On the significance of an accepted standard of living in shaping Malaya's British community, see John G. Butcher, *The British in Malaya, 1880–1941: The Social History of a European Community in Colonial South-East Asia* (New York: Oxford University Press, 1979).

30. Thus Kuklick notes that an Oxbridge education was required "not so much to receive occupational training as to acquire the social polish considered intrinsic to a commanding personality" (*Imperial Bureaucrat,* 26). See chapter 4 on what role character played in distinguishing poor Indies-born Europeans of mixed descent from those who were "really Dutch" in legal decisions about citizenship.

31. Lily E. Clerkx, *Mensen in Deli,* Publication No. 2 (Amsterdam: Sociologisch-Historisch Seminarium voor Zuidoost-Azie, 1961), 10–12; Rob Nieuwenhuys, *Mirror of the Indies: A History of Dutch Colonial Literature,* trans. Frans van Rosevelt (Amherst: University of Massachusetts Press, 1982), 154.

32. Breman, *Koelies,* 63–67.

33. The transformation of a greenhorn into a seasoned planter is a central theme in a number of the memoirs and novels cited in note 28.

34. *De Planter,* April 1, 1909, 19; H. Mohammad Said, *Sejarah Pers di Sumatera Utara* (Medan: Waspada, 1976), 51–52; cf. Breman, *Koelies,* 65–66.

35. Marinus and van der Laan, *Veertig Jaren Ervaring,* 47.

36. *Kroniek,* Ooskust van Sumatra-Instituut (Amsterdam: J. H. de Bussy, 1917), 39.

37. *De Planter,* April 1, 1909; September 1, 1909.

38. Said, *Sejarah,* 51.

39. Algemene Rijksarchief, Afdeeling II, Verbaal, January 19, 1921, no. 71.

40. This policy was not specific to Deli; it was simply enforced at a much later date there than elsewhere in the Indies. The migration of European women to the Dutch East Indies was actively discouraged from the seventeenth to the mid-nineteenth century, and until the late 1800s European marriages in the army were restricted to the officer corps. See Hanneke Ming, "Barracks-Concubinage in the Indies, 1887–1920," *Indonesia* 35 (April 1983): 65–93; Jean

Taylor, *The Social World of Batavia: European and Eurasian in Dutch Asia* (Madison: University of Wisconsin Press, 1983), 26.

41. Sumatra *Post,* 1913; *Kroneik,* 1917, 50.

42. Butcher, *British in Malaya,* 93.

43. Ibid., 26.

44. *De Planter,* May 1, 1909. See also Nieuwenhuys, *Mirror of the Indies,* 144, on the importance of maintaining a moral colonial society to assuage the fears of mothers in the Netherlands.

45. Said, *Sejarah,* 51–52.

46. J. H. Marinus, for example, in noting that distinctions between assistants and administrators were sharper thirty years earlier, writes: "The historical facts that the assistant might not ride in a four-wheeled carriage, or wear a gray helmet, as did the administrator are long forgotten and something most of the young assistants today know nothing about" (*Veertig Jaren Ervaring,* 12, 112).

47. For a detailed discussion of the shift in corporate strategy to "family formation," or *gezinvorming,* see Stoler, *Capitalism and Confrontation,* 31–46.

48. *Kroniek,* 1917, 36.

49. *Kroniek,* 1925, 72.

50. Spear, *The Nabobs,* 140.

51. Ashis Nandy, *The Intimate Enemy: Loss and Recovery of Self under Colonialism* (New York: Oxford University Press, 1983), 9–10. Also see Woodcock (*The British,* 163), who argues that with the arrival of Englishwomen, "racial distinctions . . . became more sharply defined"; and Hank Nelson (*Taim Bilong Masta: The Australian Involvement with Papua New Guinea* [Sydney: Australian Broadcasting Commission, 1982], 47), who asserts that new racial barriers were created when New Guinea's patrol officers (*kiaps*) were accompanied by their European wives.

52. Beidelman, *Colonial Evangelism,* 13.

53. Gann and Duignan, *Rulers of British Africa,* 242; also see Rita Cruise O'Brien, *White Society in Black Africa: The French in Senegal* (London: Faber and Faber, 1972), 59.

54. More convincing accounts suggest that expatriate women were more than symbols of white male power. They also "served to define men in relationship to one another" (Elaine Silverman, quoted in Boutilier, "European Women," 196; see also Amirah Inglis, *The White Women's Protection Ordinance: Sexual Anxiety and Politics in Papua* [London: Sussex University Press, 1975]; Pat Barr, *The Memsahibs: The Women of Victorian India* [London: Secker & Warburg, 1976]). Boutilier argues that the racist inclinations were not imported by women from Europe but were derived from prejudices previously brought to the metropole by colonial men ("European Women").

55. David Arnold, "White Colonization and Labour in Nineteenth-Century India," *Journal of Imperial and Commonwealth History* 10, no. 2 (1979): 154.

56. Inglis, *White Women's Protection Ordinance,* 11.

57. Ibid., vii.

58. Boutilier, "European Women," 196.

59. Company and government authorities were concerned with interracial sexual contact but primarily as it related to prostitution. In the Indies, venereal disease had become endemic among subordinate white men. In 1930 it was estimated that more than 47,000 European men, mostly soldiers, were hospitalized with syphilis (A. de Braconier, "Het Prostitutie-Vraagstuk in Nederlandsch-Indie," *Indische Gids* 55, no. 2 [1933]: 923). New restrictions imposed on concubinage in army barracks apparently led to an increase in paid sexual service and incidence of venereal disease. Concubinage and prostitution thus were seen to create different sorts of problems: the former, a major source of European pauperism (by creating a large class of impoverished barrack children); the latter, a health hazard and social evil (Ming, "Barracks-Concubinage," 74).

60. The number of European women in the Dutch East Indies rose from 18.7 to 40.6 percent of the total European population between 1905 and 1915 (Nieuwenhuys, *Oost-Indische Spiegel*, 166).

61. *De Planter*, April 9, 1910, 52; Groupe d'Etudes Coloniales, "La femme blanche au Congo," *Bulletin de la Société Belge d'Etudes Coloniales* 5 (May 1910): 7.

62. Madelon Székely-Lulofs, *Rubber* (Amsterdam: Elsevier [1931] 1946).

63. Compare, for example, the fiction of Madelon Székely-Lulofs with that of her husband, Ladislao Székely. Also see Jo Manders, *De Boedjang-Club*, whose account of planter excesses won her much disfavor from those who deemed her portrait damaging to "colonial prestige at home and abroad" (Nieuwenhuys, *Oost-Indische Spiegel*, 173). On the hierarchy in African colonial communities and the constraints it imposed on European women's lives, see Yvonne Knibiehler and Régine Goutalier, *La femme au temps des colonies* (Paris: Stock, 1985), 13–36.

64. Also see Kuklick, *Imperial Bureaucrat*; Nicole Lucas, "Trouwverbod, Inlandse Huishoudsters en Europese Vrouwen: Het Concubinaat in de Planterswereld aan Sumatra's Oostkust, 1860–1940" in *Vrouwen in de Nederlandse Kolonien*, ed. Reijs Jeske et al. (Nijmegen: SUN, 1986), 78–97.

65. Jacquelyn Dowd Hall, " 'The Mind That Burns in Each Body': Women, Rape, and Racial Violence," *Southern Exposure* 12, no. 6 (1984): 61–71.

66. Barr, *Memsahibs*, 170; Kenneth Ballhatchet, *Race, Sex, and Class under the Raj: Imperial Attitudes and Policies and Their Critics, 1793–1905* (New York: St. Martin's Press, 1980), 7.

67. *Kroniek*, 1929, 43–48. For a fuller account of this event and the political issues that surrounded it, see Stoler, *Capitalism and Confrontation*, 82–86. Also see my "Perceptions of Protest," which contrasts this 1929 reaction to the murder of an estate manager's wife sixty years earlier.

68. A. Grenfell Price, *White Settlers in the Tropics* (New York: American Geographical Society of New York, 1939), 6–8; J. E. Spencer and W. L. Thomas, "The Hill Stations and Summer Resorts of the Orient," *Geographical Review* 38, no. 4 (1948): 637.

69. *Kroniek,* 1923, 78; Arnold, "White Colonization and Labour," 141; Patricia Grimshaw, " 'Christian Woman, Pious Wife, Faithful Mother, Devoted Missionary': Conflicts in Roles of American Missionary Women in Nineteenth-Century Hawaii," *Feminist Studies* 9, no. 3 (1983): 508.

70. Mercier, "European Community," 287.

71. Groupe d'Etudes Coloniales, "La femme blanche," 10.

72. David Arnold, "European Orphans and Vagrants in India in the Nineteenth Century," *Journal of Imperial and Commonwealth History* 7, no. 2 (1979): 113.

73. Arnold, "White Colonization and Labour," 139.

74. *Kroniek,* 1933, 181.

75. Arnold, "European Orphans," 104, 122.

76. *Encyclopaedie van Nederlandsch-Indie,* 2d ed. (The Hague: Martinus Nijhoff and E. J. Brill, [1919] 1921), 366–68.

77. Jill Sheppard, *The "Redlegs" of Barbados* (New York: KTO Press, 1977), 43; Hilary Beckles, " 'Black Men in White Skins': The Formation of a White Proletariat in West Indian Slave Society," *Journal of Imperial and Commonwealth History* 15, no. 1 (1986): 7.

78. Mercier, "European Community," 292–93; O'Brien, *White Society,* 66–91; Daniel Leconte, *Les pieds noirs* (Paris: Seuil, 1980), 71–83.

79. J. R. Albertyn, *Die Armblanke ein die Maatskappy: Verslag van die Carnegie-Kommissie* (Stellenbosch: Pro-ecclesia-drukkery, 1932), vii.

80. Ibid., 33–38.

81. *Kroniek,* 1917, 51.

82. Ibid., 49.

83. Ibid., 1922, 50.

84. Clerkx, *Mensen in Deli,* 13.

85. Kantoor van Arbeid, *Werkloosheid in Nederlandsch-Indie* (Batavia: Landsdrukkerij, 1935), 1–94.

86. *Kroniek,* 1930, 22.

87. J. S. Furnivall, *Netherlands India: A Study of Plural Economy* (New York: Macmillan, 1944), 444.

88. *Kroniek,* 1931, 79.

89. Ibid., 1932, 82.

90. Frances Fox Piven and Richard A. Cloward, *Regulating the Poor: The Functions of Public Welfare* (New York: Vintage, 1971), 49–60.

91. *Kroniek* 1932, 82.

92. Furnivall, *Netherlands India,* 444.

93. *Kroniek,* 1931, 80.

94. Ibid., 1933, 85.

95. J. de Waard, "De Oostkust van Sumatra," *Tijdschrift voor Economische Geographie* 25 (1934): 272.

96. *Kroniek,* 1935, 94–96.

97. See " 'Uit den Volksraad—De Werkloosheid," *Onze Stem* 8 (February 20, 1931): 187.

98. A. van Marle, "De groep der Europeanen in Nederlands-Indie, iets over Ontstaan en Groei," *Indonesie* 5, no. 2(1952): 108.

99. Ibid., 98, 109.

100. Butcher, *British in Malaya*, 25.

101. The alternating fluidity and rigidity with which these divisions were drawn is illustrated in June Nash's work on interracial marriage in sixteenth-century Mexico. Mixed marriages between Spanish men and Christianized Indian women were condoned by the colonial state and later condemned to exclude mestizos from tribute rights and thus restrict their control over Indian labor. Nash, "Aztec Women: The Transition from Status to Class in Empire and Colony," in *Women and Colonization: Anthropological Perspectives*, ed. Mona Etienne and Eleanor Leacock (New York: Praeger, 1980), 140–41. Also see Dominguez, *White by Definition*, for a fine-grained analysis of the history of social classification and its changing legal specification in creole Louisiana.

102. Taylor, *Social World of Batavia*, 16.

103. Beidelman, *Colonial Evangelism*, 2

104. Frantz Fanon, *The Wretched of the Earth*, trans. Constance Farrington (New York: Grove Press, 1963); Memmi, *Portrait du colonisé*; Aimé Césaire, *Discourse on Colonialism*, trans. Joan Pinkham (New York: Monthly Review Press, 1972); Nandy, *Intimate Enemy*.

105. V. S. Naipaul, *The Middle Passage: Impressions of Five Societies, British, French and Dutch, in the West Indies and South America* (London: Penguin, 1978), 65.

CHAPTER 3. CARNAL KNOWLEDGE AND IMPERIAL POWER

The research for the material in this chapter was supported by an NSF Postdoctoral Fellowship for the International Exchange of Scientists (Grant INT-8701561), by a NATO Postdoctoral Fellowship in Science (Grant RCD-8751159), and by funding from the Centre National de la Recherche Scientifique in France. The Center for Asian Studies Amsterdam (CASA) and the Centre d'Etudes Africaines in Paris generously extended their facilities and collegial support. I owe particular thanks to the following people whose comments on various versions I have tried to take into account: Julia Adams, Etienne Balibar, Pierre Bourdieu, Robert Connell, Frederick Cooper, Linda Gordon, Lawrence Hirschfeld, Micaela di Leonardo, Gerda Lerner, and George Mosse. This chapter first appeared as "Carnal Knowledge and Imperial Power: Gender, Race, and Morality in Colonial Asia," in *Gender at the Crossroads of Knowledge: Feminist Anthropology in the Postmodern Era*, ed. Micaela di Leonardo (Berkeley: University of California Press, 1991).

1. See, for example, Mona Etienne and Eleanor Leacock, eds., *Women and Colonization: Anthropological Perspectives* (New York: Praeger, 1980); Nancy J. Hafkin and Edna G. Bay, eds., *Women in Africa: Studies in Social and Economic Change* (Stanford, Calif.: Stanford University Press, 1976); Claire Robertson and Martin Klein, *Women and Slavery in Africa* (Madison:

University of Wisconsin Press, 1983); Irene Silverblatt, *Moon, Sun, and Witches: Gender Ideologies and Class in Inca and Colonial Peru* (Princeton: Princeton University Press, 1987). For a review of some this literature in an African context, see Belinda Bozzoli, "Marxism, Feminism and South African Studies," *Journal of South African Studies* 9, no. 2 (1983): 139–71; Claire Robertson, "Developing Economic Awareness: Changing Perspectives in Studies of African Women, 1765–1985," *Feminist Studies* 13, no. 1 (1987): 97–135; and Luise White, Book review, *Signs* 13, no. 2 (1988): 360–64.

2. Hilary Callan and Shirley Ardener, eds., *The Incorporated Wife* (London: Croom Helm, 1984); Yvonne Knibiehler and Régine Goutalier, *La femme au temps des colonies* (Paris: Stock, 1985), and *"Femmes et colonisation": Rapport terminal au Ministère des Rélations Extérieures et de la Coopération* (Aix-en-Provence: Institut d'Histoire des Pays d'Outre-Mer, 1987); Helen Callaway, *Gender, Culture and Empire: European Women in Colonial Nigeria* (Oxford: Macmillan, 1987); Margaret Strobel, "Gender and Race in the Nineteenth- and Twentieth-Century British Empire," in *Becoming Visible: Women in European History*, 2d ed., ed. Renate Bridenthal, Claudia Koonz, and Susan Stuard (Boston: Houghton Mifflin, 1987), 389–414.

3. Callan and Ardener, *Incorporated Wife*; Knibiehler and Goutalier, *La femme au temps*; Jeske Reijs, E. Kloek, U. Jansz, A. de Wildt, S. van Norden, and M. de Bat, *Vrouwen in de Nederlandse Kolonien* (Nijmegen: SUN, 1986); Callaway, *Gender, Culture and Empire*.

4. Some women's sojourns in the colonies did allow them to pursue career possibilities and independent lifestyles barred to them in metropolitan Europe at the time. However, the experience of professional women in South Asia and Africa highlights how quickly they were shaped into "cultural missionaries" or, in resisting that impulse, were marginalized in their work and social life. See Callaway, *Gender, Culture and Empire*, 83–164; Barbara Ramuschack, "Cultural Missionaries, Maternal Imperialists, Feminist Allies: British Women Activists in India, 1865–1945," in *Western Women and Imperialism: Complicity and Resistance*, ed. Nupur Chaudhwi and Margaret Strobel, 119–36 (Bloomington: Indiana University Press, 1992).

5. On contrasts and commonalities in how European women and men represented and experienced the social, psychological, and sexual tensions of colonial life, see the papers from the conference, "Feminism, Imperialism and Race: India and Britain," University of Cincinnati, 1992.

6. See, e.g., Frederick Cooper, *From Slaves to Squatters: Plantation Labor and Agriculture in Zanzibar and Coastal Kenya, 1890–1925* (New Haven: Yale University Press, 1980); P. J. Drooglever, *De Vaderlandse Club, 1929–1942: Totoks en de Indische Politiek* (Franeker: Wever, 1980); Hugh Ridley, *Images of Imperial Rule* (New York: Croom Helm, 1981); Jean Comaroff and John Comaroff, "Christianity and Colonialism in South Africa," *American Ethnologist* 13, no. 1 (1986): 1–22; Dane Kennedy, *Islands of White: Settler Society and Culture in Kenya and Southern Rhodesia, 1890–1939* (Durham, N.C.: Duke University Press, 1987); David Prochaska, *Making Algeria French:*

Colonialism in Bône, 1870–1920 (Cambridge: Cambridge University Press, 1990).

7. See Verena Martinez-Alier, *Marriage, Class and Colour in Nineteenth-Century Cuba: A Study of Racial Attitudes and Sexual Values in a Slave Society* (Cambridge: Cambridge University Press, 1974), for a subtle analysis of the changing criteria by which color was perceived and assigned; and for the Indies, Jean Taylor, *The Social World of Batavia: European and Eurasian in Dutch Asia* (Madison: University of Wisconsin Press, 1983), on the changing cultural markers of European membership, A. van Marle ("De groep der Europeanen in Nederlands-Indie, iets Over Ontstaan en Groei," *Indonesie* 5, no. 2 [1952]: 77–121; 5, no. 3 [1952]: 314–41; 5, no. 5 [1952]: 481–507) offers a fascinating description of racial classification, conjugal patterns, and sexual relations for the colonial Indies.

8. Martinez-Alier, *Marriage, Class and Colour;* Hanneke Ming, "Barracks-Concubinage in the Indies, 1887–1920," *Indonesia* 35 (April 1983): 65–93; Taylor, *Social World.*

9. E. Pujarniscle, *Philoxène ou de la littérature coloniale* (Paris: Firmin-Didot, 1931),106; Martine Loutfi, *Littérature et colonialisme: L'expansion coloniale vue dans la littérature romanesque française, 1871–1914* (Paris: Mouton, 1971), 36.

10. Loutfi, *Littérature;* Sander L. Gilman, *Difference and Pathology: Stereotypes of Sexuality, Race, and Madness* (Ithaca: Cornell University Press, 1985), 79. See Winthrop D. Jordan, *White over Black: American Attitudes toward the Negro, 1550–1812* (Chapel Hill: University of North Carolina Press, 1968), 32–40, on Elizabethan attitudes toward black African sexuality; and Gilman, *Difference and Pathology,* 76–108, on the sexual iconography of Hottentot women in European art of the eighteenth and nineteenth centuries. On colonial sexual imagery, see Louis Malleret, *L'exotisme indochinois dans la littérature française depuis 1860* (Paris: Larose, 1934), 216–41; and Sharon W. Tiffany and Kathleen J. Adams, *The Wild Woman: An Inquiry into the Anthropology of an Idea* (Cambridge, Mass.: Schenkman, 1985), 13, who argue that "the romance of the wild woman" expressed critical distinctions between civilization and the primitive, culture and nature, and the class differences between the repressed middle-class woman and "her regressively primitive antithesis, the working-class girl."

11. Ronald Hyam, "Concubinage and the Colonial Service: The Crewe Circular (1909)," *Journal of Imperial and Commonwealth History* 14, no. 3 (1986): 170–86.

12. Lewis H. Gann and Peter Duignan, *The Rulers of British Africa, 1870–1914* (London: Croom Helm, 1978), 240.

13. Edward W. Said, *Orientalism* (New York: Pantheon Books, 1978), 6; my emphasis.

14. Ibid., 207.

15. In Dutch and French colonial novels of the nineteenth century heightened sensuality is the recognized reserve of Asian and Indo-European mis-

tresses and only of those European women born in the colonies and loosened by its moral environment. See P. A. Daum, *Ups and Downs of Life in the Indies,* trans. Elsje Qualms Sturtevant and Donald W. Sturtevant (Amherst: University of Massachusetts Press, 1987); Loutfi, *Littérature.*

16. Loutfi, *Littérature,* 108–9.

17. Kenneth Ballhatchet, *Race, Sex and Class under the Raj: Imperial Attitudes and Policies and Their Critics, 1793–1905* (New York: St. Martin's Press, 1980).

18. Jean J. Van Helten and K. Williams, " 'The Crying Need of South Africa': The Emigration of Single British Women to the Transvaal, 1901–1910," *Journal of South African Studies* 10, no. 1 (1983): 11–38; Knibiehler and Goutalier, *La femme au temps;* Callaway, *Gender, Culture and Empire;* Strobel, "Gender and Race."

19. Taylor, *Social World;* Knibiehler and Goutalier, *La femme au temps;* Callan and Ardener, *Incorporated Wife;* Callaway, *Gender, Culture and Empire.*

20. Knibiehler and Goutalier, *La femme au temps;* Nancy Hunt, " 'Le bébé en brousse': European Women, African Birth Spacing, and Colonial Intervention in Breast Feeding in the Belgian Congo," in *Tensions of Empire: Colonial Cultures in a Bourgeois World,* ed. Frederick Cooper and Ann Laura Stoler (Berkeley: University of California Press, 1988), 287–321.

21. Ellen Ross and Rayna Rapp, "Sex and Society: A Research Note from Social History and Anthropology," *Comparative Studies in Society and History* 22, no. 1 (1980): 54.

22. Deborah Gaitskell, "Housewives, Maids or Mothers: Some Contradictions of Domesticity for Christian Women in Johannesburg, 1903–39," *Journal of African History* 24 (1983): 241–56; Elizabeth B. Van Heyningen, "The Social Evil in the Cape Colony, 1868–1902: Prostitution and the Contagious Disease Act," *Journal of Southern African Studies* 10, no. 2 (1984): 170–97; Elizabeth Schmidt, "Ideology, Economics, and the Role of Shona Women in Southern Rhodesia, 1850–1939" (Ph.D. dissertation, University of Wisconsin, 1987); Karen Tranberg Hansen, *Distant Companions: Servants and Employers in Zambia, 1900–1985* (Ithaca: Cornell University Press, 1989); Luise White, *The Comforts of Home: Prostitution in Colonial Nairobi* (Chicago: University of Chicago Press, 1990). For the Indies, see Ming, "Barracks-Concubinage"; and Liesbeth Hesselink, "Prostitution, a Necessary Evil, Particularly in the Colonies: Views on Prostitution in the Netherlands Indies," in *Indonesian Women in Focus: Past and Present Notions,* ed. Elsbeth Locher-Scholten and Anke Niehof (Dordrecht: Foris, 1987). For India, see Dagmar Engels, "The Age of Consent Act of 1891: Colonial Ideology in Bengal," *South Asia Research* 3, no. 2 (1983): 107–34.

23. Ronald T. Takaki, *Iron Cages: Race and Culture in Nineteenth-Century America* (New York: Knopf, 1977).

24. Jordan, *White over Black,* 141.

25. Gilman, *Difference and Pathology.*

26. Ibid., 25.

27. Octavio Mannoni, *Prospero and Caliban: The Psychology of Colonization*, trans. Pamela Powesland (New York: Praeger, 1956); Frantz Fanon, *Black Skin, White Masks*, trans. Charles Lam Markmann (New York: Grove Press, [1952] 1967); Ashis Nandy, *The Intimate Enemy: Loss and Recovery of Self under Colonialism* (New York: Oxford University Press, 1983).

28. The relationship among sexual control, racial violence, and political power has been most directly addressed by historians of the U.S. South. See Jordan, *White over Black*; Gerda Lerner, *Black Women in White America: A Documentary History* (New York: Pantheon, 1972); Jacquelyn Dowd Hall, " 'The Mind That Burns in Each Body': Women, Rape, and Racial Violence," *Southern Exposure* 12, no. 6 (1984): 61–71; and the analyses by turn-of-the-century African American women intellectuals discussed in Hazel Carby, "On the Threshold of Woman's Era: Lynching, Empire and Sexuality in Black Feminist Theory," *Critical Inquiry* 12, no. 1 (1985): 262–77. Nell Irvin Painter argues that the treatment of rape as a symbol of male power was an interpretation held by both white and black male authors: " 'Social Equality': Miscegenation, Labor and Power," in *The Evolution of Southern Culture*, ed. Numan V. Bartley (Athens: University of Georgia Press, 1988), 59.

29. Ronald Hyam, "Empire and Sexual Opportunity," *Journal of Imperial and Commonwealth History* 4, no. 3 (1986): 75.

30. Taylor, *Social World*, 12.

31. Leonard Blussé, *Strange Company: Chinese Settlers, Mestizo Women and the Dutch in VOC Batavia* (Riverton, N.J.: Foris Publications, 1986), 161.

32. Taylor, *Social World*, 14.

33. Fear of trade competition from European women is alluded to frequently in historical work on eighteenth-century colonies. In the French trading centers (factories) of the Middle East, for example, the Marseille Chamber of Commerce went to great lengths to ensure that no marriages would take place in their trading domain, fearing that European women and children would pose a threat to the French monopoly. In 1728 any French national married in a French entrepôt was prohibited from trading directly or indirectly with the royal government. M. Cordurie, "Résidence des françaises et mariage des français dan les échelles du Levant au XVIIIe siècle," in *La femme dans les sociétés coloniales: Table ronde, CHEE, CRHSE, IHPOM: Groningen-Amsterdam, Septembre 1982, Centre d'histoire de l'expansion Européenne, Université de Leiden*, ed. Rijksuniversiteit te Leiden and Werkgroep voor de Geschiedenis van de Europese Expansie Centre de Recherche d'Histoire Socio-Economique and Institut d'Histoire des Pays d'Outre-Mer Université de Provence (Aix-en-Provence: Institut d'Histoire des Pays d'Outre-Mer, Université de Provence, 1984), 42.

34. Taylor, *Social World*, 14.

35. Ibid., 16. European-born women also were excluded from much of the Portuguese empire from the sixteenth through eighteenth centuries. C. R. Boxer, *The Portuguese Seaborne Empire, 1415–1825* (New York: Knopf, 1969), 129–30.

36. Ming, "Barracks-Concubinage," 69; Taylor, *Social World*, 16; Blussé, *Strange Company*, 173.

37. W. L. Ritter, *De Europeaan in Nederlandsch Indie* (Leiden: Sythoff, 1856), 21.

38. van Marle, *De Groep der Europeanen*, 485.

39. Ming, "Barracks-Concubinage,"70.

40. Algemene Rijksarchief, Mailrapport 91, March 23, 1903, no. 972.

41. van Marle, *De groep der Europeanen*, 486.

42. The homoerotic tendencies Hyam ("Empires and Sexual Opportunity") notes in British political biography are not paralleled in the Dutch colonial literature. The dangers of homosexuality were frequently invoked to justify prostitution among Chinese plantation workers and concubinage among European soldiers, but such arguments were rarely applied to higher-ranking European staff. J. van den Brand, *No geens: De Millionen uit Deli* (Amsterdam: Hoveker & Wormser, 1904); W. Middendorp, *De Poenale Sanctie* (Haarlem: Tjeenk Willink, 1924), 51; Ming, "Barracks-Concubinage,"69, 83. Some sources suggest that as many as 31 percent of the European colonial troops in the Indies had venereal disease. See J. F. H. Kohlbrugge, "Prostitutie in Nederlandsch Indie," *Indisch Genootschap* 19 (February 1901): 2–36.

43. Kohlbrugge, "Prostitutie in Nederlandsch-Indie"; Ballhatchet, *Race, Sex and Class*; Ming, "Barracks-Concubinage."

44. Malleret, *L'exotisme indochinois*, 216; William B. Cohen, *Rulers of Empire: The French Colonial Service in Africa* (Stanford, Calif.: Hoover Institution Press, 1971), 122.

45. A. de Braconier, "Het Prostitutie-Vraagstuk in Nederlandsch-Indie," *Indische Gids* 55, no. 2 (1933): 906–28.

46. Rob Nieuwenhuys, *Tussen Twee Vaderlanden* (Amsterdam: G. A. van Oorschot, 1959), 19; C. J. Dixon, *De Assistent in Deli* (Amsterdam: J. H. de Bussy, 1913), 77.

47. John Butcher, *The British in Malaya, 1886–1941: The Social History of a European Community in Colonial South-East Asia* (New York: Oxford University Press, 1979), 200, 202. The danger of sexual abstinence for young men was often invoked to license both concubinage and government-regulated prostitution at different times (Hesselink, "Prostitution," 208–9).

48. Hyam, "Concubinage"; Callaway, *Gender, Culture and Empire*, 49; Kennedy, *Islands of White*, 175.

49. Lily E. Clerkx, *Mensen in Deli*, Publication no. 2 (Amsterdam: Sociologisch-Historisch Seminarium voor Zuidoost Azie, 1961), 87–93; Ann Laura Stoler, *Capitalism and Confrontation in Sumatra's Plantation Belt, 1870–1979* (New Haven: Yale University Press, 1985), 31–34; Nicole Lucas, "Trouwverbod, Inlandse Huishoudsters en Europese Vrouwen: Het Concubinaat in de Planterswereld aan Sumatra's Oostkust, 1860–1940," in *Vrouwen in de Nederlandse Kolonien*, ed. Reijs Jeske et al. (Nijmegen: SUN, 1986), 84.

50. As Tessel Pollmann suggests, the term *nyai* glossed several functions: household manager, servant, housewife, wife, and prostitute ("Bruidstraantjes: De Koloniale Roman, de Njai en de Apartheid," in Reijs, *Vrouwen in de Nederlandse Kolonien*, 100). Which of these was most prominent depended on a complex economic, social, and affective equation that included the prosperity of the European man, the resources of a woman so positioned, and the local conventions of the communities in which they each lived.

51. Taylor, *Social World*, 148.

52. Lucas, "Trouwverbod," 186.

53. Nieuwenhuys, *Tussen Twee Vaderlanden*, 17; Lucas, "Trouwverbod," 86; Taylor, *Social World*.

54. C. Chivas-Baron, *La femme française aux colonies* (Paris: Larose, 1929), 103.

55. When concubinage was condemned in the 1920s in India, Malaysia, and Indonesia, the rapid spread of venereal disease prompted renewed efforts to reorder the domestic arrangements of European men. Butcher, *British in Malaya*; Ming, "Barracks-Concubinage"; Jean Taylor, "The World of Women in the Colonial Dutch Novel," *Kabar Seberang* 2 (1977): 26–41; Ballhatchet, *Race, Sex and Class*.

56. Stoler, *Capitalism and Confrontation*, 33; Lucas, "Trouwverbod," 90–91.

57. Hesselink, "Prostitution," 216.

58. In the mid-nineteenth century these arrangements are described as a "necessary evil" with no emotional attachments to native women, for whom "the meaning of our word 'love' is entirely unknown" (Ritter, *De Europeaan*, 21). This portrayal of concubinage as a loveless practical union contrasted sharply with the image of the nyai in Chinese literature in the Indies. M. Bocquet-Siek argues that it was precisely the possibility of romantic love that made concubinage with Javanese or Sudanese women so attractive to Chinese men ("Some Notes on the Nyai Theme in Pre-war Peranakan Chinese Literature," paper presented for the Asian Studies Association of Australia, University of Adelaide, May 13, 1984, 8–9). Cf. Eugene D. Genovese's discussion of the categorical denial that love could enter into relations between slaveholder and slave in the American South: "[T]he tragedy of miscegenation lay not in its collapse into lust and sexual exploitation, but in the terrible pressure to deny the delight, affection and love that so often grew from tawdry beginnings" (*Roll, Jordan, Roll: The World the Slaves Made* [New York: Pantheon, 1976], 419).

59. Nieuwenhuys, *Tussen Twee Vaderlanden*, 21.

60. Taylor, "World of Women," 29.

61. In the case of the Indies, interracial marriages increased at the same time that concubinage fell into sharp decline (van Marle, "De Groep"). This rise was undoubtedly restricted to Indisch Europeans (those born in the Indies) who may have been eager to legalize preexisting unions in response to the moral shifts accompanying a more European cultural climate of the 1920s (Jacobus van Doorn, *A Divided Society: Segmentation and Mediation in Late-Colonial*

Indonesia [Rotterdam: CASPA, 1985]). It should not be taken as an indication of less closure among the highly endogamous European-born (totok) population of that period (I owe this distinction in conjugal patterns to Wim Hendrik).

62. Cf. George Fredrickson, *White Supremacy: A Comparative Study in American and South African History* (New York: Oxford University Press, 1981), 109.

63. Ming, "Barracks-Concubinage," 70.

64. Butcher, *British in Malaya*, 138.

65. B. J. Moore-Gilbert, *Kipling and "Orientalism"* (New York: St. Martin's Press, 1986), 48.

66. Ibid., 48; George Woodcock, *The British in the Far East* (New York: Atheneum, 1969), 164.

67. A. Tirefort, " 'Le bon temps' ": La communauté française en basse Côte d'Ivoire pendant l'entre-deux guerres, 1920–1940," Troisième Cycle (Centre d'Etudes Africaines, 1979), 134. In British Africa "junior officers were not encouraged to marry, and wives' passages to Africa were not paid" (Gann and Duignan, *Rulers of British Africa*, 240) .

68. Taylor, *Social World*, 128.

69. *Koloniale Verslag*, quoted in Lucas, "Trouwverbod," 82.

70. Tirefort, " 'Le bon temps,' " 31.

71. Gilles de Gantes, *La population française au Tonkin entre 1931 et 1938*, Mémoire de Maitrise (Aix-en-Provence: Université de Provence, Centre d'Aix, Institut d'Histoire des Pays d'Outre-Mer, 1981), 138.

72. Butcher, *British in Malaya*.

73. Janice N. Brownfoot, "Memsahibs in Colonial Malaya: A Study of European Wives in a British Colony and Protectorate, 1900–1940," in Callan and Ardener, *Incorporated Wife*, 191.

74. Het Pauperisme Commissie, *Het Pauperisme onder de Europeanen* (Batavia: Landsdrukkerij, 1901); Nieuwenhuys, *Tussen Twee Vaderlanden*, 20–23; Hesselink, "Prostitution," 208.

75. Jordan, *White over Black*, 140. Carl N. Degler made a similar point when contrasting the shortage of European women in the Portuguese colonies to the family emigration policy of the British in North America. He argued that the former gave rise to widespread miscegenation and a vast population of mulattos, the "key" to contrasting race relations in the United States and Brazil (*Neither Black nor White: Slavery and Race Relations in Brazil and the United States* [New York: Macmillan, (1971) 1986], 226–38).

76. Despite differences between French assimilationist rhetoric, Dutch tolerance of intermarriage, and Britain's overtly segregationist stance, similar perceptions and practices that tied the maintenance of racial distinctions to sexual control are striking in these otherwise varied contexts. See, for example, Pierre-Jean Simon, *Rapatriés d'Indochine: Un village franco-indochinois en Bourbonnais* (Paris: L'Harmattan, 1981), 46–48), who argues that although French colonial rule was generally thought to be more racially tolerant than that of the British, racial distinctions in French Indochina were vigorously

maintained in practice. John Laffey also has argued that the cultural relativistic thinking tied to associationist rhetoric was used by Indochina's French colon to uphold inequalities in law and education ("Racism in Tonkin before 1914," *French Colonial Studies* 8 [1977]: 65–81).

77. Malleret, *L'exotisme indochinois;* Robert J. Gordon and Mervyn J. Meggitt, "The Decline of the Kipas," in *Law and Order in the New Guinea Highlands: Encounters with Enga,* ed. Robert J. Gordon and Mervyn J. Meggitt (Hanover, N.H.: University Press of New England, 1985), 39–70. Also see chapter 2.

78. James Boutilier, "European Women in the Solomon Islands, 1900–1942: Accommodation and Change on the Pacific Frontier," in *Rethinking Women's Roles: Perspectives from the Pacific,* ed. Denise O'Brien and Sharon W. Tiffany (Berkeley: University of California Press, 1984), 173–99; Thomas George Percival Spear, *The Nabobs: A Study of the Social Life of the English in Eighteenth-Century India* (London: Oxford University Press, 1963); Woodcock, *The British;* Cohen, *Rulers of Empire.*

79. Ch. Grall, *Hygiène coloniale appliquée: Hygiène de l'Indochine* (Paris: Ballière, 1908), 74.

80. Beverley Gartrell, "Colonial Wives: Villains or Victims?" in Callan and Ardener, *Incorporated Wife,* 165–85; Knibiehler and Goutalier, *La femme au temps;* Callaway, *Gender, Culture and Empire.*

81. Strobel, "Gender and Race," 378–79.

82. Spear, *The Nabobs;* Pierre Nora, *Les français d'Algérie* (Paris: R. Julliard, 1961).

83. Nora, *Les français d'Algérie,* 174.

84. Mannoni, *Prospero and Caliban,* 115.

85. Raymond Kennedy, *The Ageless Indies* (New York: John Day, 1947), 164.

86. Tirefort, " 'Le bon temps,' " 197.

87. Gann and Duignan, *Rulers of British Africa,* 242; also see Rita Cruise O'Brien, *White Society in Black Africa: The French in Senegal* (London: Faber and Faber, 1972), 59.

88. Nandy, *Intimate Enemy,* 9–10.

89. Cohen, *Rulers of Empire,* 122.

90. J. de Vere Allen, "Malayan Civil Service, 1874–1941: Colonial Bureaucracy/Malayan Elite," *Comparative Studies in Society and History* 12, no. 2 (1970): 169.

91. Ibid., 168. According to Degler the tenor of race relations was set by attitudes of European women who were not inherently more racist but were able to exert more influence over the extramarital affairs of their men. Contrasting race relations in Brazil and the United States, he contends that British women in the English settlements had more social power than their Portuguese counterparts and therefore slave-holding men could and did less readily acknowledge their mulatto offspring (*Neither Black nor White,* 238).

92. Strobel, "Gender and Race," 378; Degler, *Neither Black nor White*, 189.

93. Brownfoot, "Memsahibs," 191.

94. Strobel, "Gender and Race," 378.

95. See p. 31.

96. Knibiehler and Goutalier, *La femme au temps*, 76.

97. Taylor, "World of Women," 27.

98. Clerkx, *Mensen in Deli*.

99. Lucas, "Trouwverbod," 94–95.

100. Taylor, "World of Women," 31–32; Lucas, "Trouwverbod," 95.

101. Tiffany and Adams, *Wild Woman*.

102. Strobel, "Gender and Race," 379; Schmidt, "Ideology," 411.

103. Deborah Kirkwood, "Settler Wives in Southern Rhodesia: A Case Study," in Callan and Ardener, *Incorporated Wife*, 158; Schmidt, "Ideology," 412; Kennedy, *Islands of White*, 128–147; Hansen, *Distant Companions*.

104. Amirah Inglis, *The White Women's Protective Ordinance: Sexual Anxiety and Politics in Papua* (London: Sussex University Press, 1975), vi.

105. Boutilier, "European Women," 197.

106. Schmidt, "Ideology"; Inglis, *White Women's Protective Ordinance*; Kirkwood, "Settler Wives"; Kennedy, *Islands of White*, 1987; Boutilier, "European Women."

107. Philip Mason, *The Birth of a Dilemma: The Conquest and Settlement of Rhodesia* (New York: Oxford University Press, 1958), 246–47.

108. Charles van Onselen, "Prostitutes and Proletarians, 1886–1914," in *Studies in the Social and Economic History of the Witwatersrand, 1886–1914*, vol. 1 (New York: Longman, 1982); Schmidt, "Ideology"; Inglis, *White Women's Protective Ordinance*; Strobel, "Gender and Race"; Kennedy, *Islands of White*, 128–47.

109. Thomas R. Metcalf, *The Aftermath of Revolt: India, 1857–1870* (Princeton: Princeton University Press, 1964), 290.

110. van Onselen, "Prostitutes."

111. Inglis, *White Women's Protective Ordinance*, 8, 11.

112. Emmanuel Sivan, *Interpretations of Islam, Past and Present* (Princeton: Darwin Press, 1983), 178.

113. Boutilier, "European Women," 197; Inglis, *White Women's Protective Ordinance*, 11; Schmidt, "Ideology," 413.

114. van Onselen, "Prostitutes," 51.

115. Kennedy, *Islands of White*, 138.

116. Stoler, *Capitalism and Confrontation*.

117. Strobel, "Gender and Race."

118. Jean-Luc Vellut, "Matériaux pour une image du blanc dan la société coloniale du Congo Belge," in *Stéréotypes nationaux et préjugés raciaux aux XIXe et XXe Siècles: Sources et méthodes pour une approche historique*, ed. Jean Pirotte, Recueil de travaux d'histoire et de philologie, 6. sér., fasc. 24 (Louvain-La-Neuve: Collège Erasme, Bureau du Recueil, 1982).

119. Inglis, *White Women's Protective Ordinance*, 80.

120. Gartrell, "Colonial Wives," 169.

121. Mason, *Birth of a Dilemma*, 247.

122. Kennedy, *Islands of White*, 140.

123. Dowd Hall, " 'The Mind That Burns,' " 64.

124. March Baroli, *La vie quotidienne des français en Algérie* (Paris: Hachette, 1967), 159; O'Brien, *White Society*.

125. Tirefort, " 'Le bon temps,' " 112.

126. Paul Mercier, "The European Community of Dakar," in *Africa: Social Problems of Change and Conflict: Readings*, ed. Pierre L. Van den Berghe (San Francisco: Chandler, 1965), 292.

127. Caroline Ralston, *Grass Huts and Warehouses: Pacific Beach Communities of the Nineteenth Century* (Canberra: Australian National University Press, 1977); Knibiehler and Goutalier, *La femme au temps*; Callaway, *Gender, Culture and Empire*, 111.

128. Dowd Hall, " 'The Mind That Burns,' " 1984.

129. Jean Marie Antoine de Lanessan, *L'indo-chine française* (Paris: F. Alcan, 1889), 450; Grace Corneau, *La femme aux colonies* (Paris: Librairie Nilsson, 1900), 12.

130. Gantes, *La population française*, 45.

131. Archive d'Outre Mer GG9903, 1893–1894; GG7663 "Emigration des femmes aux colonies 1897–1904."

132. See the Archive d'Outre Mer, Series S.65, "Free Passage Accorded to Europeans," including dossiers on "free passage for impoverished Europeans," GG 9925, 1897; GG 2269, 1899–1903.

133. Boutilier, "European Women," 179.

134. Ming, "Barracks-Concubinage," 84–85.

135. Het Pauperisme, 1901.

136. Knibiehler and Goutalier, *La femme au temps*.

137. European prostitutes and domestics-turned-prostitutes were not banned from South Africa, where at the turn of the century there were estimated to be more than one thousand. Van Onselen argues that their presence was secured by a large white working-class population and a highly unstable labor market for white working-class women ("Prostitutes," 103–62). Also see Van Heyningen, "Social Evil," 192–95, which traces the history of prostitution among continental women in the Cape Colony, arguing that its prohibition was led by white middle-class women "secure . . . in their respectability" and only came about with new notions of racial purity and the large-scale urbanization of blacks after the turn of the century.

138. Hervé Le Bras, "Histoire secrète de la fécondité," *Le Débat* 8 (1981): 77. On the close ties between eugenics and anthropology, see, for France, William Schneider, "Toward the Improvement of the Human Race: The History of Eugenics in France," *Journal of Modern History* 54 (June 1982): 269–91; for the Netherlands, H. Biervliet et al., "Biologism, Racism and Eugenics in the Anthropology and Sociology of the 1930s," *Netherlands Journal of Sociology* 16, no. 1 (1980): 69–92; and for Britain, Paul B. Rich, "The Long Victorian

Sunset: Anthropology, Eugenics and Race in Britain, c. 1900–48," *Patterns of Prejudice* 18, no. 3 (1984): 3–17.

139. George L. Mosse, *Toward the Final Solution: A History of European Racism* (New York: H. Fertig, 1978), 82. As Mosse notes, the concept of racial degeneration had been tied to miscegenation by Gobineau and others by the mid-nineteenth century but gained common currency in the decades that followed, entering European medical and popular vocabulary at the turn of the century (82–88).

140. Morel, quoted in Mosse, *Final Solution*, 83.

141. Ibid., 87; Daniel J. Kevles, *In the Name of Eugenics: Genetics and the Uses of Human Heredity* (New York: Knopf, 1985), 70–84.

142. Schneider, "Human Race," 1982.

143. Ernest Rodenwaldt, "Eugenetische Problemen in Nederlandsch-Indie," in *Ons Negeslact*, Orgaan van de Eugenetische Vereeniging in Nederland-Indie (1928), 1–8.

144. Mosse, *Final Solution*, 87; Nancy Stepan, *The Idea of Race in Science: Great Britain, 1886–1960* (London: Macmillan in association with St. Anthony's College, Oxford, 1982), 122. British eugenists petitioned to refuse marriage licenses to the mentally ill, vagrants, and the chronically unemployed (Anna Davin, "Imperialism and Motherhood," in Cooper and Stoler, *Tensions of Empire*, 16; Stepan, *Idea of Race*, 123). In the United States a model eugenic sterilization law from 1922 targeted among others "the delinquent, the blind, orphans, homeless and paupers" (Carl Bajema, ed., *Eugenics Then and Now* [Stroudsberg, Pa.: Dowden, Hutchinson & Ross, 1976], 138). In Germany during the same period, "sterilization was widely and passionately recommended as a solution to shiftlessness, ignorance, laziness in the workforce, . . . prostitution[,] . . . illegitimate birth, the increasing number of ill and insane[,] . . . poverty[,] and the rising costs of social services" (Gisela Bock, "Racism and Sexism in Nazi Germany: Motherhood, Compulsory Sterilization, and the State," in *When Biology Became Destiny: Women in Weimar and Nazi Germany*, ed. Renate Bridenthal, Atina Grossmann, and Marion Kaplan [New York: Monthly Review Press, 1984], 27). However, in pronatalist France, the sterilization of social deviants was never widely embraced (Jacques Leonard, "Les origines et les conséquences de l'eugenique en France," *Annales de Démographie Historique* [1985]: 203–14).

145. Linda Gordon, *Woman's Body, Woman's Right: A Social History of Birth Control in America* (New York: Grossman, 1976), 395; Davin, "Imperialism and Motherhood"; A. James Hammerton, *Emigrant Gentlewomen: Genteel Poverty and Female Emigration, 1830–1914* (London: Croom Helm, 1979).

146. Gordon, *Woman's Body*, 134.

147. Ridley, *Images of Imperial Rule*, 91.

148. Davin, "Imperialism and Motherhood," 12.

149. Eric Hobsbawm, *The Age of Empire, 1875–1914* (London: Weidenfeld and Nicolson, 1987), 253.

150. J. Th. Koks, *De Indo* (Amsterdam: H. J. Paris, 1931), 179–89.

151. A. de Braconier, *Kindercriminaliteit en de Verzorging van Misdadig Aangelegde en Verwaarloosde Minderjarigen in Nederlandsche-Indie* (Baarn: Hollandia-Drukkerij, 1918), 11.

152. Bock, "Racism and Sexism," 1986, 274.

153. Taylor, *Social World;* van Doorn, *Divided Society.*

154. Rodenwaldt, "Eugenetisch Problemen," 1.

155. Pujarniscle, *Philoxène,* 72; also see Robert Louis Delavignette, *Service africain* (Paris: Gallimard, 1946), 41.

156. The articles published in the bulletin of the Netherlands Indies Eugenics Society give some sense of the range of concerns: "bio-genealogical" investigations, the complementarity of Christian thought and eugenic principles, ethnographic studies of mestizo populations, and the role of Indo-Europeans in the anti-Dutch rebellions (see *Ons Nageslacht,* a eugenic review, from the years 1928–32).

157. David Arnold, "European Orphans and Vagrants in India in the Nineteenth Century," *Journal of Imperial and Commonwealth History* 7, no. 2 (1979): 133–58; Vellut, "Matériaux," 97.

158. Taylor, *Social World;* Heather Sutherland, "Ethnicity and Access in Colonial Macassar," in *Papers of the Dutch-Indonesian Historical Conference,* Dutch and Indonesian Steering Committees of the Indonesian Studies Programme (Leiden: Bureau of Indonesian Studies, 1982), 250–77.

159. *Encyclopaedie van Nederland-Indie,* 2d ed. (The Hague: Martinus Nijhoff and E. J. Brill, [1919] 1921), 367.

160. Quoted in David Arnold, "White Colonization and Labour in Nineteenth-Century India," *Journal of Imperial and Commonwealth History* 10, no. 2 (1983): 139.

161. Loutfi, *Littérature,* 112–113; Ridley, *Images of Imperial Rule,* 104. See George L. Mosse, *Nationalism and Sexuality: Respectability and Abnormal Sexuality in Modern Europe* (New York: H. Fertig, 1985), on the relationship among manliness, racism, and nationalism in a European context.

162. Said, *Orientalism,* 42.

163. *Kroniek,* 1917, 49.

164. F. Cool, "De Bestrijding der Werkloosheidsgevolgen in Nederlandsch-Indie Gedurende 1930–1936," *De Economist* 87 (1938): 135–47, 217–43; A. G. Veerde, "Onderzoek Naar den Onivang der Werkloosheid op Java (November 1930–June 1931)," *Koloniale Studien* 16 (1931): 242–73, 503–33; Kantoor van Arbeid, *Werkloosheid in Nederlandsch-Indie* (Batavia: Landsdrukkerij, 1935).

165. A. Dupuy, "La personnalité du colon," *Revue d"Histoire Economique et Sociale* 33, no. 1 (1955): 188.

166. M. René Maunier, *Sociologie coloniale,* (Paris: Domat-Montchrestien, 1932); Pujarniscle, *Philoxène.* Linking physical appearance to moral depravity was not applied to European colonials alone. Eugenic studies abounded with speculations on the constellation of physical traits that signaled immorality in the European lower orders, while detailed descriptions of African and Asian in-

digenous populations paired their physical attributes with immoral tendencies and debased character. See, for example, Pierre-Jean Simon, "Portraits coloniaux des Vietnamiens (1858–1914)," *Pluriel* 10, no. 1 (1977): 29–54, on French colonial descriptions of physical features of Indochinese populations.

167. Maunier, *Sociologie coloniale,* 169.

168. Hughes Le Roux, *Je deviens colon: Moeurs algériennes* (Paris: Calmann Lévy, 1898), 222.

169. Dupuy, "La personnalité," 184–85.

170. Maunier, *Sociologie coloniale,* 174; Jaurequiberry, *Les blancs en pays chauds* (Paris: Maloine, 1924), 25. Historical analyses of earlier colonial ventures followed the same explanatory convention. Thus a 1939 publication of the American Geographical Society used the Portuguese colonies to "illustrate the factors that defeated the whites in the eastern hemisphere":

> The unbridled passions of the lower types of invaders, who included outlaws and prostitutes, brought scandal upon the Portuguese name. As few European women came out to India, miscegenation was common, and even the higher classes degenerated. . . . [L]ife in Goa became orientalized. The whites left all hard work to slaves and fell into luxury, vanity, and sloth. . . . [T]he whites adopted the enervating doctrines that trade disgraces a man and domestic work is beneath a woman's social status. These evils are still rampant in British India, as in most of the Eastern tropics where the Europeans hold sway. (A. Grenfell Price, *White Settlers in the Tropics* [New York: American Geographical Society of New York, 1939], 16)

171. Hartenberg, "Les troubles nerveux et mentaux chez les coloniaux" (Paris, 1910); S. Abbatucci, "Le milieu africain considéré au point de vue de ses effets sur le système nerveux de l'européen," *Annales d'Hygiène et de Médecine Coloniale* 13 (1910): 328–35.

172. C. W. F. Winckel, "The Feasibility of White Settlements in the Tropics: A Medical Point of View," in *Comptes Rendus du Congrès International de Géographie,* Amsterdam, vol. 2, sec. 3c (Leiden: Brill, 1938), 352.

173. Gilman, *Difference and Pathology,* 199, 202.

174. Elaine Showalter, *The Female Malady: Women, Madness, and Culture in England, 1830–1980* (New York: Penguin, 1987), 135.

175. Ch. Joyeux and A. Sice, "Affections exotiques du système nerveux," *Précis de Médecine Coloniale* (Paris: Masson, 1937), 335. Not all medical practitioners adhered to the idea that "tropical neurasthenia" was a specific malady. Those who suggested that use of the term be discontinued considered it is a psychopathology caused by social, not physiological, maladjustment (Millais Culpin, "An Examination of Tropical Neurasthenia," 1926, cited in Price, *White Settlers,* 211).

176. J. E. Spencer and W. L. Thomas, "The Hill Stations and Summer Resorts of the Orient," *Geographical Review* 38, no. 4 (1948): 637–51; Anthony D. King, *Colonial Urban Development: Culture, Social Power, and Environment* (London: Routledge & Kegan Paul, 1976), 165.

177. On the social geography of hill stations in British India and on the pre-dominance of women and children in them, see King, *Colonial Urban Development*, 156–79.

178. Price, *White Settlers*.

179. Joyeux and Sice, "Affections exotiques," 335; Pujarniscle, *Philoxène*, 28.

180. Grall, *Hygiène coloniale*, 51; Price, *White Settlers*; also see Kennedy, *Islands of White*, 123.

181. B. Raptchinsky, *Kolonisatie van Blanken in de Tropen* (The Hague: Bibliotheek van Weten en Denken, 1941), 46. Contrast this thinking on appro-priate colonial lifestyles to that of a Jamaican historian writing in 1793 on the physical characteristics of "tropical whites":

> The women lived calm and even lives, marked by habitual temperance and self-denial. They took no exercise . . . and had no amusement or avocation to compel them to much exertion of either mind or body. . . . Their mode of life and the hot oppressive atmo-sphere produced lax fiber and pale complexions. They seemed to have just risen from a bed of sickness. Their voices were soft and spiritless, and every step betrayed languor and lassitude. Eminently and deservedly applauded for heart and disposition, *no women on earth made better wives or better mothers*. (Quoted in Price, *White Settlers*, 31; my emphasis)

182. Chivas-Baron, *La femme française*; J.-L. Favre, *La vie aux colonies* (Paris: Larose, 1938).

183. Maunier, *Sociologie coloniale*, 171.

184. Dupuy, "La personnalité," 198.

185. Pujarniscle, *Philoxène*, 107.

186. Jacques Mazet, *La condition juridique des métis dans les possessions françaises* (Paris: Domat-Montchrestien, 1932), 8.

187. Douchet, *Métis et congaies d'Indochine* (Hanoi, 1928), 10.

188. Nieuwenhuys, *Tussen Twee Vaderlanden*, 23; A. M. N. Brou, "Le métis franco-annamite," *Revue Indochinois* (July 1907): 897–909; Ming, "Barracks-Concubinage," 75.

189. When children were recognized by a European father, a native mother could neither prevent them from being taken from her nor contest paternal suitability for custody.

190. Het Pauperisme Commissie, *Rapport der Pauperisme-Commissie* (Batavia: Landsdrukkerij, 1903).

191. *Encyclopaedie*, 367.

192. W. Mansvelt, "De Positie der Indo-Europeanen," *Kolonial Studien* 16 (1932): 295. The term *pauperism* was applied in the Indies only to those indi-viduals legally classified as "European" (Ming, "Barracks-Concubinage"). At the turn of the century it referred primarily to a class of Indo-Europeans mar-ginalized from the educated and "developed" elements in European society (J. Th. Petrus Blumberger, *De Indo-Europeesche Beweging in Nederlandsch-Indie* [Haarlem: Tjeenk Willink, 1939], 19). However, pauperism was by no means synonymous with Eurasian status as 75 percent of the "Dutch" community were of mixed descent, some with powerful political and economic standing (A.

de Braconier, "Het Pauperisme Onder de in Ned. Oost-Indie levende Europeanen," *Nederlandsch-Indie* [1917]: 291). As van Doorn notes, "It was not the Eurasian as such, but the 'kleine Indo' [poor Indo] who was the object of ridicule and scorn in European circles" (*Divided Society,* 8). One could argue that the denigration of "poor Indos" coincided with a political bid for increased civil liberties among the wider Indo-European population, that it was as much Eurasian *empowerment* as pauperism that had to be checked.

193. Braconier, "Het Pauperisme," 298.

194. Mansvelt, "De positie"; Blumberger, *De Indo-Europeesche,* 1939.

195. Vellut, "Matériaux," 103.

196. Claire Goldberg Moses, *French Feminism in the Nineteenth Century* (Albany: State University of New York Press, 1984), 208.

197. Knibiehler and Goutalier, *"Femmes et colonisation,"* 37.

198. Ch. Chenet, "Le rôle de la femme française aux colonies: Protection des enfants métis abandonnés," *Le Devoir des Femmes* (February 15, 1936): 8; Knibiehler and Goutalier, *"Femmes et colonisation,"* 35; Henri Sambuc, "Les métis franco-annamites en Indochine," *Revue du Pacifique* (1931): 261.

199. Quoted in Braconier, "Het Pauperisme," 293.

200. Arnold, "European Orphans," 108.

201. Chenet, "Le rôle"; Sambuc, "Les métis," 256–72; Malleret, *L'exotisme indochinois,* 220. Such support did not indicate a liberalization of colonial policy. Conservative colonial architects such as van den Bosch (who instituted the forced cultivation system on Java) were among those most concerned that the government take responsibility for neglected European offspring (Mansvelt, "De Positie," 292).

202. Taylor, *Social World.*

203. In colonial India "orphanages were the starting-point for a lifetime's cycle of institutions" (Arnold, "European Orphans," 113). "Unseemly whites," paupers, the sick, the aged, "fallen women," and the insane were protected, removed from Asian sight, and placed under European control. In Indonesia *Pro Juventute* branches supported and housed together "neglected and criminal" youth with special centers for Eurasian children. In French Indochina, colonial officials debated the advantages of providing segregated education for métis youth "to protect" them from discrimination.

204. Braconier, "Het Pauperisme," 293; Gabriel Louis Angoulvant, *Les Indies Néerlandaises, leur rôle dans l'économie internationale* (Paris: Monde Nouveau, 1926), 102; Albert de Pouvourville, "Le métis," in *Le mal d'Argent* (Paris: Monde Moderne, 1926), 97–114; Sambuc, "Les métis," 261; Malleret, *L'exotisme indochinois.*

205. Grall, *Hygiène coloniale,* 66; M. J. Chailley-Bert, *L'émigration des femmes aux colonies,* Union Coloniale Française Conference, January 12 (Paris: Armand Colin, 1897).

206. Favre, *La vie,* 217.

207. Ibid., 256; Travaux du Groupe d'Etudes Coloniales, *La femme blanche au Congo* (Brussels: Misch and Thron, 1910), 10.

208. Travaux du Groupe d'Etudes Coloniales, *La femme blanche,* 7.

209. Georges Hardy, *Ergaste ou la vocation coloniale* (Paris: Armand Colin, 1929), 78.

210. Delavignette, *Service africain;* Loutfi, *Littérature,* 112; Ridley, *Images of Imperial Rule;* Mosse, *Final Solution,* 86.

211. Mosse, *Final Solution,* 10, 133–52.

212. Ibid., 5.

213. On the importance of cleanliness and cooking in structuring domestic relations from the perspective of Javanese women who worked in Dutch colonial households, see chapter 7.

214. Ridley, *Images of Imperial Rule,* 77.

215. Stoler, *Capitalism and Confrontation,* 42–44.

216. Grall, *Hygiène coloniale,* 65.

217. Davin, "Imperialism and Motherhood," 13; Carol Smith-Rosenberg and Charles Rosenberg, "The Female Animal: Medical and Biological Views of Woman and Her Role in Nineteenth-Century America," *Journal of American History* 60, no. 2 (1973): 351; Bock, "Racism and Sexism," 274; Siep Stuurman, *Verzuiling, Kapitalisme en Patriarchaat: Aspecten van de Ontiwikkeling van de Moderne Staat in Nederland* (Nijmegen: SUN, 1985).

218. Le Bras, "Histoire secrète," 1981, 90.

219. Ridley, *Images of Imperial Rule,* 90.

220. Hunt, " 'Le bébé en brousse,' " 1988.

221. Rodenwaldt, "Eugenetische Problemen," 3. Not everyone agreed with this evaluation. Cf. the following medical report from 1875: "[I]f the white race does not perpetuate itself in Senegal, one need not attribute it to the weakened reproductive properties of the individuals but to the thousands of other bad conditions against which they fight a desperate and incessant battle" (L. Bérenger-Féraud, *Traité clinique des maladies des européens au Sénégal* [Paris: Adrien Delahaye, 1875], 491).

222. Knibiehler and Goutalier, *La femme au temps,* 92; Vellut, "Matériaux," 100.

223. Grall, *Hygiène coloniale,* 65.

224. Price, *White Settlers,* 204.

225. Dorothy Harwood, "The Possibility of White Colonization in the Tropics," in *Comptes Rendus du Congrès International de Geographie* (Leiden: Brill, 1938), 132; Ripley quoted in George W. Stocking, Jr., *Race, Culture, and Evolution: Essays in the History of Anthropology* (New York: Free Press, [1968] 1982), 54; Cranworth, quoted in Kennedy, *Islands of White,* 115.

226. E. H. Hermans, *Gezondscheidsleer voor Nederlandsche-Indie* (Amsterdam: Meulenhoff, 1925), 123.

227. Angoulvant, *Indies Néerlandaises*101.

228. Rodenwaldt, "Eugenetische Problemen," 4.

229. Winckel, "White Settlements"; Price, *White Settlers.* In the search for a way to alleviate metropolitan unemployment, a surge of scientific reports ap-

peared reassessing the medical arguments against European settlement in the tropics (as in the proceedings of the 1938 International Congress of Geography).

230. Hammerton, *Emigrant Gentlewomen.*

231. P. Grimshaw, " 'Christian Woman, Pious Wife, Faithful Mother, Devoted Missionary': Conflicts in Roles of American Missionary Women in Nineteenth-Century Hawaii," *Feminist Studies* 9, no. 3 (1983): 507.

232. Murdoch Mackinnon, "European Children in the Tropical Highlands," *Lancet* 199 (1920): 944.

233. P. Wanderken, "Zoo Leven Onze Kinderen," in *Zoo Leven Wij in Indonesia* (Deventer: W. van Hoeve, 1943), 173.

234. Dominique Chrétien Marie Bauduin, *Het Indische Leven* ('s-Gravenhage: H. P. Leopold, 1941); Bérenger-Féraud, *Traité clinique,* 491.

235. Price, *White Settlers,* 204.

236. Grimshaw, " 'Christian Woman,' " 507.

237. Bauduin, *Het Indische Leven,* 63.

238. Ibid., 63–64.

239. Angoulvant, *Les Indies,* 101.

240. Malleret, *L'éxotisme indochinois,* 164; Grimshaw, " 'Christian Woman,' " 507; Callaway, *Gender, Culture and Empire,* 183–184.

241. June Nash, "Aztec Women: The Transition from Status to Class in Empire and Colony," in Etienne and Leacock, *Women and Colonization,* 140.

242. Martinez-Alier, *Marriage, Class and Colour,* 39.

243. Degler, *Neither Black nor White,* 185.

244. Michael Adas, *Machines as the Measure of Men: Science Technology, and Ideologies of Western Dominance* (Ithaca: Cornell University Press, 1989).

245. Henrika Kuklick, *The Imperial Bureaucrat: The Colonial Administrative Service in the Gold Coast, 1920–1939* (Stanford, Calif.: Hoover Institution Press, 1979).

246. I thank Barney Cohn for pressing me on this issue.

CHAPTER 4. SEXUAL AFFRONTS AND RACIAL FRONTIERS

This material was originally printed in *Comparative Studies in Society and History* 34 (1992): 154–51. Reprinted with permission of Cambridge University Press. An earlier version of this chapter was presented at the American Anthropological Association meetings, Papers in Honor of Eric Wolf, in December 1990, and at the Transnational Institute conference, The Decolonization of Imagination: The New Europe and Its Others, Amsterdam, May 1991. I thank Talal Asad, Val Daniel, Geoff Eley, Lawrence Hirschfeld, Barbara Laslett, Jeffrey Weeks, Luise White, and fellows of the Histories of Sexuality Seminar at the Institute of the Humanities, the University of Michigan, for their comments.

1. Uday Mehta outlines some features of this relationship in "Liberal Strategies of Exclusion," in *Tensions of Empire,* ed. Frederick Cooper and Ann Laura Stoler (Berkeley: University of California Press, 1997), 59–86. He co-

gently argues the more radical claim that the theoretical underpinnings of liberalism were exclusionary and cannot be explained as "an episodic compromise with the practical constraints of implementation" (429).

2. Cochinchina's European population only increased from 594 in 1864 to 3,000 by 1900 (Charles Meyer, *Le français en Indochine: 1860–1910* [Paris: Hachette, (1996) 1985], 70). By 1914 only 149 planters qualified as electors in the Chamber of Agriculture of Tonkin and Annam (John Laffey, "Racism in Tonkin before 1914," *French Colonial Studies* 8 [1977]: 65–81). On Java alone there were several thousand. In 1900 approximately 91,000 persons were classified as European in the Indies. As late as 1931 there were just under 10,500 French civilians in Indochina, whereas the Indies census counted 244,000 Europeans for the same year. See A. van Marle, "De Groep der Europeanen in Nederlands-Indie, Iets over Ontstaan en Groei,"*Indonesie* 5 (1952): 490; and Gilles de Gantes, *La population française au Tonkin entre 1931 et 1938*, Mémoire de Maitrise (Aix-en-Provence: Université de Provence, Centre d'Aix, Institut d'Histoire des Pays d'Outre-Mer, 1981), 23.

3. The label *Indisch* is dense with connotation. According to Jean Taylor, it is a cultural marker of a person who "partook of Mestizo culture in marriage, practice, habit and loyalty" (*The Social World of Batavia: European and Eurasian in Dutch Asia* [Madison: University of Wisconsin Press, 1983], xx). It was most often used in contrast to the lifestyle and values of those Dutch *(totok)* born and bred in Europe who refused such cultural accommodations and retained a distinct distance from native customs and social practice. For example, the European *blivjers* (those who stayed in the Indies) were commonly referred to as *Indisch* as opposed to *vertrekkers* (those Europeans who treated their residence in the Indies as a temporary assignment away from their native metropolitan homes).

4. See Martin Lewis, "One Hundred Million Frenchmen: The 'Assimilation' Theory in French Colonial Policy," *Comparative Studies in Society and History* 3, no. 4 (1961): 129–51. While the social positioning of Eurasians in India is often contrasted to that in the Indies, there are striking similarities in their changing and contradictory legal and social status in the late nineteenth century. See Mark Naidis, "British Attitudes toward the Anglo-Indians," *South Atlantic Quarterly* 62, no. 3 (1963): 407–22; and Noel Pitts Gist and Roy Dean Wright, *Marginality and Identity: Anglos-Indians as a Racially Mixed Minority in India* (Leiden: E. J. Brill, 1973), esp. 7–20.

5. For further discussion of degeneracy and the eugenics of empire, see chapter 3.

6. The following section draws on Etienne Balibar's "Fichte et la frontière intérieure: A propos des *Discours á la nation allemande*," *Les Cahiers de Fontenay* (June 1990): 58–59.

7. Fichte quoted in Balibar, "Fichte et la frontière," 4.

8. See Andre-Pierre Taguieff's discussion of "la hantise du métissage" in *La force du préjugé: Essai sur le racisme et ses doubles* (Paris: Découverte, 1987), where he argues that the métis problem is not about being "of mixed blood" but about the indeterminate "social identity" that métissage implies (345).

9. French and Dutch rejection of métis as a legal category did not follow the same trajectory or occur in the same way. The legal status of métis children with unknown parents was still a subject of French juridical debate in the 1930s in a discourse in which race and upbringing were offered as two alternative criteria for judging whether a métis child should be granted the rights of a French citizen. See Jacques Mazet, *La condition juridique des métis dans les possession françaises* (Paris: Domat-Montchrestien, 1932).

10. Paul B. Rich, *Race and Empire in British Politics* (New York: Cambridge University Press,1986), has argued that the antiblack riots in Liverpool and Cardiff in 1919 represented "the extension of rising colonial nationalism into the heart of the British metropolis itself at a time when nationalist ferment was being expressed in many parts of the empire" (122).

11. The many French juridical tracts in the 1930s debating whether métis should be made a separate legal category (distinct from "European" and "native") and the political effects of doing so were produced in the tense environment in which Vietnamese nationalists were making their opposition more strongly felt. See David G. Marr's two important studies of the Vietnamese nationalist movements: *Vietnamese Anticolonialism, 1885–1925* (Berkeley: University of California Press, 1971); and *Vietnamese Tradition on Trial, 1920–1945* (Berkeley: University of California Press, 1981). Marr makes no reference to the métis problem (generally or as it related to citizenship, immigration, and education) in either text.

12. Battles for legal reform regarding paternity suits, illegitimate children, and family law waged by jurists, feminists, and religious organizations in the Netherlands and the Indies at the turn of the century were animated by the same political projects and fears. In the colonies, the social menace of illegitimate children was less about future criminals and prostitutes than about their mixed-blood origins, unverified European paternity, and the influence of their native mothers. These were debates about race and the protection of European men by the colonial state. For contrasting discourses on paternity suits in the Indies and Holland, compare Selma Sevenhuijsen's discussion of this political debate, *De Orde van het Vaderschap: Politieke Debatten over Ongehuwd Moederschap, Afstamming en Huwelijk in Nederland, 1870–1900* (Amsterdam: Stichting Beheer IISG, 1987), to R. Kleyn's "Onderzoek Naar het Vaderschap," *Het Recht in Nederlandsch-Indie* 67 (1896): 130–50. On paternity suits in French colonies, see Jean E. Pedersen, " 'Special Customs': Paternity Suits and Citizenship in France and the Colonies, 1870–1912," in *Domesticating the Empire: Race, Gender, and Family Life in French and Dutch Colonialism,* ed. Julia Clancy-Smith and Frances Gouda (Charlottesville: University Press of Virginia, 1998), 43–64.

13. On the relationship between racial supremacy and new conceptions of British motherhood at the turn of the century, see Anna Davin, "Imperialism and Motherhood,"in Cooper and Stoler, *Tensions of Empire,* 87–151; and Lucy Bland, " 'Guardians of the Race' or 'Vampires upon the Nation's Health'? Female

Sexuality and Its Regulations in Early Twentieth-Century Britain," *Netherlands Journal of Sociology* 16, no. 1 (1982): 69–92. On the European maternalist discourse of the emerging welfare states, see Seth Koven and Sonya Michel, "Womanly Duties: Maternalist Politics and the Origins of Welfare States in France, Germany, Great Britain, and the United States, 1980–1920," *American Historical Review* 95 (October 1990): 1076–1108.

14. See Eugene Weber, *Peasants into Frenchmen: The Modernization of Rural France, 1870–1914* (Stanford, Calif.: Stanford University Press, 1976), 114. Despite refutations of Weber's argument that much of France's rural population neither considered itself French nor embraced a national identity, his ancillary argument holds that debates over the nature of French citizenship and identity were contested at the time.

15. Ibid., 110.

16. Raoul Girardet, ed., *Le nationalisme français, 1871–1914* (Paris: Seuil, [1966]1983), 30–31; and Robert A. Nye, *Crime, Madness, and Politics in Modern France: The Medical Concept of National Decline* (Princeton: Princeton University Press, 1984), 140.

17. See Pierre Nora, *Les français d'Algerie* (Paris: R. Julliard, 1961).

18. French fertility rates began to decline in the late eighteenth century, much earlier than in other European countries, but then decreased most sharply after 1881. See Claire Moses, *French Feminism in the Nineteenth Century* (Albany: State University of New York Press, 1984), 20–24.

19. See Nora's *Les français d'Algérie* and Stephen Wilson's study of French antisemitism at the turn of the century, where he argues that violent cultural racism in the colonies against Jews provided a "model" for antisemitism at home: *Ideology and Experience: Antisemitism in France at the Time of the Dreyfus Affair* (London: Associated University Presses, 1982), esp. 230–42.

20. See Ali de Regt, "De Vorming van een Opvoedings-Traditie: Arbiederskinderen Rond 1900," in *Geschiedenis van Opvoeding en Onderwijs*, ed. B. Kruithof, J. Nordman, and Piet de Rooy (Nijmegen: SUN, 1982), 394–409. On the new focus on family morality and motherhood in the development of the modern Dutch state, see Siep Stuurman, *Verzuiling, Kapitalisme en Patriarchaat: Aspecten van de Ontiwikkeling van de Moderne Staat in Nederland* (Nijmegen: SUN, 1985). But compare Jacques Donzelot's *The Policing of Families* (New York: Pantheon, 1979), which traces state interventions in French family life and child-rearing practices to a half century earlier.

21. See I. Schoffer, "Dutch 'Expansion' and Indonesian Reactions: Some Dilemmas of Modern Colonial Rule (1900–1942)," in *Expansion and Reaction: Essays on European Expansion and Reaction in Asia and Africa*, ed. H. L. Wesseling (Leiden: Leiden University Press, 1978); and Maarten Kuitenbrouwer, *The Netherlands and the Rise of Modern Imperialism: Colonies and Foreign Policy, 1870–1902*, trans. Hugh Beyer (New Yort: St. Martin's Press, 1991), 220.

22. See Colin Bundy, "Vagabond Hollanders and Runaway Englishmen: White Poverty in the Cape before Poor Whiteism," in *Putting a Plough to the Ground: Accumulation and Dispossession in Rural South Africa, 1850–1930,* ed. William Beinart, Peter Delius, and Stanley Trapido (Johannesburg: Ravan Press, (1987), 101–28. On the colonial state's concern about Dutch paupers in the Indies, see *Rapport der Pauperisme-Commissie* (Batavia: Landsdrukkerij, 1902). These issues are discussed further in chapter 5.

23. See Kuitenbrouwer, *The Netherlands,* 223.

24. For the Netherlands, compulsory education was only instituted in 1900, about the same time it was introduced in the Indies. See Jan Romein, *The Watershed of Two Eras: Europe in 1900,* trans. Arnold J. Pomerans (Middletown, Conn.: Wesleyan University Press, 1978), 278.

25. See T. H. Marshall, *Class, Citizenship, and Social Development: Essays* (Westport, Conn.: Greenwood Press, [1963] 1973), 81.

26. See Gerald Sider, "When Parrots Learn to Talk, and Why They Can't: Domination, Deception, and Self-Deception in Indian-White Relations," *Comparative Studies in Society and History* 29, no. 1 (1987): 3–23.

27. See Mary Poovey, *Uneven Developments: The Ideological Work of Gender in Mid-Victorian England* (Chicago: University of Chicago Press, 1988).

28. Benedict Anderson, *Imagined Communities: Reflections on the Origin and Spread of Nationalism* (London: Verso, 1983), 136.

29. For more on the protean quality of racial categories, see my "Racial Histories and Their Regimes of Truth," *Political Power and Social Theory* 11 (1997): 183–255.

30. Archives d'Outre-Mer [hereafter AOM], Protectorat de l'Annam et du Tonkin, no. 1506, 17 December 1898.

31. See AOM, December 1898, No. 39127, Report from Monsieur E. Issaud, Procureur-Général to the Résident Superieure in Tonkin.

32. "Rélations immorales qui ont pu éxister entre le détenue et celui qui s'est déclaré son père" AOM, Fonds Amiraux, No. 1792, 12 December 1898.

33. AOM, Fonds Amiraux, No. 1792, 12 December 1898, Report of M. Villemont, Procureur in Haiphong, to the Procureur-Général, Head of the Judicial Service in Hanoi.

34. According to the procureur-général, Raoul Abor, these fraudulent acknowledgments were threatening to submerge the French element by a deluge of naturalized natives. Raoul Abor, *Des reconnaisances frauduleuses d'enfants naturels en Indochine* (Hanoi: Imprimerie Tonkinoise, 1917), 25.

35. George L. Mosse, *Nationalism and Sexuality: Respectability and Abnormal Sexuality in Modern Europe* (New York: H. Fertig, 1985).

36. See Etats-Généraux du Féminisme, *Exposition coloniale internationale de Paris 1931, rapport général présenté par le Gouverneur Général Olivier* (Paris: Imprimerie Nationale, 1931), esp. 133–41.

37. John Boswell, *The Kindness of Strangers: The Abandonment of Children in Western Europe from Late Antiquity to the Renaissance* (New York:

Pantheon, 1988). According to Boswell, this relinquishment might occur by "leaving them somewhere, selling them, or legally consigning authority to some other person or institution" (24). Abandonment in colonial practice did not fit this definition.

38. See Donzelot, *The Policing of Families*, 29.

39. I use this term to suggest the definitive exile from European society that abandonment implied (not social death in the sense employed by Orlando Patterson with regard to slavery).

40. AOM, Amiraux 7701, 1899, Statute of the Société de protection et d'éducation des Jeunes Métis Français de la Cochinchine et du Cambodge.

41. AOM, No. 164, 11 May 1904 (my emphasis).

42. AOM, 13 November 1903.

43. Letter from the Administrative Resident in Bac-giang to the Résident Supérieur in Hanoi.

44. AOM, No. 151, to Governor-General in Hanoi from Monsieur Paris, President of the Société de Protection et d'Éducation des Jeunes Métis Français Abandonnés, 29 February 1904. This concern over the entrapment of European young women in the colonies coincided with campaigns against the white slave trade in Europe. See Frank Mort, *Dangerous Sexualities: Medico-Moral Politics in England since 1830* (New York: Routledge & Kegan Paul, 1987), 126–27.

45. For such recommendations, see A. M. N. Brou, "Le métis franco annamite," *Revue Indochinois* (July 1907): 897–909; Douchet, *Métis et congaies d'Indochine* (Hanoi, 1928); Mazet, *La condition juridique;* Philippe Gossard, *Etudes sur le métissage principalement en A.O.F.* (Paris: Presses Modernes, 1934).

46. Etats-Généraux du Féminisme, *Exposition coloniale*, 139.

47. AOM, Amiraux 7701, *Report on Métis in the Dutch East Indies* (1901).

48. "Courte notice sur les métis d'Extreme Orient et un particulier sur ceux de l'Indochine," Firmin Jacques Montagne, AOM, Amiraux 1669 (1903), 1896–1909.

49. Concern over poor whites was evident in a number of colonies at this time, in part because social welfare was coming to be perceived in metropole and colony in new ways. In Calcutta nearly one-fourth of the Anglo-Indian community in the late nineteenth century was on poor relief (Gist and Wright, *Marginality and Identity*). Colin Bundy argues that white poverty in South Africa was redefined "as a social problem to be tackled by state action rather than as a phenomenon of individual failure to be assuaged by charity" ("Vagabond Hollanders," 104). In the Indies this reassignment of poor relief from civic to state responsibility was resisted and only partially made.

50. *Rapport der Pauperisme-Commissie*, 1902; *Uitkomsten der Pauperisme-Enquete: Algemeen Verslag* (Batavia: Landsdrukkerij, 1902); *Het Pauperisme onder de Europeanen in Nederlandsch-Indie*, pts. 3, 5 (Batavia: Landsdrukkerij, 1901); *Uitkomsten der Pauperisme-Enquete: Gewestelijke Verslagen* (Batavia:

Landsdrukkerij, 1901); *De Staatsarmenzorg voor Europeanen in Nederlandsch-Indie* (Batavia: Landsdrukkerij, 1901).

51. See J. Th. Petrus Blumberger, *De Indo-Europeesche Beweging in Nederlandsch-Indie* (Haarlem: Tjeenk Willink, 1939), 26.

52. J. M. Coetzee has argued that the British railed against Boer idleness precisely because they refused the possibility that an alternative, native milieu may have been preferred by some European men and may have held a real attraction: *White Writing: On the Culture of Letters in South Africa* (New Haven: Yale University Press, 1988).

53. *Encyclopedie van Nederlandsch-Indie,* 2d ed. (The Hague: Martinus Nijhoff and E. J. Brill, [1919] 1921), 367.

54. AOM, Archives Centrales de l'Indochine, Nos. 9147, 9273, 7770, 4680.

55. In 1900 an educational survey carried out in Dutch elementary schools in the Indies among fifteen hundred students found that only 29 percent of those with European legal standing knew some Dutch and more than 40 percent knew none at all. Paul van der Veur, "Cultural Aspects of the Eurasian Community in Indonesian Colonial Society," *Indonesia* 6 (October 1968): 45.

56. See Izaak Johannes Brugmans, *Geschiedenis van her Onderwijs in Nederlandsch-Indie* (Groningen: J. B. Wolters, 1938).

57. See J. F. Kohlbrugge, "Prostitutie in Nederlandsch-Indie," *Indisch Genootschap* 19 (February 1901): 2–36.

58. Abor, *Des reconnaissance frauduleuses.*

59. B. V. Houthuysen, *Het Betwisten eener Erkenning als Natuurlijk Kind* (Batavia: G. Kolff, 1898), 5–6.

60. See "Ons Pauperisme," *Mededeelingen der Vereeniging "Soeria Soemirat,"* no. 2 (1892): 8. One proof offered to confirm the falsity of these claims was that fathers conferred on these children "repulsive and obscene" names frequently enough that a government ruling stipulated that no family name could be given that "could humiliate the child" (G. H. Koster, "Aangenomen Kinderen en Staatsblad Europeanen," *De Amsterdammer,* July 15, 1922).

61. AOM, Letter No. 164, ll May 1904, from the administrative résident in Bac-giang to the résident superieure, Hanoi.

62. See Mazet, *La condition juridique.*

63. Kohlbrugge, "Prostitutie," 23.

64. Linda Gordon discusses this issue in *Heroes of Their Own Lives: The Politics and History of Family Violence: Boston, 1880–1960* (New York: Vintage, 1988).

65. See Mazet, *La condition juridique,* 37, 42.

66. Debates over the legal status of métis and its political consequences were not confined to the French. The International Colonial Institute in Brussels created by Joseph Chailley-Bert in 1893 discussed the issue in at least three of its international meetings in 1911, 1920, and 1924. See *Comptes Rendus de l'Institut Colonial International* (1911, 1920, 1924).

67. Mazet, *La condition jurdique,* 114.

68. Ibid., 80.

69. Ibid., 90.

70. Statute of the "Société de Protection des Enfants Métis," 18 May 1904, Article 37.

71. There were similar debates at the International Colonial Congress of 1889, where scholars and administrators compared and contrasted pedagogic strategies for natives in the colonies to those for the peasants in France. See Lewis, "One Hundred Million Frenchmen," 140.

72. J. Kohlbrugge, "Het Indische Kind en Zijne Karaktervorming," in *Blikken in het Zielenleven van den Javaan en Zijner Overheerschers* (Leiden: E. J. Brill, 1907).

73. For a colonial reading of Foucault's analysis of the historical shift from a "symbolics of blood" to an "analytics of sexuality" in the mid- and late nineteenth century see my *Race and the Education of Desire: Foucault's History of Sexuality and the Colonial Order of Things* (Durham, N.C.: Duke University Press, 1995), esp. chaps. 1, 2.

74. See, for example, Paul Gilroy, "*There Ain't No Black in the Union Jack*": *The Cultural Politics of Race and Nation* (London: Hutchinson, 1987). Also compare Etienne Balibar's discussion of nationalism and racism in France where he argues for a new intensification of cultural difference in marking the interior frontiers of the modern nation-state: Etienne Balibar and Immanuel Wallerstein, *Race, Nation, Class: Ambiguous Identities*, trans. Chris Turner (London: Verso, 1991).

75. Gilroy ("*There Ain't No Black*," 43) argues that the "novelty" of the new racism "lies in the capacity to link discourses of patriotism, nationalism, xenophobia, Englishness, Britishness, militarism, and gender differences into a complex system which gives 'race' its contemporary meaning. These themes combine to provide a definition of 'race' in terms of culture and identity. . . . Race differences are displayed in culture which is reproduced in educational institutions and, above all, in family life. Families are therefore not only the nation in microcosm, its key components, but act as the means to turn social processes into natural, instinctive ones."

76. This is precisely the period for which George Stocking identifies a semantic shift of culture in the social sciences from its singular humanistic sense of refinement to the plural anthropological notion of cultures as shared values of specific human groups. Stocking may be right that Franz Boas made the analytic leap from culture to cultures as an antiracist response, but these two connotations were not so clearly distinct: both defined the exclusionary tenets of nationalist and racist projects. See George W. Stocking, Jr., *Race, Culture, and Evolution: Essays in the History of Anthropology* (New York: Free Press, [1968] 1982), esp. 200–4.

77. In *French Modern: Norms and Forms of the Social Environment* (Cambridge, Mass.: MIT Press, 1989), esp. 126–67, Paul Rabinow traces the effects of neo-Lamarckian thinking on colonial pacification policies. My concern

is more with how this attention to milieu fixed the boundaries of the European community and identified threats to it.

78. Note the similarity to Pierre Bourdieu's notion of "habitus" as a stylization of life, an unconsciously embodied set of rules of behavior that engenders durable schemes of thought and perception. These colonial discussions of milieu denote both a social ecology of acquired competencies and a psychological environment in which certain dispositions are promoted and affective sensibilities are shaped. Pierre Bourdieu, *Outline of a Theory of Practice*, trans. Richard Nice (Cambridge: Cambridge University Press, 1977), 82.

79. "In de beschaafd wereld, niemand zonder staatsverband mag zijn" (K. H. Beyen, *Het Nederlanderschap in verband met het international recht* [Utrecht, 1890], quoted in J. A Nederburgh, *Wet en Adat* [Batavia: Kolff, 1898b], 83). The word *staatsverband* literally means "relationship to the state." Nederburgh distinguishes it from nationality and defines it as "the tie that exists between the state and each of its members, the membership of the state" (91). Dutch scholars of colonial history say the term is rarely used but connotes citizenship.

80. Nederburgh, *Wet en Adat*, 87–88.

81. Ibid., 87.

82. See Willem Wertheim's incisive review of R. D. Kollewijn's *Intergentiel Recht* in *Indonesie* 19 (1956): 169–73. Nederburgh's name comes up in this critique of Kollewijn, whose liberal rhetoric and opposition to such conservatives as Nederburgh belied the fact that he praised the virtues of the Indies mixed-marriage legislation of 1898, despite the racist principles that underwrote it.

83. Nederburgh, *Wet en Adat*, 88.

84. Ibid., 90.

85. Kooreman, 1906.

86. Ibid.

87. William Edward van Mastenbroek, *De Historische Ontwikkeling van de Staatsrechtelijke Indeeling der Bevolking van Nederlandsch-Indie* (Wageningen: H. Veenman & Zonen, 1934), 70.

88. See W. Prins, "De Bevolkingsgroepen in het Nederlandsch-Indische Recht," *Koloniale Studien* 17 (1933): esp. 677.

89. Ibid., 677; van Marle, "De groep der Europeanen," 110.

90. See Mastenbroek, *De Historische Ontwikkeling*, 87.

91. See Karen Offen, "Depopulation, Nationalism and Feminism in Fin-de-Siècle France," *American Historical Review* 89, no. 3 (1984): 648–76.

92. The following discussion is based on several documents (abbreviated as indicated below): *Verslag van het Verhandelde in de Bijeenkomsten der Nederlandsch-Indische Juristen-Vereeniging* on 25, 27, and 29 June 1887 in Batavia [hereafter *JV*]; "Voldoet de wetgeving betreffende huwelijken tusschen personen behoorende tot de beide staatkundige categorien der Nederlandsch Indische bevolking (die der Europeanen en met hen, en die der Inlanders-, en met hen gelijkgestelden) aan de maatschappelijke behoefte? Zoo neen, welke wijzigingen zijn noodig? (1887) [hereafter *VW*]; J. A. Nederburgh, *Gemengde*

Huwelijken, Staatsblad 1898, No. 158: Officiele Bescheiden met Eenige Aanteekeningen [hereafter *GH*].

93. Wertheim, *Intergentiel Recht*.

94. The term *mixed marriages* (*gemengde huwelijken*) had two distinct but overlapping meanings in the Indies at the turn of the century. In common usage it referred to a contract between a man and a woman of different racial origin. The state defined it as "a marriage between persons who were subject to different laws in the Netherlands Indies" with no reference to race. The distinction is significant for at least two reasons: (1) because the designations of legal standing as inlander versus European cut across the racial spectrum, with generations of mixed-bloods falling on different sides of this divide; and (2) because *adat* (customary) and Dutch law followed different rulings with respect to the marriage contract, divorce, inheritance, and child custody.

95. Gender and racial hierarchies may only partly account for the fact that in 1895 more than half of the European men in the Indies still lived with native women outside of marriage. The juridical debates on the legal reform of mixed marriages suggest that there were women who chose cohabitation over legal marriage. Thus concubinage may not have been an appropriate term for some of these arrangements, nor does it necessarily reflect what options women may have perceived by taking that route.

96. Prins, "De Bevolkingsgroepen," 665. That some women chose cohabitation over legal mixed marriages is rarely addressed on the assumption that all forms of cohabitation could be subsumed by the term *concubinage*, signaling the moral degradation of a "kept woman" that the later term implies. References in these legal debates to the fact that some women chose not to marry beg for further study.

97. Nederburgh, *GH*, 17.

98. As the chairman of the commission poignantly illustrated, a woman with native legal standing could be arrested for wearing European attire at the very moment she emerged from the building in which she had just married a European. Nor could a European man and his wife of native standing take the short boat trip from Soerabaya to Madura without permission of the authorities as sea passage for natives was forbidden by law (*JV*, 29–30).

99. Nederburgh, *GH*, 20.

100. Ibid., 13.

101. Ibid.

102. *JV*, 39.

103. Ibid.

104. Ibid., 51.

105. Ibid., 40. The arguments presented over the mixed-marriage ruling are many more and more elaborate than this short account suggests. There were indeed those such as Abendanon (the lawyer friend of Kartini) whose proposals raised yet a whole different set of options than those offered in these accounts. He argued that both man and woman should be given European status, except in those cases in which a native man preferred to retain his rights under

adat law. Abendanon also boldly refuted the claim that any European woman who chose to marry a native man was already debased and pointed out that for many Dutch girls in the Netherlands this was not the case. But these arguments were peripheral to the main debate and had little sway in the final analysis.

106. Nederburgh, *GM*, 64.

107. See van Marle's "De Groep der Europeanen," 322, 328. Van Marle suggests that the much larger number of illiterate women of European standing in central Java and the Moluccas compared to the rest of the Indies indicates that there were not a significant number of mixed marriages in these regions (330). But this was not the case everywhere. In East Java, European men acknowledged more of their métis children but continued to cohabit with the native mothers of their children outside of marriage (495).

108. Douaire Klerck, *Eenige Beschouwingen over Oost-Indische Toestanden* (Amsterdam: Versluys, 1898), 3–19.

109. S. S. J. Ratu-Langie, *Sarekat Islam* (Baam: Hollandia Drukkerij, 1913), 21.

110. A woman who had contracted a mixed marriage could, on divorce or the death of her husband, declare her desire to reinstate her original nationality as long as she did so within a certain time. However, a native woman who married a European man and subsequently married and divorced a man of non-European status could not recoup her European status.

111. Ernest Rodenwalt, "Eugenetische Problemen in Nederlandsch-Indie," in *Ons Nageslacht, Orgaan van de Eugenetische Vereeninging in Nederland-Indie* (1928): 1–8.

112. Johan Winsemius, *Nieuw-Guinee als Kolonisatie-Gebied voor Europeanen en van Indo-Europeanen* (Purmerend: J. Muusses, 1936), 227. [Ph.D. dissertation, Faculty of Medicine, University of Amsterdam, 1936.]

113. Articles on "rassenwaan" (racialism), "rassenbewustzijn" (racial consciousness), and "rassenhaat" (racial hatred) appeared in various short-lived and more enduring publications such as *De Taak, De Opwekker,* and *De Banier* in the teens and 1920s. The well-established *Koloniaal Tijdschrift* published a set of long articles on "racial feelings, racial consciousness, and racial policy" in 1928 and 1929.

114. H. H. F. van de Wall, "Rassenhaat," *Jong Indie* 1 (1908): 120–22.

115. Jacques van Doorn emphasizes the dualistic policy on poverty in the 1930s in *De Laatste Eeuw van Indie: Ontwikkeling en Ondergang van een Koloniaal Project* (Amsterdam: Bert Bakker, 1994). I would refer to it rather as a three-tiered policy, not a dualistic one.

116. Blumberger, *De Indo-Europeesche,* 5.

117. See Paul van der Veur, "The Eurasians of Indonesia: A Problem and Challenge in Colonial History," *Journal of Southeast Asian History* 9, no. 2 (1966): 191–207; and "Cultural Aspects."

118. On the various currents of Eurasian political activity, see van der Veur, "Eurasians of Indonesia." On the importance of Indo individuals in the early Malay press and nationalist movement, see Takashi Shiraishi, *An Age in*

Motion: Popular Radicalism in Java, 1912–1926 (Ithaca: Cornell University Press, 1990), esp. 37, 58–59. Neither account addresses Eurasian class differences and diverse political allegiances.

119. Blumberger, *De Indo-Europeesche*, 50.

120. Rudolph Mrazek suggests that the early silent rejection of the Indo-European community from the Indonesian nationalist movement turned explicit under Sukarno in the mid-1920s, when Indo-Europeans were barred from membership in nationalist organizations. He argues that this silence among Dutch-educated nationalist leaders on the Indo question should be understood as a response to their own culturally hybrid friendships, formation, and identification (pers. com.).

121. On this failed effort, see P. J. Drooglever, *De Vaderlandse Club 1929–1942: Totoks en de Indische Politiek* (Franeker: Wever, 1980).

122. Ibid., 285.

123. *Verbond Nederland en Indie*, no. 3, September 1926. In the late 1920s, the subtitle *A Fascist Monthly* was appended to the title.

124. Liisa Malkki explores the meanings attached to displacement and uprootedness in the national order of things in "National Geographic: The Rooting of Peoples and the Territorialization of National Identity among Scholars and Refugees," *Cultural Anthropology* 7, no. 1 (1992): 24–44. André-Pierre Taguieff examines the French National Front's rhetoric on the dangers of rootless immigrant workers in "The Doctrine of the National Front in France (1972–1989)," *New Political Science* 16–17 (1985): 28–68.

125. See A. de Braconier, "Het Pauperisme onder de in Ned. Oost-Indie levende Europeanen," *Nederlandsch-Indie* (1917): 293.

126. AOM, Amiraux, Enquetê sur Métissage, 53.50.6.

127. René Martial, *Les métis* (Paris: Flammarion, 1942), 58.

128. See Taguieff, "The Doctrine of the National Front." Also see my "Racist Visions for the Twenty-first Century: On the Cultural Politics of the French Radical Right," in *Rethinking Post-Colonialism*, ed. David Goldberg and Ato Quayson (Oxford: Blackwell, forthcoming).

129. On the recent British discourse on Britishness and the cultural threat of Islam to that identity, see Talal Asad, "Multiculturalism and British Identity in the Wake of the Rushdie Affair," *Politics & Society* 18, no. 4 (1990): 455–80.

130. Hazel Carby, in "On the Threshold of Woman's Era: Lynching, Empire and Sexuality," *Critical Inquiry* 12, no. 1 (1985): 262–77, argues that African American women intellectuals at the turn of the century focused on the mixed race figure because it enabled an exploration of relations between the races and demythologized concepts of pure blood and pure race and debunked the notion of degeneracy through amalgamation. Pauline Hopkins was one who embraced the mulatto to argue that miscegenation was not the inmost desire of the non-white peoples but rather a result of white rape (274). In both the Indies and the United States, the figure of the Indo-mulatto served to convey strategic social dilemmas and political messages.

131. Taylor, *Social World*, 155.

132. As Carole Pateman argues, the sexual contract was fundamental to the functioning of European civil society, with the principle of patriarchal right defining the social contract between men and the individual and citizen as male: *The Sexual Contract* (Cambridge: Polity, 1988).

133. For a recent study of métissage, see Françoise Vergès, *Monsters and Revolutionaries: Colonial Family Romance and Métissage* (Durham, N.C.: Duke University Press, 1999).

134. I thank Luise White for pressing me on this point.

CHAPTER 5. A SENTIMENTAL EDUCATION

This chapter is a much revised, expanded, and reconceived version of "A Sentimental Education: Native Servants and the Cultivation of European Children in the Netherlands Indies," in *Fantasizing the Feminine in Indonesia*, ed. Laurie J. Sears (Durham, N.C.: Duke University Press, 1997).

1. Dr. J. J. Nieuwenhuis, "Lichamelijke Opvoeding en Onderwijs Hervorming in Nederlands-Indie," *Koloniale Studien*, pt. 1 (1920): 482–536.

2. J. A. Nederburgh, *Wet en Adat* (Batavia: Kolff, 1898), 88.

3. W. Prins, "De Bevolkingsgroepen in het Nederlandsche-Indisch Recht," *Koloniale Studien* 17 (1933): 677.

4. Jean Taylor, *The Social World of Batavia: European and Eurasian in Dutch Asia* (Madison: University of Wisconsin Press, 1983), 144.

5. Carolyn Steedman, *Landscape for a Good Woman: A Story of Two Lives* (New Brunswick, N.J.: Rutgers University Press, 1985), 14.

6. *Encylopaedie van Nederlandsche-Indie*, 2d ed. (The Hague: Martinus Nijhoff and E. J. Brill, [1919] 1921), 782–83.

7. A. Wilkens, *Het Inlandsche Kind in Oost-Indie en Iets over den Javaan* (Amsterdam: Van Kampen, 1849), 22–24.

8. *Algemeen Schoolversalg onder ultimo 1849*, quoted in *Het Pauperisme Onder de Europeanen in Nederlandsch-Indie, Eerste Gedeelte: Algemeen Overzicht* (Batavia: Landsdrukkerij, 1902), 56–57.

9. Pieter Johannes Veth, *Over den Toestand en de Behoeften van het Onderwijs der Jeugd in Nederlandsch Indie* (Amsterdam: Spin and Zoon, 1850), 22.

10. See Jeroen H. H. Dekker, "Transforming the Nation and the Child: Philanthropy in the Netherlands, Belgium, France and England, c.1780–c.1850," in *Charity, Philanthropy and Reform: From the 1690s to 1850*, ed. Hugh Cunningham and Joanne Innes (London: Macmillan, 1998), 130–47.

11. A. de Braconier, *Kindercriminaliteit en de Verzorging van Misdadig Aangeledge en Verwaarloosde Minderjarigen in Nederlandsch Indie* (Baarn: Hollandia-Drukkerij, 1918), 20–21.

12. Ibid., 20.

13. Ibid., 20.

14. Ibid., 20–21, 25, 26.

15. Wilkens, *Het Inlandsche Kind*, 38.

16. Doris Sommer, *Foundational Fictions: The National Romances of Latin America* (Berkeley: University of California Press, 1991).

17. Benedict Anderson, *Imagined Communities: Reflections on the Origin and Spread of Nationalism* (London: Verso, 1983).

18. Norbert Elias, *Power and Civility* (New York: Pantheon, [1939] 1982), 328.

19. In "On Acquiring Social Categories: Cognitive Development and Anthropological Wisdom," *Man* 23 (December 1988): 611–38, Lawrence Hirschfeld argues against the common view that children's cognitions are "ready-made from previous generations" (Bloch, quoted on 613). Also see William A. Corsaro and Donna Eder, "Children's Peer Cultures," *Annual Review of Sociology* 16 (1990): 197–220, which holds that children's socialization is a process of altering and reshaping the cultural environments of their parents and peers.

20. Carolyn Steedman, *Childhood, Culture, and Class in Britain: Margaret McMillan, 1860–1931* (London: Virago, 1990), 62. For the United States, some historians date the increased interest in child-rearing problems as occurring between the 1820s and the 1860s. See, for example, Robert Sunley, "Early Nineteenth-Century American Literature on Child-rearing," in *Childhood in Contemporary Cultures*, ed. Margaret Mead and Martha Wolfenstein (Chicago: University of Chicago Press, 1955), 150–68.

21. The transnational exchange and creation of new knowledge about infant care in the mid-nineteenth century suggests an already globalized discourse of social reform. For example, histories of day care centers for the poor in the Netherlands looked to and referenced similar initiatives in New York, Boston, London, South Africa, and France, as in J. W. Elink Sterk's history of nurseries: *Proeve Eener Geschiedenis der Armen-Bewaarscholen* (Arhem: J. G. Stenfert Kroese, 1849).

22. For a useful review of this debate, see Francisco O. Ramirez and John Boli, "The Political Construction of Mass Schooling: European Origins and Worldwide Institutionalization, " *Sociology of Education* 60, no. 1 (1987): 2–17.

23. The "uplifting" of native women as a common focus of colonial administrations and European women's organizations is well documented. Nancy Rose Hunt, for example, notes that the "foyer sociaux" in the Belgian Congo were domestic training institutions for African women from the urban elite, or "evolué": "Domesticity and Colonialism in Belgian Africa: Usumbara's *Foyer Social*, 1945–1960," *Signs* 15, no. 3 (1990): 447–74. My point here is the marked absence of this uplifting project for mothers of illegitimate métis children. The focus was rather on the *removal* of children from their care and uplifting of the children alone.

24. This distinction was suggested to me by Linda Gordon. See the discussion of this issue in her *Heroes of Their Own Lives: The Politics and History of Family Violence: Boston, 1880–1960* (New York: Vintage, 1988).

25. Dr. D. R. Horst, "Opvoeding en Onderwijs van Kinderen van Europeanen en Indo-Europeanen in Indie," *De Indische Gids* 2 (1900): 989–96. Also see W. Philippus Coolhaas, "Zorg voor Bepaalde Bevolkingsgroepen," in *Insulinde: Mensch en Maatschappij* (Deventer: W. van Hoeve, 1944), 147.

26. Th. J. A. Hilgers and H. Douma, *De Indische Lagere School Toegepaste Opvoedkunde en Methodeleer ten Dienste van Onderwijzers en Kweekelingen* (Weltevreden, 1908), 11–12.

27. See Ann Taylor Allen, "Gardens of Children, Gardens of God: Kindergartens and Daycare Centers in 19th Century Germany," *Journal of Social History* 19, no. 3 (1986): 433–50.

28. Little of the literature on the history of childhood in the United States addresses questions of race. See, for example, N. Ray Hiner, "The Child in American Historiography: Accomplishments and Prospects," *Psychohistory Review* 7 (Summer 1978): 13–23, and the extensive bibliography therein that includes neither bibliograpical reference to race, child care, and childhood nor a comment by the author on that absence. This is all the more striking because the article begins with a quote on family life in eighteenth-century Virginia by Edmund Morgan, author of the classic study of race and republican policies on the mixing of slave men and indentured white women in the seventeenth century South. Also see Bruce Bellingham, "The History of Childhood since the 'Invention of Childhood': Some Issues in the Eighties," *Journal of Family History* 13, no. 2 (1988): 347–58, which urges a focus on "politicized meanings of childhood" but with no reference to the making of race.

29. Lily E. [van Rijswijk-]Clerkx dates the first bewaarschool to 1827, under the initiative of the Maatschappij tot Nut van 't Algemeen. See her *Moeders, Kinderen en Kinderopvang* (Nijmegen: Socialistsche Uitgeverij, 1981), 50.

30. Allen, "Gardens of Children," 446.

31. For a history of how Froebel's theories informed kindergarten movements throughout Europe and the United States, see Michael Steven Shapiro, *Child's Garden: The Kindergarten Movement from Froebel to Dewey* (University Park: Pennsylvania State University Press, 1983).

32. See Nancy Cott, "Notes toward an Interpretation of Antebellum Childrearing," *Psychohistory Review* 7, no. 4 (1973): 4–20.

33. Shapiro makes the similar point that for Froebel, "ironically, women from diverse social backgrounds came to share the same misfortune: poor child management" (*Child's Garden*, 25).

34. For England, see Nanette Whitbread, *The Evolution of the Nursery-Infant School: A History of Infant and Nursery Education in Britain, 1800–1970* (London: Routledge and Kegan Paul, 1972); for the Netherlands, see Lily E. Clerkx, "De Kinderjuffrouw: Opvoedster en Dienstbode tussen Ouders en Kinderen," *Sociologisch Tijdschrift* 10, no. 4 (1984): 671–715; for Germany, see Allen, "Gardens of Children"; for the United States, see Elizabeth Dale Ross, *The Kindergarten Crusade: The Establishment of Preschool Education in the United States* (Athens: Ohio University Press, 1976).

35. Izaak Johannes Brugmans, *Geschiedenis van het Onderwijs in Nederlandsch-Indie* (Groningen: J. B. Wolters, 1938), 110. Also see *Algemeen Schoolverslag Onder Ultimo 1849*, quoted in *Het Pauperisme onder de Europeanen* (1902), 56–57.

36. Brugmans, *Geschiedenis*, 110.

37. *Algemeen Verslag (1858) van den Staat van het Schoolwezen in Nederlandsch-Indie*, 1859,16–17.

38. Quoted in *Nota's over het Armwezen en het Pauperisme* (Batavia: Landsdrukkerij, 1902), 39.

39. *Het Pauperisme onder de Europeanen* (1902), 57.

40. Horst, "Opvoeding en Onderwijs," 989–96.

41. *Het Pauperimse onder de Europeanen* (1902), 61.

42. *Nota's over het Armwezen en het Pauperisme*, 27.

43. As Horst clearly put it, "The equivalence of all Indo-Europeans with Dutch-born Nederlanders was an evident act of generosity and liberalism toward the Indies, but the Nederlander runs the risk of degenerating through this fraternization [verbroedering] and this must be guarded against with all the power that is in us" ("Opvoeding en Onderwijs," 989).

44. "Nota van het lid der commissie, den Heer J. van der Steur, gedagteekend Magelang, 14 Augustus 1902," in *Nota's over het Armwezen en het Pauperisme*, 39.

45. On the "unbridled freedom" that Indies administrations feared in the wake of the May 1848 demonstration by Dutch city fathers in Batavia against government educational policy and its imagined ties to the revolutions in Germany and France earlier that year, see my chapter "States of Sentiment, Reasons of State" in my *Along the Archival Grain: Colonial Cultures and Their Affective States* (Princeton: Princeton University Press, forthcoming); and Cees Fasseur's discussion of this "demonstration" (*gisting*) in *De Indologen: Ambtenaren voor de Oost, 1825–1950* (Amsterdam: Bert Bakker, 1993), esp. 116–30.

46. Horst, "Opvoeding en Onderwijs," 990.

47. M. G. Dumontier, "Du rôle politique de l'éducation dans l'enseignement français en Indochine," in *Congrès Colonial International de Paris* (Paris: Challamel, 1889), 185–98.

48. Clerkx has argued that many middle-class women preferred and chose to keep their children at home with "uncultured" servants rather than place them in the Froebel schools because they associated them with the bewaarscholen that were designed to contain and discipline children of the unemployed and laboring poor. "De Kinderjuffrouw," 681.

49. These letters were collected in the organization's brochure, "Clerkx-Methode voor Schriftelijk Voortgezet Onderwijs," 1931.

50. Brugmans, *Geschiedenis*.

51. According to the 1849 Annual General Report on Education in the Indies (*Algemeen Verslag van den Staat van het Schoolwezen in Nederlandsche-Indie* [1849], 16), in 1833, of the 760 students attending, 400 enjoyed gratis status.

52. Brugmans, *Geschiedenis.*

53. L. J. Hissink-Snellebrand, "Wat is ten doen in het Belang van de Indische Paupermeisjes en tot Verstreking van het Nederlandsche Element in Nederlandsch-Indie," *Indische Genootschap* (1910): 37–57.

54. Braconier, *Kindercriminaliteit,* 24.

55. H. van Kol, *Uit Onze Kolonien* (Leiden: A. W. Sijthoff, 1903), 770.

56. Hissink-Snellebrand, "Wat is ten doen," 40.

57. Braconier, *Kindercriminaliteit,* 39.

58. "Moeten Onze Kinderen naar Holland?" *'t Onderwijs* 36 (15 September 1906): 420.

59. In *The Politics and Poetics of Trangression* (Ithaca: Cornell University Press, 1986), esp. 5–6, Peter Stallybrass and Allon White identify features of this servant-child relationship that figured in the Indies as well.

60. James Clifford, *The Predicament of Culture: Twentieth-Century Ethnography, Literature, and Art* (Cambridge, Mass.: Harvard University Press, 1988), 4.

61. J. J. Pigeaud, *Iets over Kinderopvoeding: Raadgevingen voor Moeders in Indie* (Samarang: G. C. T. van Dorp, 1896).

62. See chap. 5, "Domestic Subversions and Children's Sexuality," in Ann Laura Stoler, *Race and the Education of Desire: Foucault's History of Sexuality and the Colonial Order of Things* (Durham, N.C.: Duke University Press, 1995), 137–64.

63. Plantersschoolvereeniging "Brastagi," *De Opvoeding van het Europeesche Kind in Indie* (Brastagi, 1934), 10.

64. P. Wanderken, "Zoo Leven Onze Kinderen," in *Zoo Leven wij in Indonesia* (Deventer: W. van Hoeve, 1943), 173.

65. See, for example, Douglas Medin's lucid discussion of pyschological essentialism in "Concepts and Conceptual Structure," *American Psychologist* (December 1989): 1469–81.

66. See Lawrence Hirschfeld, *Race in the Making: Cognition, Culture, and the Child's Construction of Human Kinds* (Cambridge, Mass.: MIT Press, 1996); and Dan Sperber, "Anthropology and Psychology: Towards an Epidemiology of Representations," *Man* 20 (March 1985): 73–89.

67. A. de Braconier, Kindercriminaliteit en de Verzorging van Misdadig Aangelegde en Verwaarloosde Minderjarigen in Nederlandsch Indie (Baarn: Hollandia Drukkerij, 1918), 8.

68. Nieuwenhuis, "Lichamelijke Opvoeding," 519–20.

69. J. Kohlbrugge, "Het Indische Kind en Zijne Karaktervorming," in *Blikken in het Zielenleven van den Javaan en Zijner Overheerschers* (Leiden: E. J. Brill, 1907), 112.

70. Horst, "Opvoeding en Onderwijs."

71. Dominique Chrétien Marie Bauduin, *Het Indische Leven* ('s-Gravenhage: H. P. Leopold, 1941), 63.

72. Arjun Appardurai uses this concept to a different end in "Topographies of the Self: Praise and Emotion in Hindu India," in *Language and the Politics*

of Emotion, ed. Catherine A. Lutz and Lila Abu-Lughod (Cambridge: Cambridge University Press, 1990), 92–112.

CHAPTER 6. A COLONIAL READING OF FOUCAULT

This chapter is based on a much revised text of two addresses delivered in 1997, the first at the conference, Gender and Imperialism, at the University of the Western Cape in Cape Town, South Africa; and then at the conference, Foucault Goes Troppo, at Australian National University in Canberra. Both were public lectures for an interdisciplinary audience, some of whom had read *Race and the Education of Desire,* more of whom had not. Parts of the middle section draw directly on the book with commentary, sometimes with little modification. In both cases, I was asked to discuss the book. The self-referential quality of the chapter derives from the fact that the second conference was prompted by and in part devoted to it.

1. Michel Foucault, *The History of Sexuality,* vol. 1: *An Introduction* (New York: Vintage, 1978), 103 [hereafter *HS*].

2. I discuss this relationship between sentiment and the state through the venue of moral philosophy in my *Along the Archival Grain: Colonial Cultures and Their Affective States* (Princeton: Princeton University Press, forthcoming).

3. On Nietzsche's notion of history in the comfort zone, see "On the Uses and Disadvantages of History for Life," in *Untimely Meditations,* trans. R. J. Hollingdale (Cambridge: Cambridge University Press, 1996), 57–124.

4. Michel Foucault, "Nietzsche, Genealogy, History," in *The Foucault Reader,* ed. Paul Rabinow (New York: Pantheon, 1972), 76.

5. See Christian Delacampagne's review titled "Foucault, genealogie du bio-pouvoir," *Le Monde des Livres* (February 21, 1997): 1.

6. On Foucault's productive and political period in Tunisia, see David Macey, *The Lives of Foucault* (New York: Pantheon, 1993), 183–208.

7. Ann Laura Stoler, "Colonial Aphasia and the Place of Race in France," Keynote Address at the conference, 1951–2000: Transatlantic Perspectives on *The Colonial Situation,* New York University, April 2001.

8. It should be noted that some of Foucault's thinking on subjugated knowledge has been widely available for some time under the title "Two Lectures" in *Power/Knowledge: Selected Interviews and Other Writings, 1972–1977,* ed. Colin Gordon (Brighton, Sussex: Harvester Press, 1977); and more recently in Nicholas B. Dirks, Geoff Eley, and Sherry B. Ortner, eds., *Culture/Power/History: A Reader in Contemporary Social Theory* (Princeton: Princeton University Press, 1994). Out of context, there is no mention in either volume that these "two lectures" are the first two from the 1976 series on race.

9. See my "Racial Histories and Their Regimes of Truth," *Political Power and Social Theory* 11 (1997): 183–255.

10. *HS,* 3.

11. Ibid.

12. See chapter 3 in this volume; Anne McClintock, *Imperial Leather: Race, Gender, and Sexuality in the Colonial Conquest* (New York: Routledge, 1995); and Robert Young, *Colonial Desire: Hybridity in Theory, Culture and Race* (London: Routledge, 1995).

13. *HS*, 57–58.

14. Timothy Mitchell, *Colonising Egypt* (Cambridge: Cambridge University Press, 1991).

15. Paul Rabinow, *French Modern: Norms and Forms of the Social Environment* (Cambridge, Mass.: MIT Press, 1989); Gwendolyn Wright, *The Politics of Design in French Colonial Urbanism* (Chicago: University of Chicago Press, 1991).

16. Mary Louise Pratt, *Imperial Eyes: Travel Writing and Transculturation* (New York: Routledge, 1991).

17. Etienne Balibar, "Foucault et Marx: L'enjeu du nominalisme," in *Michel Foucault, Philosophe: Rencontre Internationale, Paris, 9, 10, 11 Janvier 1988* (Paris: Seuil, 1989).

18. See my "Racist Visions for the Twenty-first Century: On the Cultural Politics of the Radical Right in France," in *Relocating Postcolonialism*, ed. David Goldberg and Ato Quayson (Oxford: Blackwell, 2002).

19. Despite the recent rash of books on racism and the radical Right documenting the French National Front's rise, split, and fall, texts used in middle schools (college) and lycées categorically avoid mention of the history of racism in France.

20. More sophisticated analyses can be found in Jean-Yves Camus, *Le front national: Histoire et analyses* (Paris: O. Laurens, 1997), and on the National Front as an integral product of French history and politics, see the journalist Hubert Huertas's *FN: Made in France* (Paris: Editions Autrestemps, 1997).

21. Michel Foucault, *"Il faut défendre la société": Cours au Collège de France (1975–1976)* (Paris: Seuil/Gallimard, 1997). Delacampagne's review ("Foucault, genealogie") remarks on the appropriateness of the 1976 lectures' appearance in the first of a thirteen-year series because they are a turning point, a "pause" in Foucault's trajectory.

22. See, for example, Delacampagne, "Foucault, genealogie," 1.

23. Yves Charles Zarka, "Michel Foucault: De la guerre des races au biopouvoir," in *Cités: Philosophe, politique, histoire* (Paris: Presses Universitaires de France, 2000).

24. *HS*, 54.

25. Michel Foucault, *Difendere la società* (Florence: Pont alle Gracie, 1990), 66.

26. *HS*, 118–19.

27. *HS*, 123.

28. See Nicholas Thomas, *Colonialism's Culture: Anthropology, Travel, and Government* (Princeton: Princeton University Press, 1994).

29. *HS*, 123; emphasis added.

30. Uday Mehta, "Liberal Strategies of Exclusion," in *Tensions of Empire: Colonial Cultures in a Bourgeois World*, ed. Frederick Cooper and Ann Laura Stoler (Berkeley: University of California Press, 1997), 59–86.

31. Doris Sommer, "Irresistible Romance: The Foundational Fictions of Latin America," in *Nation and Narration*, ed. Homi K. Bhabha (Berkeley: University of California Press, 1990), 87.

32. *HS*, 121.

33. *HS*, 47.

34. Michel Foucault, *Résumé des cours, 1970–1982* (Paris: Julliard, 1989), 78.

35. Michel Foucault, *The Archaeology of Knowledge*, trans. A. M. Sheridan Smith (New York: Pantheon, 1972), 36–37.

36. Ibid., 152.

37. See my "Racial Histories," footnote 5.

CHAPTER 7. MEMORY-WORK IN JAVA

This chapter appeared in a slightly different version in *Comparative Studies in Society History*, January 2000. It was written with support from the Luce Foundation and the Rackham Discretionary Fund, University of Michigan. Special thanks are due the following friends and colleagues who wrestled with its earlier versions: Julia Adams, Lauren Berlant, Leonoor Broeder, Victoria Ebin, Andrew Goss, Nancy Florida, Lawrence Hirschfeld, Laura Kunreuther, Janet McIntosh, Penelope Papailias, Peter Pels, Julie Skurski, Peggy Somers, and Doris Sommer, as well as Shula Marks, Megan Vaughan, Robert Young, Catherine Hall, and the audiences at the University of Michigan, Nuffield College, Oxford University, the University of Essex, the University of London, and the University of Amsterdam for their critical and engaged discussions.

In collaboration with Karen Strassler, a Ph.D. candidate in anthropology at the University of Michigan, I carried out interviews in 1996 and 1997. We were assisted by two Indonesian researchers, Nita Kariani Purwanti, an anthropologist, and Didi Kwartanada, a historian, as well as Dias Pradadimara, a Ph.D. candidate in history at the University of Michigan.

The research was focused in Yogyakarta, a city best known as the seat of Javanese culture and for its crucial role in the nationalist revolution. In the 1930s it was a provincial capital surrounded by sugar plantations. There was a clearly marked European area, surrounded by the dense urban *kampung* neighborhoods where many of the people we interviewed were still living. A few people we interviewed lived outside of the city, having worked as house servants for employees of the sugar estates.

Discussions among the five of us yielded inevitable differences of opinion that appear here principally in our effort to keep a wide range of interpretive possibilities in play. Nevertheless, my and Strassler's interests shaped the chapter's argument and final form, and we alone are responsible for its shortcomings.

1. Renato Rosaldo, *Culture and Truth: The Remaking of Social Analysis* (Stanford, Calif.: Stanford University Press, 1985), 68.

2. Ibid.

3. Friedrich Nietzsche, "The Uses and Advantages of History," in *Untimely Meditations*, trans. R. J. Hollingdale (Cambridge: Cambridge University Press, [1874] 1996), 68.

4. As E. M. Beekman has noted in his introduction to E. Breton de Nijs's fictionalized memoir, *Faded Portraits*, some of the most powerful Dutch colonial memoirs and novels are marked by "an evocation of a place with its tactile and olfactory peculiarities" (3). Also see Ernest Hillen, *The Way of a Boy: A Memoir of Java* (London: Penguin, 1993).

5. We know of no autobiographies written by Indonesian men and women who worked in domestic service. Most of the Indonesian memoirs of life in the colonial period, such as *Verboden voor Honden en Inlanders: Indonesiers Vertellen over hun Leven in de Koloniale Tijd* [Forbidden for Dogs and Natives: Indonesians Recount Their Lives in the Colonial Period], ed. H. C. Beynon (Amsterdam: Jan Mets, 1995), are accounts of people who, though sometimes of humble origins, were well educated—often in Dutch schools.

6. A *slendang* is a cloth worn across the chest over one shoulder so that an infant can lie across the front of the body. Somewhat older children often straddle with one leg behind and the other in front so that the child's weight is on the hip while still able to breast-feed.

7. This memory is that of an Indo-Dutch woman whose Javanese aunt ("Bibi Koetis") was the object of her warmest recollections of being a child in Java. See Lin Scholte, *Bibi Koetis voor Altijd* (Amsterdam: E. Querido, 1974), 43–44.

8. Robert Nieuwenhuys, *De Schim van Nenek Tidjah* (Amsterdam: Huis Clos, 1995), 56. This is the prelude to his forthcoming autobiography, *Sinjo Robbie*.

9. Ibu Tinem, March 24, 1997, interview with Didi Kwartanada and Nita Kariani Purwanti.

10. Raymond Williams, *Marxism and Literature* (London: Oxford University Press, 1977), 134.

11. See my chapter, "States of Sentiment, Reasons of State," in *Along the Archival Grain: Colonial Cultures and Their Affective States* (Princeton: Princeton University Press, forthcoming).

12. See Paul Stoller, *Embodying Colonial Memories: Spirit Possession, Power, and the Hauka in West Africa* (New York: Routledge,1995); on "the sensory experience of history," see C. Nadia Seremetakis, ed., *The Senses Still: Perception and Memory as Material Culture in Modernity* (Boulder, Colo.: Westview Press, 1994).

13. We were inspired here by Carolyn Steedman's *Landscape for a Good Woman: A Story of Two Lives* (New Brunswick, N.J.: Rutgers University Press, 1987).

14. Although many postcolonial intellectuals do not discuss memory per se, analysis of postcolonial subject formation can be considered an investigation of remembering and the enduring effects of colonialism. Here we are looking at something different: explicit articulations of past experience (rather than sub-

ject-effects) among a population of largely uneducated, nonelites (rather than postcolonial intellectuals). See, among others, Frantz Fanon, *Black Skin, White Masks*, trans. Charles Lam Markmann (New York: Grove Press, [1952] 1967); Homi K. Bhabha, *The Location of Culture* (New York: Routledge, 1994); and Gayatri Chakravorty Spivak, *In Other Worlds: Essays in Cultural Politics* (New York: Methuen, 1987).

15. See, among others, Michel-Rolph Trouillot, *Silencing the Past: Power and the Production of History* (Boston: Beacon Press, 1995); and Joanne Rappaport, *Cumbe Reborn: An Andean Ethnography of History* (Chicago: University of Chicago Press, 1994). On how colonial archives "remember," see Ann Laura Stoler, " 'In Cold Blood': Hierarchies of Credibility and the Politics of Colonial Narratives," *Representations* 37 (Winter 1992): 151–89.

16. See Stoler, *Embodying Colonial Memories*; Shahid Amin, *Event, Metaphor, Memory: Chari Chaura, 1922–1992* (Berkeley: University of California Press, 1995); Gyanendra Pandey, *Memory, History and the Question of Violence: Reflections on the Reconstruction of Partition* (Calcutta: K. P. Bagchi, 1999) and "Violence 'Out There': Memories of Partition," paper presented at the conference, Religion and Nationalism in Europe and Asia, Amsterdam, November (1995). For work on how the colonial is "remembered" in contemporary cultural discourse, see Michael T. Taussig, "Culture of Terror—Space of Death: Roger Casement's Putamaya Report and the Explanation of Terror," *Comparative Studies in Society and History* 26 (July 1994): 467–97; John Pemberton, *On the Subject of "Java"* (Ithaca: Cornell University Press, 1994); Fernando Coronil and Julie Skurski, "Dismembering and Remembering the Nation: The Semantics of Political Violence in Venezuela," *Comparative Studies in Society and History* 33, no. 2 (1991): 288–377; E. Valentine Daniel, *Charred Lullabies: Chapters in an Anthropography of Violence* (Princeton: Princeton University Press, 1996). Jennifer Cole's "The Work of Memory in Madagascar," *American Ethnologist* 25, no. 4 (1998): 610–33, critiques the assumption that the experience of the colonial pervades postcolonial subjectivities and cultural discourse. While we are concerned here with present-day memories of the mundane routines of colonial life, Cole raises important questions about how colonial memories figure in everyday contemporary life.

17. The neurocognitive psychologist Daniel L. Schacter uses this term to refer to the simultaneous durability and malleability of personal memory in *Searching for Memory: The Brain, the Mind, and the Past* (New York: Basic Books, 1996).

18. For a critique of the retrieval model in psychology, see Asher Koriat and Morris Goldsmith, "Memory Metaphors and the Laboratory/Real-Life Controversy: Correspondence versus Storehouse Conceptions of Memory," *Behavioral and Brain Sciences* 19, no. 2 (1996): 167–228; in historical anthropology, see Trouillot, *Silencing the Past*.

19. On the notion of the archives as a source waiting to be tapped, see my "Colonial Archives and the Arts of Governance: On the Content in the Form," in *Refiguring the Archive*, ed. Carolyn Hamilton (Cape Town: David Philip,

2002). Obviously this hydraulic model of memory is indebted to a Freudian tradition in which memory-work involves releasing repressed memories in a redemptive exercise.

20. Or as Luise White, Stephan Miescher, and David William Cohen put it so well: "The African voice—cradled, massaged, and authenticated within the expert approaches of the African historian—comes to represent (or at least presents the opportunity to reach for) truth while it provisions scholarly claims to objectivity." *African Words, Voices: Critical African Practices in Oral History* (Bloomington: Indiana University Press, 2001).

21. See, for example, Amin's careful account, in *Event, Metaphor, Memory*, of how the murder of twenty-three constables at Chauri Chaura in 1922 has been remembered nationally. Amin draws on testimonies of former participants and observers to rectify dominant versions of a major nationalist event but is less concerned with either the crafting of these acts of remembering or the context of their retelling.

22. Ranajit Guha, "The Small Voice of History," in *Subaltern Studies X: Writings on South Asian History and Society*, ed. Gautam Bhadra, Gyan Prakash, and Susie Tharu (Delhi: Oxford University Press, 1996), 1–12.

23. See Lila Abu-Lughod, "The Romance of Resistance: Tracing Transformations of Power through Bedouin Women," *American Ethnologist* 17, no. 1 (1990): 41–55.

24. See James C. Scott, *Weapons of the Weak: Everyday Forms of Peasant Resistance* (New Haven: Yale University Press, 1985), and *Domination and the Arts of Resistance: Hidden Transcripts* (New Haven: Yale University Press, 1990); Michael T. Taussig, *Shamanism, Colonialism, and the Wild Man: A Study in Terror and Healing* (Chicago: University of Chicago Press, 1987).

25. Ted Swedenburg's compelling study of Palestinian nationalism and selective forgetting takes as its explicit subject the nature of acts of memory. Nevertheless, the frame is still the event-centered history of nationalist narratives and alternative versions stored in "subaltern circuits." *Memories of Revolt: The 1936–1939 Rebellion and the Palestinian National Past* (Minneapolis: University of Minnesota Press, 1995). In a noncolonial context, Luisa Passerini begins from the premise that popular memory contains "stories handed down and kept alive and adapted for the interview": *Fascism in Popular Memory: The Cultural Experience of the Turin Working Class*, trans. Robert Lumley and Jude Bloomfield (Cambridge: Cambridge University Press, 1987), 19.

26. See Gyan Prakash, "Writing Post-Orientalist Histories," *Comparative Studies in Society and History* 32, no. 2 (1990): 383–408; Dipesh Chakrabarty, "Postcoloniality and the Artifice of History: Who Speaks for 'Indian' Pasts?" *Representations* 37 (Winter 1992): 1–26.

27. Thus Boyarin argues that "identity and memory are virtually the same concept." Jonathan Boyarin, ed., *Remapping Memory: The Politics of Timespace* (Minneapolis: University of Minnesota Press, 1994), 23.

28. It is Michel Foucault's notion of "polyvalent mobility" that we think of here. See *The Archaeology of Knowledge*, trans. A. M. Sheridan Smith (New York: Pantheon, 1972), 36–37.

29. Hillen, *Way of a Boy*, 3.

30. Ibu Rubi, February 27, 1997, interview with Kwartanada.

31. On the polarity between sensational, narratable, and thus memorable events and the sensory structure of the everyday as a zone of inattention and forgetfulness, see Seremetakis, *Senses Still*, 19–20.

32. Emphasis on domestic memories may reflect discomfort in Holland with memories of the war against the emergent Indonesian republic as well as other violent aspects of Dutch rule. See Vincent Houben, "A Torn Soul: The Dutch Public Discussion of the Colonial Past in 1995," *Indonesia* 63 (1997): 67–90.

33. Annie Salomons, *Het Huis in de Hitte: Drie Jaar Deli* (Amsterdam: Nederlandsche Keurboejerij, 1932), 5. See also Hein Buitenweg, *Op Java Staat en Huis* (The Hague: Servire, 1960); Maria Dermoût, *Nog Pas Gisteren* (Amsterdam: E. Querido, 1964).

34. See Rudy Kousbroek, *Terug naar Negri Pan Erkoms* (Amsterdam: Meulenhoff, 1995), 243; and the film *Het Meer der Herinnering*. Similarly, Frances Gouda's study of the Dutch in colonial Indonesia dramatically begins a section on colonial nostalgia with an anecdote about a young Dutch girl asking herself why her babu refused to read with her on her bed because she "belonged below on the floor," in *Dutch Culture Overseas: Colonial Practice in the Netherlands Indies 1900–1942* (Amsterdam: Amsterdam University Press, 1995), 1–38, 237–42.

35. Dorothée Buur's annotated bibliography on Indische children's literature lists more than eighty-six stories in which "servants" appear and sixty-eight with babus (*Indische Jeugdliteratuur: Geannoteerde Bibliografie van Jeugdboeken over Nederlands-Indië en Indonesië, 1825–1991* [Leiden: KITLV, 1992). Also see her essay, "Het 'Indische' Element in de Nederlandse Jeugdliteratuur," in *Indische Letteren*, vol. 1 (1986), in which she notes:

> The babu played an especially important role in the lives of children in the Indies. They functioned as a "trait d'union" between mother and child. Sometimes they were brought in if the mother had died. The child learned its first Malay words from the babu and through her came into contact with the native world. From that often developed a loving bond. But there was also a dark side to this bond, if the child continually acquired its appetites from the babu and resisted that from its own parents. (189)

36. As in de Nijs's *Faded Portraits* and in Louis Couperus's *The Hidden Force*, trans. Alexander Teixeira de Mattos (Amherst: University of Massachusetts Press, [1900] 1985). On servants as "the [only] point of contact for Dutch colonials," see C. van Heekeren, *Trekkers en Blijvers: Kroniek van een Haags-Indische Familie* (Amsterdam: Franeker, 1980).

37. See, for example, Hillen, *Way of a Boy*, 24.

38. Elsbeth Locher-Scholten takes this position when she writes:

Of all dominated groups in the former colonies, dominated servants were the most "subaltern." Silenced by the subservient nature of their work and the subordinated social class they came from, Indonesian and Javanese servants in the former Dutch East Indies were neither expected nor allowed to speak for themselves. . . . For all these reasons, it is impossible to present these servants' historical voices and experiences directly from original source material. "Orientalism and the Rhetoric of the Family: Javanese Servants in European Household Manuals and Children's Fiction," *Indonesia* 58 (October 1994): 19

39. See Anne McClintock, *Imperial Leather: Race, Gender and Sexuality in the Colonial Contest* (New York: Routledge, 1995), for a nuanced reading of servant-employer dependencies in imperial Britain and the colonies.

40. Ibu Kilah, June 13, 1996, interview with Karen Strassler.

41. The overt display of feelings in Java is a sign of being immature, "a not fully developed person." On this aspect of Javanese culture, see Hildred Geertz's classic, *The Javanese Family: A Study of Kinship and Socialization* (New York: Free Press of Glencoe, 1961). Control of feelings is a sign of power as well as refinement; see, for example, Ward Keeler, *Javanese Shadow Plays, Javanese Selves* (Princeton: Princeton University Press, 1987).

42. See Greta Uehling's Ph.D. dissertation on memory and sentiment among Crimean Tatars: "Building Memories: Recalling the Deportation, Exile and Repatriation of Crimean Tatars to Their Historic Homeland" (University of Michigan, 2000).

43. Hayden V. White, *The Content of the Form: Narrative Discourse and Historical Representation* (Baltimore: Johns Hopkins University Press, 1987).

44. On the important distinction that psychology draws between "retelling" and "remembering," see Maurice Bloch, *How We Think They Think: Anthropological Approaches to Cognition, Memory, and Literacy* (Boulder, Colo.: Westview Press, 1998).

45. From fieldnotes of July 9, 1997.

46. The Japanese occupied Indonesia from 1942 to 1945. During the occupation, all Europeans (except Germans) were placed in Japanese internment camps (an estimated 170,000 people). Indonesians, meanwhile, were subjected to forced labor and extreme shortages of food, cloth, and other basic necessities.

47. In *Dutch Culture Overseas,* Gouda notes the New Order's tendency to "gloss . . . over the long history of Dutch control" (35) and not to dwell on "troubling historical events" in official versions (36–37).

48. In late New Order Indonesia's licensed version of Indonesian history, the welcoming of the Japanese as liberators was excised while the very real and widely shared suffering of the period was richly elaborated.

49. Some people, for example, would go so far as to say that "the canals and rivers were full of blood," but they would rarely locate themselves more precisely as witnesses to (or participants in) the massacres of an estimated 500,000 to 1,000,000 suspected communists.

50. See Pemberton, *On the Subject of "Java."*

51. James T. Siegel, *Fetish, Recognition, Revolution* (Princeton: Princeton University Press, 1997).

52. Some servants were able, for a time, to go in and out of the camps. One former servant had worked as a guard at a Japanese internment camp for women.

53. Ibu Kilah, June 13 and July 7, 1996, interviews with Strassler; and September 28, 1996, interview with Stoler and Strassler. It was not until the third interview that she explicitly stated this was why she had left.

54. Pak Mulyo, March 18, 1997, interview with Purwanti and Kwartanada.

55. Among many Javanese it is considered impolite—as well as impolitic— to assert an opinion too directly. For the classic treatment of Javanese tendencies to prize group harmony over personal expression, see Clifford Geertz, *The Religion of Java* (Glencoe, Ill.: Free Press, 1960). For more recent discussion of calibrated Javanese conversation styles, see Laine Berman, *Speaking through the Silence: Narratives, Social Conventions, and Power in Java* (New York: Oxford University Press, 1998).

56. "Mas" is a polite Javanese term of address for a young man; "Mbah" is a polite term for an elder.

57. The idiom typically used to mean "to work for" (*ikut*) literally means "to follow," or "to go along with," connoting loyalty as well as employment. One woman told of escaping harassment by Dutch troops during the 1948 siege of Yogyakarta by telling them that she had once worked for the Dutch (*ikut Blanda*) (Ibu Kasan, July 30, 1997, interview with Strassler).

58. Pak Purwo, March 22, 1997, interview with Kwartanada and Purwanti. Interestingly, it was only when Nita momentarily left the room soon after the interview had begun that Pak Purwo began his anxious questioning of Didi.

59. Mary Steedly, *Hanging without a Rope: Narrative Experience in Colonial and Postcolonial Karoland* (Princeton: Princeton University Press, 1993), 225.

60. Rudolph Mrazek, December 9, 1997, pers. com. Although not enough interviews were done with men to make assertions about how memories were differently gendered, men seemed to work harder to place themselves in heroic histories. They were also more anxious about how their work in Dutch homes might be construed, perhaps reflecting their greater sense of political risk and need to assert nationalist credentials.

61. Ibu Tinem, July 9, 1997, interview with Stoler, Strassler, and Kwartanada.

62. Renato Rosaldo, *Ilongot Headhunting, 1883–1974: A Study in Society and History* (Stanford, Calif.: Stanford University Press, 1980), 231.

63. See Pramoedya Ananta Toer's "Djongos + Babu," originally published in *Tjerita Dari Djakarta: Sekumpulan Karikatur Keadaan dan Manusianya* (Djakarta: Grafica, 1957), in which domestic servants are paradigmatic figures for a colonized mentality: self-hating, subservient, and opportunistic. There are more recent translations by James T. Siegel, in *Indonesia* 61 (1996); and Nancy Florida, in *Tenggara* 33 (1997). Urban-placed Indonesian novels and short stories, from those of Mas Marco in the 1930s to Toer's, frequently locate the life

tragedies of the urban poor—illegitimate births, rapes, impoverishment—in the domestic service sector. For the figure of the nyai, see Toer, *This Earth of Mankind: A Novel [Bumi Manusia]*, trans. Max Lane (New York: Penguin, [1975] 1990), in which the positive depiction of Nyai Ontosoroh is an explicit reworking of the negative stereotype. Jean Taylor has traced portrayals of the legendary figure Nyai Dasima in "Nyai Dasima: Portrait of a Mistress in Literature and Film," in *Fantasizing the Feminine*, ed. Laurie Sears (Durham, N.C.: Duke University Press, 1996), 225–48. On *This Earth of Mankind* and *Child of All Nations*, see Keith Foulcher, "*Bumi Manusia* and *Anak Semua Bangsa*: Pramoedya Ananta Toer Enters the 1980s," *Indonesia* 32 (October 1981): 1–15.

64. The "tainting" might be political as well. In the 1920s, during the early years of the nationalist movement, men with daughters who were huishoud-sters (in domestic/sexual service) for Dutch men were denied access to some nationalist organizations. At a demonstration of the Sarekat Islam (an early anticolonial Islamic organization) in 1913, huishoudsters were stoned and stripped of their clothes by the mob. See *Bintang Soerabaja*, no. 162, referenced in *Koloniaal Tijdschrift* 2 (1913): 1472.

65. Ibu Soekati, June 17, 1996, interview with Strassler; and October 3, 1996, interview with Strassler, Stoler, and Dias Pradadimara.

66. Ibu Kilah, June 13 and July 7, 1996, interviews with Strassler; September 28, 1996, interview with Stoler and Strassler.

67. Pak Hardjo, September 30, 1996, interview with Stoler, Strassler, and Pradadimara.

68. Doris Sommer's subtle and powerful discussion of "strategic refusal" should be de rigueur for all students of memory. See her *Proceed with Caution, When Engaged by Minority Writing in the Americas* (Cambridge, Mass.: Harvard University Press, 1999).

69. David William Cohen, *The Combing of History* (Chicago: University of Chicago Press, 1994), 18.

70. In the first interview, Ibu Sastro avoided the topic of sex. But in two subsequent interviews (April 4, 1997, with Purwanti and Kwartanada; July 10, 1997, with Purwanti, Strassler, and Stoler) she told the same account, almost verbatim.

71. The word used for "marry" here is *kawin*, which can be used to mean formal marriage or simply being engaged in a (usually long-term) sexual relationship. In our July 10, 1997, interview, she clarified that in this context *kawin* meant "play around" (*main-main saja*) sexually only, not marriage.

72. Ibu Sastro, April 4, 1997, interview with Purwanti and Kwartanada.

73. Hein Buitenweg, *Omong Kosong Lagi: Vreugde uit het Oude Indie II* (Amsterdam: Van der Peet, 1956), 18l.

74. Ibu Tinem, March 24, 1997, and April 3, 1997, interviews with Kwartanada and Purwanti; July 5, 1997, interview with Purwanti, Kwartanada, and Stoler.

75. Ibu Patmi, October 1, 1996, interview with Pradadimara, Stoler, and Strassler. In two previous interviews with Strassler, Ibu Patmi had shown no such anxiety. It was only when an Indonesian member of our team took part in the interview that she became nervous. These critical comments were made before the catastrophic drop in the value of the rupiah in early 1998.

76. Ibu Patmi, June 18, 1996, interview with Strassler.

77. How photography was enlisted in colonial rule and its cultural imaginary is the subject of a growing number of works. Among the many, see Elizabeth Edwards, ed., *Anthropology and Photography, 1860–1920* (New Haven: Yale University Press in association with the Royal Anthropological Institute, London, 1992); Elizabeth Edwards, ed., *Anthropology and Colonial Endeavor,* special issue, *History of Photography* 21, no. 1 (1997); Christopher Pinney, *Camera Indica: The Social Life of Indian Photographs* (Chicago: University of Chicago Press, 1998). Still, little has been written specifically on colonial era family photography. The majority of photographs reproduced here were selected from a collection of thousands of photos from family albums of people who lived in the Indies between the late nineteenth century and the 1940s. This collection was made available for me and prepared for reproduction with the generosity of Leo Haks (who owns this collection) and with funding from the Rackham Discretionary Fund at the University of Michigan (figs. 2, 4, 5, 6, 9–14, 16). Others are from the Koninklijk Instituut Voor de Tropen (figs. 1, 3, 7, 15); fig. 8 is from E. Breton de Nijs's *Tempo Doeloe: Fotografische Documenten uit het Oude Indie, 1870–1914* (Amsterdam: E. Querido, 1973); the photograph of Ibu Sastro holding her certificate (fig. 42) was taken by Karen Strassler, July 10, 1997.

78. "Tempo Doeloe" is a key term in the lexicon of Dutch (and Indonesian) colonial nostalgia. Several volumes of colonial era photographs appear under this title.

79. On servants in colonial era photographs, see Arjun Appadurai, "The Colonial Backdrop," *Afterimage* 24, no. 5 (1997): 4–7.

80. A good example is the collection of photographs archived at the Koninklijk Instituut voor Taal-, Land- en Volkenkunde under the title "Indo-Europese familie" (1915). Out of some fifty photographs, a servant appears in only one (but see fig. 35).

81. Ibu Kamsih, November 14, 1996, interview with Purwanti and Kwartanada.

82. Ibu Rubi, February 27 1997, interview with Kwartanada.

83. Ibu Rubi, March 4 1997, interview with Purwanti and Kwartanada.

84. Genduk Ginem, March 1, 1997, interview with Kwartanada and Purwanti.

85. Ibu Darmo, March 31, 1997, interview with Kwartanada and Purwanti.

86. Ibu Sastro, April 4, 1997, interview with Purwanti and Kwartanada.

87. Bruce Robbins, *The Servant's Hand: English Fiction from Below* (New York: Columbia University Press, 1993), 33.

88. Benedict Anderson's notion that the Javanese word *londo* for "Dutch" and more generally for "whites" carried no "derogatory secondary distinctions" is curious given the range of terms in use in Java today. The appellation *bulai* (albino), shouted on the streets by the young to whites, and the older but still invoked description of *londos* as those who "smell of ripened cheese" (*bau keju*), attest to a rich repertoire of pejoratives. Our interviews suggest that even the apparently benign "good" could be used to convey a derogatory evaluation. See Benedict Anderson, *Imagined Communities: Reflections on the Origin and Spread of Nationalism* (London: Verso, 1983), 153, and footnote 25 where he writes: "I have never heard of an abusive argot word in Indonesian or Javanese for either 'Dutch' or 'white.' "

89. Ibu Soekati, June 17, 1996, interview with Strassler. Similarly, Pak Ardjo, who had worked as a gardener, when asked whether his employers had ever been abusive answered, "Oh no, my employers were all good," but later commented, "So the Dutch towards Javanese people, you know it was like they really derided them, whatever your work was, that was your name" (Pak Ardjo, November 19, 1996, interview with Purwanti and Kwartanada).

90. Clearly, if Ambonese soldiers in the Dutch army were called "Black Dutch," then the term "Dutch" (Belanda) was by itself not an unambiguous racial marker. Similarly, while some people called those of mixed parentage "red Dutch" (*Belanda merah*) or "Dutch descendants" (*Belanda peranakan*), others referred to them simply as "mixed" (*campuran*), thereby not always marking them as belonging to the category "Dutch." As we saw in chapter 4, in practice many poorer Indos who were not recognized by their Dutch fathers and were not accorded European legal status by the colonial state.

91. Ibu Sastro, July 10, 1997, interview with Stoler, Strassler, and Purwanti. The construction of Dutch colonial nostalgia rests in part on belief in a distinction drawn by Indonesians themselves between "the colonial system" and individual Dutch persons who happened to be employed in the colonies. Dutch too make the distinction. On this perception of anticolonial violence as something directed at "the system" and not at themselves see chapter 4 of *Capitalism and Confrontation in Sumatra's Plantation Belt, 1870–1979* (New Haven: Yale University Press, 1985). Also see Karen Tranberg Hansen, *Distant Companions: Servants and Employers in Zambia, 1900–1985* (Ithaca: Cornell University Press, 1989).

92. Ibu Kilah, September 28, 1996, interview with Stoler and Strassler.

93. Ibu Darmo, July 12, 1997, interview with Kwartanada, Purwanti, Stoler, and Strassler.

94. Ibu Kasan, October 3, 1996, interview with Strassler, Stoler, and Pradadimara.

95. To have worked for so many employers was not unusual; many people with whom we spoke emphasized how they had repeatedly "moved on" (*pindah-pindah*) once they became "bored" or "fed up" (*bosan*) with an employer. Such comments offset the equally frequent comment that one worked because

"one had to eat." Stressing mobility and self-determination, they challenged stereotypes of the loyal domestic servant.

96. Ibu Rubi, 27 February 1997, interview with Kwartanada.

97. She also humorously related how she used butter to "clean" her Dutch employers' shoes when she couldn't find the polish. February 28, 1997, interview with Kwartanada.

98. Ibu Rubi, February 27 1997, interview with Kwartanada.

99. Here we cannot know to what extent the apparent "salience" of Dutch cleanliness indicates how important this quality seemed then and how much it reflects the term's contemporary currency. On salience as a "treacherous concept," see Marigold Linton, "Ways of Searching and the Contents of Memory," in *Autobiographical Memory*, ed. David C. Rubin (Cambridge: Cambridge University Press, 1986), 50–67.

100. On emotion as part of the vocabulary of appraisal and criticism, see Francis Dunlop, *The Education of Feeling and Emotion* (London: Allen & Unwin, 1984), 7; and my discussion of the sentiments as expressions of feeling and of judgment in "States of Sentiment, Reasons of State," in *Along the Archival Grain*.

101. Ibu Kilah, September 28, 1996, interview with Stoler and Strassler.

102. Genduk Ginem, March 1, 1997, interview with Kwartanada and Purwanti.

103. Ibu Rubi, February 27, 1997, interview with Kwartanada.

104. Ibu Adi, November 12, 1996, interview with Kwartanada.

105. Ibu Patmi, June 18, 1996, interview with Strassler.

106. Ibu Sastro, April 4, 1997, interview with Kwartanada and Purwanti.

107. Ibu Adi, November 12, 1996, interview with Kwartanada.

108. Not only do Javanese rarely have pets, but in Islamic Java to serve a dog is a singularly lowly job.

109. Pak Mulyo, March 18, 1997, interview with Kwartanada and Purwanti.

110. See Berman's *Speaking through Silence* for an analysis of Javanese women's narrative styles (conducted in Yogyakarta). She argues that in lower-class Javanese women's narratives, repetition and the relating of mundane details are crucial ways in which speakers invite group participation.

111. As Barbara Hernstein Smith writes:

> Our knowledge of past events is usually not narrative in structure or given in story-like sequences: on the contrary, that knowledge is most likely to be in the form of general or imprecise recollections, scattered and possibly inconsistent pieces of verbal information, and various visual, auditory, and kinesthetic images—some of which, at any given time, will be organized . . . as a specific "set" of events only in and through the very act by which we narrate them as such. "Narrative Versions, Narrative Theories," in *On Narrative*, ed. W. J. T. Mitchell (Chicago: University of Chicago Press, 1981), 225

112. But see also Marilyn R. Waldman, " 'The Otherwise Unnoteworthy Year 711': A Reply to Hayden White," in Mitchell, *On Narrative*, 242, for a discussion of the "implicit stories" embedded in lists.

113. Genduk Ginem, March 1, 1997, interview with Purwanti and Kwartanada.

114. On anxiety about mastery of language as a central preoccupation in Javanese culture, see James T. Siegel, *Solo in the New Order: Language and Hierarchy in a Javanese City* (Princeton: Princeton University Press, 1986). Ibu Sastro imitated an overheard argument between her employers, the husband berating his wife for her abusive anger at a servant. She quoted him asking his wife, "Ben je is zo gek?" which she translated as "Why are you like that?" (literally, the Dutch phrase means: "Why are you so crazy?"), then followed her translation with a laugh and the disclaimer "I don't know." Ibu Sastro, March 11, 1997, interview with Kwartanada and Purwanti.

115. Ibu Darmo, July 12 1997, interview with Kwartanada, Purwanti, Stoler, and Strassler; and March 31, 1997, interview with Purwanti and Kwartanada.

116. Ibu Rubi, February 27, 1997, interview with Kwartanada.

117. On refusal to become an ethnographic subject, see Kamala Visweswaran, *Fictions of Feminist Ethnography* (Minneapolis: University of Minnesota Press, 1994).

118. Ibu Darmo, July 12, 1997, interview with Kwartanada, Purwanti, Stoler, and Strassler.

119. Arjun Appardurai, "The Past as a Scarce Resource," *Man*, no. 2 (1981): 201–19; Nicholas B. Dirks, *Colonialism and Culture* (Ann Arbor: University of Michigan Press, 1992), introd.

EPILOGUE. CAVEATS ON COMFORT ZONES AND COMPARATIVE FRAMES

1. Take such a seemingly transparent term as "colonial policy" that does not even merit the stature of a concept, despite its ubiquitous use to cover practices, agents, and events. It may designate plan or procedure, tactics or techniques, conduct or course. It can signal different micro-processes that go into the imagining of governance as opposed to the making of it—different styles of authorization and agents of them. In treating it as a catchall for a range of different referents, we miss the opportunity to identify the contingent space that distinguished design from implementation and vision from effects.

2. Bernard Cohn, "History and Anthropology: The State of Play," *Comparative Studies in Society and History* 22, no. 2 (1980): 219.

3. Ian Hacking, *The Social Construction of What?* (Cambridge, Mass.: Harvard University Press, 1999).

4. On the imperial quest for comprehensive knowledge, see Thomas Richards, *The Imperial Archive: Knowledge and the Fantasy of Empire* (New York: Verso, 1993). Also see Peter Pels's discussion of taxonomies and the art of government in "The Anthropology of Colonialism: Culture, History, and the Emergence of Western Governmentality," *Annual Review of Anthropology* 26 (1997): 163–83.

5. I owe my first formulation of "taxonomic states" to discussions with Roger Rouse on the differences between identity politics and the state's politics of identification.

6. James C. Scott, *Seeing Like a State: How Certain Schemes to Improve the Human Condition Have Failed* (New Haven: Yale University Press, 1998).

7. On what Ian Hacking refers to as a "historical ontological" methodology for studying the making of human kinds, see "The Looping Effects of Human Kinds," in *Causal Cognition: A Multidisciplinary Debate*, ed. Dan Sperber, David Premack, and Ann Premack (Oxford: Oxford University Press, 1995); and "Historical Ontology: From the Creation of Phenomena to the Formation of Character" (n.d.).

8. I owe this formulation to Gary Wilder's careful reading of an earlier draft.

9. A large body of scholarship starts and ends with that assumption. See, for example, Cecily Forde-Jones's "Mapping Racial Boundaries: Gender, Race, and Poor Relief in Barbadian Plantation Society," *Journal of Women's History* 10, no. 3 (1998): 9–31, where she argues that in eighteenth-century Barbados "any intermixing of the races clearly represented a threat to white supremacism" (p. 18). For a recent discussion of whether métissage was a subversive site or a merely a point of assimilation, see Françoise Vergès, *Monsters and Revolutionaries: Colonial Family Romance and Métissage* (Durham, N.C.: Duke University Press, 1999).

10. See my "Racial Histories and Their Regimes of Truth," *Political Power and Social Theory* 11 (1997): 183–255.

11. Michel Foucault, *The Archaeology of Knowledge*, trans. A. M. Sheridan Smith (New York: Pantheon, 1972), 36–37.

12. I think here of edited volumes such as Nicholas Dirk's *Culture and Colonialism* (Ann Arbor: University of Michigan Press, 1992); Frederick Cooper and Ann Laura Stoler's *Tensions of Empire: Colonial Cultures in a Bourgeois World* (Berkeley: University of California Press, 1997); Antoinette M. Burton's *Gender, Sexuality and Colonial Modernities* (London: Routledge, 1999); or Julia Clancy-Smith and Frances Gouda's *Domesticating the Empire: Race, Gender, and Family Life in French and Dutch Colonialism* (Charlottesville: University Press of Virginia, 1998). Each of these compilations contains potentially comparable cases, but none of the studies included explicitly works off the others or is comparative in itself.

13. For an informed discussion of "colonial humanism" as a particular form of political rationality, see Gary Wilder, "The Politics of Failure: Historicising Popular Front Colonial Policy in French West Africa," in *French Colonial Empire and the Popular Front: Hope and Disillusion*, ed. Tony Chafer and Amanda Sackur (New York: Macmillan, 1999), 33–55. Carol Summers also argues that "social programs" (such as that which promoted a "new motherhood" in colonial Uganda in the 1920s) "were not mere sideshows to the public politics and economic maneuvering of imperialism . . . [but] integral to the holding of power": "Intimate Colonialism: The Imperial Production of Reproduction in Uganda, 1907–1925," *Signs* 16, no. 4 (1991): 787–807.

14. For more on the politics of comparison, see my "Tense and Tender Ties: The Politics of Comparison in North American History and (Post) Colonial Studies," *Journal of American History* 88 (2001): 829–65, 893–97. On the fact that common relations are essential to processes of making analogy and comparison whereas common objects are not, see Dedre Gentner and Arthur B. Markman, "Structure Mapping in Analogy and Similarity," *American Psychologist* 52, no. 1 (1997): 45–56. Also see Rodney Needham's discussion of Kant's observation that is not the similarities of things but the similarities of relations to which we should attend: "Analogical Classifications," in *Reconnaissances* (Toronto: University of Toronto Press, 1980), 41–62. The intersection between "our epistemologies" and those we study is a critical and troubled subject in anthropology and has been for decades. For a classic collection on the subject, see Bryan R. Wilson, ed., *Rationality* (Oxford: Blackwell, 1979). For an ambitious effort to rebuild "macronarratives from the perspective of coloniality" and as a "post-occidental reason," see Walter Mignolo, *Local Histories, Global Designs: Coloniality, Subaltern Knowledges, and Border Thinking* (Princeton: Princeton University Press, 2000), 22.

15. Frederick Cooper and I make this point in the introduction to *Tensions of Empire*.

16. See, for example, the essays in Clancy-Smith and Gouda, *Domesticating the Empire*.

17. Lynn Hunt, *The Family Romance of the French Revolution* (Berkeley: University of California Press, 1992), 196.

18. David Scott, *Refashioning Futures: Criticism after Postcoloniality* (Princeton: Princeton University Press, 1999), 7.

19. Mary Steedly is right that the category "gender" is made more problematic than "the state" in studies of Southeast Asia. Still, two of the most interesting studies of state and family ties (by Jean Taylor and Julia Adams) have been done for the Indies colonial state and its familial politics. See Mary Steedly, "The State of Culture Theory in the Anthropology of Southeast Asia," *Annual Review of Anthropology* 28 (1999): 431–54.

20. On the relationship between subjugated and erudite knowledge, see Michel Foucault's "Two Lectures," in *Power/Knowledge: Selected Interviews and Other Writings, 1972–1977*, ed. C. Gordon (New York: Pantheon, 1980), 78–101; and my discussion of them in *Race and the Education of Desire: Foucault's History of Sexuality and the Colonial Order of Things* (Durham, N.C.: Duke University Press, 1995), 63–69.

21. Luise White, *The Comforts of Home: Prostitution in Colonial Nairobi* (Chicago: University of Chicago Press, 1990).

22. On colonial prostitution and the international traffic in women, see Kenneth Ballhatchet, *Race, Sex and Class under the Raj: Imperial Attitudes and Policies and Their Critics, 1793–1905* (New York: St. Martin's Press, 1980); Elizabeth B. van Heyningen, "The Social Evil in the Cape Colony, 1868–1902: Prostitution and the Contagious Disease Acts," *Journal of Southern African Studies* 10, no. 2 (1984): 170–97; James Francis Warren, "Prostitution and the

Politics of Venereal Disease: Singapore, 1870–98," *Journal of Southeast Asian Studies* 21, no. 2 (1990): 360–83; Leonore Manderson, "Colonial Desires: Sexuality, Race, and Gender in British Malaya," *Journal of the History of Sexuality* 7, no. 3 (1994): 372–88. Also see Andrew Abalahin's forthcoming Ph.D. dissertation, "Prostitution Policy and the Project of Modernity: A Comparison of Colonial Indonesia and the Philippines, 1850–1940" (Cornell University).

23. For a brief description of its work and why one active member thought more Dutch women should be recruited to it, see M. Misset-Stein, "De Vrouw in het Pro Juventute Werk," in *Indische Vrouwen Jaarboek* (Yogyakarta: Kolff-Buning, 1936).

24. Vereeniging Pro Juventute Jogjakarta, *Verslag* 1934, 1937, 1940.

25. Enrique Dussel, *The Underside of Modernity* (Atlantic Highlands, N.J.: Humanities Press, 1996).

26. See, for example, the essays in Burton, *Gender, Sexuality and Colonial Modernities*, especially Burton's "Introduction: The Unfinished Business of Colonial Modernities," which emphasizes the "unstable foundations" of colonial gender and sexual politics and thus the maneuverability of those living within it. This is somewhat different from my emphasis here on a modern colonialism that subsumed rejected models of an older, "nonmodern" set of colonial relations.

Bibliography

ARCHIVES

Algemene Rijksarchief. The Hague, the Netherlands.
Archives d'Outre-Mer. Protectorat de l'Annam et du Tonkin.

BOOKS, ARTICLES, AND DISSERTATIONS

Abalahin, Andrew. "Prostitution Policy and the Project of Modernity: A Comparison of Colonial Indonesia and the Philippines, 1850–1940." Ph.D. dissertation, Cornell University, forthcoming.

Abbatucci, S. "Le milieu africain considéré au point de vue de ses effets sur le système nerveux de l'européen." *Annales d'Hygiène et de Médicine Coloniale* 13 (1910): 328–35.

Abor, Raoul. *Des reconnaisances frauduleuses d'enfants naturels en Indochine,* 25. Hanoi: Imprimerie Tonkinoise, 1917.

Abu-Lughod, Lila. "The Romance of Resistance: Tracing Transformations of Power through Bedouin Women." *American Ethnologist* 17, no. 1 (1990): 41–55.

Adams, Julia. "The Familial State: Family Practices and State-making in the Early Modern Netherlands." *Theory and Society* 23, no. 4 (1994): 505–39.

Adas, Michael. *Machines as the Measure of Men: Science, Technology, and Ideologies of Western Dominance.* Ithaca: Cornell University Press, 1989.

Alatas, Syed Hussein. *The Myth of the Lazy Native: A Study of the Image of the Malays, Filipinos and Javanese from the 16th to the 20th Century and Its Function in the Ideology of Colonial Capitalism.* London: Cass, 1977.

Albertyn, J. R. *Die Armblanke ein die Maatskappy: Verslag van die Carnegie-Kommissie.* Stellenbosch: Pro-ecclesia-drukkery, 1932.

Algemeen Schoolverslag onder ultimo 1849. Quoted in *Het Pauperisme onder der Europeanen in Nederlandsch-Indie, Eerste Gedeelte: Algemeen Overzicht* Batavia: Landsdrukkerij, 1902.

Algemeen Verslag (1858) van den Staat van het Schoolwezen in Nederlandsch-Indie. [1849 Annual General Report on Education in the Indies.] Batavia: Lange & Co., 1859.

Allen, Ann Taylor. "Gardens of Children, Gardens of God: Kindergartens and Daycare Centers in 19th-Century Germany." *Journal of Social History* 19, no. 3 (1986): 433–50.

The American Heritage Dictionary. 2d ed. Boston: Houghton Mifflin, 1991.

Amin, Shahid. *Event, Metaphor, Memory: Chauri Chaura, 1922–1992.* Berkeley: University of California Press, 1995.

Anderson, Benedict. *Imagined Communities: Reflections on the Origin and Spread of Nationalism.* London: Verso, 1983.

Anderson, Warwick. "The Trespass Speaks: White Masculinity and Colonial Breakdown." *American Historical Review* 102, no. 5 (1997): 1343–70.

Angoulvant, Gabriel Louis. *Les Indes Néerlandaises, leur rôle dans l'économie internationale.* Paris: Le Monde Nouveau, 1926.

Anthropological Research. "Anthropological Research in British Colonies." *Anthropological Forum* 4, no. 2 (1977): 1–112.

Appadurai, Arjun. "The Colonial Backdrop." *Afterimage* 24, no. 5 (1997): 4–7.

———. *Modernity at Large: Cultural Dimensions of Globalization.* Minneapolis: University of Minnesota Press, 1996.

———. "Numbers in the Colonial Imagination." In *Modernity at Large,* 114–35. Minneapolis: University of Minnesota Press, 1996.

———. "The Past as a Scarce Resource." *Man* 6, no. 2 (1981): 201–19.

———. "Topographies of the Self: Praise and Emotion in Hindu India." In *Language and the Politics of Emotion,* ed. Catherine A. Lutz and Lila Abu-Lughod, 92–112. Cambridge: Cambridge University Press, 1990.

Arnold, David. "European Orphans and Vagrants in India in the Nineteenth Century." *Journal of Imperial and Commonwealth History* 7, no. 2 (1979): 104–27.

———. "White Colonization and Labour in Nineteenth-Century India." *Journal of Imperial and Commonwealth History* 10, no. 2 (1983): 133–58.

Asad, Talal. "Multiculturalism and British Identity in the Wake of the Rushdie Affair." *Politics & Society* 18, no. 4 (1990): 455–80.

———. "Two European Images of Non-European Rule." In *Anthropology and the Colonial Encounter,* ed. Talal Asad, 102–30. London: Ithaca Press, 1975.

———, ed. *Anthropology and the Colonial Encounter.* London: Ithaca Press, 1973.

Bagley, Christopher. *The Dutch Plural Society: A Comparative Study in Race Relations.* London: Oxford University Press, 1973.

Bajema, Carl, ed. *Eugenics Then and Now.* Stroudsburg, Pa.: Dowden, Hutchinson & Ross, 1976.

Balandier, Georges. "The Colonial Situation: A Theoretical Approach." In *Africa: Social Problems of Change and Conflict,* ed. Pierre L. Van den Berghe, 34–61. San Francisco: Chandler, 1965.

Balibar, Etienne. "Fichte et la frontière intérieure: A propos des *Discours á la nation allemande.*" *Les Cahiers de Fontenay* (June 1990): 58–59.

———. "Foucault et Marx: L'enjeu du nominalisme." In *Michel Foucault, Philosophe: Rencontre Internationale, Paris, 9, 10, 11 Janvier 1988,* 54–75. Paris: Seuil, 1989.

Balibar, Etienne, and Immanuel Wallerstein. *Race, Nation, Class: Ambiguous Identities.* Trans. Chris Turner. London: Verso, 1991.

Ballhatchet, Kenneth. *Race, Sex, and Class under the Raj: Imperial Attitudes and Policies and Their Critics, 1793–1905.* New York: St. Martin's Press, 1980.

Baroli, March. *La vie quotidienne des français en Algérie.* Paris: Hachette, 1967.

Barr, Pat. *The Memsahibs: The Women of Victorian India.* London: Secker & Warburg, 1976.

Bartley, Numan V., ed. *The Evolution of Southern Culture.* Athens: University of Georgia Press, 1988.

Bauduin, Dominique Chrétien Marie. *Het Indische Leven.* 's-Gravenhage: H. P. Leopold, [1927] 1941.

Beckles, Hilary. " 'Black Men in White Skins': The Formation of a White Proletariat in West Indian Slave Society." *Journal of Imperial and Commonwealth History* 15, no. 1 (1986): 5–21.

Beekman, E. M. Introduction to E. Breton de Nijs, *Faded Portraits.* Ed. E. M. Beekman. Amherst: University of Massachusets Press, [1954] 1982.

———, ed. *Fugitive Dreams: An Anthology of Dutch Colonial Literature.* Amherst: University of Massachusetts Press, 1988.

Beidelman, T. O. *Colonial Evangelism: A Socio-Historical Study of an East African Mission at the Grassroots.* Bloomington: Indiana University Press, 1982.

Bellingham, Bruce. "The History of Childhood Since the 'Invention of Childhood': Some Issues in the Eighties." *Journal of Family History* 13, no. 2 (1988): 347–58.

Bérenger-Féraud, L. *Traité clinique des maladies des européens au Sénégal.* Paris: Adrien Delahaye, 1875.

Berghe, Pierre L. Van den, ed. *Africa: Social Problems of Change and Conflict: Readings.* San Francisco: Chandler, 1965.

Berman, Laine. *Speaking through the Silence: Narratives, Social Conventions, and Power in Java.* New York: Oxford University Press, 1998.

Berreman, Gerald. *The Politics of Truth: Essays in Critical Anthropology.* New Delhi: South Asian Publishers, 1981.

Beyen, K. H. *Het Nederlanderschap in Verband met het International Recht.* Utrecht, 1890.

Beynon, H. C., ed. *Verboden voor Honden en Inlanders: Indonesiers Vertellen over Hun Leven in de Koloniale Tijd.* [Forbidden for Dogs and Natives: Indonesians Recount Their Lives in the Colonial Period.] Amsterdam: Jan Mets, 1995.

Bhabha, Homi K. *The Location of Culture.* New York: Routledge, 1994.

———. *Nation and Narration.* New York: Routledge, 1990.

———. "Of Mimicry and Man: The Ambivalence of Colonial Discourse." In *Tensions of Empire: Colonial Cultures in a Bourgeois World,* ed. Frederick Cooper and Ann Laura Stoler, 152–60. Berkeley: University of California Press, 1997.

Biervliet, H., et al. "Biologism, Racism and Eugenics in the Anthropology and Sociology of the 1930s." *Netherlands Journal of Sociology* 16, no. 1 (1980): 69–92.

Bland, Lucy. " 'Guardians of the Race' or 'Vampires upon the Nation's Health'? Female Sexuality and Its Regulations in Early Twentieth-Century Britain." In *The Changing Experience of Women,* ed. Elizabeth Whitelegg and Open University, 373–88. Oxford: M. Robertson in association with the Open University, 1982.

Bloch, Maurice. *How We Think They Think: Anthropological Approaches to Cognition, Memory, and Literacy.* Boulder, Colo.: Westview Press, 1998.

Blumberger, I. J. *Geschiedenis van her Onderwijs in Nederlandschh-Indie.* Batavia: Wolters, 1938.

Blumberger, J. Th. Petrus. *De Indo-Europeesche Beweging in Nederlandsch-Indie.* Haarlem: Tjeenk Willink, 1939.

Blussé, Leonard. *Strange Company: Chinese Settlers, Mestizo Women and the Dutch in VOC Batavia.* Riverton, N.J.: Foris, 1986.

Bock, Gisela. "Racism and Sexism in Nazi Germany: Motherhood, Compulsory Sterilization, and the State." In *When Biology Became Destiny: Women in Weimar and Nazi Germany,* ed. Renate Bridenthal, Atina Grossmann, and Marion Kaplan, 271–96. New York: Monthly Review Press, 1984.

Bocquet-Siek, M. "Some Notes on the Nyai Theme in Pre-war Peranakan Chinese Literature." Paper presented for the Asian Studies Association of Australia, Adelaide University, May 13, 1984.

Boswell, John. *The Kindness of Strangers: The Abandonment of Children in Western Europe from Late Antiquity to the Renaissance.* New York: Pantheon, 1988.

Bourdieu, Pierre. *Outline of a Theory of Practice.* Trans. Richard Nice. Cambridge: Cambridge University Press, 1977.

Boutilier, James. "European Women in the Solomon Islands, 1900–1942: Accommodation and Change on the Pacific Frontier." In *Rethinking Women's Roles: Perspectives from the Pacific,* ed. Denise O'Brien and Sharon W. Tiffany, 173–99. Berkeley: University of California Press, 1984.

Boxer, C. R. *The Portuguese Seaborne Empire, 1415–1825.* New York: Knopf, 1969.

Boyarin, Jonathan, ed. 1994. *Remapping Memory: The Politics of Timespace.* Minneapolis: University of Minnesota Press, 1994.

Bozzoli, Belinda. "Marxism, Feminism and South African Studies." *Journal of Southern African Studies* 9, no. 2 (1983): 139–71.

Braconier, A. de. "Het Kazerne-Concubinaat in Ned-Indie." *Vragen van den Dag* 28 (1913): 974–95.

————. "Het Pauperisme onder de in Ned. Oost-Indie Levende Europeanen." *Nederlandsch-Indie* (1917): 291–300.

————. "Het Prostitutie-Vraagstuk in Nederlandsch-Indie." *Indische Gids* 55, no. 2 (1933): 906–28.

————.*Kindercriminaliteit en de Verzorging van Misdadig Aangelegde en Verwaarloosde Minderjarigen in Nederlandsche-Indie.* Baarn: Hollandia-Drukkerij, 1918.

Brand, J. van den. *Nog eens: De Millionen uit Deli.* Amsterdam: Hoveker & Wormser, 1904.

Brandt, Willem. *De Aarde van Deli.* The Hague: W. van Hoeve, 1948.

Breman, Jan. *Koelies, Planters en Koloniale Politiek.* Dordrecht: Foris, 1987.

Bridenthal, Renate, Claudia Koonz, and Susan Stuart, eds. *Becoming Visible: Women in European History.* Boston: Houghton Mifflin, 1987.

Brink, K. B. M. ten. *Indische Gezondheid: Wenken voor Totoks, en ook voor anderen bewerkt onder Toezicht.* Batavia: Nederlandsch-Indische Levensverzekeringen Lijfrente-Maatschappij, 1920.

Brou, A. M. N. "Le métis franco-annamite." *Revue Indochinois* (July 1907): 897–909.

Brownfoot, Janice N. "Memsahibs in Colonial Malaya: A Study of European Wives in a British Colony and Protectorate, 1900–1940." In *The Incorporated Wife,* ed. Hilary Callan and Shirley Ardener, 186–218. London: Croom Helm, 1984.

Brugmans, Izaak Johannes. *Geschiedenis van het Onderwijs in Nederlandsch-Indie.* Groningen: J. B. Wolters, 1938.

Buitenweg, Hein. *Omong Kosong Lagi: Vreugde uit het Oude Indie II.* Amsterdam: Van der Peet, 1956.

————.*Op Java Staat een Huis.* The Hague: Servire, 1961.

Bundy, Colin. "Vagabond Hollanders and Runaway Englishmen: White Poverty in the Cape before Poor Whiteism." In *Putting a Plough to the Ground: Accumulation and Dispossession in Rural South Africa, 1850–1930,* ed. William Beinart, Peter Delius, and Stanley Trapido, 101–28. Johannesburg: Ravan Press, 1987.

Burton, Antoinette M. *At the Heart of the Empire: Indians and the Colonial Encounter in Late-Victorian Britain.* Berkeley: University of California Press, 1998.

————.*Burdens of History: British Feminists, Indian Women, and Imperial Culture, 1865–1915.* Chapel Hill: University of North Carolina Press, 1994.

————, ed. *Gender, Sexuality and Colonial Modernities.* London: Routledge, 1999.

Butcher, John G. *The British in Malaya, 1880–1941: The Social History of a European Community in Colonial South-East Asia.* New York: Oxford University Press, 1979.

Buur, Dorothée. "Het 'Indische' Element in de Nederlandse Jeugdliteratuur." In *Indische Letteren,* vol. 1 (1986): 173–92.

————.Indische Jeugdliteratuur: Geannoteerde Bibliografie van Jeugdboeken over Nederlands-Indië en Indonesië, 1825–1991. Leiden: KITLV, 1992.

Callan, Hilary, and Shirley Ardener, eds. The Incorporated Wife. London: Croom Helm, 1984.

Callaway, Helen. Gender, Culture, and Empire: European Women in Colonial Nigeria. Oxford: Macmillan, 1987.

Camus, Jean-Yves. Le front national: Histoire et analyses. Paris: O. Laurens, 1997.

Carby, Hazel. "On the Threshold of Woman's Era: Lynching, Empire and Sexuality in Black Feminist Theory." Critical Inquiry 12, no. 1 (1985): 262–77.

Césaire, Aimé. Discourse on Colonialism. Trans. Joan Pinkham. New York: Monthly Review Press, 1972.

Chafer, Tony, and Amanda Sackur, eds. French Colonial Empire and the Popular Front: Hope and Disillusion. New York: St. Martin's Press, 1999.

Chailley-Bert, M. J. L'émigration des femmes aux colonies. Union Coloniale Française Conference, January 12, 1897. Paris: Armand Colin, 1897.

Chakrabarty, Dipesh. "Postcoloniality and the Artifice of History: Who Speaks for 'Indian' Pasts?" Representations 37 (Winter 1992): 1–26.

Chance, John, and William Taylor. "Estate and Class in a Colonial City: Oaxaca in 1792." Comparative Studies in Society and History 19, no. 4 (1977): 454–87.

Chatterjee, Indrani. "Colouring Subalternity: Slaves, Concubines, and Social Orphans in Early Colonial India." In Subaltern Studies X: Writings on South Asian History and Society, ed. Gautam Bhadra, Gyan Prakash, and Susie Tharu, 49–97. New Delhi: Oxford University Press, 1996.

Chenet, Ch. "Le rôle de la femme française aux colonies: Protection des enfants métis abandonnés." Le Devoir des Femmes (February 15, 1936): 8.

Chivas-Baron, C. La femme française aux colonies. Paris: Larose, 1929.

Chowdhury, Indira. The Frail Hero and Virile History: Gender and the Politics of Culture in Colonial Bengal. New York: Oxford University Press, 1998.

Clammer, John. "Colonialism and the Perception of Tradition." In Anthropology and the Colonial Encounter, ed. Talal Asad, 192–222. London: Ithaca Press, 1975.

Clancy-Smith, Julia, and Frances Gouda, eds. Domesticating the Empire: Race, Gender, and Family Life in French and Dutch Colonialism. Charlottesville: University Press of Virginia, 1998.

Clerkx, H. G. "Clerkx-Methode voor schriftelijk voortgezet Onderwijs." Brochure. 's-Gravenhage, 1931.

Clerkx, Lily E. "De Kinderjuffrouw: Opvoedster en Dienstbode tussen Ouders en Kinderen." Sociologisch Tijdschrift 10, no. 4 (1984): 671–715.

————. Living in Deli: Its Society as Imaged in Colonial Fiction. Amsterdam: Vrije Universiteit Press, 1991.

————. Mensen in Deli. Publication No. 2. Amsterdam: Sociologisch-Historisch Seminarium voor Zuidoost-Azie, 1961.

———— [van-Rijswijk-]. *Moeders, Kinderen en Kinderopvang*. Nijmegen: Socialistsche Uitgeverij, 1981.

Clifford, James. *The Predicament of Culture: Twentieth-Century Ethnography, Literature, and Art*. Cambridge, Mass.: Harvard University Press, 1988.

Cock, Jacklyn. *Maids and Madams: Domestic Workers under Apartheid*. Johannesburg: Raven Press, 1980.

Coetzee, J. M. *White Writing: On the Culture of Letters in South Africa*. New Haven: Yale University Press, 1988.

Cohen, David William. *The Combing of History*. Chicago: University of Chicago Press, 1994.

Cohen, William B. *The French Encounter with Africans: White Response to Blacks, 1530–1880*. Bloomington: Indiana University Press, 1980.

————. *Rulers of Empire: The French Colonial Service in Africa*. Stanford, Calif.: Hoover Institution Press, 1971.

Cohn, Bernard. "The Census, Social Structure and Objectification in South Asia." In *An Anthropologist among the Historians and Other Essays*, 224–53. Delhi: Oxford University Press, 1987.

————. "History and Anthropology: The State of Play." *Comparative Studies in Society and History* 22, no. 2 (1980): 198–221.

————. "Representing Authority in Victorian India." In *The Invention of Tradition*, ed. Eric Hobsbawm and Terence Ranger, 165–210. Cambridge: Cambridge University Press, 1983.

Cole, Jennifer. "The Work of Memory in Madagascar." *American Ethnologist* 25, no. 4 (1998): 610–33.

Comaroff, Jean. *Body of Power, Spirit of Resistance: The Culture and History of a South African People*. Chicago: University of Chicago Press, 1985.

Comaroff, Jean, and John Comaroff. "Christianity and Colonialism in South Africa." *American Ethnologist* 13, no. 1 (1986): 1–22.

————. "Home-made Hegemony: Modernity, Domesticity, and Colonial in South Africa." In *African Encounters with Domesticity*, ed. Karen Tranberg Hansen, 37–74. New Brunswick, N.J.: Rutgers University Press, 1992.

Comaroff, John. "Images of Empire, Contests of Conscience: Models of Colonial Domination in South Africa." In *Tensions of Empire: Colonial Cultures in a Bourgeois World*, ed. Frederick Cooper and Ann Laura Stoler, 163–97. Berkeley: University of California Press, [1989] 1997.

Comptes Rendus de l'Institut Colonial International. Brussels: Bibliothèque Coloniale Internationale, 1911, 1920, 1924.

Cool, F. "De Bestrijding der Werkloosheidsgevolgen in Nederlandsch-Indie Gedurende 1930–1936." *De Economist* 87 (1938): 135–47, 217–43.

Coolhaas, W. Philippus. *Insulinde: Mensch en Maatschappij*. Deventer: W. van Hoeve, 1944.

————. "Zorg voor Bepaalde Bevolkingstoepen." In *Insulinde: Mensch en Maatschappij*, 989–96. Deventer: W. van Hoeve, 1944.

Cooper, Frederick. *From Slaves to Squatters: Plantation Labor and Agriculture in Zanzibar and Coastal Kenya, 1890–1925.* New Haven: Yale University Press, 1980.

———. *On the African Waterfront: Urban Disorder and the Transformation of Work in Colonial Mombasa.* New Haven: Yale University Press, 1987.

Cooper, Frederick, and Ann Laura Stoler, eds. *Tensions of Empire: Colonial Cultures in a Bourgeois World.* Berkeley: University of California Press, 1997.

Cordurie, M. "Résidence des françaises et mariage des français dans les échelles du Levant au XVIIIe siècle." In *La femme dans les sociétés coloniales: Table ronde, CHEE, CRHSE, IHPOM : Groningen-Amsterdam, Septembre 1982, Centre d'histoire de l'expansion Européenne, Université de Leiden,* ed. Rijksuniversiteit te Leiden and Werkgroep voor de Geschiedenis van de Europese Expansie Centre de Recherche d'Histoire Socio-Economique and Institut d'Histoire des Pays d'Outre-Mer Université de Provence, 35–47. Aix-en-Provence: Institut d'Histoire des Pays d'Outre-Mer, Université de Provence, 1984.

Corneau, Grace. *La femme aux colonies.* Paris: Librairie Nilsson, 1900.

Coronil, Fernando, and Julie Skurski. "Dismembering and Remembering the Nation: The Semantics of Political Violence in Venezuela." *Comparative Studies in Society and History* 33, no. 2 (1991): 288–337.

Corsaro, William A., and Donna Eder. "Children's Peer Cultures." *Annual Review of Sociology* 16 (1990): 197–220.

Cott, Nancy. "Notes toward an Interpretation of Antebellum Childrearing." *Psychohistory Review* 7, no. 4 (1973): 4–20.

Couperus, Louis. *The Hidden Force.* Trans. Alexander Teixeira de Mattos. Amherst: University of Massachusetts Press, [1900] 1985.

Courtois, E. "Des règles hygiéniques que doit suivre l'européen au Tonkin." *Revue Indochinoise* 83 (1900): 539–41, 564–66, 598–601.

Crapanzano, Vincent. *Waiting: The Whites of South Africa.* New York: Vintage, 1985.

Cribb, Robert, ed. *The Late Colonial State in Indonesia: Political and Economic Foundations of the Netherlands Indies, 1880–1942.* Leiden: KITLV, 1994.

Culpin, Millais. "An Examination of Tropical Neurasthenia." *Proceedings of the Royal Society of Medicine* 26 (1933): 911–22.

Daniel, E. Valentine. *Charred Lullabies: Chapters in an Anthropography of Violence.* Princeton: Princeton University Press, 1996.

Daum, P. A. *Ups and Downs of Life in the Indies.* Trans. Elsje Qualms Sturtevant and Donald W. Sturtevant. Amherst: University of Massachusetts Press, 1987.

Davin, Anna. "Imperialism and Motherhood." In *Tensions of Empire: Colonial Cultures in a Bourgeois World,* ed. Frederick Cooper and Ann Laura Stoler, 87–151. Berkeley: University of California Press, [1978] 1997.

Dawson, Graham. *Soldier Heroes: British Adventure, Empire, and the Imagining of Masculinities.* New York: Routledge, 1994.

De Staatsarmenzorg voor Europeanen in Nederlandsch-Indie. Batavia: Landsdrukkerij, 1901.

Degler, Carl N. *Neither Black nor White: Slavery and Race Relations in Brazil and the United States.* New York: Macmillan, [1971] 1986.

Dekker, Jeroen H. H. "Transforming the Nation and the Child: Philanthropy in the Netherlands, Belgium, France and England, c. 1789–c.1850." In *Charity, Philanthropy and Reform: From the 1690s to 1850,* ed. Hugh Cunningham and Joanne Innes, 130–47. London: Macmillan, 1998.

Delacampagne, Christian. "Foucault, genealogie du bio-pouvoir." *Le Monde des Livres* (February 21, 1977): 1.

Delavignette, Robert Louis. *Service africain.* Paris: Gallimard, 1946.

Dermoût, Maria. *Nog Pas Gisteren.* Amsterdam: E. Querido, 1964.

Dirks, Nicholas B. *The Hollow Crown: Ethnohistory of an Indian Kingdom.* Cambridge: Cambridge University Press, 1987.

———, ed. *Colonialism and Culture.* Ann Arbor: University of Michigan Press, 1992.

Dirks, Nicholas B., Geoff Eley, and Sherry B. Ortner, eds. *Culture/Power/History: A Reader in Contemporary Social Theory.* Princeton: Princeton University Press, 1994.

Dixon, C. J. *De Assistent in Deli.* Amsterdam: J. H. de Bussy, 1913.

Dodwell, Henry. *The Nabobs of Madras.* London: Williams and Norgate, 1926.

Domínguez, Virginia R. *White by Definition: Social Classification in Creole Louisiana.* New Brunswick, N.J.: Rutgers University Press, 1986.

Donzelot, Jacques. *The Policing of Families.* Trans. Robert Hurley. New York: Pantheon, 1979.

Doorn, Jacobus van. *A Divided Society: Segmentation and Mediation in Late-Colonial Indonesia.* Rotterdam: CASPA, 1983.

———. "Indie als Koloniale Maatschappy." In *De Nederlandse Samenleving sinds 1815,* ed. F. L. van Holthoon, 139–57. Assen: Maastricht, 1985.

———. *De Laatste Eeuw van Indie: Ontwikkeling en Ondergang van een Koloniaal Project.* Amsterdam: Bert Bakker, 1994.

Douchet. *Métis et congaies d'Indochine.* Hanoi, 1928.

Dowd Hall, Jacquelyn. " 'The Mind That Burns in Each Body': Women, Rape, and Racial Violence." *Southern Exposure* 12, no. 6 (1984): 61–71.

Drooglever, P. J. *De Vaderlandse Club 1929–1942: Totoks en de Indische Politiek.* Franeker: Wever, 1980.

Dumontier, M. G. "Du rôle politique de l'education dans l'enseignement française en Indochine." In *Congrès Colonial International de Paris,* 185–98. Paris: Challamel, 1898.

Dunlop, Francis. *The Education of Feeling and Emotion.* London: Allen & Unwin, 1984.

Dupuy, A. "La personnalité du colon." *Revue d'Histoire Economique et Sociale* 33, no. 1 (1955): 77–103.

Duras, Marguerite. *The Lover.* Trans. Barbara Bray. New York: Pantheon, 1985.

———. *The Sea Wall*. Trans. Herma Briffault. New York: Harper and Row, 1952.

Dussel, Enrique. *The Underside of Modernity*. Atlantic Highlands, N.J.: Humanities Press, 1996.

Edwardes, Michael. *Bound to Exile: The Victorians in India*. London: Sidgwick & Jackson, 1969.

Edwards, Elizabeth, ed. *Anthropology and Photography, 1860–1920*. New Haven: Yale University Press in association with the Royal Anthropological Institute, London, 1992.

———, ed. "Anthropology and the Colonial Endeavor." Special issue of *History of Photography* 21, no. 1 (1997).

Elias, Norbert. *Power and Civility*. New York: Pantheon, [1939] 1982.

Emmanuel, Arghiri. "White-Settler Colonialism and the Myth of Investment Imperialism." *New Left Review* 73 (May–June 1972): 35–57.

Encyclopaedie van Nederlandsch-Indie. 2d ed. The Hague: Martinus Nijhoff and E. J. Brill, [1919] 1921.

Engels, Dagmar. "The Age of Consent Act of 1891: Colonial Ideology in Bengal." *South Asia Research* 3, no. 2 (1983): 107–34.

Etats-Généraux du Féminisme. *Exposition coloniale internationale de Paris 1931, rapport général présenté par le Gouverneur Général Olivier*. Paris: Imprimerie Nationale, 1931.

Etienne, Mona, and Eleanor Leacock, eds. *Women and Colonization: Anthropological Perspectives*. New York: Praeger, 1980.

Fanon, Frantz. *Black Skin, White Masks*. Trans. Charles Lam Markmann. New York: Grove Press, [1952] 1967.

———. *The Wretched of the Earth*. Trans. Constance Farrington. New York: Grove Press, 1963.

Fasseur, Cees. "Cornerstone and Stumbling Block: Racial Classification and the Late Colonial State in Indonesia." In *The Late Colonial State in Indonesia: Political and Economic Foundations of the Netherlands Indies, 1880–1942*, ed. Robert Cribb, 31–56. Leiden: KITLV, 1994.

———. *De Indologen: Ambtenaren voor de Oost, 1825–1950*. Amsterdam: Bert Bakker, 1993.

Favre, J.-L. *La vie aux colonies*. Paris: Larose, 1938.

Feuilletau de Bruyn, W. K. H. "Over de Economische Mogelijkheid van een Kolonisatie van Blanken op Nederlandsch Nieuw-Guinea." In *Comptes Rendus du Congrès International de Géographie, Amsterdam, 1938. Tome Premier Actes du Congrès*, ed. International Geographical Congress, 21–29. Leiden: E. J. Brill, 1938.

Forde-Jones, Cecily. "Mapping Racial Boundaries: Gender, Race, and Poor Relief in Barbadian Plantation Society." *Journal of Women's History* 10, no. 3 (1998): 9–31.

Foster-Carter, Aidan. "The Modes of Production Controversy." *New Left Review* 107 (January–February 1978): 47–78.

Foucault, Michel. *The Archaeology of Knowledge.* Trans. A. M. Sheridan Smith. New York: Pantheon, 1972.

———. *Difendere la società.* Florence: Pont alle Grazie, 1990.

———. *"Il faut défendre la société": Cours au Collège de France (1975–1976).* Paris: Seuil/Gallimard, 1997.

———. *The History of Sexuality.* Vol. 1, *An Introduction.* New York: Vintage, 1978.

———. "Nietzsche, Genealogy, History." In *The Foucault Reader,* ed. Paul Rabinow, 76–100. New York: Pantheon, [1972] 1984.

———. *Power/Knowledge: Selected Interviews and Other Writings, 1972–1977.* Trans. Colin Gordon. Brighton, Sussex: Harvester Press, 1980.

———. *Résumé des cours, 1970–1982.* Paris: Julliard, 1989.

———. "Two Lectures." In *Power/Knowledge: Selected Interviews and Other Writings, 1972–1977,* ed. C. Gordon, 78–108. New York: Pantheon, 1980.

Foulcher, Keith. *"Bumi Manusia* and *Anak Semua Bangsa:* Pramoedya Ananta Toer enters the 1980s." *Indonesia* 32 (October 1981): 1–15.

Fredrickson, George. *White Supremacy: A Comparative Study in American and South African History.* New York: Oxford University Press, 1981.

Furnivall, J. S. *Netherlands India: A Study of Plural Economy.* New York: Macmillan, 1944.

Gaitskell, Deborah. "Housewives, Maids or Mothers: Some Contradictions of Domesticity for Christian Women in Johannesburg, 1903–39." *Journal of African History* 24 (1983): 241–56.

Gann, Lewis H., and Peter Duignan. *The Rulers of British Africa, 1870–1914.* London: Croom Helm, 1978.

Gantes, Gilles de. 1981. *La population française au Tonkin entre 1931 et 1938.* Mémoire de Maitrise, Aix-en-Provence: Université de Provence, Centre d'Aix, Institut d'Histoire des Pays d'Outre-Mer.

Gartrell, Beverley. "Colonial Wives: Villains or Victims?" In *The Incorporated Wife,* ed. Hillary Callan and Shirley Ardener, 165–85. London: Croom Helm, 1984.

Geertz, Clifford. *Agricultural Involution: The Process of Ecological Change in Indonesia.* Berkeley: University of California Press, 1963.

———. *The Religion of Java.* Glencoe, Ill.: Free Press, 1960.

Geertz, Hildred. *The Javanese Family: A Study of Kinship and Socialization.* New York: Free Press of Glencoe, 1961.

Genovese, Eugene D. *Roll, Jordan, Roll: The World the Slaves Made.* New York: Pantheon, 1976.

Gentner, Dedre, and Arthur B. Markman. "Structure Mapping in Analogy and Similarity." *American Psychologist* 52, no. 1 (1997): 45–56.

George, Rosemary M. "Homes in the Empire, Empires in the Home." *Cultural Critique* (Winter 1994): 95–127.

Gilman, Sander L. *Difference and Pathology: Stereotypes of Sexuality, Race, and Madness.* Ithaca: Cornell University Press, 1985.

Gilroy, Paul. *"There Ain't No Black in the Union Jack": The Cultural Politics of Race and Nation.* London: Hutchinson, 1987.

Girardet, Raoul, ed. *Le nationalisme français, 1871–1914.* Paris: Seuil, [1966] 1983.

Gist, Noel Pitts, and Roy Dean Wright. *Marginality and Identity: Anglo-Indians as a Racially Mixed Minority in India.* Leiden: E. J. Brill, 1973.

Gordon, Linda. *Heroes of Their Own Lives: The Politics and History of Family Violence: Boston, 1880–1960.* New York: Vintage, 1988.

———. *Woman's Body, Woman's Right: A Social History of Birth Control in America.* New York: Grossman, 1976.

Gordon, Robert J., and Mervyn J. Meggitt. "The Decline of the Kipas." In *Law and Order in the New Guinea Highlands: Encounters with Enga,* ed. Robert J. Gordon and Mervyn J. Meggitt, 39–70. Hanover, N.H.: University Press of New England, 1985.

Gorter, Hendrik. *Delianen: Schetsen uit het Plantersleven op Sumatra's Oostkust.* Amsterdam: L. J. Veen, 1941.

Gossard, Philippe. *Etudes sur le métissage principalement en A.O.F.* Paris: Presses Modernes, 1934.

Gouda, Frances. *Dutch Culture Overseas: Colonial Practice in the Netherlands Indies, 1900–1942.* Amsterdam: Amsterdam University Press, 1995.

———. "Gender and 'Hyper-masculinity' as Post-Colonial Modernity during Indonesia's Struggle for Independence, 1945–49." In *Gender, Sexuality and Colonial Modernities,* ed. Antoinette Burton, 161–74. New York: Routledge, 1999.

———. *Poverty and Political Culture: The Rhetoric of Social Welfare in the Netherlands and France, 1815–1854.* Lanham, Md.: Rowman & Littlefield, 1995.

Gough, Kathleen. "Anthropology and Imperialism." *Current Anthropology* 9, no. 5 (1968): 403–7.

Grall, Charles. *Hygiène coloniale appliquée: Hygiène de l'Indochine.* Paris: Baillière, 1908.

Grimshaw, Patricia. " 'Christian Woman, Pious Wife, Faithful Mother, Devoted Missionary': Conflicts in Roles of American Missionary Women in Nineteenth-Century Hawaii." *Feminist Studies* 9, no. 3 (1983): 489–521.

———. *Paths of Duty: American Missionary Wives in Nineteenth-Century Hawaii.* Honolulu: University of Hawaii Press, 1989.

Groupe d'Etudes Coloniales. "La femme blanche au Congo." *Bulletin de la Société Belge d'Etudes Coloniales* 5 (May 1910): 1–12.

Guha, Ranajit. "The Small Voice of History." In *Subaltern Studies X: Writings on South Asian History and Society,* ed. Gautam Bhadra, Gyan Prakash, and Susie Tharu, 1–12. Delhi: Oxford University Press, 1996.

Gunew, Sneja, and Anna Yeatman, eds. *Feminism and the Politics of Difference.* Boulder: Westview Press, 1993.

Gupta, Akhil. 1995. "Blurred Boundaries: The Discourse of Corruption, the Culture of Politics, and the Imagined State." *American Ethnologist* 22, no. 2 (1995): 375–402.

Gutiérrez, Ramón A. *When Jesus Came, the Corn Mothers Went Away: Marriage, Sexuality, and Power in New Mexico, 1500–1846*. Stanford, Calif.: Stanford University Press, 1991.

Hacking, Ian. "The Looping Effects of Human Kinds." In *Causal Cognition: A Multidisciplinary Debate*, ed. Dan Sperber, David Premack, and Ann Premack, 351–83. Oxford: Oxford University Press, 1995.

———. "Historical Ontology: From the Creation of Phenomena to the Formation of Character." Manuscript.

———. *The Social Construction of What?* Cambridge, Mass.: Harvard University Press, 1999.

Hafkin, Nancy J., and Edna G. Bay, eds. *Women in Africa: Studies in Social and Economic Change*. Stanford, Calif.: Stanford University Press, 1976.

Hall, Catherine. *Cultures of Empire: A Reader*. Manchester: Manchester University Press, 2000.

———. "Missionary Stories: Gender and Ethnicity in the 1830s and 1840s." In *White, Male and Middle Class*, 205–54. Cambridge: Polity Press, 1992.

———. *White, Male and Middle Class: Explorations in Feminism and History*. Cambridge: Polity Press, 1992.

Hammerton, A. James. *Emigrant Gentlewomen: Genteel Poverty and Female Emigration, 1830–1914*. London: Croom Helm, 1979.

Hanagan, Michael, and Charles Stephenson, eds. *Proletarians and Protest: The Roots of Class Formation in an Industrializing World*. Westport, Conn.: Greenwood Press, 1986.

Hansen, Karen Tranberg. *African Encounters with Domesticity*. New Brunswick, N.J.: Rutgers University Press, 1992.

———. *Distant Companions: Servants and Employers in Zambia, 1900–1985*. Ithaca: Cornell University Press, 1989.

———. "Negotiating Sex and Gender in Urban Zambia." *Journal of Southern African Studies* 10, no. 2 (1984): 218–38.

Hardy, Georges. *Ergaste ou la vocation coloniale*. Paris: Armand Colin, 1929.

Harris, Marvin. *Patterns of Race in the Americas*. New York: Norton, 1964.

———. "Referential Ambiguity in the Calculus of Brazilian Racial Identity." *Southwestern Journal of Anthropology* 26, no. 1 (1970): 1–14.

Harris, Marvin, and Conrad Kottak. "The Structural Significance of Brazilian Racial Categories." *Sociologia* 25 (1963): 203–9.

Hartenberg. "Les troubles nerveux et mentaux chez les coloniaux." Paris, 1910.

Harwood, Dorothy. "The Possibility of White Colonization in the Tropics." In *Comptes Rendu du Congrès International de Géographie*, 131–40. Leiden: E. J. Brill, 1938.

Heekeren, C. van. *Trekkers en Blijvers: Kroniek van een Haags-Indische Familie*. Amsterdam: Franeker, 1980.

Hermans, E. H. *Gezondscheidsleer voor Nederlandsche-Indie.* Amsterdam: Meulenhoff, 1925.

Hesselink, Liesbeth. "Prostitution, a Necessary Evil, Particularly in the Colonies: Views on Prostitution in the Netherlands Indies." In *Indonesian Women in Focus: Past and Present Notions,* ed. Elsbeth Locher-Scholten and Anke Niehof, 205–24. Dordrecht: Foris, 1987.

Het Pauperisme Commissie. *Rapport der Pauperisme-Commissie.* Batavia: Landsdrukkerij, 1903.

Het Pauperisme onder de Europeanen in Nederlandsch-Indie, pts. 1, 3, 5. Batavia: Landsdrukkerij, 1901.

Heyningen, Elizabeth B. Van. "The Social Evil in the Cape Colony 1868–1902: Prostitution and the Contagious Disease Acts." *Journal of Southern African Studies* 10, no. 2 (1984): 170–97.

Hilgers, Th. J. A., and H. Douma. *De Indisch Lagere School toegepaste Opvoedkunde en Methodeleer ten Dienste van Onderwijzers en Kweekelingen.* Weltevreden, 1908.

Hillen, Ernest. *The Way of a Boy: A Memoir of Java.* London: Penguin, 1993.

Hiner, N. Ray. "The Child in American Historiography: Accomplishments and Prospects." *Psychohistory Review* 7 (Summer 1978): 13–23.

Hirsch, E. D. *Cultural Literacy: What Every American Needs to Know.* Boston: Houghton Mifflin, 1987.

Hirschfeld, Lawrence. "On Acquiring Social Categories: Cognitive Development and Anthropological Wisdom." *Man* 23 (December 1988): 611–38.

———. *Race in the Making: Cognition, Culture, and the Child's Construction of Human Kinds.* Cambridge, Mass.: MIT Press, 1996.

Hissink-Snellebrand, L. J. "Wat is ten doen in het Belang van de Indische Paupermeisjes en tot Verstreking van het Nederlandsche Element in Nederlandsch-Indie." Indische Genootschap, Algemeene vergadering van 22 November 1910, 37–57.

Hobsbawm, Eric. *The Age of Empire, 1875–1914.* London: Weidenfeld and Nicolson, 1987.

Hobsbawn, Eric, and Terence Ranger, eds. 1983. *The Invention of Tradition.* Cambridge: Cambridge University Press, 1983.

Holthoon, F. L. van, ed. *De Nederlandse Samenleving Sinds 1815.* Assen: Maastricht, 1985.

Horst, D. W. "Opvoeding en Onderwijs van Kinderen van Europeanen en Indo-Europeanen in Indie." *De Indische Gids* 2 (1900): 989–96.

Houthuysen, B. V. *Het Betwisten eener Erkenning als Natuurlijk Kind.* Batavia: G. Kolff, 1898.

Houben, Vincent. "A Torn Soul: The Dutch Public Discussion of the Colonial Past in 1995." *Indonesia* 63 (1997): 67–90.

Huertas, Hubert. *FN: Made in France.* Paris: Editions Autrestemps, 1997.

Hughes, Robert. *The Fatal Shore: A History of the Transportation of Convicts to Australia, 1787–1868.* New York: Knopf, 1987.

Hunt, Lynn. *The Family Romance of the French Revolution.* Berkeley: University of California Press, 1992.

Hunt, Nancy Rose. " 'Le bébé en brousse': European Women, African Birth Spacing, and Colonial Intervention in Breast Feeding in the Belgian Congo." In *Tensions of Empire: Colonial Cultures in a Bourgeois World,* ed. Frederick Cooper and Ann Laura Stoler, 287–321. Berkeley: University of California Press, 1997.

———. *A Colonial Lexicon of Birth Ritual, Medicalization, and Mobility in the Congo.* Durham, N.C.: Duke University Press, 1999.

———. "Domesticity and Colonialism in Belgian Africa: Usumbura's *Foyer Social,* 1946–1960." *Signs* 15, no. 3 (1990): 447–74.

———. Introduction to special issue, "Gendered Colonialism in African History." *Gender and History* 8, no. 3 (1996): 323–37.

Hyam, Ronald. "Concubinage and the Colonial Service: The Crewe Circular (1909). *Journal of Imperial and Commonwealth History* 14, no. 3 (1986): 170–86.

———. "Empire and Sexual Opportunity." *Journal of Imperial and Commonwealth History* 14, no. 2 (1986): 34–90.

Hymes, Dell H., ed. *Reinventing Anthropology.* New York: Vintage, 1969.

Ingelson, John. " 'Bound Hand and Foot': Railway Workers and the 1923 Strike in Java." *Indonesia* 31 (April 1981): 53–88.

Inglis, Amirah. *The White Women's Protection Ordinance: Sexual Anxiety and Politics in Papua.* London: Sussex University Press, 1975.

International Geographical Congress, ed. *Comptes Rendus du Congrès International de Géographie, Amsterdam, 1938. Tome Premier Actes du Congrès.* Leiden: E. J. Brill, 1938.

Jarequiberry. *Les blancs en pays chauds.* Paris: Maloine, 1924.

Jeske, Reijs, et al., eds. *Vrouwen in de Nederlandse Kolonien.* Nijmegen: SUN, 1986.

Jolly, Margaret. "Colonizing Women: The Maternal Body and Empire." In *Feminism and the Politics of Difference,* ed. Sneja Gunew and Anna Yeatman, 103–27. Sydney: Allen & Unwin, 1993.

Jordan, Winthrop D. *White over Black: American Attitudes toward the Negro, 1550–1812.* Chapel Hill: University of North Carolina Press, 1968.

Joyeux, Ch., and A. Sice. "Affections exotiques du système nerveux." *Précis de Médecine Coloniale.* Paris: Masson, 1937.

Kantoor van Arbeid. *Werkloosheid in Nederlandsch-Indie.* Batavia: Landsdrukkerij, 1935.

Keeler, Ward. *Javanese Shadow Plays, Javanese Selves.* Princeton: Princeton University Press, 1987.

Kelly, John Dunham. *A Politics of Virtue: Hinduism, Sexuality, and Countercolonial Discourse in Fiji.* Chicago: University of Chicago Press, 1991.

Kennedy, Dane. *Islands of White: Settler Society and Culture in Kenya and Southern Rhodesia, 1890–1939.* Durham, N.C.: Duke University Press, 1987.

Kennedy, Raymond. *The Ageless Indies.* New York: John Day, 1947.

Kevles, Daniel J. *In the Name of Eugenics: Genetics and the Uses of Human Heredity.* Berkeley: University of California Press, 1985.

Kincaid, Dennis. *British Social Life in India, 1608–1937.* New York: Kennikat Press, 1971.

King, Anthony D. *Colonial Urban Development: Culture, Social Power, and Environment.* London: Routledge & Kegan Paul, 1976.

Kirkwood, Deborah. "Settler Wives in Southern Rhodesia: A Case Study." In *The Incorporated Wife,* ed. Hilary Callan and Shirley Ardener, 106–19. London: Croom Helm, 1984.

Kleian, J. *Deli-Planter.* The Hague: W. van Hoeve, 1936.

Klerck, Douaire. *Eenige Beschouwingen over Oost-Indische Toestanden.* Amsterdam: Versluys, 1898.

Kleyn, R. "Ondezoek Naar het Vaderschap." *Het Recht in Nederlandsch-Indie* 67 (1896): 130–50.

Knapman, Claudia. *White Women in Fiji, 1835–1930: The Ruin of Empire?* Boston: Allen & Unwin, 1986.

Knibiehler, Yvonne, and Régine Goutalier. *La femme au temps des colonies.* Paris: Stock, 1985.

———. *"Femmes et colonisation": Rapport terminal au Ministère des Relations Extérieures et de la Coopération.* Aix-en-Provence: Institut d'Histoire des Pays d'Outre-Mer, 1987.

Kohlbrugge, J. *Blikken in het Zieleleven van den Javaan en Zijner Overheerschers.* Leiden: E. J. Brill, 1907.

———. "Het Indische Kind en Zijne Karaktervorming." In *Blikken in het Zielenleven van den Javaan en Zijner Overheerschers.* Leiden: E. J. Brill, 1907.

———. "Prostitutie in Nederlandsch-Indie." *Indisch Genootschap* (February 19, 1901): 2–36.

Koks, J. Th. *De Indo.* Amsterdam: H. J. Paris, 1931.

Kol, H. van. *Uit Onze Kolonien.* Leiden: A. W. Sijthoff, 1903.

Koriat, Asher, and Morris Goldsmith. "Memory Metaphors and the Laboratory/Real-Life Controversy: Correspondence versus Storehouse Conceptions of Memory." *Behavioral and Brain Sciences* 19, no. 2 (1996): 167–228.

Koster, G. H. "Aangenomen Kinderen en Staatsblad Europeanen." *De Amsterdammer,* July 15, 1922.

Kousbroek, Rudy. *Terug naar Negri Pan Erkoms.* Amsterdam: Meulenhoff, 1995.

Koven, Seth, and Sonya Michel. "Womanly Duties: Maternalist Politics and the Origins of Welfare States in France, Germany, Great Britain, and the United States, 1880–1920." *American Historical Review* 95 (October 1990): 1076–1108.

Kuitenbrouwer, Maarten. *The Netherlands and the Rise of Modern Imperialism: Colonies and Foreign Policy, 1870–1902.* Trans. Hugh Beyer. New York: St. Martin's Press, 1991.

Kuklick, Henrika. *The Imperial Bureaucrat: The Colonial Administrative Service in the Gold Coast, 1920–1939.* Stanford, Calif.: Hoover Institution Press, 1979.

La femme dans les sociétés coloniales: Table Ronde CHEE, CRHSE, IHPOM: Groningen-Amsterdam, Septembre 1982, Centre d'Histoire de l'Expansion Européenne, Université de Leiden (P.B.). 1984. Aix[-en-Provence]: Institut d'Histoire des Pays d'Outre-Mer, Université de Provence.

Laffey, John. "Racism in Tonkin before 1914." *French Colonial Studies* 8 (1977): 65–81.

Lanessan, Jean Marie Antoine de. *L'Indo-Chine française.* Paris: F. Alcan, 1889.

Le Bras, Hervé. "Histoire secrète de la fécondité." *Le Débat* 8 (1981): 76–100.

Leconte, Daniel. *Les pieds noirs.* Paris: Seuil, 1980.

Le Roux, Hughes. *Je deviens colon: Moeurs algériennes.* Paris: Calmann Lévy, 1898.

Leonard, Jacques. "Les origins et les conséquences de l'eugenique en France." *Annales de Démographie Historique* (1985): 203–14.

Leonardo, Micaela di, ed. *Gender at the Crossroads of Knowledge: Feminist Anthropology in the Postmodern Era.* Berkeley: University of California Press, 1991.

Lerner, Gerda. *Black Women in White America: A Documentary History.* New York: Pantheon, 1972.

Lévi-Strauss, Claude. *Le regard éloigné.* Paris: Plon, 1983.

Lewis, Martin. "One Hundred Million Frenchmen: The 'Assimilation' Theory in French Colonial Policy." *Comparative Studies in Society and History* 3, no. 4 (1961): 129–51.

Linton, Marigold. "Ways of Searching and the Contents of Memory." In *Autobiographical Memory,* ed. David C. Rubin, 50–67. Cambridge: Cambridge University Press, 1986.

Locher-Scholten, Elsbeth. "Orientalism and the Rhetoric of the Family: Javanese Servants in European Household Manuals and Children's Fiction." *Indonesia* 58 (October 1994): 19–39.

———. *Women and the Colonial State: Essays on Gender and Modernity in the Netherland Indies, 1900–1942.* Amsterdam: Amsterdam University Press, 2000.

Locher-Scholten, Elsbeth, and Anke Niehof, eds. *Indonesian Women in Focus: Past and Present Notions.* Dordrecht: Foris, 1987.

Lonsdale, John, and Bruce Berman. "Coping with the Contradictions: The Development of the Colonial State in Kenya, 1895–1914." *Journal of African History* 20 (1979): 487–505.

Loutfi, Martine. *Littérature et colonialisme: L'expansion coloniale vue dans la littérature romanesque française, 1871–1914.* Paris: Mouton, 1971.

Lucas, Nicole. "Trouwverbod, Inlandse Huishoudsters en Europese Vrouwen: Het Concubinaat in de Planterswereld aan Sumatra's Oostkust, 1860–1940." In *Vrouwen in de Nederlandse Kolonien,* ed. Reijs Jeske et al., 78–97. Nijmegen: SUN, 1986.

Macey, David. *The Lives of Michel Foucault.* New York: Pantheon, 1983.

Mackinnon, Murdoch. "European Children in the Tropical Highlands." *Lancet* 199 (1920): 944–45.

Malinowski, Bronislaw. "Dynamics of Culture Change." In *Social Change: The Colonial Situation,* ed. I. Wallerstein, 11–24. New York: Wiley, 1966.

Malkki, Liisa. "National Geographic: The Rooting of Peoples and the Territorialization of National Identity among Scholars and Refugees." *Cultural Anthropology* 7, no. 1 (1992): 24–44.

Malleret, Louis. *L'éxotisme indochinois dans la littérature française depuis 1860.* Paris: Larose, 1934.

Manders, Jo. *De Boedjang-Club: Delische Roman.* 's-Gravenhage: H. P. Leopold, 1933.

Manderson, Leonore. "Colonial Desires: Sexuality, Race, and Gender in British Malaya." *Journal of the History of Sexuality* 7, no. 3 (1997): 372–88.

Mani, Lata. *Contentious Traditions: The Debate on Sati in Colonial India, 1780–1833.* Berkeley: University of California Press, 1999.

Manicom, Linzi. "Ruling Relations: Rethinking State and Gender in South African History." *Journal of African History* 33 (1992): 441–65.

Mannoni, Octavio. *Prospero and Caliban: The Psychology of Colonization.* Trans. Pamela Powesland. New York: Praeger, 1956.

Mansvelt, W. "De Positie der Indo-Europeanen." *Kolonial Studien* 16 (1932): 290–311.

Marinus, J. H., and J. J. van der Laan. *Veertig Jaren Ervaring in de Delicultures.* Amsterdam: J. H. de Bussy, 1929.

Marks, Shula, ed. *Not Either an Experimental Doll: The Separate Worlds of Three South African Women.* Bloomington: Indiana University Press, 1987.

Marks, Shula, and Stanley Trapido, eds. *The Politics of Race, Class, and Nationalism in Twentieth-Century South Africa.* London: Longman, 1986.

Marle, A. van. "De Groep der Europeanen in Nederlands-Indie, Iets over Ontstaan en Groei." *Indonesie* 5, no. 2 (1952): 77–121; 5, no. 3 (1952): 314–41; 5, no. 4 (1952): 481–507.

Marr, David G. *Vietnamese Anticolonialism, 1885–1925.* Berkeley: University of California Press, 1971.

———. *Vietnamese Tradition on Trial, 1920–1945.* Berkeley: University of California Press, 1981.

Marshall, T. H. *Class, Citizenship, and Social Development: Essays.* Westport, Conn.: Greenwood Press, [1963] 1973.

Martial, René. *Les métis.* Paris: Flammarion, 1942.

Martinez-Alier [Stolcke], Verena. *Marriage, Class and Colour in Nineteenth-Century Cuba: A Study of Racial Attitudes and Sexual Values in a Slave Society.* Cambridge: Cambridge University Press, 1974.

Mason, Philip. *The Birth of a Dilemma: The Conquest and Settlement of Rhodesia.* New York: Oxford University Press, 1958.

Mastenbroek, William Edward van. *De Historische Ontwikkeling van de Staatsrechtelijke Indeeling der Bevolking van Nederlandsch-Indie.* Wageningen: H. Veenman & Zonen, 1934.

Maunier, M. René. *Sociologie coloniale.* Paris: Domat-Montchrestien, 1932.

Mazet, Jacques. *La condition juridique des métis dans les possessions françaises.* Paris: Domat-Montchrestien, 1932.

McClintock, Anne. *Imperial Leather: Race, Gender, and Sexuality in the Colonial Conquest.* New York: Routledge, 1995.

McClure, John A. *Kipling and Conrad: The Colonial fiction.* Cambridge, Mass.: Harvard University Press, 1981.

Mead, Margaret. *Letters from the Field, 1925–1975.* New York: Harper and Row, 1977.

Mead, Margaret, and Martha Wolfenstein, eds. *Childhood in Contemporary Cultures.* Chicago: University of Chicago Press, 1955.

Medin, Douglas. "Concepts and Conceptual Structure." *American Psychologist* (December 1989): 1469–81.

Mehta, Uday. "Liberal Strategies of Exclusion." In *Tensions of Empire: Colonial Cultures in a Bourgeois World,* ed. Frederick Cooper and Ann Laura Stoler, 59–86. Berkeley: University of California Press, 1997.

Memmi, Albert. *The Colonizer and the Colonized.* Boston: Beacon Press, [1957] 1967.

———. *Portrait du colonisé, précédé du portrait du colonisateur.* Paris: Payot, [1957] 1973.

Mercier, Paul. "The European Community of Dakar." In *Africa: Social Problems of Change and Conflict: Readings,* ed. Pierre L. Van den Berghe, 283–304. San Francisco: Chandler, 1965.

Metcalf, Thomas R. *The Aftermath of Revolt: India, 1857–1870.* Princeton: Princeton University Press, 1964.

Meyer, Charles. *Les français en Indochine: 1860–1910.* Paris: Hachette, [1985] 1996.

Middendorp, W. *De Poenale Sanctie.* Haarlem: Tjeenk Willink, 1924.

Mignolo, Walter. *Local Histories, Global Designs: Coloniality, Subaltern Knowledges, and Border Thinking.* Princeton: Princeton University Press, 2000.

Ming, Hanneke. "Barracks-Concubinage in the Indies, 1887–1920." *Indonesia* 35 (April 1983): 65–93.

Mintz, Sidney W. *Caribbean Transformations.* Chicago: Aldine, 1974.

———. "Groups, Group Boundaries, and the Perception of 'Race.'" *Comparative Studies in Society and History* 13 (Fall 1971): 437–50.

———. *Sweetness and Power: The Place of Sugar in Modern History.* New York: Penguin, 1985.

Misset-Stein, M. "De Vrouw in het Pro Juventute-werk." In *Indische Vrouwen Jaarboek, 1936,* ed. M. A. E. van Lith-van Schreven and H. H. Hooykaas-van Leeuwen Boomkamp, 27–30. Jogjakarta: Kolff-Buning, 1936.

Mitchell, Timothy. *Colonising Egypt.* Cambridge: Cambridge University Press, 1988.

———. "The Limits of the State: Beyond Statist Approaches and Their Critics." *American Political Science Review* 85, no. 1 (1991): 77–96.

"Moeten onze Kinderen naar Holland?" *'t Onderwijs* 36 (September 15, 1906): 420.

Moore-Gilbert, B. J. *Kipling and "Orientalism."* New York: St. Martin's Press, 1986.

Mort, Frank. *Dangerous Sexualities: Medico-Moral Politics in England since 1830.* New York: Routledge and Kegan Paul, 1987.

Moses, Claire Goldberg. *French Feminism in the Nineteenth Century.* Albany: State University of New York Press, 1984.

Mosse, George L. *Nationalism and Sexuality: Respectability and Abnormal Sexuality in Modern Europe.* New York: H. Fertig, 1985.

———. *Toward the final Solution: A History of European Racism.* New York: H. Fertig, 1978.

Murphy, Agnes. *The Ideology of French Imperialism, 1871–1881.* New York: H. Fertig, 1968.

Naidis, Mark. "British Attitudes toward the Anglo-Indians." *South Atlantic Quarterly* 62, no. 3 (1963): 407–22.

Naipaul, V. S. *The Middle Passage: Impressions of five Societies, British, French and Dutch, in the West Indies and South America.* London: Penguin, 1974.

Nandy, Ashis. *The Intimate Enemy: Loss and Recovery of Self under Colonialism.* New York: Oxford University Press, 1983.

Nash, June. "Aztec Women: The Transition from Status to Class in Empire and Colony." In *Women and Colonization: Anthropological Perspectives,* ed. Mona Etienne and Eleanor Leacock, 134–48. New York: Praeger, 1980.

———. "Ethnographic Aspects of the World Capitalist System." *Annual Review of Anthropology* 10 (1981): 393–423.

Nazzari, Muriel. "Concubinage in Colonial Brazil: The Inequalities of Race, Class and Gender." *Journal of Family History* 21, no. 2 (1996): 107–24.

Nederburgh, J. A. *Gemengde Huwelijken, Staatsblad 1898, No. 158: Officiele Bescheiden met eenige Aanteekeningen.*

———. *Wet en Adat.* Batavia: Kolff, 1898.

Needham, Rodney. "Analogical Classifications." In *Reconnaissances,* 41–62. Toronto: University of Toronto Press, 1980.

———. *Belief, Language, and Experience.* Chicago: University of Chicago Press, 1972.

Nelson, Hank. *Taim Bilong Masta: The Australian Involvement with Papua New Guinea.* Sydney: Australian Broadcasting Commission, 1982.

Nietzsche, Friedrich. *Untimely Meditations.* Trans. R. J. Hollingdale. Cambridge: Cambridge University Press, 1997.

Nieuwenhuis, J. J. 1920. "Lichamelijke Opvoeding en Onderwijs Hervorming in Nederlands-Indie." *Koloniale Studien,* pt. 1 (1920).

Nieuwenhuys, Rob. *Mirror of the Indies: A History of Dutch Colonial Literature.* Trans. Frans van Rosevelt. Amherst: University of Massachusetts Press, 1982.

———. *Oost-Indische Spiegel: Wat Nederlandse Schrijvers en Dichters over Indonesië hebben geschreven, vanaf de Eerste Jaren der Compagnie tot op Heden.* Amsterdam: E. Querido, 1978.

———. *De Schim van Nenek Tidjah.* Amsterdam: Huis Clos, 1995.

———. *Sinjo Robbie.* Forthcoming.

———. *Tussen Twee Vaderlanden.* Amsterdam: G. A. van Oorschot, 1959.

Nijs, E. Breton de. *Faded Portraits.* Trans. E. M. Beekman. Amherst: University of Massachusetts Press, [1954] 1982.

———. *Tempo Doeloe: Fotografische Documenten uit het oude Indië, 1870–1914.* Amsterdam: E. Querido, 1973.

Nora, Pierre. *Les français d'Algérie.* Paris: R. Julliard, 1961.

"Nota van het lid der commissie, den Heer J. van der Steur, gedagteekend Magelang, 14 Augustus 1902." In *Nota's over het Armwezen en het Pauperisme,* 39. Batavia: Landsdrukkerij, 1902.

Nye, Robert A. *Crime, Madness, and Politics in Modern France: The Medical Concept of National Decline.* Princeton: Princeton University Press, 1984.

O'Brien, Denise, and Sharon Tiffany, eds. *Rethinking Women's Roles: Perspectives from the Pacific.* Berkeley: University of California Press, 1984.

O'Brien, Rita Cruise. *White Society in Black Africa: The French in Senegal.* London: Faber and Faber, 1972.

Offen, Karen. "Depopulation, Nationalism and Feminism in fin-de-Siècle France." *American Historical Review* 89, no. 3 (1984): 648–76.

"Ons Pauperisme." *Mededeelingen der Vereeniging "Soeria Soemirat,"* no. 2 (1892).

Onselen, Charles van. "Prostitutes and Proletarians, 1886–1914." In *Studies in the Social and Economic History of the Witwatersrand, 1886–1914.* Vol 1. New York: Longman, 1982.

Orwell, George. "Shooting an Elephant." In *Collected Essays,* 154–62. London: Secker & Warburg, 1961.

Painter, Nell Irvin. " 'Social Equality': Miscegenation, Labor and Power." In *The Evolution of Southern Culture,* ed. Numan V. Bartley, 47–67. Athens: University of Georgia Press, 1988.

Pandey, Gyanendra. *Memory, History and the Question of Violence: Reflections on the Reconstruction of Partition.* Calcutta: K. P. Bagchi, 1999.

———. "Violence 'Out There': Memories of Partition." Paper presented at the conference, Religion and Nationalism in Europe and Asia, Amsterdam, November 1995.

Passerini, Luisa. *Fascism in Popular Memory: The Cultural Experience of the Turin Working Class.* Trans. Robert Lumley and Jude Bloomfield. Cambridge: Cambridge University Press, 1987.

Pateman, Carole. *The Sexual Contract.* Cambridge: Polity Press, 1988.

Pedersen, Jean E. " 'Special Customs': Paternity Suits and Citizenship in France and the Colonies, 1870–1912." In *Domesticating the Empire: Race, Gender, and Family Life in French and Dutch Colonialism*, ed. Julia Clancy-Smith and Frances Gouda, 43–64. Charlottesville: University Press of Virginia, 1998.

Pels, Peter. "The Anthropology of Colonialism: Culture, History, and the Emergence of Western Governmentality." *Annual Review of Anthropology* 26 (1997): 163–83.

Pemberton, John. *On the Subject of "Java."* Ithaca: Cornell University Press, 1994.

Perron, Edgar du. *Country of Origin.* Trans. Francis Bulhof and Elizabeth Daverman. Amherst: University of Massachusetts Press, [1935] 1984.

Petersen, H. Tscherning. *Tropical Adventure: Sumatra, Land of Loveliness and Stern Destiny.* Trans. Eugene Gay-Tifft. London: J. Rolls, 1948.

Pigeaud, J. J. *Iets over Kinderopvoeding: Raadgevingen voor Moeders in Indie.* Samarang: G. C. T. van Dorp, 1896.

Pinney, Christopher. *Camera Indica: The Social Life of Indian Photographs.* Chicago: University of Chicago Press, 1998.

Piven, Frances Fox, and Richard A. Cloward. *Regulating the Poor: The Functions of Public Welfare.* New York: Vintage, 1971.

Plantersschoolvereeniging "Brastagi." *De Opvoeding van het Europeesche Kind in Indie.* Brastagi, 1934.

Pollmann, Tessel. "Bruidstraantjes: De Koloniale Roman, de Njai en de Apartheid." In *Vrouwen in de Nederlandse Kolonien*, ed. Jeske Reijs et al., 98–125. Nijmegen: SUN, 1986.

Poovey, Mary. *Uneven Developments: The Ideological Work of Gender in Mid-Victorian England.* Chicago: University of Chicago Press, 1988.

Pouvourville, Albert de. "Le métis." In *Le mal d'Argent*, 97–114. Paris: Monde Moderne, 1926.

Powdermaker, Hortense. *Stranger and Friend: The Way of an Anthropologist.* New York: Norton, 1966.

Prakash, Gyan. Introduction to *After Colonialism: Imperial Histories and Postcolonial Displacements*, ed. Gyan Prakash, 3–20. Princeton: Princeton University Press, 1995.

———. "Science "Gone Native' in Colonial India." *Representations* 40 (1992): 153–78.

———. "Writing Post-Orientalist Histories." *Comparative Studies in Society and History* 32, no. 2 (1990): 383–408.

Pratt, Mary Louise. *Imperial Eyes: Travel Writing and Transculturation.* New York: Routledge, 1992.

Price, A. Grenfell. *White Settlers in the Tropics.* New York: American Geographical Society of New York, 1939.

Prins, W. "De Bevolkingsgroepen in het Nederlandsche-Indische Recht." *Koloniale Studien* 17 (1933): 652–88.

Prochaska, David. *Making Algeria French: Colonialism in Bône, 1870–1920.* Cambridge: Cambridge University Press, 1989.

Pujarniscle, Eugène. *Philoxène ou de la littérature coloniale.* Paris: firmin-Didot, 1931.

Rabinow, Paul. *French Modern: Norms and Forms of the Social Environment.* Cambridge, Mass.: MIT Press, 1989.

Rafael, Vicente L. "Colonial Domesticity: White Women and United States Rule in the Philippines." *American Literature* 67 (December 1995): 639–66.

———. *Contracting Colonialism: Translation and Christian Conversion in Tagalog Society under Early Spanish Rule.* Ithaca: Cornell University Press, 1988.

———. *White Love and Other Events in Filipino History.* Durham, N.C.: Duke University Press, 2000.

———, ed. *Discrepant Histories: Translocal Essays on Filipino Cultures.* Philadelphia: Temple University Press, 1995.

Rai, Amat. *The Rule of Sympathy.* New York: St. Martin's Press, 2002.

Ralston, Caroline. *Grass Huts and Warehouses: Pacific Beach Communities of the Nineteenth Century.* Canberra: Australian National University Press, 1977.

Ramirez, Francisco O., and John Boli. "The Political Construction of Mass Schooling: European Origins and Worldwide Institutionalization." *Sociology of Education* 60, no. 1 (1987): 2–17.

Ramuschack, Barbara. "Cultural Missionaries, Maternal Imperialists, Feminist Allies: British Women Activists in India, 1865–1945." In *Western Women and Imperialism: Complicity and Resistance,* ed. Nupur Chaudhwi and Margaret Strobel, 119–36. Bloomington: Indiana University Press, 1992.

Rappaport, Joanne. *Cumbe Reborn: An Andean Ethnography of History.* Chicago: University of Chicago Press, 1994.

Rapport der Pauperisme-Commissie. Batavia: Landsdrukkerij, 1902.

Raptchinsky, B. *Kolonisatie van Blanken in de Tropen.* The Hague: Bibliotheek van Weten en Denken, 1941.

Ratu-Langie, S. S. J. *Sarekat Islam.* Baam: Hollandia Drukkerij, 1913.

Regt, Ali de. "De Vorming van een Opvoedings-Traditie: Arbiederskinderen Rond 1900." In *Geschiedenis van Opvoeding en Onderwijs,* ed. B. Kruithof, J. Nordman, and Piet de Rooy, 394–409. Nijmegen: SUN, 1982.

Reijs, Jeske, E. Kloek, U. Jansz, A. de Wildt, S. van Norden, and M. de Bat, eds. *Vrouwen in de Nederlandse Kolonien.* Nijmegen: SUN, 1986.

Rich, Paul B. "The Long Victorian Sunset: Anthropology, Eugenics and Race in Britain, c. 1900–48." *Patterns of Prejudice* 18, no. 3 (1984): 3–17.

———. *Race and Empire in British Politics.* New York: Cambridge University Press, 1986.

Richards, Thomas. *The Imperial Archive: Knowledge and the Fantasy of Empire.* New York: Verso, 1993.

Ricoeur, Paul. *Time and Narrative.* Vol. 1. Trans. Kathleen McLaughlin and David Pellauer. Chicago: University of Chicago Press, 1984.

Ridley, Hugh. *Images of Imperial Rule.* New York: Croom Helm, 1981.

Rijksuniversiteit te Leiden and Werkgroep voor de Geschiedenis van de Europese Expansie Centre de Recherche d'Histoire Socio-Economique and Institut d'Histoire des Pays d'Outre-Mer Université de Provence. *La femme dans les sociétés coloniales: Table ronde, CHEE, CRHSE, IHPOM: Groningen-Amsterdam, Septembre 1982, Centre d'Histoire de l'Expansion Européenne, Université de Leiden.* Aix-en-Provence: Institut d'Histoire des Pays d'Outre-Mer, Université de Provence, 1984.

Ritter, W. L. *De Europeaan in Nederlandsch Indie.* Leiden: Sythoff, 1856.

Robbins, Bruce. *The Servant's Hand: English Fiction from Below.* New York: Columbia University Press, 1986.

Robertson, Claire. "Developing Economic Awareness: Changing Perspectives in Studies of African Women, 1976–1985." *Feminist Studies* 13, no. 1 (1987): 97–135.

Robertson, Claire, and Martin Klein, eds. *Women and Slavery in Africa.* Madison: University of Wisconsin Press, 1983.

Rodenwaldt, Ernest. "Eugenetische Problemen in Nederlandsch-Indie." In *Ons Nageslacht,* 1–8. Orgaan van de Eugenetische Vereeniging in Nederland-Indie, 1928.

Romein, Jan. *The Watershed of Two Eras: Europe in 1900.* Trans. Arnold J. Pomerans. Middletown, Conn.: Wesleyan University Press, 1978.

Rosaldo, Renato. *Culture and Truth: The Remaking of Social Analysis.* Stanford, Calif.: Stanford University Press, 1985.

———. *Ilongot Headhunting, 1883–1974: A Study in Society and History.* Stanford, Calif.: Stanford University Press, 1980.

Roseberry, William. *Coffee and Capitalism in the Venezuelan Andes.* Austin: University of Texas Press, 1983.

———. "Images of the Peasant in the Consciousness of the Venezuelan Proletariat." In *Proletarians and Protest: The Roots of Class Formation in an Industrializing World,* ed. Michael Hanagan and Charles Stephenson, 149–69. Westport, Conn.: Greenwood Press, 1986.

Ross, Elizabeth Dale. *The Kindergarten Crusade: The Establishment of Preschool Education in the United States.* Athens: Ohio University Press, 1976.

Ross, Ellen, and Rayna Rapp. "Sex and Society: A Research Note from Social History and Anthropology." *Comparative Studies in Society and History* 22, no. 1 (1980): 51–72.

Rubin, David C., ed. *Autobiographical Memory.* Cambridge: Cambridge University Press, 1986.

Saada, Emmanuelle. "Enfants de la colonie: Batards raciaux, batards sociaux." In *Enquête d'Ariel: Discours sur le métissage, identites métisse,* ed. Sylvie Kandé, 75–96. Paris: L'Harmattan, 1999.

Sahlins, Marshall. *Historical Metaphors and Mythical Realities: Structure in the Early History of the Sandwich Islands Kingdom.* Ann Arbor: University of Michigan Press, 1981.

Said, Edward W. *Orientalism.* New York: Pantheon, 1978.

Said, H. Mohammad. *Sejarah Pers di Sumatera Utara*. Medan: Waspada, 1976.

Salomons, Annie. *Het Huis in de Hitte: Drie Jaar Deli*. Amsterdam: Nederlandsche Keurboekerij, 1932.

Sambuc, Henri. "Les métis franco-annamites en Indochine." *Revue du Pacifique* (1931): 256–72.

Sartre, Jean-Paul. *Critique of Dialectical Reason: Theory of Practical Ensembles*. Trans. Alan Sheridan Smith. London: New Left Books, 1976.

Schacter, Daniel L. *Searching for Memory: The Brain, the Mind, and the Past*. New York: Basic Books, 1996.

Schmidt, Elizabeth. "Ideology, Economics, and the Role of Shona Women in Southern Rhodesia, 1850–1939." Ph.D. dissertation, University of Wisconsin, 1987.

———. "Race, Sex and Domestic Labour: The Question of African Female Servants in Southern Rhodesia, 1900–1939." Manuscript.

Schneider, William. "Toward the Improvement of the Human Race: The History of Eugenics in France." *Journal of Modern History* 54 (June 1982): 269–91.

Schoevers, T. "Het Leven en Werken van den Assistant bij de Tabakschultuur in Deli." *Jaarboek der Vereeniging "Studiebelangen,"* 3–43. Wageningen: Zomer, 1913.

Schoffer, I. "Dutch 'Expansion' and Indonesian Reactions: Some Dilemmas of Modern Colonial Rule (1900–1942)." In *Expansion and Reaction: Essays on European Expansion and Reaction in Asia and Africa*, ed. H. L. Wesseling. Leiden: Leiden University Press, 1978.

Scholte, Lin. *Bibi Koetis voor Altijd*. Amsterdam: E. Querido, 1974.

Schwarz, Bill. "Decolonizing England," in *Memories of Empire in Twentieth-Century England*. London: Verso, forthcoming.

Scott, David. *Refashioning Futures: Criticism after Postcoloniality*. Princeton: Princeton University Press, 1999.

Scott, James C. *Domination and the Arts of Resistance: Hidden Transcripts*. New Haven: Yale University Press, 1990.

———. *The Moral Economy of the Peasant: Rebellion and Subsistence in Southeast Asia*. New Haven: Yale University Press, 1976.

———. *Seeing Like a State: How Certain Schemes to Improve the Human Condition Have Failed*. New Haven: Yale University Press, 1998.

———. *Weapons of the Weak: Everyday Forms of Peasant Resistance*. New Haven: Yale University Press, 1985.

Sears, Laurie J. *Fantasizing the Feminine in Indonesia*. Durham, N.C.: Duke University Press, 1996.

Seed, Patricia. "Social Dimensions of Race: Mexico City, 1753." *Hispanic American Historical Review* 62, no. 4 (1982): 590–606.

———. *To Love, Honor, and Obey in Colonial Mexico: Conflicts over Marriage Choice, 1574–1821*. Stanford, Calif.: Stanford University Press, 1988.

Seigel, James T. *Fetish, Recognition, Revolution*. Princeton: Princeton University Press, 1997.

Seremetakis, C. Nadia, ed. *The Senses Still: Perception and Memory as Material Culture in Modernity*. Boulder, Colo.: Westview Press, 1994.

Sevenhuijsen, Selma. *De Orde van het Vaderschap: Politieke Debatten over Ongehuwd Moederschap, Afstamming en Huwelijk in Nederland 1870–1900*. Amsterdam: Stichting Beheer IISG, 1987.

Shapiro, Michael Steven. *Child's Garden: The Kindergarten Movement from Froebel to Dewey*. University Park: Pennsylvania State University Press, 1983.

Sheppard, Jill. *The "Redlegs" of Barbados*. New York: KTO Press, 1977.

Shiraishi, Takashi. *An Age in Motion: Popular Radicalism in Java, 1912–1926*. Ithaca: Cornell University Press, 1990.

Showalter, Elaine. *The Female Malady: Women, Madness, and Culture in England, 1830–1980*. New York: Penguin, 1987.

Sider, Gerald. "When Parrots Learn to Talk, and Why They Can't': Domination, Deception, and Self-Deception in Indian-White Relations." *Comparative Studies in Society and History* 29, no. 1 (1987): 3–23.

Siegel, James T. *Fetish, Recognition, Revolution*. Princeton: Princeton University Press, 2002.

———. *Solo in the New Order: Language and Hierarchy in an Indonesian City*. Princeton: Princeton University Press, 1986.

Silverblatt, Irene. *Moon, Sun, and Witches: Gender Ideologies and Class in Inca and Colonial Peru*. Princeton: Princeton University Press, 1987.

Simon, Pierre-Jean. "Portraits coloniaux des Vietnamiens (1858–1914)." *Pluriel* 10, no. 1 (1977): 29–54.

———. *Rapatriés d'Indochine: Un village franco-indochinois en Bourbonnais*. Paris: L'Harmattan, 1981.

Sinha, Mrinalini. *Colonial Masculinity: The "Manly Englishman" and the "Effeminate Bengali" in the Late Nineteenth Century*. Manchester: Manchester University Press, 1995.

Sivan, Emmanuel. *Interpretations of Islam, Past and Present*. Princeton: Darwin Press, 1985.

Smith, Barbara Hernstein. "Narrative Versions, Narrative Theories." In *On Narrative*, ed. W. J. T. Mitchell, 209–32. Chicago: University of Chicago Press, 1981.

Smith, Raymond T. "Hierarchy and the Dual Marriage System in West Indian Society." In *Gender and Kinship*, ed. Jane Collier and Sylvia Yanagisako, 163–96. Stanford, Calif.: Stanford University Press, 1987.

Smith-Rosenberg, Carroll, and Charles Rosenberg. "The Female Animal: Medical and Biological Views of Woman and Her Role in Nineteenth-Century America." *Journal of American History* 60, no. 2 (1973): 332–56.

Société de Protection des Enfants Métis. Statute, May 18, 1904, Article 37.

Sommer, Doris. *Foundational Fictions: The National Romances of Latin America*. Berkeley: University of California Press, 1991.

———. "Irresistible Romance: The Foundational Fictions of Latin America." In *Nation and Narration*, ed. Homi K. Bhabha, 71–98. Berkeley: University of California Press, 1990.

———. *Proceed with Caution, When Engaged by Minority Writing in the Americas.* Cambridge, Mass.: Harvard University Press, 1999.

Spear, Thomas George Percival. *The Nabobs: A Study of the Social Life of the English in Eighteenth-Century India.* London: Oxford University Press, 1963.

Spencer, J. E., and W. L. Thomas. "The Hill Stations and Summer Resorts of the Orient." *Geographical Review* 38, no. 4 (1948): 637–51.

Sperber, Dan. 1985. "Anthropology and Psychology: Towards an Epidemiology of Representations." *Man* 20 (March 1985): 73–89.

Spivak, Gayatri Chakravorty. *In Other Worlds: Essays in Cultural Politics.* New York: Methuen, 1987.

Stallybrass, Peter, and Allon White. *The Politics and Poetics of Transgression.* Ithaca: Cornell University Press, 1986.

Steedly, Mary. *Hanging without a Rope: Narrative Experience in Colonial and Postcolonial Karoland.* Princeton: Princeton University Press, 1993.

———. "The State of Culture Theory in the Anthropology of Southeast Asia." *Annual Review of Anthropology* 28 (1999): 431–54.

Steedman, Carolyn. *Childhood, Culture, and Class in Britain: Margaret McMillan, 1860–1931.* London: Virago, 1990.

———. *Landscape for a Good Woman: A Story of Two Lives.* New Brunswick, N.J.: Rutgers University Press, 1985.

Stepan, Nancy. *The Idea of Race in Science: Great Britain, 1800–1960.* London: Macmillan, in association with St. Anthony's College, Oxford, 1982.

Sterk, J. W. Elink. *Proeve Eener Geschiedenis der Armen-Bewaarscholen.* Arhem: J. G. Stenfert Kroese, 1849.

Steward, Julian H. *The People of Puerto Rico: A Study in Social Anthropology.* Urbana: University of Illinois Press, 1956.

Stocking, George W., Jr. *Race, Culture, and Evolution: Essays in the History of Anthropology.* New York: Free Press, [1968] 1982.

Stoler, Ann Laura. *Along the Archival Grain: Colonial Cultures and Their Affective States.* Princeton: Princeton University Press, forthcoming.

———. *Capitalism and Confrontation in Sumatra's Plantation Belt, 1870–1979.* New Haven: Yale University Press, 1985.

———. "Carnal Knowledge and Imperial Power: Matrimony, Race and Morality in Colonial Asia." In *Gender at the Crossroads of Knowledge: Feminist Anthropology in the Postmodern Era*, ed. Micaela di Leonardo, 51–101. Berkeley: University of California Press, 1991.

———. "Colonial Aphasia and the Place of Race in France." Keynote address at the conference, 1951–2000: Transatlantic Perspectives on *The Colonial Situation*, New York University, April 2001.

———. "Colonial Archives and the Arts of Governance: On the Content in the Form." In *Refiguring the Archive*, ed. Carolyn Hamilton. Cape Town: David Philip Publishers, 2002.

———. " 'In Cold Blood': Hierarchies of Credibility and the Politics of Colonial Narratives." *Representations* 37 (Winter 1992): 151–89.

———. "Making Empire Respectable: The Politics of Race and Sexual Morality in 20th-Century Colonial Cultures." *American Ethnologist* 16, no. 4 (1989): 634–60.

———. "Perceptions of Protest: Defining the Dangerous in Colonial Sumatra." *American Ethnologist* 12, no. 4 (1985): 642–58.

———. *Race and the Education of Desire: Foucault's History of Sexuality and the Colonial Order of Things.* Durham, N.C.: Duke University Press, 1995.

———. "Racial Histories and Their Regimes of Truth." *Political Power and Social Theory* 11 (1997): 183–255.

———. "Racist Visions for the Twenty-first Century: On the Cultural Politics of the French Radical Right." In *Relocating Postcolonialism,* ed. David Goldberg and Ato Quayson, 103–21. Oxford: Blackwell, 2002.

———. "Rethinking Colonial Categories: European Communities and the Boundaries of Rule." *Comparative Studies in Society and History* 31, no. 1 (1989): 134–61.

———. "A Sentimental Education: Native Servants and the Cultivation of European Children in the Netherlands Indies." In *Fantasizing the Feminine: Sex and Death in Indonesia,* ed. Laurie Sears, 71–91. Durham, N.C.: Duke University Press, 1996.

———. "Sexual Affronts and Racial Frontiers: European Identities and the Politics of Exclusion in Colonial Southeast Asia." *Comparative Studies in Society and History* 34, no. 3 (1992): 514–51.

———. "Tense and Tender Ties: The Politics of Comparison in North American History and (Post) Colonial Studies." *Journal of American History* 88 (2001): 829–65, 893–97.

Stoler, Ann Laura, and Frederick Cooper. "Between Metropole and Colony: Toward a New Research Agenda." In *Tensions of Empire: Colonial Cultures in a Bourgeois World,* ed. Frederick Cooper and Ann Laura Stoler, 1–56. Berkeley: University of California Press, 1997.

Stoller, Paul. *Embodying Colonial Memories: Spirit Possession, Power and the Hauka in West Africa.* New York: Routledge, 1995.

Stora, Benjamin. *Le transfer d'une mémoire: De "l'Algérie française" au racisme anti-arabe.* Paris: Découverte.

Strobel, Margaret. "Gender and Race in the Nineteenth- and Twentieth-Century British Empire." In *Becoming Visible: Women in European History,* 2d ed., ed. Renate Bridenthal, Claudia Koonz, and Susan Stuard, 389–414. Boston: Houghton Mifflin, 1987.

Stuurman, Siep. *Verzuiling, Kapitalisme en Patriarchaat: Aspecten van de Ontiwiddeling van de Moderne Staat in Nederland.* Nijmegen: SUN, 1985.

Suarez Findlay, Eileen J. *Imposing Decency: The Politics of Sexuality and Race in Puerto Rico, 1870–1920.* Durham, N.C.: Duke University Press, 1999.

Summers, Carol. "Intimate Colonialism: The Imperial Production of Reproduction in Uganda, 1907–1925." *Signs* 16, no. 4 (1991): 787–807.

Sunley, Robert. "Early Nineteenth-Century American Literature on Child-rearing." In *Childhood in Contemporary Cultures*, ed. Margaret Mead and Martha Wolfenstein, 150–68. Chicago: University of Chicago Press, 1955.

Sutherland, Heather. "Ethnicity and Access in Colonial Macassar." In *Papers of the Dutch-Indonesian Historical Conference*, Dutch and Indonesian Steering Committees of the Indonesian Studies Programme, 250–77. Leiden: Bureau of Indonesian Studies, 1982.

Swedenburg, Ted. *Memories of Revolt: The 1936–1939 Rebellion and the Palestinian National Past*. Minneapolis: University of Minnesota Press, 1995.

Székely, Ladislao. *Tropic Fever: The Adventures of a Planter in Sumatra*. Kuala Lumpur: Oxford in Asia, [1937] 1979.

Székely-Lulofs, Madelon. *De Andere Wereld*. Amsterdam: Elsevier, 1931.

———. *Rubber*. Amsterdam: Elsevier, 1932.

Taguieff, Pierre-André. "The Doctrine of the National Front in France (1972–1989)." *New Political Science* 16–17 (1985): 28–68.

———. *La force du préjugé: Essai sur le racisme et ses doubles*. Paris: Découverte, 1987.

Takaki, Ronald T. *Iron Cages: Race and Culture in Nineteenth-Century America*. New York: Knopf, 1977.

———. *Pau Hana: Plantation Life and Labor in Hawaii, 1835–1920*. Honolulu: University of Hawaii Press, 1983.

Tanner, R. E. S. "Conflict within Small European Communities in Tanganyika." *Human Organization* 23, no. 4 (1964): 319–27.

Taussig, Michael T. "Culture of Terror—Space of Death: Roger Casement's Putamayo Report and the Explanation of Terror." *Comparative Studies in Society and History* 26 (July 1994): 467–97.

———. *The Devil and Commodity Fetishism in South America*. Chapel Hill: University of North Carolina Press, 1980.

———. *Shamanism, Colonialism, and the Wild Man: A Study in Terror and Healing*. Chicago: University of Chicago Press, 1987.

Taylor, Jean. "Nyai Dasima: Portrait of a Mistress in Literature and film." In *Fantasizing the Feminine*, ed. Laurie Sears, 225–48. Durham, N.C.: Duke University Press, 1996.

———. *The Social World of Batavia: European and Eurasian in Dutch Asia*. Madison: University of Wisconsin Press, 1983.

———. "The World of Women in the Colonial Dutch Novel." *Kabar Seberang* 2 (1977): 26–41.

Theweleit, Klaus. *Male Fantasies*. Trans. Stephen Conway, in collaboration with Erica Carter and Chris Turner. Minneapolis: University of Minnesota Press, 1989.

Thomas, Nicholas. *Colonialism's Culture: Anthropology, Travel, and Government*. Princeton: Princeton University Press, 1994.

Tiffany, Sharon W., and Kathleen J. Adams. *The Wild Woman: An Inquiry into the Anthropology of an Idea*. Cambridge, Mass.: Schenkman, 1985.

Tirefort, A. " 'Le bon temps': La communauté française en basse Côte d'Ivoire pendant l'entre-deux guerres, 1920–1940." Troisième Cycle, Centre d'Etudes Africaines, 1979.

Todorov, Tzvetan. *The Conquest of America: The Question of the Other.* Trans. Richard Howard. New York: Harper and Row, 1985.

Toer, Pramoedya Ananta. *Child of All Nations: A Novel.* Trans. Max Lane. Melbourne: Penguin Books Australia, 1984.

———. "Djongos + Babu." Trans. Nancy Florida. *Tenggara* 33 (1997). [Originally trans. James T. Siegel in *Indonesia* 61 (1996). Originally published in *Tjerita Dari Djakarta, 1957.*]

———. *Footsteps.* Trans. Max Lane. New York: W. Morrow, 1994.

———. *House of Glass: A Novel.* Trans. Max Lane. New York: Penguin, 1992.

———. *This Earth of Mankind: A Novel* [Bumi Manusia]. Trans. Max Lane. New York: Penguin, [1975] 1990.

———. *Tjerita Dari Djakarta: Sekumpulan Karikatur Keadaan dan Manusianya.* Djakarta: Grafica, 1957.

Travaux du Groupe d'Études Coloniales. *La femme blanche au Congo.* Brussels: Misch and Thron, 1910.

Treille, G. *De l'acclimatation des Européens dans les pays chaud.* Paris: Octave Doin, 1888.

Trouillot, Michel-Rolph. *Silencing the Past: Power and the Production of History.* Boston: Beacon Press, 1995.

Uehling, Greta. "Building Memories: Recalling the Deportation, Exile and Repatriation of Crimean Tatars to Their Historic Homeland." Ph.D. dissertation, University of Michigan, 2000.

"Uit den Volksraad—De Werkloosheid." *Onze Stem* 8 (February 20, 1931): 187.

Uitkomsten der Pauperisme-Enquête: Algemeen Verslag. Batavia: Landsdrukkerij, 1902.

Uitkomsten der Pauperisme-Enquête: Gewestelijke Verslagen. Batavia: Landsdrukkerij, 1901.

Union Géographique International. *Comptes Rendus du Congrès International de Géographie, Amsterdam 1938.* Leiden: E. J. Brill, 1938.

Van Helten, Jean J., and K. Williams. 1983. " 'The Crying Need of South Africa': The Emigration of Single British Women to the Transvaal, 1901–1910." *Journal of South African Studies* 10, no. 1 (1983): 11–38.

Veerde, A.G. "Onderzoek naar den omvang der Werkloosheid op Java (November 1930–June 1931)." *Koloniale Studien* 16 (1931): 242–73, 503–33.

Vellut, Jean-Luc. "Matériaux pour une image du blanc dans la société coloniale du Congo Belge." In *Stéréotypes nationaux et préjugés raciaux aux XIXe et XXe siècles: Sources et méthodes pour une approche historique,* ed. Jean Pirotte. Recueil de Travaux d'Histoire et de Philologie, 6 sér., fasc. 24. Louvain and La-Neuve: Collège Erasme, Bureau du Recueil, 1982.

Verbond Nederland en Indie. No. 3 (September 1926).

Vere Allen, J. de. "Malayan Civil Service, 1874–1941: Colonial Bureaucracy/Malayan Elite." *Comparative Studies in Society and History* 12, no. 2 (1970): 149–78.

Vergès, Françoise. *Monsters and Revolutionaries: Colonial Family Romance and Métissage.* Durham, N.C.: Duke University Press, 1999.

Verslag van het Verhandelde in de Bijeenkomsten der Nederlandsch-Indische Juristen-Vereeniging. June 25, 27, 29. Batavia, 1887.

Veth, Pieter Johannes. *Over den Toestand en de Behoeften van het Onderwijs der Jeugd in Nederlandsch Indie.* Amsterdam: Spin and Zoon, 1850.

Veur, Paul van der. "Cultural Aspects of the Eurasian Community in Indonesian Colonial Society." *Indonesia* 6 (October 1968): 38–53.

———. "The Eurasians of Indonesia: A Problem and Challenge in Colonial History." *Journal of Southeast Asian History* 9, no. 2 (1966): 191–207.

Vincent, Joan. *Teso in Transformation: The Political Economy of Peasant and Class in Eastern Africa.* Berkeley: University of California Press, 1982.

Visweswaran, Kamala. *Fictions of Feminist Ethnography.* Minneapolis: University of Minnesota Press, 1994.

Waard, J. de. "De Oostkust van Sumatra." *Tijdschrift voor Economische Geographie* 25 (1934): 213–21, 255–75, 182–301.

Waldman, Marilyn R. " 'The Otherwise Unnoteworthy Year 711': A Reply to Hayden White." In *On Narrative,* ed. W. J. T. Mitchell. Chicago: University of Chicago Press, 1981.

Wall, H. H. F. van de. "Rassenhaat." *Jong Indie* 1 (1908): 120–22.

Wallerstein, I. *Social Change: The Colonial Situation.* New York: Wiley, 1966.

Wanderken, P. "Zoo leven onze Kinderen." In *Zoo leven wij in Indonesia,* 172–87. Deventer: W. van Hoeve, 1943.

Ware, Vron. *Beyond the Pale: White Women, Racism and History.* New York: Verso, 1992.

Warren, James Francis. "Prostitution and the Politics of Venereal Disease: Singapore, 1870–98." *Journal of Southeast Asian Studies* 21, no. 2 (1990): 360–83.

Wasserstrom, Robert. "Ethnic Violence and Indigenous Protest: The Tzeltal (Maya) Rebellion of 1712." *Journal of Latin American Studies* 12, no. 1 (1980): 1–19.

Weber, Eugene. *Peasants into Frenchmen: The Modernization of Rural France, 1870–1914.* Stanford, Calif.: Stanford University Press, 1976.

Wertheim, Willem. *Indonesian Society in Transition.* The Hague: W. van Hoeve, 1959.

———. Review of *Intergentiel Recht,* by R. D. Kollewijn. *Indonesie* 19 (1956): 169–73.

Wesseling, H. L., ed. *Expansion and Reaction: Essays on European Expansion and Reaction in Asia and Africa.* Leiden: Leiden University Press, 1978.

Whitbread, Nanette. *The Evolution of the Nursery-Infant School: A History of Infant and Nursery Education in Britain, 1800–1970.* London: Routledge and Kegan Paul, 1972.

White, Hayden V. *The Content of the Form: Narrative Discourse and Historical Representation*. Baltimore: Johns Hopkins University Press, 1987.

White, Luise. *The Comforts of Home: Prostitution in Colonial Nairobi*. Chicago: University of Chicago Press, 1990.

———. Review of *Empire and Opportunity*, by Ronald Hyam. *Signs* 13, no. 2 (1988): 360–64.

———. *Speaking with Vampires: Rumor and History in Colonial Africa*. Berkeley: University of California Press, 2000.

White, Luise, Stephan Miescher, and David William Cohen. *African Words, African Voices: Critical Practices in Oral History*. Bloomington: Indiana University Press, 2001.

Wilder, Gary. "The Politics of Failure: Historicising Popular Front Colonial Policy in French West Africa." In *French Colonial Empire and the Popular Front: Hope and Disillusion*, ed. Tony Chafer and Amanda Sackur, 33–55. New York: Macmillan, 1999.

Wilkens, A. *Het Inlandsche Kind in Oost-Indie en Iets over den Javaan*. Amsterdam: Van Kampen, 1849.

Williams, Raymond. *Marxism and Literature*. London: Oxford University Press, 1977.

Wilson, Bryan R., ed. *Rationality*. Oxford: Blackwell, 1979.

Wilson, Stephen. *Ideology and Experience: Antisemitism in France at the Time of the Dreyfus Affair*. London: Associated University Presses, 1982.

Winckel, C. W. F. "The Feasibility of White Settlements in the Tropics: A Medical Point of View." In *Comptes Rendus du Congrès International de Géographie*, Amsterdam, vol. 2, sec. 3c, 345–56. Leiden: E. J. Brill, 1938.

Winsemius, Johan. *Nieuw-Guinee als Kolonisatie-Gebied voor Europeanen en van Indo-Europeanen*. Purmerend: J. Muusses, 1936. [Ph.D. dissertation, Faculty of Medicine, University of Amsterdam, 1936.]

Wolf, Eric R. *Europe and the People without History*. Berkeley: University of California Press, 1982.

———. *Sons of the Shaking Earth*. Chicago: University of Chicago Press, 1959.

Woodcock, George. *The British in the Far East*. New York: Atheneum, 1969.

Wright, Gwendolyn. *The Politics of Design in French Colonial Urbanism*. Chicago: University of Chicago Press, 1991.

———. "Tradition in the Service of Modernity: Architecture and Urbanism in French Colonial Policy, 1900–1930." In *Tensions of Empire: Colonial Cultures in a Bourgeois World*, ed. Frederick Cooper and Ann Laura Stoler, 322–45. Berkeley: University of California Press, 1977.

Young, Robert. *Colonial Desire: Hybridity in Theory, Culture and Race*. London: Routledge, 1995.

Zarka, Yves Charles. "Michel Foucault: De la guerre des races au biopouvoir." In *Cités: Philosophe, politique, histoire*. Paris: Presses Universitaires de France, 2000.

NEWSPAPERS

Deli Courant. Medan, Sumatra.
Kroniek. 1916–39. Oostkust van Sumatra-Instituut. Amsterdam: J. H. de Bussy.
Ons Nageslacht: Orgaan van de Eugenetische Vereeniging in Ned-Indie. Batavia.
De Planter. 1909–22. Organ of the *Vakvereeniging voor Assistenten in Deli.* Medan, Sumatra.
Sumatra Post. Medan, Sumatra.

Index

histories *(continued)*
179–83; of race and sexuality,
145–51. *See also* anthropology;
archives; memories
History of Sexuality (Foucault), 14,
140–61
Holland. *See* Netherlands
home education, 75, 129–30
homosexuality, 10, 56, 86; prostitution
and concubinage preventing, 2, 48,
239n42
honor, female, 32–34
Horst, D. W., 128, 129, 266n43
housekeeping manuals, 6, 17, 70–72,
130, 136, 163. *See also* domesticity
housewives association, Indies, 130
housing: after European women arrived, 55; servants' quarters, 165;
Sumatra plantation labor, 31
humanitarianism, 111
Hunt, Lynn, 210
Hyam, Ronald, 44
hybridity: cultural, 110–11, 151–52.
See also mixed-bloods

identities: chromatic, 13; cultural,
109; male, 1–6, 42, 44, 62, 65;
memory modeled on, 170, 273n27;
sexuality as core aspect of, 46. *See
also* categories; class; classification,
politics of; gender; national identity; race
"imagined communities," 13–14, 24,
27, 41. *See also* Anderson, Benedict
immigration: studies of, 15. *See also*
European colonials
Immorality Act (1916), Rhodesia, 60
imperial power: carnal knowledge and,
41–78, 140–61, 213; genealogies,
140–61
"imperial prude," Foucault on, 145,
146
India: British class distinctions,
230n29; Eurasian social positioning,
252n4; European women's racism,
32–33; orphanages, 69–70, 249n203;
poor whites, 35, 36, 256n49; post-

colonial, 19; racial segregation, 33,
36, 45, 77–78; resistance to colonial-
ism, 33, 58–59, 77–78; sexual man-
agement, 45, 77–78; sexual mutila-
tion of British women, 58–59
Indies Civil Code (1848), 49
Indies Pauperism Commission, 93,
128–30
Indisch, 96–97, 106–7, 108, 252n3
Indische Bond, 106, 108
Indische Partij, 107
Indo, 106, 117. *See also* mixed-bloods
Indochina. *See* French Indochina
Indochine (film), 14
Indo-Europeesch Verbond (IEV), 107,
108
Indonesia: child rearing, 114–19;
Japanese occupation, 173–74,
175–79, 184, 195, 275nn46,48; labor
resistance, 33, 59; nationalism, 29,
81, 96–97, 104–8, 118–19, 176–78,
262n120, 276n60, 277n64; New
Order, 175–76, 179, 184, 197–98,
275nn47,48; photographs of colonial domesticity, 2–5*fig*, 113*fig*,
166–67*figs*, 171–72*figs*, 184–94*figs*,
278n77; postcolonial memories,
19–20, 162–203, 270–81; Pro Juventute, 213–16, 249n203; servants, 7,
19–20, 162–203. *See also* colonialism; Dutch colonials; Java; Netherlands Indies; New Guinea; Sumatra
inspectorate, labor, 31
intellectuals: African American
women, 262n130; postcolonial, 40,
163, 210–11, 271–72n14
interior frontiers, 75, 80, 205. *See also*
national identity
internment camps, Japanese, 173–74,
177, 275n46, 276n52
interpretation: memory and, 170, 174,
270; "ready-made syntheses," 206
interracial sexuality: European
women/native men, 58–61, 96, 100,
101–5, 153, 260–61n105; forced,
58–59, 180–83, 195, 262n130;
mixed-marriage law, 101–6,

Compositor: Impressions Book and Journal Services, Inc.
Text: 10/13 Aldus
Display: Aldus
Printer and binder: Sheridan Books, Inc.